ROBERT GRAVES

Richard Perceval Graves was born in Brighton in 1945. A full-time biographer, he has written on T. E. Lawrence, A. E. Housman, and most recently on the Powys brothers – a book described by Philip Larkin as 'a remarkable piece of craftsmanship'.

ROBERT GRAVES

THE ASSAULT
HEROIC
1895–1926

RICHARD PERCEVAL GRAVES

PAPERMAC

First published 1986 by George Weidenfeld & Nicolson
Limited

First published in paperback 1987 by
PAPERMAC
a division of Macmillan Publishers Limited
4 Little Essex Street London WC2R 3LF
and Basingstoke

Associated companies in Auckland, Delhi, Dublin,
Gaborone, Hamburg, Harare, Hong Kong,
Johannesburg, Kuala Lumpur, Lagos, Manzini,
Melbourne, Mexico City, Nairobi, New York,
Singapore and Tokyo

British Library Cataloguing in Publication Data
Graves, Richard Perceval
Robert Graves: the assault heroic
1895–1926.
1. Graves, Robert——Biography   2. Authors,
English——20th century——Biography
I. Title
821'.912   PR6013.R35Z/

ISBN 0-333-43217-7

Printed in Hong Kong

FOR ALL THE DESCENDANTS OF

JOHN CROSBIE GRAVES AND HELENA PERCEVAL

AND ESPECIALLY FOR

MY CHILDREN

DAVID JOHN PERCEVAL GRAVES

PHILIP MACARTNEY GRAVES

AND

LUCIA MARY GRAVES

ACKNOWLEDGEMENTS

Grateful acknowledgement is made to the Executors of the Estate of Robert Graves for permission to quote from the works of Robert Graves; to Sam Graves for permission to quote from writings by Nancy Nicholson; and to Lord Bridges for permission to quote from a letter written by Robert Graves to Robert Bridges.

For permission to quote from the following, grateful acknowledgement is made to: the Virginia Woolf Estate, Chatto & Windus, and Harcourt Brace Jovanovich, Inc. for the *Diary of Virginia Woolf*, Volume 3, edited by A. Olivier Bell; Anthony Sheil Associates Ltd. for *Robert Graves* by M. Seymour-Smith, published by Hutchinson and by Abacus; Faber and Faber Ltd. and the K.S. Giniger Co. Inc. for *Memoirs of an Infantry Officer* by Siegfried Sassoon; Faber and Faber Ltd. for *Old Soldiers Never Die* by F. Richard, for *Ottoline at Garsington 1915–1918*, edited by Gathorne-Hardy, and for Volumes 1–3 of *Siegfried Sassoon Diaries*, edited by R. Hart Davis; David Higham Associates Ltd. for *A Biography of Sir Edward Marsh* by C. Hassall, published by Longman; Oxford University Press for *Wilfred Owen: Collected Letters* (1967), edited by H. Owen and J. Bell; Victor Gollancz Ltd. for *Memoirs 1897–1948: Through Diplomacy to Politics* by L. Pearson.

The author would like to thank the Trustees of the Imperial War Museum for allowing him access to their collection of letters by Robert Graves.

CONTENTS

BOOK FOUR

MILITARY SERVICE

1914–1919

BOOK FIVE

HARLECH AND BOAR'S HILL

1919–1921

BOOK SIX
THE WORLD'S END
1921–1926

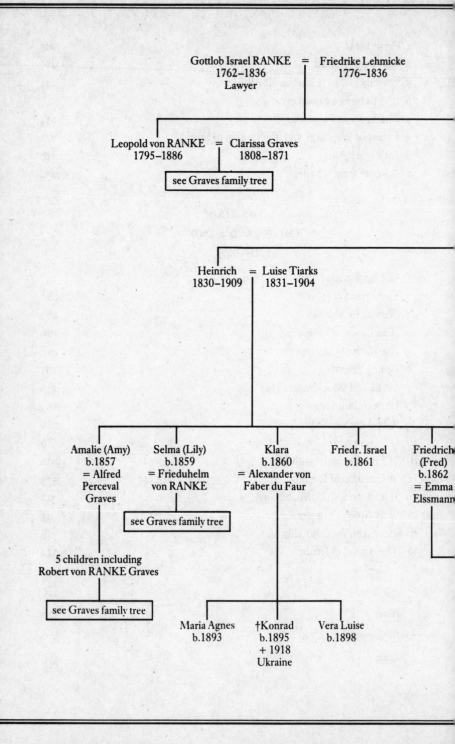

Gottlob Israel RANKE = Friedrike Lehmicke
1762–1836   1776–1836
Lawyer

Leopold von RANKE = Clarissa Graves
1795–1886   1808–1871

see Graves family tree

Heinrich = Luise Tiarks
1830–1909   1831–1904

Amalie (Amy)   Selma (Lily)   Klara   Friedr. Israel   Friedrich
b.1857   b.1859   b.1860   b.1861   (Fred)
= Alfred   = Frieduhelm   = Alexander von   b.1862
Perceval   von RANKE   Faber du Faur   = Emma
Graves   Elssmann

                              see Graves family tree

5 children including
Robert von RANKE Graves

see Graves family tree

                              Maria Agnes   †Konrad   Vera Luise
                              b.1893   b.1895   b.1898
                                                     + 1918
                                                     Ukraine

RANKE *as of January 1926*

†Great War Casualties

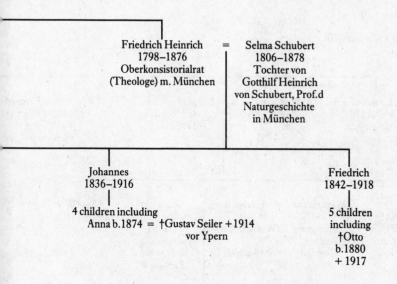

Friedrich Heinrich
1798–1876
Oberkonsistorialrat
(Theologe) m. München

=

Selma Schubert
1806–1878
Tochter von
Gotthilf Heinrich
von Schubert, Prof.d
Naturgeschichte
in München

Johannes
1836–1916

4 children including
Anna b.1874 = †Gustav Seiler +1914
vor Ypern

Friedrich
1842–1918

5 children
including
†Otto
b.1880
+ 1917

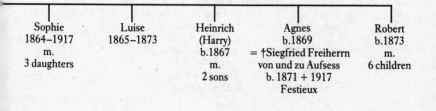

Sophie
1864–1917
m.
3 daughters

Luise
1865–1873

Heinrich
(Harry)
b.1867
m.
2 sons

Agnes
b.1869
= †Siegfried Freiherrn
von und zu Aufsess
b. 1871 + 1917
Festieux

Robert
b.1873
m.
6 children

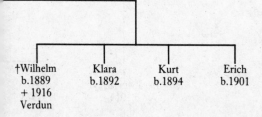

†Wilhelm
b.1889
+ 1916
Verdun

Klara
b.1892

Kurt
b.1894

Erich
b.1901

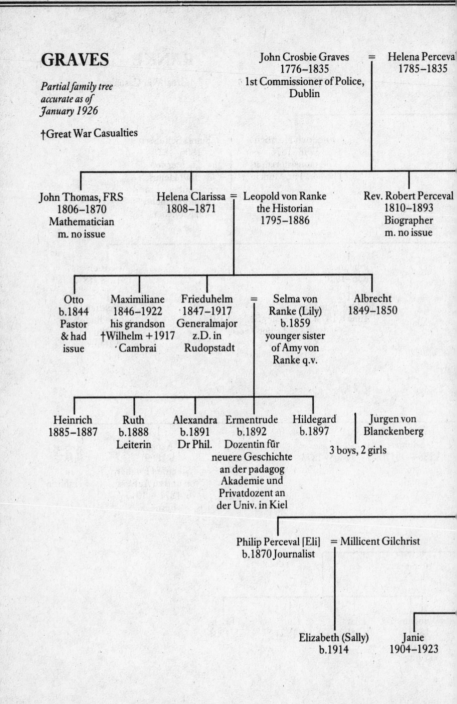

GRAVES

*Partial family tree
accurate as of
January 1926*

†Great War Casualties

John Crosbie Graves
1776–1835
1st Commissioner of Police,
Dublin
= Helena Perceval
1785–1835

John Thomas, FRS
1806–1870
Mathematician
m. no issue

Helena Clarissa = Leopold von Ranke
1808–1871   the Historian
1795–1886

Rev. Robert Perceval
1810–1893
Biographer
m. no issue

Otto
b.1844
Pastor
& had
issue

Maximiliane
1846–1922
his grandson
†Wilhelm +1917
Cambrai

Frieduhelm = Selma von
1847–1917   Ranke (Lily)
Generalmajor   b.1859
z.D. in   younger sister
Rudopstadt   of Amy von
                 Ranke q.v.

Albrecht
1849–1850

Heinrich
1885–1887

Ruth
b.1888
Leiterin

Alexandra
b.1891
Dr Phil.

Ermentrude
b.1892
Dozentin für
neuere Geschichte
an der padagog
Akademie und
Privatdozent an
der Univ. in Kiel

Hildegard
b.1897

Jurgen von
Blanckenberg

3 boys, 2 girls

Philip Perceval [Eli] = Millicent Gilchrist
b.1870 Journalist

Elizabeth (Sally)
b.1914

Janie
1904–1923

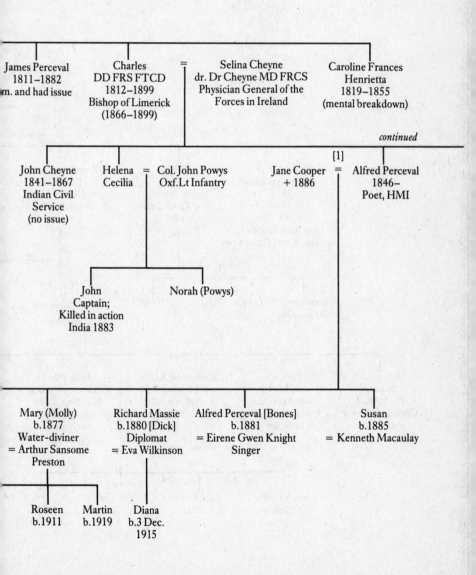

19th from Edward 1st of England;
24th from McMurrough, King of Ireland (Leinster);
22nd from Henry 1st of France and Anne of Russia;
25th from David 1st of Scotland;
26th from Robert, 1st Duke of Normany

| James Perceval 1811–1882 m. and had issue | Charles DD FRS FTCD 1812–1899 Bishop of Limerick (1866–1899) | = | Selina Cheyne dr. Dr Cheyne MD FRCS Physician General of the Forces in Ireland | Caroline Frances Henrietta 1819–1855 (mental breakdown) |

continued

[1]

| John Cheyne 1841–1867 Indian Civil Service (no issue) | Helena Cecilia = Col. John Powys Oxf.Lt Infantry | Jane Cooper + 1886 = Alfred Perceval 1846– Poet, HMI |

John
Captain;
Killed in action
India 1883

Norah (Powys)

| Mary (Molly) b.1877 Water-diviner = Arthur Sansome Preston | Richard Massie b.1880 [Dick] Diplomat = Eva Wilkinson | Alfred Perceval [Bones] b.1881 = Eirene Gwen Knight Singer | Susan b.1885 = Kenneth Macaulay |

Roseen
b.1911

Martin
b.1919

Diana
b.3 Dec.
1915

GRAVES

(continued)

†Great War Casualties

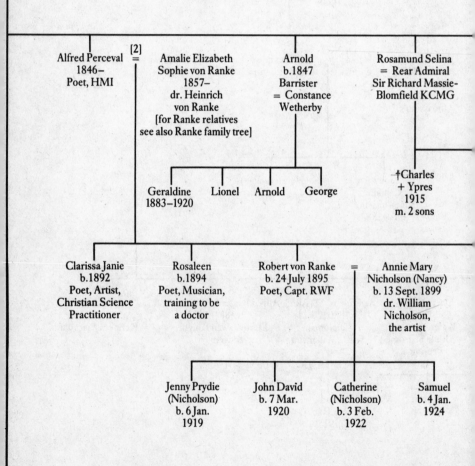

Alfred Perceval
1846–
Poet, HMI

[2] =

Amalie Elizabeth
Sophie von Ranke
1857–
dr. Heinrich
von Ranke
[for Ranke relatives
see also Ranke family tree]

Arnold
b.1847
Barrister
= Constance
Wetherby

Rosamund Selina
= Rear Admiral
Sir Richard Massie-
Blomfield KCMG

Geraldine
1883–1920

Lionel

Arnold

George

†Charles
+ Ypres
1915
m. 2 sons

Clarissa Janie
b.1892
Poet, Artist,
Christian Science
Practitioner

Rosaleen
b.1894
Poet, Musician,
training to be
a doctor

Robert von Ranke
b. 24 July 1895
Poet, Capt. RWF

=

Annie Mary
Nicholson (Nancy)
b. 13 Sept. 1899
dr. William
Nicholson,
the artist

Jenny Prydie
(Nicholson)
b. 6 Jan.
1919

John David
b. 7 Mar.
1920

Catherine
(Nicholson)
b. 3 Feb.
1922

Samuel
b. 4 Jan.
1924

Per pale Gules and Azure, an Eagle displayed ducally
crowned Or; in the dexter Chief point a Cross patonce of
the last. For Crest a demi Eagle displayed and erased Or
encircled round the body below the wings with a ducal
Coronet Gules, each wing charged with a Cross patonce,
also Gules. *And for motto* AQUILA NON CAPTAT
MUSCAS, *the whole to be borne and used for ever hereafter by
him the said* Charles Graves D.D. *and his descendants and by
the other descendants of* John Crosbie Graves *quarterly with
the arms of* Perceval.

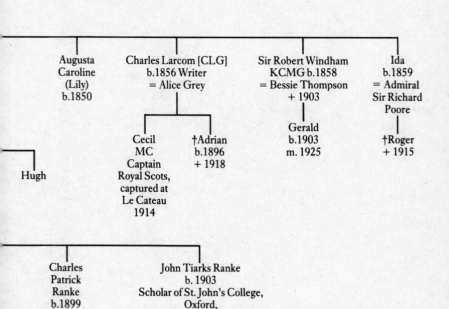

Augusta
Caroline
(Lily)
b.1850

Charles Larcom [CLG]
b.1856 Writer
= Alice Grey

Sir Robert Windham
KCMG b.1858
= Bessie Thompson
+ 1903

Ida
b.1859
= Admiral
Sir Richard
Poore

Gerald
b.1903
m. 1925

†Roger
+ 1915

Cecil
MC
Captain
Royal Scots,
captured at
Le Cateau
1914

†Adrian
b.1896
+ 1918

Hugh

Charles
Patrick
Ranke
b.1899
Journalist

John Tiarks Ranke
b. 1903
Scholar of St. John's College,
Oxford,
Tutor to son of rich American
[later to become the father of
the present author]

ILLUSTRATIONS

Unless otherwise acknowledged, all the photographs reproduced in this book belong to the author.

INTRODUCTION

A true poem is like a spring of water in a desert land; and a true poet is like the prophet who takes his staff and strikes that spring from the living rock. It is to similes like this that we must resort when describing the writing of a poem, because it is a creative and inspirational act which at its deepest level is beyond direct description. But writing a poem is also an act born out of the human experience of an individual poet; and to share as fully as possible in that human experience should bring us to a greater understanding of the truths which the poet seeks to express. That is the chief purpose of this book about my uncle, the poet Robert Graves, whom I knew and have loved since childhood.

It is the chief purpose because poetry was always Robert's principal vocation. He first attracted public attention as one of the soldier-poets of the 1914–1918 War, when he was associated with such names as Siegfried Sassoon and Wilfred Owen; until the end of 1922 he was also a contributor to Edward Marsh's volumes of 'Georgian' poetry; and since then, although he has firmly turned his back on most 'modern' developments in poetry, pouring scorn on his near contemporaries Eliot and Auden, he has come to be regarded as one of the finest poets of the twentieth century.

However, Robert's literary activities have never been confined to the writing of poetry. He wrote a remarkable autobiography, *Goodbye To All That*, whose title has become a catch-phrase; and he also achieved popular fame as the author of a number of historical novels including *I, Claudius*, of which a brilliantly successful adaptation for television has been watched by millions all over the world. In addition he has been prolific as an essayist, as a literary critic, and as a translator from the Classics; while his *The White Goddess*, an 'historical grammar of poetic myth', has a cult following.

My own principal vocation is biography, which, as a branch of history, is more of an art than a science, and comes by tradition under the kindly protection of Clio, one of the Nine Muses. Biographies should therefore never be dull: but artistic licence cannot absolve biographers from the duty of being as accurate as possible; and, since the time of Lytton Strachey, biography often been given a bad name by biographers with a higher regard for bold strokes of colour and sensation than for the truth. Biographers also have a duty to be sympathetic to their subjects. As soon as I begin to discover that a biographer is treating his subject with malice, envy, dislike or contempt,

I begin to suspect the quality both of his motives and of his human understanding. In this book, as in my previous biographies, I have done my best to be both accurate and sympathetic.

However, it is generally held to be far easier to be fair and sympathetic to comparative strangers than to members of one's own family; and if that is true, then to write the biography of a father, a mother, an uncle, or any other close relative is a particularly dangerous undertaking. Many people have said to me recently: 'I suppose it was inevitable that some day you should write about your uncle Robert.' Perhaps it was. I myself preferred not to think so until January 1980. On the seventh day of that month my father John died in a Salisbury hospital. He had always remarked that in old age all members of the Graves family begin to look alike; and when I saw him for the last time, lying in his coffin, his finely moulded features, his high brow, his long handsome face and his aquiline nose exactly resembled those of his grandfather, the Bishop of Limerick. This was fitting: like the Bishop, his cool intellectual command and his patrician manner alarmed some people at first; but John was a devout Christian, a loving father, and a most honourable, unselfish man.

In his will, knowing my interest in family history, he left me a treasured collection of letters, diaries and other papers which had been hoarded up by five generations of the family, and which dated back as far as the 1760s. They included numerous extracts from a book which my father had begun to write, and which he had provisionally entitled *My Brother Robert*. Literary work was not new to him: in his youth a romantic, and something of a poet, he had combined tutoring and teaching with travel and journalism, and was himself the author or editor of several books. In late middle age, after a spell at the Ministry of Education, he became Headmaster of a preparatory school near Wokingham: Holme Grange, a rambling Norman Shaw mansion surrounded by acres of lawns and woodland. When ill health compelled him to retire, he returned to his earlier literary interests.

I heard from my mother how evening after evening in their windswept home on the Wiltshire downs John had pored with a magnifying glass over the almost indecipherable handwriting of his own father's detailed 'page-a-day' diaries, copying out everything relevant to Robert's life between the years 1911 and 1931. Collecting material from this and other sources occupied much of his time. But his health continued to decline, and at last the work became too much for him.

After his death I found heaps of papers in which recent bills, letters from the 1800s, extracts from *My Brother Robert* and ephemera collected on John's Continental travels during the 1930s were mingled together in a confused and yet somehow deeply touching manner. Scattered among them were the distinctive tools of his trade: large paper folders, sheets of blotting paper, piles of paper clips, and old-fashioned steel-nib pens. I was then heavily occupied with other work; but I determined immediately that as soon as time permitted I would build upon what my father had done, and ensure that the labours of his old age should not have been in vain.

The appearance of Martin Seymour-Smith's pioneering biography in 1982, when I had hardly begun my own researches, blunted my determination for a while; but only until I had read the first few chapters of his book. It would be unkind to my predecessor to list all my disagreements with him at this stage, and tedious for the reader if I cluttered up the rest of the book with academic controversy. A man is entitled to his opinions; and where we differ on matters of fact I have drawn up my evidence in the decent obscurity of the reference notes.

As my researches continued, I discovered how strange and disconcerting it can be to examine in detail the lives of one's family. Some of them had been no more than a dim memory, and a few remembered stories passed on as part of the family folklore. These sprang to life, and demanded to be recognized for deeds and achievements which had long been forgotten or distorted. Others, whom I thought I knew well, revealed themselves as strangers, and not only their lives but parts of my own had to be reinterpreted before I could continue.

I owe a great debt to all those who supplied me with information, and from whom I received so much encouragement and support during the three and a half years of my labours. In particular I thank my Aunt Beryl, who welcomed me to Deya in the spring of 1982, and allowed me to spend the first few weeks of my researches sitting at the desk in Robert's study at the back of Canellun. Both then and since, she has been unfailingly helpful and encouraging. I should also like to thank my Aunt Dr Rosaleen Cooper, Robert's only surviving sister; my Aunt Betty Graves, Perceval's widow; and many of my cousins, especially Sally Chilver, Roseen Freeth, Paul Cooper, and (among Robert's children) Catherine, Sam, William and Lucia. I am also grateful to Mrs Laura (Riding) Jackson and to Mr Alan Clark, who have supplied me with information and made useful criticisms about those sections of the book relating to Mrs Jackson. Others who have helped me include R.L. Arrowsmith, J.G.A. Reith, George Baugh, Paul O'Prey, Wilf Stopp, Jim Wilkinson, Arthur Bateman, the present owners of both Red Branch House and Erinfa, and my picture-researcher Anne-Marie Ehrlich. I also thank my editor at Weidenfeld, Candida Brazil, whose suggestions for the final shaping of the book have been most valuable.

BOOK ONE

SOME PRELIMINARY SCENES IN ENGLAND, IRELAND, WALES AND BAVARIA

CHAPTER
1
A CHILDHOOD
MEMORY

On the morning of Friday 8 January 1926 Robert Graves, then half-way through his thirty-first year, boarded the P. & O. liner *Ranpura*, and set sail for Egypt, where he had been appointed Professor of Poetry at Cairo University. It was the only full-time appointment which he had accepted since he had been demobilized from the army in 1919; and although it would provide him with financial security, it might also impose upon him an official and conventional way of life which he would find deeply distasteful, so he viewed the future with mixed feelings. By Robert's side was his wife Nancy, an elegantly-dressed and independent-minded young woman who was nevertheless in a poor mental and physical condition: she had been suffering badly both from nervous depression and from a pituitary imbalance, and had been advised that she must winter in a warm climate if she wished to regain her health. She and Robert were accompanied not only by their four young children Jenny, David, Catherine and Sam, but by the children's nurse, and by Robert's new associate, the American poet Laura Riding.

During the voyage to Egypt there were gales both in the Atlantic and in the Mediterranean; and the stormy journey away from one culture and towards another is somehow symbolic of the personal journey which Robert was about to make away from the traditional world of his childhood, and towards a new world which he had often glimpsed but which he had almost despaired of reaching. On many occasions only a deeply-rooted determination to 'get through somehow' had enabled him to survive; and in one of his poems, 'The Assault Heroic', Graves explained how he had managed to 'alchemize' the worst of his experiences into literary 'lumps of gold'.

Now, as he sailed into an uncertain future, Graves carried with him as his intellectual cargo a number of strongly-held beliefs which, given the chance, he would express with great force; and which, when anchored to a coherent framework of thought, would eventually provide him with the alternative view of the Universe for which he was seeking. Among them was the belief that

3

organized religion is the enemy of freedom; that the world is a stranger and more magical place than appears at first sight; that Poetry itself is a modified descendant of primitive magic; that ordinary perception and formal logic have their limits, and that beyond them lies a timeless land which is quite at odds with conventional life; that society had once been matriarchal, and that many of our present ills could be attributed to the fact that men now ruled instead of women; that literal truth is relatively unimportant, as an artist can tell the truth by a condensation and dramatization of the facts; and that there are areas in which intellectual thought is markedly inferior to associative or 'analeptic' thought.

This is a surprising collection of ideas for someone who had been educated both at home and at school in the most traditional fashion: whose mother had intended to be a missionary; and whose father, though a poet, had also been an Inspector of Schools. As I began trying to unravel the mystery of how Robert had arrived at these ideas, and as I therefore turned my attention to the early part of his life, I found that it was dominated to a greater degree than I had expected by the figure of my grandmother, Amy Graves; and I remembered how when I was a very young child, no more than four or five years of age, we had motored up to North Wales to stay with her. She lived in Erinfa, her large and by then somewhat dilapidated home near Harlech. Known chiefly to the world as Robert Graves's mother, she was already in her nineties, but was still mentally alert, with a commanding physical presence that was all her own.

Standing to welcome us beside the massive oak bookcase in Erinfa's gloomy hall, she might easily have appeared terrifying to me, for besides being tall she was dressed from head to foot in black. However, she radiated such a warm and unselfish love that I felt instantly at home and utterly secure in her presence. Later, at tea in the dining-room, where I was allowed for the first time to hold a toasting-fork up to a blazing fire, I turned proudly to the table where she sat with my mother and father and several aunts and uncles, and it was clear to me that she was the presiding genius of the company. At the same time, she was strangely unlike anyone I had ever met before: there was something about her that was not quite of this world.

CHAPTER
2
AMALIE
VON RANKE

Robert's mother looks back at me from countless family photographs: here is the kindly, wrinkled old lady, dressed in black, whose presence I remember but whose face I had forgotten, holding my hand as we walk across the sands on Harlech beach; here is the pretty little girl of seven or eight, sitting on an elaborately carved wooden chair, smiling for the camera but looking as though she wants to jump up, and run off to play; and here is the self-confident young woman of twenty, dressed rather plainly, but evidently at the height of her beauty, with a superb figure and a lovely face, her forehead seductively fringed with ringlets, and a self-confident slightly teasing expression in her eyes.

She had been born Amalie Elizabeth Sophie Ranke on 15 December 1857 at a house in Fitzroy Square, London; so by birth she could claim to be a British subject. But her mother Luise was of Norwegian extraction, a daughter of the Greenwich astronomer Ludwig Tiarks; and her father, whom Luise had married in May 1856, was Heinrich Ranke, a doctor and a member of a distinguished German family: his uncle was the great historian Leopold von Ranke.[1]

Luise was a woman of many contradictions: naturally gentle and feminine, with warm, loving eyes and a liking for pretty clothes, she could purse her lips in an unpleasing manner, and there were moments when it was possible to see that her spirit had received some great injury from which she had never wholly recovered. She brought with her a considerable fortune, a keen interest in the arts, which she passed on to her children, and a fund of dry humour: to a young friend of hers, inordinately proud of her small waist, Luise is said to have commented: 'Really, Florence, if I had so small a waist as yours I should put a little wadding round it!'[2] She was a devoted but narrow Christian, who placed duty above happiness; but it was her faith which had enabled her to survive. She and her sister Sophie had become orphans as children of five or six; and although they were adopted by a kindly great-uncle, whose wife they learned to call Mamma, Sophie died in her early teens. This double tragedy left a permanent mark upon Luise. She was a perfectly capable wife and mother, well able to hold her own with her tough-minded husband; but her grandson Robert was right to detect in her not only saintliness, but fear.

Heinrich, a large, strong, self-reliant, vigorous man with a fiercely independent turn of mind, had led a less tragic and more exciting life. As a rather wild-looking medical student at a Prussian university he had been a liberal and an atheist, and had taken part in the political disturbances of 1848, when there was rioting in Berlin. A number of important concessions had been won from the Prussian Government, but eventually the revolutionary movements had been suppressed, and Heinrich was one of those who were compelled to flee to England for safety. He completed his medical training in London, where he rose to be Head of the German Hospital. Then in 1854, with the outbreak of the Crimean War, he travelled out to the Crimea as a surgeon attached to the Brigade of Guards; and it was on his return from that terrible conflict that he met and married Luise.[3]

Not long after Amy's birth, Heinrich decided to return to Germany, though not to Prussia, and he and Luise settled in Munich. Luise found security at the centre of a growing family: she eventually had ten children; and although she remained very much more devout than her husband, Heinrich met her religious convictions half-way, 'communicating once a year and going to church about once a quarter'.[4] Although he kept control of the purse-strings, finding Luise inclined to be almost too generous with her money, Heinrich shared her active concern for others. The former revolutionary became a Professor of Medicine at Munich University, served as Vice-President of the Agricultural Society of Bavaria, worked tirelessly for the supply of pure water and pure milk for Munich, founded and ran a children's hospital, and tried to lower the high rate of infant mortality by giving written advice urging breast-feeding to every woman who notified the birth of a child.

Amy enjoyed a happy childhood, spent partly in Munich and partly at Laufzorn, the magnificent country property only a few miles from the city which Heinrich had purchased with some of his wife's fortune. Laufzorn, or 'Be off, anger!' had been built in about 1570 as a hunting lodge of Duke Albrecht, the Elector of Bavaria. The ground floor was now a farm; an imposing outside staircase led up to a terrace on the first floor, from which one entered a banqueting hall, and the family rooms; on the top floor there was a granary, and from there one could 'climb up to the gazebo, a lantern on the roof, surrounded by a strong iron trellis and commanding a wide view over the surrounding woods to the shimmering blue chain of the Alps beyond'.[5]

With his wealth, his public spirit, and his powerful personality, Amy's father

was soon well-known in Bavarian society, went deer-shooting with the Kaiser
– one of the favourite family photographs shows Heinrich, elderly but imposing,
with a hunting rifle in his hands – and was eventually ennobled to become
Herr Geheimrat Ritter von Ranke. The former radical had developed into
'a strict disciplinarian' but was adored by his children, who had an English
nanny, and whom he and Luise had brought up to be equally fluent in both
German and English.

In October 1870, when Amy was two months short of her thirteenth birthday,
she wrote a letter in remarkably good English to Mrs Tiarks, the woman whom
her mother had called 'Mamma', and whom she therefore addressed as:

My dear Grandmama!

Many thanks for the two kind letters you wrote to me. ... My last letter
was written in Laufzorn, but now I am sitting in the school-room in Munich.
We had a great surprise on Saturday ... when the door opened, and who
do you think stood there with wide spread out arms – our dear Papa.
You can fancy how extremely pleased we were (not to say dreadfully) to
see him again, how we flew into his arms and kissed him, we were so
happy! Papa brought with him the harness and the helmet of a french
horseman; they are very beautiful particularly the helmet. He also brought
a french gun, not a Chassepot, but a 'Wallbuchs'; Papa is very pleased
with it.

...I was [at the Hirschgarten] ... the other day with my cousins. ...
There are many stags, roes and fallow deers. We had bought some bread;
and by walking backwards we at last brought three beautiful fallow-deers
to the tables of the garden....

Mamma and I read every day a portion of the book out of which Mamma
learnt when she was very little; it is called 'Natural Philosophy'; it is very
interesting and I like it very much. Freddy and we all, send you our love,
we are all so sorry that you are not coming this year, dear Grandmama.
But now goodbye. I am your affectionate
Amy Ranke

The qualities which Amy reveals in this letter, her deep and warm-hearted
love of family, her appreciation of natural beauty, and her enquiring mind
remained with her for life.

She was deeply interested in intellectual questions; and when at the age
of eighteen, as a very lovely young woman, she attended her first adult parties,
she was infuriated to find that the young men to whom she was introduced
did not think it worth while to talk about anything of importance to a mere
female. One evening was particularly grim: she had to listen the entire time

to a doctor who could 'think of nothing to talk of but the beer, for instance which was the best kind, and the good places to get it at, which did not interest me at all'.[6]

Amy had been brought up to think for herself in most things; but she had also been brought up by both parents with a strong sense of duty, and by her mother with profound religious convictions. From early childhood she had been expected to act almost like a second mother or perhaps a governess in helping to look after her numerous younger brothers and sisters; and while she was still eighteen she agreed to travel to London to become the 'companion' of her widowed 'Grandmama' Mrs Tiarks, a kindly-looking old lady of seventy-two.[7]

At the time it was assumed that Amy's younger sisters would take their turn in looking after 'Granny'. However, Mrs Tiarks liked her new companion so much that she insisted on keeping Amy by her side for the next fifteen years. To allow an eighteen-year-old's youth to be swallowed up in this manner was the kind of monstrous deed which was common enough at a time when the most extreme self-sacrifice was more widely held to be a Christian duty, and Amy herself grew devoted to the old lady who had enslaved her. It was later rumoured that Mrs Tiarks had been a natural daughter of the Duke of Kent, and was therefore a half-sister of Queen Victoria, and she certainly acted in a regal manner: 'One had to do what she said', Amy recalled, 'without any question.'[8]

Fortunately it was not all loss: Mrs Tiarks, though firm, was prepared to be perfectly friendly and agreeable provided that her wishes were obeyed. She had a wide circle of interesting friends, entertained a great deal, and insisted on taking Amy with her whenever she was invited to dine out. Amy enjoyed these dinners very much,

> not only for the food, but for the excellent opportunity for talk one had, sitting next to an interesting person for an hour and a half. ... I felt it such a compliment when in England people began to talk to me of important things, giving me credit for taking an interest in them.[9]

Amy read voraciously, and Mrs Tiarks, realizing that she had a gift for music, paid for her to have piano lessons, and to have her fine contralto voice professionally trained. One unforeseen consequence of this was that Amy began to be invited out for the evening on her own, only to discover that she literally had to sing for her supper. Mrs Tiarks, perhaps feeling some genuine sympathy for Amy's predicament, but perhaps also feeling irritated by her absence, protested that these 'friends' were taking advantage of Amy's good nature, and treating her like a servant. I should like to think that Amy's reply was carefully framed in order to protect her evenings out, which must have been enjoyable despite what was expected of her: 'Oh, that would be too much honour,' she told 'Granny'. 'Our Lord said, "He that will be chief among you, let him be your servant." '[10]

In the summer Amy sometimes went boating with friends of her own age, and she made an annual visit to Munich, where her sisters applauded her nobility of character, but wisely declined to emulate her self-sacrifice. During her fifteen years with Mrs Tiarks, Amy had several offers of marriage, but she rejected all her suitors. Perhaps they were not persistent enough; probably she did not care deeply about any of them; and in any case people who are governed by a sense of duty can grow accustomed to almost any circumstances, however depressing. She even turned down the Prime Minister of Bavaria, who fell in love with her in 1884, when at the age of twenty-six she attended her sister Clara's wedding to the aristocratic Alexander von Faber du Faur, a tall handsome man in the Bavarian consular service.

Instead she remained with 'Granny', reading, talking, writing letters, and learning how to manage on very little. For although Mrs Tiarks liked entertaining, that was her only extravagance. In all other respects she insisted upon the most rigid economy. Not even a match was to be used if a spill could be lighted from the fire. The reason for this was that Mrs Tiarks had suffered a severe financial loss not long after her husband's death way back in 1848, and this had given her such a fright that she was incapable of dealing sensibly with what remained. Both she and Amy were under the impression that there would be some ten or fifteen thousand pounds left when she died, and to encourage Amy to remain with her she allowed her to know that she had drawn up a will leaving Amy £10,000 as a reward for her years as a companion.

However, in 1890, at the age of eighty-seven, having taken no notice of her investments for over forty years, Mrs Tiarks felt that the time had come to reassess her financial situation and asked her bankers to draw up a list of her stocks and shares. When this arrived, memories of her early imprudence meant that she could not bear to look at it. Instead she took to her bed, called for Amy, and asked her to count everything up, and see how much she was worth. Amy took the package to another room, and did so. Amazed by the grand total, she

went back to the bedroom where Granny was lying in bed with a silk handkerchief round her head and said 'Granny, you are a rich woman. I make it, at par, about £100,000.' She was also taken aback by the news and moved her head in astonishment.[11]

This immense fortune was worth perhaps two and a half million pounds in present-day (mid-1980s) terms. But it was too late for Mrs Tiarks to alter her way of life. She had decided to investigate her financial situation largely because she felt that she had not long to live; and within a few months of discovering the extent of her wealth she was confined permanently to her room. She refused to have a nurse until very near the end, and for some weeks Amy had to play and sing to her during the day, and then get what rest she could on a small sofa in Granny's room, while keeping her fire alive throughout the night.

At last, in the early hours of 11 February 1891 – Ash Wednesday – Mrs Tiarks died. Amy, who ever afterwards remembered her kindnesses and forgot her tyranny, was deeply upset. Years later, in a private memoir written for her children and grandchildren, she recalled that

> When all was over the nurse asked me to help her to wash Granny & to lay her out. I never did anything so difficult in my life & have always felt, if I could do that, I could do anything I must. ... The night after the death I woke up & felt I had a choice either of letting myself go, or of making a great effort & living. You can tell which I did.[12]

Amy had been appointed as co-executor, with her father, of Mrs Tiarks's will. Heinrich, on hearing that Mrs Tiarks was dead, immediately travelled to London, assuming that he would have to take charge of things. To his surprise and pleasure he found that his saintly and apparently unworldly daughter was perfectly capable of dealing with everything, and, explaining that she had 'read a book on the subject', she did without the services of a solicitor and proved the will herself.

Shortly afterwards, on a brief return visit to Laufzorn, Amy had the new and rather pleasing experience of being 'much honoured and made much of'.[13] This was not surprising, as by her unselfish actions she had enriched them all. When Mrs Tiarks had discovered the true size of her fortune, she had decided to draw up a new will. To her credit, she wanted substantially to increase Amy's inheritance from the original £10,000, but Amy declined this offer, telling 'Granny' that if she insisted on making an extra gift, she would prefer the money to go to other members of her family. So each of Amy's nine brothers and sisters received £9,000; while her parents Heinrich and Luise, as residuary legatees, took £12,000 each. Amy had also suggested that 'Granny' should think of her own Tiarks relatives. The old lady would not hear of it: they meant nothing to her. Amy, who felt this was most unfair, had been given an additional £10,000 in bearer bonds, and on Mrs Tiarks's death she immediately divided this money equally among her ten unmarried Tiarks cousins.

Amy now had to plan her future. The will gave her a considerable breathing-space, because Mrs Tiarks had thoughtfully left her the use of 107 Gloucester Terrace for a year, together with the sum of £500 to cover her expenses during that time. Heinrich and Luise were both very keen that Amy should get married. At the age of thirty-three she was still a very good-looking woman, and Luise told her that she would pity her if she did not have the opportunity of raising a family of her own. Amy, having turned down one Prime Minister, did not find anything more pleasing about the succession of middle-aged men who were presented to her during the few weeks that she spent at Laufzorn. Eventually she announced to her father that she was thinking of going to India as a medical missionary, rather than consider which of the possible husbands she disliked least. Heinrich, 'with tears standing in his eyes', said bitterly and despairingly: 'Then we will try to forget you.'[14]

But neither Heinrich nor Luise nor Amy's sisters had any intention of letting the matter rest there. How could the family conscience have borne it? Amy had sacrificed herself, and enriched them all. She was a saint. But saints are uncomfortable people to live with, especially if they have achieved sainthood at your expense. Now, please God, let her enjoy a little ordinary human happiness! Amy had only been back in London for a few days when a family friend arrived to keep an eye on her, and then her mother Luise followed. Soon they were joined by Clara, with her husband Alexander Faber du Faur; and by another of Amy's sisters, Lily, and her husband Frieduhelm.

General Frieduhelm von Ranke, a cousin of Heinrich's and a son of the great Leopold von Ranke, was a short, well-dressed, energetic man who sported a bushy moustache, and wore a heavy gold signet ring on the third finger of his left hand. With his well-rounded, rather boyish face he looked younger than his years; but he had keen blue eyes, and his expression managed to combine great good humour with an evident determination to get things done. In the present circumstances, his objective was clear: his sister-in-law Amy was in need of a good husband; and as soon as he arrived in London he set his military mind to work, and began by gathering information on suitable candidates.

Frieduhelm's mother Clarissa, now dead, had been an Anglo-Irish beauty from Dublin, whose maiden name was Graves; and Frieduhelm discussed Amy's future with one of his Graves cousins who happened to be visiting London. This was Lily Graves, daughter of the Protestant Bishop of Limerick. She had something in common with Amy, for at the age of forty-one she too was unmarried, and she had spent the last nineteen years of her life looking after her widowed father. When Frieduhelm told her that he was looking for a husband for a woman who was, like herself, pious and hardworking, and who had in addition a considerable fortune at her disposal, Lily immediately thought of one of her own brothers, Alfred. In Alfred's present circumstances, Amy could be an ideal match.

CHAPTER
3
ALFRED
PERCEVAL
GRAVES

Alfred Perceval Graves was born on 22 July 1846 in Dublin, where his father was later to become Dean of the Chapel Royal; and after a childhood whose happiest days were spent in the remote countryside beyond Killarney, on the southern shores of the Kerry peninsula, he returned to Dublin to study at Trinity College. As a young man Alfred was good-looking and very Irish, with regular features, blue eyes, and flaming red hair. He was a romantic poet, with a dreamy, sensitive expression; and although he dressed conventionally he sported a moustache and long red sideburns.

While he was an undergraduate he fell in love with the strikingly beautiful but seemingly unattainable Jane, or 'Janie' Cooper of Cooper's Hill, a woman who combined charm and beauty with great strength of character and strong religious convictions. As Alfred's first love-letter to her suggests, she became both his inspiration and his guide:

> from Trinity College Saturday Night and Sunday Morning
> My dear Miss Cooper,
> [he began; and then, after a few lines of social chatter:]
> Before I met you my life had been that of many young men of my age – careless though not wholly irreligious – I was a dreamer with little or no purpose – ambitious to be great but not practically good enough ever to deserve to be so –
> To you I owe a great & I trust a lasting change in my character. I have become a man since I met you – I have gained purpose & energy & do not despair of becoming a useful member of society.
> The little book that you lent me – 'Jessica's First Prayer' affected me much and gave me help on my way – My College successes are due to your influence – for I never did myself any justice before – Now what

is the end of all this to be? Are you to be my good angel and yet a stranger
to me?

[and then, after several more pages in a similar vein:]

Pardon the length and persistency of this appeal & believe me until death

    Your devoted lover

      Alfred Perceval Graves[15]

Persistence was one of Alfred's great qualities; and when Janie's parents told
him that he must earn a living before he could contemplate marriage, he set
off in the mid-1860s for London, where he combined the duties of a clerkship
in the Home Office with literary work, and contributed fresh, lively poems
to *Punch*, *The Gentleman's Magazine*, and numerous other periodicals. As a
rising young poet Alfred began to move in literary circles, met Swinburne,
and was taken up by his fellow Irishman William Allingham, now chiefly remembered for his 'Up the airy mountain,/Down the rushy glen'. Allingham introduced Graves to members of the pre-Raphaelite Brotherhood including Dante
Gabriel Rossetti, William Morris and John Ruskin; and in 1873 Alfred's own
first volume of poems appeared. *Songs of Killarney*, in a handsome, green cover,
contained gloriously light-hearted songs and ballads such as 'The Invention
of Wine', whose second verse runs:

> Before Bacchus could talk
> Or dacently walk,
> Down Olympus he leaped from the arms of his nurse,
> But though three years in all
> Were consumed by the fall,
> He might have gone further and fared a deal worse;[16]

Or 'Lonesome Lovers', with its:

> Oh! Dublin is fine
> Wid her ships on the river,
> And her iligant line
> Of bridges for ever.
> But, Kitty, my dear,
> I'd exchange them this minute
> For our small little pier
> And my boat, and you in it.[17]

Songs of Killarney was well received, especially by the *Spectator*, to which
Alfred Perceval Graves now became a regular contributor. At last he appeared
to be an established figure; and in 1874, after weathering a courtship of some
six or seven years which had involved not only minor squalls in their own

relationship, but a number of force eight gales between their two families,[18] he and Janie Cooper were married.

Alfred remained at the Home Office for a few more months; but in 1875 he found work as one of Her Majesty's Inspectors of Schools in Manchester. He had taken the job largely because it was better paid; but he soon became passionately interested in education as a means of social reform. It was only five years since the Education Act of 1870 had stipulated that provision must be made for elementary education for all, and although thousands of new schools had been built, there was considerable confusion about how they should be run. Graves was one of the educational pioneers who made the 1870 Act work; and in 1879 he and his colleague Rice-Wiggins published their *The Elementary School Manager* which rapidly became the standard work in its field.[19]

Later that year Alfred was promoted to take charge of the West Riding District of Yorkshire, and he and Janie moved to Huddersfield. They took with them their two small children, Philip and Mary; and while they were living in Yorkshire, two more children were born: Richard and Perceval. But the northern winters were too much for Janie, who had begun to suffer from tuberculosis, a disease then usually fatal; and in 1882, hoping that the mild south-westerly breezes of the West Country would be better for Janie's health, they moved south to the West Somerset District where they found a house in Taunton.

Alfred loved his family but never sank into domesticity. He continued to regard poetry as his main calling, received considerable encouragement from Tennyson – whom he and Janie met while holidaying in Ireland – and in 1880 he published a new volume of *Irish Songs and Ballads*.[20] Not long afterwards he was asked by the composer Charles Villiers Stanford, who had been a boyhood companion, to provide him with words to go with a number of old Irish folk tunes. Alfred was easily able to comply, and, knowing little about the rights of authors, was persuaded to sell him fifty songs outright for only £80.[21] This was a dreadfully bad bargain, especially as one of the songs was 'Father O'Flynn', which Alfred had written while he was at the Home Office, to the Kerry version of an Irish air 'The Top of the Cork Road'. It runs like this:

> Of priests we can offer a charmin' variety
> Far renowned for larnin' and piety;
> Still, I'd advance ye widout impropriety
>   Father O'Flynn as the flower of them all.
>
> [Chorus]
>   Here's a health to you, Father O'Flynn,
>   Slainté, and slainté, and slainté agin;

Powerfulest preacher, and
Tinderest teacher, and
Kindliest creature in ould Donegal.

Don't talk of your Provost and Fellows of Trinity,
Famous for ever at Greek and Latinity,
Faix and the divels and all at Divinity,
Father O'Flynn'd make hares of them all!
Come, I vinture to give ye my word,
Never the likes of his logic was heard,
Down from mythology
Into thayology,
Troth! and conchology if he'd the call.

[Chorus]
Here's a health to you, Father O'Flynn, [etc.]

Och! Father O'Flynn, you've the wonderful way wid you,
All ould sinners are wishful to pray wid you,
All the young childer are wild for to play wid you,
You've such a way wid you, Father avick!
Still for all you've so gentle a soul,
Gad, you've your flock in the grandest control;
Checking the crazy ones,
Coaxin' onaisy ones,
Liftin' the lazy ones on wid the stick.

[Chorus]
Here's a health to you, Father O'Flynn, [etc.]

And though avoidin' all foolish frivolity,
Still at all seasons of innocent jollity,
Where was the play-boy could claim an equality
At comicality, Father, wid you?
Once the Bishop looked grave at your jest,
Till this remark set him off wid the rest:
'Is it lave gaiety
All to the laity?
Cannot the clargy be Irishmen too?'

[Chorus]
Here's a health to you, Father O'Flynn, [etc.]

Taken up by the famous baritone Charles Santley, 'Father O'Flynn' became one of the great popular successes of late-Victorian England, earning hundreds of pounds in royalties for Stanford, and thousands for the publisher. It is the song for which Alfred Perceval Graves was most widely known by his contemporaries, and for which he is still remembered in dictionaries of biography; but since he himself received no more than the original £1.12s. od. for 'Father O'Flynn', it is hardly surprising that his pleasure in the song was marred by an uncharacteristic bitterness.[22]

Following their move to Taunton in 1882, Janie's health improved, and she and Alfred had three less anxious years together. Janie was largely occupied with raising their four children, and by early 1885 was expecting a fifth; while Alfred, decried at first as 'that Irish firebrand', had won many friends in Somerset, and had heard his educational experiments praised in the House of Commons by the responsible Minister. But then came tragedy. In the summer of 1885, shortly after they had moved into a new home at Kingston St Mary, a small village just outside Taunton, their children were successively attacked by scarlet fever.

Janie, 'worn out by nursing them,' as Alfred recalled sorrowfully, 'worn out ... and near her fifth confinement, had suddenly to be moved into a cottage some fields away; and there our youngest daughter, Susan was born under disastrous circumstances.' Janie's tuberculosis had flared up again; and this time there was to be no recovery. For months she lay ill in bed, and finally on 24 March 1886 she died. A few minutes before her death she had sent for her children one by one and commended each of them to Christ's keeping. Soon afterwards, Alfred found among her papers a deeply moving letter, which she had written for him a year or two earlier, and in which she told him:[23]

in case of my death what I would like about the children – our children – & you will always remember that your first duty in life is them – you took the responsibility of them, & if God sent them it was your will to have them. I will ask you as if I asked it for myself & for the sake of the love you had for me when you were still a boy – & the love I felt for you as your wife & the duty which I tried (though failing) to fulfil to you ... to look after the children. ... Teach them to be honest, careful, exact, truthful & tell them I loved them & if wishing could do anything I would have lived or died for their good.

Janie then named the individuals to whom she bequeathed various items of her jewellery: but not her wedding ring; she asked to be buried in that, with a piece of Alfred's hair and a

lock of the children's on my heart. ... Bury me as inexpensively and quietly as possible. Give me the last kiss yourself & if you don't mind when your time comes be buried with me whoever you may after marry – though I may have been a trial to you – I have done my best & have suffered more anxiety of mind than anyone knows. I wish I had made you happier, more satisfied. ... God bless you! I will try to wish even my place may be taken but it is very hard however I wish you well – well – well.

Your loving wife
Janie Graves

Utterly devastated by Janie's death, Alfred took a month's leave and went to Ireland, where both the Coopers and the Graveses did their best to comfort him; and in Dublin he also met some of the leaders of the Irish Literary Renaissance, including Katharine Tynan, John Butler Yeats, and John's son William Butler Yeats, 'then still in his teens, but full of promise'. On his return to Somerset Alfred was accompanied by Ruth Cooper, one of his sisters-in-law, who had agreed to keep house at 'The Orchard' for a year. She was followed by two governesses who came and went in rapid succession, finding five lively children more than they could handle. Then Alfred was lucky enough to employ for some three years Miss Ada North, a clergyman's daughter. 'In her,' wrote Alfred, 'I entertained an angel. She was a splendid disciplinarian, always wise and discriminating, and her patience was inexhaustible.' But now, in the autumn of 1891, she was planning to leave the Graves household so that she could look after her elderly mother in London. Alfred was once more in need of a housekeeper, or preferably (thought his sister Lily after talking to Frieduhelm about Amy's uncertain future), a wife.

CHAPTER
4
A VICTORIAN
COURTSHIP

The discreet matchmaking campaign which Lily Graves and Frieduhelm von Ranke decided upon was nearly wrecked at the outset by a major error of judgment. Amy's sister Clara was let in on the scheme, some remnant of childhood resentment surfaced, and she could not resist asking Amy point-blank whether she would like to marry a widower with five children, to which Amy replied with a resounding 'No!'

Undeterred by this tactical setback, General Frieduhelm went smilingly down to Somerset on an apparently casual social visit to his cousin Alfred. However, in the course of their conversation over dinner on the evening of his arrival, Frieduhelm asked whether Alfred, as an Inspector of Schools, could recommend any educational work for a relative of his who had lost her employment. Alfred's first thought was that Amy might become his new housekeeper when Miss North left; but Frieduhelm, affecting surprise, told him that this would be most unsuitable, and gave him some more intriguing details about Amy's appearance, character and private means.

Alfred swallowed the bait which had been so carefully prepared for him. The very next morning he asked Frieduhelm, '"Do you think I should have any chance with her?" "I do not know," said Frieduhelm, "but in any case you must be quick as there are others about."' The spirit of competition, as Frieduhelm had hoped, gave a sharper edge to Alfred's interest. Within twenty-four hours Amy received a letter from Frieduhelm in which he announced that he was now on his way back to Germany, but that he would be staying in London for a short while; and he asked 'if he might bring his cousin Alfred to see Mother & me. Of course we agreed and they both came and dined with us.'

When Alfred was shown into Amy's drawing-room for the first time, on the evening of 22 October 1891, he arrived in a highly receptive mood, and was immediately attracted to his hostess. Amy, now within two months of her thirty-fourth birthday, looked at least five years younger, and it soon became apparent that she was also a woman of some spirit. Looking at this poet and Inspector of Schools, she did not find him particularly displeasing, with his healthy open-air complexion, his ginger moustache, and his thoughtful blue eyes; but nor was she at all impressed. For one thing, he was evidently an inch or two shorter than she. For another, he looked at her rather too closely, and she suddenly realized with annoyance and embarrassment that she was once again being put on show, and that this was the widower with five children of whom Clara had spoken so irritatingly. The rest of the evening was ruined, so far as she was concerned, by Frieduhelm's obvious efforts 'to give Alfred a chance' – especially after dinner, when Alfred turned the pages for her singing 'while Fried sat on the sofa with my Mother, with his back to us', while talking to Luise 'in his "commando" voice, much too loud'.

The following day, Alfred returned to her house, where he found that Amy continued to be discouraging, taking little notice while he talked to Luise about his children and told her something of his family history. When he left, to travel empty-handed back to Somerset, it was clear to Amy that her mother liked Mr Graves a great deal. She herself tried to avoid mentioning him; and when that was impossible, as Luise kept steering the conversation round in his direction, Amy refused to call him by his proper name, referring to him rudely as 'your friend the Tomb', and privately assuming that Alfred would soon fade away and be forgotten like her other suitors. She had reckoned without a factor that is known in our branch of the family as 'the Graves determination'.

First Alfred wrote to Amy claiming that he had lost his German dictionary, and asking her for a literal translation of a German poem which he was planning to turn into English verse. Amy was surprised by this request, and did not really believe his story about the dictionary (though later she wrote that: 'When I got to know him better I thought it quite possible!'); but she politely did as she was asked.

Then came a box of flowers, with a letter of thanks and some Latin words which meant 'I came, I saw, and was conquered.' . . .

His next move was to write that he was coming up to town, largely to see his cousin Fried, and making out that we were relations also, by marriage. I was not ready and did not like the idea.

At this crucial moment, Luise made a decisive intervention. She had gathered from Alfred that his three sons were away at boarding-school, and that Miss North had taken one daughter to Ireland for a holiday in Limerick; but that his other daughter, fourteen-year-old Mary, was still with her father in Somerset. '"I do not think it would be nice of Mr. Graves to leave his little daughter Mary alone at home", said Luise. "You ask her to stay with us, and then you will see him with much less embarrassment."' Amy thought this over, and decided that:

> As he was definitely coming ... this [was] a good idea, but when he asked me to find lodgings for him near us, I refused. So he went to the Great Western hotel for a week. When he brought his daughter to us, I felt bound to say: 'We shall be glad to see you for any meals you like, Mr. Graves.' What do you think? He turned up for breakfast next morning and for every meal after that!

To occupy their guests, Amy and Luise took them to see the sights; and each evening, when Alfred had retired to his hotel, Amy was left with Mary to look after. Mary, usually known as Molly, was described by one of her brothers as 'precocious, though not offensively so, and throughout her life a truly lovable character'.[24] From early childhood she had charmed people with her warmth, her evident delight in living, and the fey delicacy of her striking good looks. Her wide eyes were unusually beautiful, and her family remembered with affection how a gushing visitor had once told Molly, when she was a very little girl, that she had 'nice violet eyes'. Molly had 'treasured this remark in her heart, and one day in an ecstasy of joy, came out with, "I've got nice violet eyes. Smell them!"'[25] Amy, who had hardened her heart against Alfred, found it softened again by Molly's charm, and began to feel sorry for this girl who had no mother to care for her. It was at Madame Tussaud's, the famous exhibition of waxworks, that Luise took Amy aside for a moment, and said that 'Mr. Graves had told her on the way of his wishes and had asked her consent'. Amy, looking perhaps at Molly, 'took no outward notice ... but thought of it the more'.[26]

Later in the week, Alfred brought some photographs of his other children to show Amy, and asked if she and Luise would accompany him the next day to Haileybury College where Philip, now aged fifteen, was to be confirmed. Amy at first refused, but she felt sorry when she 'saw him pack up his photos with a most dejected face and sigh';[27] and when both Luise and Molly said that they wanted to go, she changed her mind. At Haileybury, Amy was very much impressed when 'at the Confirmation Service ... I saw how deeply his father prayed for him ... and I felt that he was a good father, as I could also see by Molly, who was devoted to him.'[28]

After the service Amy met Philip for the first time. A scholar of Haileybury, and 'an exceptionally brilliant boy with an almost photographic memory',[29] he had been deeply upset by his mother's death when he was only nine years old. His sensitivity was qualified by a certain nervous determination; he had his share of the notorious Graves arrogance (from which his father, said never to have made an enemy in his life, was unusually free); and his bright red hair was matched on occasion by a flaming temper. Amy thought that 'he looked untidy, and ... wanted a mother';[30] and she kindly gave him a gold coin to entertain his friends.

On returning to London that evening, Alfred, Amy and Luise went out after dinner to a vocal concert in St James's Hall, where Amy remembered that she had once heard the great Santley singing Alfred's 'Father O'Flynn'. Now she sat next to the poet, who 'look[ed] over the words with me. It was a lovely concert. At the interval Alfred went to see his friends among the singers, behind the Concert Hall, and I remained alone with my mother, and I realised that all the niceness had gone with Mr. Graves. So I began to think I might be getting fond of him.'[31] That night, Amy 'asked God's advice about it in prayer'.[32] She told herself that two great points in Alfred's favour 'were the five children, giving me a vocation which I longed for, and pleasing my Father. Nevertheless I had too much sense to think one should marry without affection, and this was only dawning.'[33]

However, the next morning she was more or less swept off her feet. When she went downstairs, she found Alfred sitting alone in the dining-room, reading *The Times*. And then,

> As I touched the flowers on the table, he jumped up and asked me the momentous question. I did not say No, and perhaps I said Yes. My mother followed into the room at once, and [Molly]. Alfred at once told my Mother that it was 'All Right'. ... I felt it hard that all should be settled so suddenly and before I barely knew my own mind. Immediately after breakfast we had a little talk in the breakfast room and then he felt bound to wire news of his engagement to his Father and Uncle Robert. Now, I felt, my bridges are burnt and I cannot go back![34]

It was less than a month since their first meeting on 22 October;[35] but Alfred had no plans for a long engagement. Their wedding was arranged for 30 December, in Munich.

Heinrich von Ranke, that tough old freethinker, was overjoyed to think that his daughter had been rescued from becoming a medical missionary. He was also pleased that Amy was marrying a Graves, telling her that Clarissa Ranke, born a Graves, had been his favourite aunt. Frieduhelm's wife Lily added that Amy's marriage would be a happy one, as it was founded on shared principles. Even Philip, who on first hearing the news of his father's engagement flew into a rage and smashed his study furniture at Haileybury, eventually calmed down, and agreed to travel out to Munich to attend the wedding with his sister Molly. Amy herself, 'though I wanted to marry [Alfred] at first to be mother to his children, yet I became so fond of him and believed in his affection so much that at the last I would have married him even without any children at all'.[36]

CHAPTER
5
A SECOND
FAMILY

Not long after their wedding-night, spent at an hotel in Regensburg, Alfred and Amy Graves stayed for a few days with Amy's sister Clara. Amy is said to have been shocked by her first experience of the sexual side of married life,[37] and in her sister's home she had 'a dreadful revulsion of feeling, and wondering why I had married Alfred'.[38] Fortunately, as she herself wrote, 'the cloud passed ... and after this shock I do not think I ever looked back again. Alfred was my share of the world of men, as I was his.'[39] She soon took a healthy pleasure in her physical relationship with Alfred; and as an old lady, after listening crossly to a sermon in which a young curate disparaged sexual pleasure in marriage, she took him aside and told him rather fiercely how very wrong he was.

The remainder of their honeymoon was spent in Ireland; and they travelled first to Dublin, where Alfred introduced Amy to his favourite uncle, Robert Perceval Graves, a very old man who retained a keenly intellectual expression. A few years before this Robert's wife had written sadly that 'Graveses are generally un-successful, in spite of their excellence and abilities';[40] and Robert had been a poor man all his life. He was now Sub-Dean of the Chapel Royal, and Vice-Warden of Alexandra College – a pioneering experiment in offering higher education to women – but he received nothing for either of these time-consuming appointments; nor had his definitive and well-received biography of the famous mathematician Sir William Rowan Hamilton made him any money. None of this had embittered Robert. He was an excellent versifier, and counted himself fortunate to have been a personal friend not only of the popular poet Felicia Hemans, but of the great William Wordsworth, whom he had met when he was for eighteen years a curate in the Lake District. When his nephew Alfred was a young man, Robert had taken endless time and trouble over his early poems, and Amy soon realized that 'Alfred was devoted to him.'[41]

Then, after a train journey westward across Ireland came what Amy described as 'the great moment of seeing my Father-in-law, the Bishop of Limerick'.[42] Alfred's father, who had signed himself 'Charles Limerick' for more than twenty-five years, was now an old man of seventy-nine, 'a little below the average height, but with a dignity of carriage that made him appear taller. He had ... blue eyes. ... His forehead was high and dome-shaped, the nose aquiline, the mouth straight and stern, though it relaxed at times into an engaging smile.'[43] Amy 'felt great reverence for him', and found him 'not formidable to talk to',[44] though Charles was indeed a man of formidable distinction.

A former Fellow of Trinity College Dublin, a classical scholar who had once conversed in Latin with one of the brothers Grimm, and a leading authority on the ancient ogham inscriptions, Charles spoke six or seven modern languages, and had a European reputation as a mathematician. He was also valued so highly by Queen Victoria as a preacher that back in the 1860s, when he had been Dean of the Chapel Royal in Dublin, she had given him a ring distinguished by five large diamonds set in the form of a cross, which he still wore on one of the fingers of his right hand. Since the death of his wife Selina, a high-spirited and beautiful woman in whose honour Mendelssohn had once improvised, the Bishop had led a comparatively lonely life in his vast palace, looked after by his daughter Lily;[45] and for some years he had only continued in office under pressure from his fellow bishops, who valued his advice and long experience. He took to Amy at once, and she was touched when at their first meeting he said: 'I hope to live a little longer to be your father-in-law.'[46]

After a lengthier stay at Limerick than they had planned, as Amy went down with influenza and lived for a few days on beef tea sent up to her rooms by Lily, the newly-weds travelled back to England. It was early in February when they reached their house at Kingston St Mary, and the Bishop soon received a letter of thanks from Amy, who told him:

> It sounds very sweet to be called 'Mother' by the children. We had such a welcome on arriving! Miss North had decorated the hall with drapery & an inscription 'Willkommen liebe Mama!' The church bells rang & the servants presented us with a silver & china butter dish.[47]

At Miss North's side was 'dear little six-year-old Susie', who had 'a most beautiful head of hair ... with ringlets of a deep chestnut hue, here and there shot with dark purplish sheen'.[48] A slight but spirited girl, who was not afraid to stand up to her elders when she felt she was in the right, she was especially welcoming to Amy, because she had no recollection at all of her real mother; and Amy in turn found her 'very clever and lovable', with 'particularly nice manners'.[49]

Molly came home from her day-school in the afternoon; but Philip, often known in the family as 'Eli', was away at Haileybury; and it was not until the start of the Easter holidays that Amy met Richard and Perceval, who were also away at boarding-school. Richard, or 'Dick', was a child of eleven who was very clever, but totally lacking in self-confidence, with 'a pathetic little face, rather sad'; while ten-year-old Perceval, nicknamed 'Bones', was an adventurous child, 'fat and cheerful-looking'. Alfred was away on one of his tours of inspection when Amy's three stepsons arrived home, and she wrote to the Bishop: 'Fancy my sitting down to each meal as the solitary parent of five children!'[50]

Years later, Susan wrote that she and her siblings had been 'clever – cheerful, & with a great delight in violence towards each other. ... I hardly remember a week of the holidays of our youth when Dick, Eli or Bones were not hammering each other for something, & I getting knocked about for butting in.'[51] Amy found them hard to handle at first. Philip never fully accepted her authority, distanced himself by always addressing her as 'Mater' rather than 'Mother', and thoroughly resented her efforts to influence his behaviour. The others were more amenable, though Amy was shocked to find that when she asked Alfred to intervene on one occasion, he only 'chased them round the dining-table, getting in a smack when he could ... but they were fleet of foot'. After this, she devised her own methods of discipline: 'When Perceval was very naughty ... I said I would not come to kiss him good-night. He howled aloud, and I thought perhaps that I had found a better way.'[52]

Before long, Amy was expecting a child of her own; and in November, writing to congratulate the Bishop on his eightieth birthday, she told him how much she wished to become 'the mother of another grandson to you, to carry on your name worthily'.[53] In the event the first child of Alfred's second family, born on the morning of 29 November 1892, was a girl. She was named Clarissa after the Bishop's sister who had, in Amy's words, 'made the first link between the Graves and Ranke families'; and Janie, which was Amy's 'special choice', as a memorial to Alfred's first wife. Although she was disappointed not to have a son, Amy was very excited to have 'reached the crown of life in real motherhood'.[54] However, she was also worried that her stepchildren would be jealous if she gave too much particular attention to Clarissa, and she therefore made the mistake of 'kiss[ing] my beautiful baby very little. ... But they were all so sweet to little Clarissa that I felt they loved her too.'[55] Possibly this lack of a really warm, loving relationship with her mother at such a crucial stage contributed to the severe emotional problems which beset Clarissa in later life.

But for the time being, at least, all seemed well; and not long after Clarissa's birth there was great excitement when Alfred secured a new appointment to a large London District which included the tough working-class areas of Southwark, Bermondsey and Rotherhithe. Inspectors of Schools were normally expected to live within their district, but Alfred was given special permission to live some miles to the south-west in Wimbledon, a far more salubrious London suburb where several of Alfred's Irish friends had already found homes.

Since their marriage, Amy had paid off a number of Alfred's debts, including the very substantial sum of £380 which he owed to the Bishop; and now she was able to make a still more important contribution. It seemed impossible to find houses with enough bedrooms for their growing family, which were not also embellished with huge stables, billiard-rooms, and other features which made them ridiculously large and expensive; and after a long and fruitless search, it was agreed that Amy would have a new house built, to their own specifications. In the meantime, in March 1893, they moved 'on the fagend of a lease' into Edenhurst, a comfortable home with a pleasant garden in Arterberry Road.

It was at Edenhurst that on 7 March 1894 Amy's second child was born, another girl, this time with lovely brown eyes and short dark curls, who was therefore named Rosaleen after the 'Dark Rosaleen' of Irish folk-song. Although Amy was still hoping for a son, she was no longer so worried about making her stepchildren jealous, and was much warmer towards Rosaleen than she had been towards Clarissa. In her own words, 'I gave my love a freer rein.'[56]

Three months after Rosaleen's birth, the family moved into the new house which Amy had built for them. Alfred described it as

> simply designed ... but. ... Large over-hanging eaves and green Cumberland slates were special features. ... We named it Red Branch House after the knights of the Red Branch, celebrated in Irish chivalry for their poetry and hospitality, and from one of whom my [maternal] grandmother was said to be descended. In further justification of the name we could soon show red hawthorn blossom, red yew and holly berries, and other red branches in the garden.[57]

Not long after moving into Red Branch House, Amy had once more become pregnant; and it was in the visitors' room overlooking the garden, in the early hours of 24 July 1895, two days after Alfred's forty-ninth birthday, that their third child was born. To Amy's great joy she had at last produced a son.

A few weeks later, the boy was taken to St John's church to be baptized. It was not difficult to choose his name. The autumn of 1893 had seen the death of Alfred's beloved Uncle Robert, who had visited them with the Bishop both at The Orchard and at Edenhurst, had charmed Amy by his poetry reading, and had bequeathed to them the sole extravagance of his generally impoverished life, a handsome oak bookcase which he had had especially made to hold his most treasured volumes. Robert was also the name of Robert Windham Graves, a younger brother of Alfred's who was then the British consul at Erzerum in Armenia; [58] and of Amy's favourite younger brother, Robert von Ranke, a twenty-one-year-old student who had visited her in Wimbledon the previous summer. So the baby was christened Robert von Ranke Graves. After the service, there was 'a festive tea in the garden', to celebrate the birth of the son for whom Amy had longed so eagerly and welcomed so gladly, and who was later to give her cause for so much pride and so much sorrow.

BOOK
TWO
ROBERT'S
CHILDHOOD
1895–1909

CHAPTER
1
UNDER THE
SILVER MOON

Childhood: a time of powerful emotions and sharp sensations, when we confront the world most directly, absorbing its light and shade, its colours and darkness, reacting to its alternate warmth and coldness with joy so piercing and with sorrow so tragic that either emotion would break an adult's heart; a time whose fulfilled hopes and unsatisfied longings establish the emotional tenor of the rest of our lives; though looking backwards we have only fragmentary memories, so that some of us are forever haunted by a lost world and a lost reality.

In November 1895, when he was four months old, Robert was taken by his parents to Russell & Sons of Hill Road, Wimbledon, the distinguished firm of photographers to Her Majesty the Queen, and to their Royal Highnesses the Prince and Princess of Wales. Sitting on Amy's lap, his left hand clutching one of her fingers, his head leaning securely upon her breast, Robert stares quizzically at the camera, while his mother holds him proudly and tenderly. Beside him, sitting comfortably on their father's left knee, is fifteen-month-old Rosaleen, looking plump and healthy. Alfred himself smiles confidently and perhaps a little roguishly towards us. Clarissa, a slender elfin child of three, with a far-away look in her eyes, stands on her father's right; while nine-year-old Susie, pretty and mischievous, stands at the back between Alfred and Amy. Each of the three youngest children already has its own highly individual share of Graves and Ranke characteristics, though many of these are at this stage latent rather than apparent.

From the Graves side of his family, Robert has inherited charm, warmth, good-humour, a bad business sense, a great love of words, a seemingly endless capacity for hard work, enormous pride, great sensitivity, an occasional cool arrogance, and a brain so quick and changeable that half-finished sentences are left abandoned and forgotten in mid-air. From the Rankes he has both the iron constitution and the robust spirit of his grandfather Heinrich, whose youthful iconoclasm and later acceptance by the establishment are to be mirrored to some extent in his own life; and from his mother and maternal grandmother, a high-minded and rather narrow idealism which is to be constantly at war with other aspects of his personality.

Robert's first experience of foreign travel came as early as May 1896, when he was not quite ten months old, a sturdy child with intelligent grey eyes and curly brown hair. Amy, who had not returned to Germany since her wedding, took Clarissa, Rosaleen and Robert to visit their grandparents. She found it 'a great treat to get home to our beautiful old home Laufzorn, where my children could now pick up the coloured lights from the [stained-glass] windows [in the banqueting hall] as I had done before them'.¹ Robert, approved of by Heinrich, and made much of by Luise, was carried around the cavernous depths of the ancient hunting lodge, and taken out for picnics under the sweet-smelling pines.

Red Branch House had been let for the summer; and when Amy and her children returned to London at the beginning of July, they spent a night in a London hotel, where they were joined by Alfred with Molly and Susan. The next morning Philip, Richard and Perceval arrived. Eli was in excellent spirits: his schooldays were over, and he was now a scholar of Oriel College, Oxford. Dick was also in good form: since winning a scholarship to Haileybury his former lack of confidence had evaporated almost overnight, and he was now as lively though not as rebellious as his elder brother. When Nurse Sutterly and their two housemaids were also ready, they all set out for the station, on the first leg of their journey to Ireland.

Alfred, remembering the summers he had enjoyed as a child on the Irish coast, had rented The Mill House at Buncrana, in a remote part of Donegal. As he had hoped, it was a wonderful place for children. He took the older ones fishing in the hills, while Amy took the others to Lough Swilly, a beautiful sea-inlet on whose shores Robert learned to walk.

Their holiday was enlivened by a visit from Alfred's brother Arnold, another literary Graves who lived in Dublin where he combined play-writing with official duties and voluntary work. However, there was a great deal more worry than pleasure so far as Amy was concerned. The house was extremely damp; as so often in the country it was difficult to buy fresh vegetables, the drinking-water and the sanitation both failed, and eleven-year-old Susie had a very narrow escape: she had put up a swing in an outhouse, and the beam to which she had attached it came down with her weight. Amy also worried about her children drowning: not only at Buncrana, where it was said that the young child of the last family to have lived there had drowned in the stream which flowed through the garden; but on the voyage back across the Irish Sea, when Robert, showing an early streak of independence, ran away from his parents and could not be found for some time.

Robert's earliest distinct memories dated from the following year. In May 1897, when he was two months short of his second birthday, he was 'held up to the window to watch a carnival procession for the Diamond Jubilee [of Queen Victoria]'.[2] By this time, he had learned to find his way around Red Branch House.[3] Through the front door, one entered a large hall, from which doors led left into the dining-room, right and half-right to Alfred's study and a small drawing-room, and opposite into a large drawing-room. From there, french windows opened on to the garden, where the children were given small flower-beds of their own, and where Robert showed an early preference for double red daisies.

Down a side passage beyond the dining-room were the kitchen, scullery, and back staircase. The main staircase was at the end of the hall, and led up to the first floor, on which the family bedrooms were to be found. Here Robert's parents had a large double room, with a bathroom attached; there was another bathroom and lavatory, a linen room, three smaller bedrooms, and a nursery at the end of the passage, facing the front of the house; while opposite Alfred and Amy's room was the visitors' room in which Robert had been born.

Above, on the second floor, there were bedrooms for the cook, the kitchen-maid, the parlourmaid Emily Dykes, and old Nurse Sutterly. Heating was by coal fire; but Amy, remembering how exhausting it had once been for her to keep a fire going in 'Granny's' room, had installed an ingenious hand-lift by which coal could be hauled from the cellar to whichever floor was required.

Nurse Sutterly took Robert out for regular walks in a perambulator. Red Branch House was the first house to be built in Lauriston Road, so if she turned right, they found themselves almost immediately in narrow Ridgway Road. This ran from north to south through the most select part of Wimbledon, a largely residential area with two main groups of shops, and an occasional public house: one of them, the Swan Inn, within a stone's throw of their garden.

But more often they turned left, and walked eastward along Lauriston Road until after a few hundred yards they reached the edge of Wimbledon Common, a large unspoiled area of grassland and small woods, criss-crossed with sandy walks. It was here that they sometimes met the ageing poet Swinburne, on his way to the Rose and Crown for a daily pint of beer: all that his companion Watts-Dunton allowed him, after he had nearly drunk himself to death some years earlier. Swinburne had a great affection for small children, and would stop Robert's perambulator to pat him on the head and kiss him.

Robert disliked being made a fuss of in this way, and later recalled these meetings with irritation; though his feelings were soothed to some extent when he realized that Swinburne's pats on the head gave him a link through only three people with Queen Anne, who had lived two centuries before him. She had touched the young Dr Johnson in an attempt to cure his scrofula; Johnson as an old man had patted Walter Savage Landor on the head; and Landor as a very old man had given a poetic blessing to the young Swinburne.

In the summer of 1897 there was another family holiday. After all the difficulties at Buncrana, Amy refused to holiday in Ireland again; and one of their Wimbledon friends advised them, if they did not mind 'roughing it a little', to try the hillside village of Harlech, on the coast of Merionethshire in North Wales. They found it a remarkably unspoiled village of small granite houses with slate roofs, dominated then as now by the ruined shell of a magnificent mediaeval castle. Several hundred feet below the village was the flat sandy plain of the Morfa, where 'Golf was starting, but there was no club-house'; and beyond the golf-links were sand-dunes, and then a wide, safe, sandy beach.

They all liked Harlech so much that Amy began to think that it would be a good idea to 'invest in [building] a house & take the summer holiday as interest, & let it at other times'. Finding a site was not easy; but one day, when the children were picking blackberries on the rocky slopes above the road to the north of Harlech, Amy 'finally climbed up after them and seeing the world spread out before me and heaven so near as it seemed, I said "I should like to die here!" Alfred said "We had better live here first." On enquiry the owner of the land ... was willing to sell it for £100, with a little trickling stream running through it.'[4] At the end of the summer, leaving the conveyancing in the hands of solicitors, the Graveses returned to Wimbledon.

Before long, another important decision was taken. Nurse Sutterly, who had been unwell for some time, retired; and after interviewing a number of candidates whom she considered quite unsuitable, Amy decided to replace her with Emily Dykes, the young house-parlourmaid. 'She was excellent,' Amy recalled, 'truly good & nice ... a Christian in word & deed & kind but firm with the children.'[5] It was important because 'Master Robert, Miss Rosaleen, and Miss Clarissa', as they were called by Emily, spent far more time with her than they did with their mother. 'We had a nurse, and we had each other,' Robert was to write later, 'and that was companionship enough.'[6] Emily was a 'bridge between the servants and ourselves'; and Robert liked to recall the verse which she used to recite about herself:

> Emily Dykes is my name;
> England is my nation;
> Netheravon is my dwelling-place,
> And Christ is my salvation.[7]

Under Emily's firm but benevolent control, the children's life in the nursery was usually a happy one; though Robert recalled one day 'looking up with a sort of despondent terror at a cupboard in the nursery, which stood accidentally open, and which was filled to the ceiling with octavo volumes of Shakespeare'.[8]

Every day, as was customary in the better Victorian households, the children spent at least an hour with their mother in the drawing-room. Here she talked to them, played with them, and sometimes, as a special treat, reached down *Picture Lessons in Natural History*, each page of which was over two feet wide, and in which they gazed with fascinated wonder upon huge pictures of Rhinoceros, Reindeer, Ostrich and Elephant.[9] On Sundays this volume would be replaced by a German picture book containing thirty large and vividly coloured illustrations such as 'Geburt Jesu' or 'Christus im Sturm', with which Amy taught them stories from the New Testament.[10]

Robert had been busily talking since the spring, retailing to Amy various sayings of his sisters, and he was usually lively and animated. Only on one occasion did Clarissa notice that Robert was strangely subdued: he went to stand at the back of their mother's armchair and began earnestly 'groping in [her] back hair'. Apparently he had misheard some lines of the hymn which runs:

> Our earthly friends may fail us
> And change with changing years,

and he was trying to make sure that Amy's ears were still in good condition! Robert adored his mother; and he was also very strongly attached to Molly. Aged twenty, Molly was now studying at Swanley Horticultural College with the aim of becoming a professional gardener; but when she was at home she was like a second mother to Robert, who therefore named his doll 'Molly Amy' in their joint honour.[11]

In the autumn, with most of the children away at school, college or university, Amy took Robert and the other young ones back to Harlech where she hoped to supervise the building of their holiday home. But the owner of the land would not allow the sale of the land to be completed, and did not even answer letters, until after several wasted months she realized that he was 'waiting for me to offer to pay all expenses, his solicitor as well as my own, & when I agreed to this all went swimmingly'.[12]

In the meantime Red Branch House had been let for the winter, and Alfred, separated from his family, spent a miserable time lodging with a Wimbledon cleric, and had a severe attack of shingles. He was now only fifty-one, but his health had been a worry to Amy since an incident during the summer.

His younger brother Charles, then assistant editor of the *Spectator*, and a witty versifier with several published volumes to his credit, had been with them on the beach at Harlech. Alfred was bathing, when, as Amy described it, he was suddenly 'taken with a violent nose-bleeding & his brother Charlie & I helped him in. He had to go to bed & have his nose plugged & then a holiday ... was suggested. I could not leave the family ... so let Molly take him to Quellyn Hotel at the foot of Snowdon, where he could rest & have some fishing.'13 Alfred had come back from that holiday looking 'all the better'; but when Amy and the children spent Christmas with him in London – they rented a furnished house in the Royal Crescent – it was clear that Alfred was far from well. Doctors were consulted, and advised Alfred that his arteries were hardening, and that he must give up drinking.

For a while, Alfred considered early retirement; but his health began to improve again, and the only lasting consequence was that he signed the pledge, vowing never to touch alcohol again. Up to this time he had enjoyed a glass of whiskey, and he and Amy had usually had wine with their evening meal. Now that came to an end for both of them, because Amy, to make it easier for Alfred to continue to abstain from alcohol, signed the pledge as well. So, incidentally, did five-year-old Clarissa, who went along with them for the signing. As an adult she was to complain with justifiable bitterness that she had been 'far too young to know what I was doing'; but a promise was a promise, and for the rest of her life her strict conscience would allow her to accept a drink only on rare occasions, and 'on medical grounds'.14

By March 1898 Alfred was in much better health, the conveyancing of the Harlech property had been completed, and Amy took her three young children back to North Wales. Soon she had engaged an architect from Caernarvon, and was able to see the site being levelled, and the foundations laid. It was an exciting time for the children, who 'used to talk of going to see the ruins, for so our house in the building looked'.15

Heinrich came over from Munich to visit them for a few days in their lodgings at Gomerian House; and although he was known as a strict disciplinarian, he taught Amy a lesson in humanity which she never forgot. On returning from a long walk over the hills one evening, they found Amy's cook 'smiling happily, but unable to talk. She was hopelessly drunk.' Heinrich and Amy had to carry her up to her room, and Amy decided that next morning she would give her the sack. Heinrich pleaded for mercy; one mistake should be forgiven. Amy agreed to this, the cook stayed on for another few years, 'and I never saw her tipsy again'.16

With her children, Amy was loving but firm. It was at Gomerian House that she had my only real trouble with Rosaleen. We were returning from the seaside and had to pass a stile, which Rosaleen could just manage, but remembered having been lifted over. Now I had heavy Robert to attend to and told her to get over it or through it alone. This infuriated her and with her little fists she struck me as hard as she could to make me put Robert down and get her over. 'Rosaleen,' I said, 'you must be punished for this when you get home.'[17]

Almost as soon as they arrived back, the dinner-bell rang, and the punishment had to be deferred; but Amy, taking it as axiomatic that 'one must never threaten punishment to children without carrying it out', later called the four-year-old Rosaleen into her bedroom. 'She came like a little lamb and I smacked her, hard though it was. After a short interval we walked away to find the others. She never smacked me again.'

Besides demanding good behaviour, Amy encouraged her children to develop artistic interests. Alfred's preoccupation with poetry and song naturally gave their household a literary and musical flavour, and in February 1898 Amy had noted that Susie was 'writing [a] play, clever child'.[18] Soon afterwards five-year-old Clarissa had also 'dictated a wonderful play for her age, to me'.[19] In addition, Amy taught them to sing, and encouraged them to make up rhymes. Alfred noticed that Robert 'showed a taste for music and singing when very young',[20] and Amy made a special note about his singing as early as May 1898. Three months later, a few weeks after his third birthday, she proudly recorded his first rhyming couplet, perhaps referring to something he had seen in Harlech Castle:

> Two little flowers
> In the towers.[21]

The only unfortunate aspect of all this artistic endeavour was that Amy was so obviously proud of success, and so obviously disappointed by failure of any kind, that her children grew up feeling that they were loved by her not for themselves but for whatever special talents they possessed. This placed them under a pressure which was far more severe than Amy can have realized, and which has had serious consequences not only in their generation of the family, but in the next.

After Easter, Amy had left the new house being built, and had returned to Wimbledon, where she was soon caught up in her usual round of household duties and social obligations. Robert later commented drily that his mother was so taken up with these concerns that they 'did not see her continuously, unless on Sunday or when we happened to be ill'.[22] Holidays were a further exception. That summer they went down to Littlehampton on the south coast, where Robert was photographed on his mother's lap still wearing a baby's smock, but proudly clasping a bucket and spade.

The following spring, Robert and his sisters caught whooping cough, and again saw more of Amy than usual. In between dosing them with a sweet-tasting mixture of castor oil, honey and lemon, Amy entitled a slim red notebook *The Red Branch Song Book*, and began writing verses to amuse her children. The first of these, 'The Lost Child', contained some powerful images: a small boy with no clothes on is savagely beaten by a giant; though all ends well, because:

> The giant got tired of this very soon
> And left him under the silver moon.
> I need not say he ran home very fast
> And was safe in his mother's arms at last.

Next, Amy wrote and illustrated a poem about 'The Sick Children' themselves:

> Three little children were ill in bed
> And paid no attention to what I said.
> They showed their pink legs & kicked about
> And with their feet played in & out.
> I don't know how many times I said
> Roberty you must be covered in bed.
> And when he & Ros in a fight were found
> You might have heard a whipping sound.

She described them building brick towers, making a garden for their dolls; and using a thimble on the peel of an orange:

> To punch out sovereigns nice & thin.
> You lay the peel upon a board
> And soon increase your golden hoard.

Amy insisted that they should stay in their own beds in the nursery, to keep out of any draughts; and the poem ends with Clarissa asking for the three of them to be allowed 'a really proper play' together, which they could have if they were put into a single bed,

> 'Two at the foot & one at the head.
> 'It would be such a delightful plan

'And we'll promise to be as good as we can.'
While two of them played with their coloured bricks
Rosaleen gave them some underclothes kicks
But Robert proceeded with too much haste
The brilliant hues of those bricks to taste,
As if he hoped it were sugar-candy
Until I smacked his handy-pandy
And Rosaleen asked with a cough and a sneeze
From under the clothes, 'Whose feet are these?'

A few pages further on in *The Red Branch Song Book* there are some amusing
nonsense rhymes dictated by Clarissa and Rosaleen; and then come two verses
by Robert. The first reads simply:

My fingers are very tall
And I put my soapy fingers on the wall.

This is of little interest, and probably relates to the erasing of some pencil
scrawls which Amy had complained about in 'The Sick Children'. However,
the second verse is worth examining. It shows that a few months before his
fourth birthday Robert already had a considerable interest in words, and a
lively imagination. He also had one of the most crucial attributes for a budding
poet, which is a good ear. Some of his lines are obviously derived from the
nursery rhyme 'Who killed Cock Robin?'; and he has also remembered phrases
like 'under the silver moon' from Amy's 'The Lost Child'.

Who did that?
Said the grown-up cat.
I not
Said the dot
I did, said the spider
With my glass of cider
Then came the fox
With his little box
Then in the room where the four were placed
Came a very big girl with some nasty paste
Then she pasted the four
Against the door
She said my dears
I have my fears

My Mother will scold me soon
For she has gone
To Wimbledon
Under the silver moon.

CHAPTER
2
AN IRISH
FUNERAL

Charles, Bishop of Limerick, Robert's grandfather, died in July 1899. Alfred
set out at once for Ireland, followed shortly by Amy, and they spent a week
or ten days at Limerick, where they attended the funeral and heard the reading
of the will. Although the Bishop's death made a decisive break with the Anglo-
Irish past of the Graves family, memories of that past haunted Red Branch
House, and lay like an oppressive weight upon Robert's childhood.

Besides receiving a substantial inheritance of some £3,700, Alfred inherited
not only trunkloads of family papers, some of them dating as far back as the
1760s, but numerous portraits, family heirlooms, and items of furniture with
some sentimental family interest. In the drawing-room, on the wall beside
Robert Perceval Graves's massive oak bookcase, with its signed edition of
Wordsworth's poems, there were now huge framed portraits in marble both
of the Bishop and of his wife Selina.[23] The Bishop was held up by Amy as
an example of virtuous living; while Alfred, who was deeply interested in family
history, told the children that the lovely Selina had been the daughter of the
Physician-General to the Forces in Ireland, and that her Cheyne pedigree
was flawless back to the thirteenth century.

For the dining-room, Alfred brought back from Ireland a set of solidly-
upholstered dining-chairs whose backs had been stamped with the Bishop's
mitre and initials; and an oval glass case containing gold medals won by the
Bishop and his brothers, set on three leaves of a green velvet shamrock, and
inscribed: 'Charles Graves, John Graves, Robert Graves: First Gold Medallists
in Mathematics and Classics, Dublin University.' These medals were not only
a record of past family successes, but showed the children what was expected
of them in their own day.

Oil portraits of the Bishop's parents also arrived: here was John Crosbie
Graves, a mild-looking man, and a barrister who had risen to be Chief Magis-
trate of Police in Dublin; and there, beside him, his beautiful and ambitious
wife Helena, who had been a leader of Dublin society in the 1820s and 1830s.

It was through Helena, born Helena Perceval, that the family claimed its most distinguished ancestors, whose deeds were often on Alfred's lips. A distant cousin of Spencer Perceval, the Prime Minister who was assassinated in the year 1812, Helena was descended from Richard Perceval, who had won the favour of Queen Elizabeth I when he deciphered letters which gave her 'the first certain intelligence' about the destination of the Spanish Armada; and from Sir Walter Perceval, who as a young man of nineteen had been knighted on the field of Crecy by King Edward III. Beyond Walter, the line ran back to such notables as Henry I of France, and Anne of Russia.

The Graves family tree was more doubtful. Beyond John Crosbie Graves, the line ascended through a dean, a rector, and a Sheriff of Limerick – and then, above the 1690s, was lost in uncertainty; though Alfred passed on to his children the romantic tradition that the Irish branch of the family had been founded by Colonel William Graves, the Roundhead who had been put in charge of Charles I at Holmby House, and was converted by him into an ardent Royalist. There was some old family silver to support a link between the Irish Graveses and their more illustrious English namesakes; they also shared an eagle as their crest, and the aristocratic motto: 'Aquila non captat muscas', or 'The Eagle does not trouble itself with flies'. The Bishop, after prolonged researches had led nowhere, received a new grant of arms from the College of Arms in Dublin, confirming the armorial ensigns 'used by his family (long settled in Ireland) and borne without dispute'; and entitling all the descendants of John Crosbie Graves and Helena Perceval to quarter those arms with the arms of the Perceval family.

This brightly coloured grant of arms, rolled up in a tin document case, was occasionally brought out to show to Robert and his siblings; and after the Bishop's death Alfred also inherited a great deal of family silver, which was used regularly at table. It was mainly nineteenth-century plate, but there were also some solid silver spoons from the eighteenth century, and all of them were marked on the handle with an engraving of the Graves eagle.

So rich an inheritance gave each individual member of the family a great deal to live up to, and for some the burden was too much. But there was a highly positive side to all this for a future historical novelist. People long dead were talked about as familiarly as though they had only just left the room; and the house was full of their portraits and their most treasured possessions. History was not something only to be found in books for Robert and his brothers and sisters. It flowed constantly about them, as an essential part of the fabric of family culture.

The summer of 1899 was spent at Harlech, where at last the new house had been completed. Alfred, mourning his father's loss, was comforted by a letter from Archbishop Alexander, Primate of All Ireland, who wrote that Charles Limerick had been 'one of the finest specimens of a dignified Irish clergyman of the old school whom I have ever seen. He had the graceful courtesy of a perfect gentleman.'[24] The new house faced westward, and it was now that Alfred, feeling particularly drawn towards his Irish past, 'asked a good authority the Welsh for "towards Ireland", and on his advice named our new home, "Erinfa"'.[25]

Amy, at the age of forty-two, was expecting her fourth child. She had a happy time at Erinfa: 'Every day', she wrote, 'we made new discoveries in the beauty of our surroundings & Alfred & I would call to each other, while dressing, to notice a fresh aspect of the scene which we had not noticed before';[26] and when they returned to Wimbledon at the beginning of September everything was made as easy as possible for her. Philip, with whom she still had occasional rows, and who was now studying for the Indian Civil Service exams, began boarding out in London near his work; while Susan lodged with one of her friends from the Wimbledon High School, coming home only on Sundays.

At last, on the evening of 1 December, the doctor was sent for. Appropriately enough, he arrived dressed for a dinner party, in white tie and tails; for within a few minutes Amy had given birth to the boy who was to become the *bon viveur* of the family. As a last mark of respect for the Bishop whose funeral they had attended earlier in the year, Alfred and Amy named their new son Charles.

CHAPTER
3
CLOUDS
AND SUNSHINE

Clarissa, whose seventh birthday had fallen on the eve of Charles's birth, took a personal interest in the new baby, commenting that 'she did not mind Mother taking him, but she felt sure that the new baby was a late birthday present for her!'[27] Robert, aged four and a half, had no such warm feelings either then or later about his brother's birth.

It was natural for Robert to feel jealous of the child who appeared to have supplanted him in his mother's affections; but by an unlucky chance the wound which he suffered went far deeper than normal. Within a few days of Charles's arrival, Robert went down with scarlet fever. He could not be nursed at home because of the danger to the new baby; and within a few hours of the illness being diagnosed, an ambulance drew up to the front door of Red Branch House, and Robert was sent away by himself to a public fever hospital. 'The moment he understood why he had to go,' Alfred recalled admiringly, 'he was extraordinarily brave and went off without a complaint or whimper.'[28]

For the next two months or so, Robert was isolated from his family in a hospital ward which he shared with:

> only one other bourgeois child ... the rest were all proletarians. I did not notice particularly that the attitude of the nurses or the other patients to me was different; I accepted the kindness and spoiling easily, because I was accustomed to it. But I was astonished at the respect and even reverence that this other little boy, a clergyman's child, was given. 'Oh!' the nurses would cry after he had gone; 'Oh!' they cried, 'he did look a little gentleman in his pretty white pellisse when they came to take him away.' 'He was a fair toff,' echoed the little proletarians.[29]

On his return to Red Branch House, far from being welcomed with open arms, Robert's 'accent was commented on and [he] was told that the boys in [his] ward had been very vulgar'.[30] In addition, all his toys had been burned in case they were contaminated. And as if this were not enough, his parents

were in a state of depression about events which were happening thousands
of miles away in South Africa. 'The Boer War clouded my early childhood',[31]
Robert wrote later; and Amy recalled that 'a great gloom lay over us during
the siege of Ladysmith'.[32] During February 1900 the tide of battle began to
turn in the British favour; and when the news came that Ladysmith had been
relieved, Perceval was involved in the famous 'Ladysmith Rag' at Haileybury,
which was followed by the systematic flogging of almost two-thirds of the school.

A sunnier time followed during the early part of the summer, when Robert,
coming up to his sixth birthday, was taken with some of his brothers and
sisters on another visit to Laufzorn. It was an enchanted place. Clarissa's strong-
est memory in later years was:

> of the darkness and the profound silence of the surrounding pinewoods,
> broken only by the sighing of the wind in the upper boughs, or the occasional
> fall of a cone to the carpet of pine-needles beneath. Where the trunks
> thinned one might come upon a clearing with sheets and sheets of scented
> lilies of the valley, with their leaves standing up like green, pointed wings.
> At the wood's edge hearts-ease looked out at one with diminutive faces,
> and forget-me-nots gazed up with celestial eyes.[33]

And Robert declared that:

> Our summers there were easily the best things of my early childhood. Pine
> forests and hot sun, red deer and black and red squirrels, acres of blue-
> berries and wild strawberries; nine or ten different kinds of edible mush-
> rooms that we went into the forest to pick, and unfamiliar flowers in the
> fields ... the farm with all the usual animals except sheep, and drives through
> the countryside in a brake behind my grandfather's greys. And bathing
> in the Iser under a waterfall; the Iser was bright green and said to be
> the fastest river in Europe.[34]

Back in England, the newspapers were still filled with news of the Boer
War, which dragged on and on; and Robert noticed that it caused 'great tension
at the breakfast-table' between his father, 'whose political views were always
orthodox', and Philip, who openly supported the Boers.[35] Philip, who had passed
the first of his Indian Civil Service exams, had joined the family in North
Wales, where they were spending part of the summer at Erinfa. After breakfast,
Amy would sometimes see him through the drawing-room window,

> walking up & down the Erinfa terrace, often talking to pretty nurse Parker,
> who was in charge of baby Charles, & coughing & coughing & expectorating.
> Nurse Parker was a trained Nurse & did not at all like the sound, but
> to us all the shock came, when at his second medical exam, he was rejected,
> as suffering from incipient tuberculosis.[36]

Philip spent the next year at Arosa, then the highest sanatorium in Switzerland. Uncertain for a long time whether he would live or die, he drank 'blood and iron' (stout and champagne) on Christmas Day, began writing a book which he hoped would be read in Ireland; and like Hans Castorp in Thomas Mann's *The Magic Mountain*, he found in the company of his fellow patients a microcosm of an increasingly troubled Europe: 'From what I've seen here,' he wrote home to his father, 'I'm convinced that the Germans are the most dangerous enemies to Great Britain in the future. They all admit their hostility & they're much more persistent than the French.'[37]

While Philip lay on his hospital bed in Switzerland, Molly, the first woman to pass the Royal Horticultural Society's examinations, was working as a professional gardener in charge of the orchid house at Glasnevin in Ireland; and Dick, aged twenty, tall and a trifle arrogant, was up at Magdalen College, Oxford. So the only two of Robert's half-brothers and sisters who were much at home were Perceval and Susan. On leaving school, Perceval had been articled as a clerk to a London firm of solicitors, but he did not care much for office life, and spent as much time as possible playing cricket or rugger, and going to theatres and music-halls, where he was an ardent fan of 'Marie Lloyd in her directoire velvet gown, with lots of leg showing and that wink of hers which pepped up some of her naughtiest numbers'. Fourteen-year-old Susan, Perceval's favourite sister, was still at Wimbledon High School, where she was famous for having thrown an atlas at her form-mistress, 'a passing shot which found its mark as the lady made her exit through the classroom door'.[38]

Nine-year-old Clarissa and seven-year-old Rosaleen had also begun attending the Wimbledon High School; so during term time Robert, smartly dressed in his sailor suit, had few friends to play with. In any case, Wimbledon must have seemed very dull after holidays at Laufzorn or Harlech, and Robert later looked back on Wimbledon as a 'wrong place, neither town nor country'. He particularly disliked Wednesdays, when Amy was 'At Home', and he and Rosaleen and Clarissa had to join their mother and her guests for tea in the drawing-room. 'We were called down in our Sunday clothes to eat cakes, be kissed, and be polite. My sisters were made to recite.'[39]

They were prepared for this on Sundays, when Amy gave them their religious instruction, and they learned a number of hymns. Robert sometimes found this dull, and years later Clarissa reminded him of the time when:

Mother had been giving us our Sunday lessons under great difficulties. You had been so tiresome that she had been obliged to send you out of her bed-room. Even so, she could not get on with Rosaleen and me, for you refused to stay outside but opened the door and continued to look in. When she remonstrated with you, you replied: 'I had rather be a door-keeper in the house of my God: than to dwell in the tents of ungodliness.'[40]

Besides making them learn hymns, Amy told her children 'stories about inventors and doctors who gave their lives for the suffering, and poor boys who struggled to the top of the tree, and saintly men who made examples of themselves'.[41] She was also in charge of light 'Punishments, such as being sent to bed early or being stood in the corner'; while Alfred dealt with corporal punishment, which was 'never severe and given with a slipper'.[42] But it seemed to Robert that his father's

> chief part in our education was to insist on our speaking grammatically, pronouncing words correctly, and using no slang ... we children saw practically nothing of him except during the holidays. Then he was very sweet and playful and told us stories with the formal beginning ... 'and so the old gardener blew his nose on a red pocket handkerchief.'[43]

A number of outside interests, including in particular the Irish Literary Society, certainly kept Alfred away from home a great deal in the evenings. As far back as 1891 he had presided over the inaugural meeting of the I.L.S.; but at that time he had been living too far away from London to attend subsequent meetings with any regularity. Then, not long after Alfred and his family moved to Wimbledon, the Secretary of the I.L.S. found work in Ireland, and resigned. Alfred was persuaded to succeed him, and soon discovered that his secretarial duties were arduous in the extreme. After his official work was over, he 'had to spend some hours most days of the week at the rooms of the society', and Amy later wrote that she was 'sometimes jealous of its hold on my husband's time and interest. I remember saying that I had only one rival in his affection, and that was the Irish Literary Society.'[44]

There were some compensations: Amy's intellectual curiosity was as great as ever, and she thoroughly enjoyed joining Alfred in town for the I.L.S. 'special lectures', or the 'original nights' at which an author's work would be read aloud and discussed. In this way she came into contact with 'a very pleasant circle' of scholars, writers, artists and poets, and once had the satisfaction, at a garden party given at Edenhurst in 1893, of observing Eleanor Hull, the Irish scholar, making 'a complete conquest of the young poet Yeats, who walked about with her alone'.[45]

Alfred's involvement with literature had a still greater effect upon Robert, which went far beyond teaching him how to speak grammatically, how to pronounce words correctly, and how to treat books properly: though Alfred did all this, and indeed one of the few things which enraged him was to see a corner of a page folded down to mark a place, or – still worse – a book left open and face down. When he was not hard at work on his educational duties or his various committees, Alfred would often be found by his children sitting in his study-library, surrounded by his books, and writing one of the songs or poems for which he continued to find a ready market in the press. In this atmosphere Robert naturally acquired the conviction that literature is not just a distraction, but an essential part of life. More than this, Alfred provided him with the model of a literary career involving constant hard work for the sake of brief periods of especially important creativity.

Robert's delight in words was exceptional; and when he was a young man he wrote a poem describing an incident from his childhood which perfectly reflects that delight. The 'youngest poet' is of course himself; and 'the ancient poet' is Alfred, by then already in his late fifties, and sporting a white beard:

THE POET IN THE NURSERY

The youngest poet down the shelves was fumbling
    In a dim Library, just behind the chair
From which the ancient poet was mum-mumbling
    A song about some Lovers at a Fair,
Pulling his long white beard and gently grumbling
    That rhymes were beastly things and never there.

And as I groped, the whole time I'd been thinking
    About the tragic poem I'd been writing –
An old man's life of beer and whisky drinking,
    His years of kidnapping and wicked fighting;
And how at last, into a fever sinking,
    Remorsefully he died, his bedclothes biting.

But suddenly I saw the bright green cover
    Of a thin pretty book right down below;
I snatched it up and turned the pages over,
    To find it full of poetry and so
Put it down my neck with quick hands like a lover
    And turned to watch if the old man saw it go.

The book was full of funny muddling mazes
    Each rounded off into a lovely song,
And most extraordinary and monstrous phrases
    Knotted with rhymes like a slave-driver's thong,
And metre twisting like a chain of daisies
    With great big splendid words a sentence long.

I took the book to bed with me and gloated,
    Learning the lines that seemed to sound most grand,
So soon the pretty emerald green was coated
    With jam and greasy marks from my hot hand,
While round the nursery for long months there floated
    Wonderful words no one could understand.[46]

Amy continued to have an important share in Robert's early education.
She, like Alfred, told her children entertaining stories; and sometimes she
would sit at the piano, and accompany herself as she sang for them 'folk-songs
in French, German and Italian and of course, Irish, Scots and Welsh songs'.[47]
And by the early months of 1902 Amy had launched a family magazine to
which all the children who were still at home contributed stories or poems.
Robert was utterly devoted to his mother, and once asked her to leave him
money in her will: not for any selfish purpose, but so that he could buy a
bicycle and ride upon it to her grave.

CHAPTER
4
AN EDWARDIAN
UPBRINGING

Robert's formal education began in the spring of 1902, when at the age of six and a half he was sent to a 'dame's school' in Wimbledon. Classical and especially Spartan influences in English education have given it a particularly dismal record when it comes to looking after the interests of brighter and more sensitive children, and hating one's schooldays was for many years almost a *sine qua non* of the artistic life. Robert's first school was worse than most, an unsatisfactory establishment where he records, 'I once wet myself for nervousness' under the torture of doing 'mental arithmetic to a metronome'.[48] The most interesting discovery which he made during the next few months was the existence of a rigid class system. He met Arthur, a boy of about nine who had been in the fever hospital with him, and had taught him how to play cricket when he was convalescent: 'In hospital we had all worn the same hospital nightgown, and I had not realized that we came off such different shelves. But now I suddenly realized with my first shudder of gentility that there were two sorts of people – ourselves and the lower classes.'[49] Robert was later saddened to recall that he had 'accepted this class separation as naturally as I had accepted religious dogma',[50] and felt that it was partly the 'uncouthness' of the servants' quarters at the top of the house, the only rooms with no carpet or linoleum, which 'made me think of the servants as somehow not quite human'.[51]

Robert only spent two terms at the dame's school. Alfred found him 'crying one day at the difficulty of the twenty-three-times table',[52] and removed him, declaring that the school was hopelessly out of date. So in the autumn of 1902, at the age of seven, Robert was sent instead to King's College, Wimbledon.

It was at about this time that Philip returned from Switzerland 'practically cured'; but as the winter advanced there was renewed anxiety about his health, and eventually he was sent out to Egypt, where Alfred's sister Rosy lived with her husband, Rear-Admiral Sir Massie-Blomfield. The Rear-Admiral gave him introductions to a number of editors, and Philip found that he could make a living as a journalist. Before long he was followed out to Egypt by Molly. Her large violet eyes had already surrounded her with admirers in Dublin, and she had been involved in at least one very unhappy love affair. In Egypt she met and soon afterwards married Arthur Preston, a decent and handsome young barrister with a practice in Alexandria.

Amy was now expecting her fifth child; and on 24 February 1903, on a day of violent storms, she gave birth to another son, 'a fine fellow, clean & sound in wind and limb'.[53] Robert celebrated his arrival with the lines:

> This Shrove Tuesday there was born
> On a February morn
> Mother and Father's youngest son
> And for name they called him John.[54]

After John's birth Amy, now in her forty-sixth year, was ill with violent attacks of neuralgia;[55] and when she had completed the standard two weeks of being confined to bed, it was only a strong sense of duty which compelled her to get up every morning to sit in a chair for a few minutes. Her bed was then made, and honour was satisfied by the fact that she spent the rest of the day sitting on it, rather than in it![56]

Robert, in his second term at King's College, Wimbledon, liked it even less than the dame's school. As the youngest child in an establishment which took boys up to the age of nineteen, he felt 'oppressed by the huge hall, the enormous boys, the frightening rowdiness of the corridors, and compulsory Rugby football of which nobody told me the rules'.[57] To make matters worse, he did not understand the lessons. Alfred had been preoccupied with worries first about Philip and then about Amy; but when he realized that Robert's new school was a failure – perhaps after hearing him use 'strings of naughty words' – he took him away.

From the summer term of 1903, Robert went instead to Rokeby, a local preparatory school where he stayed

> for about three years. Here I began playing games seriously, was quarrel-some, boastful, and talkative, won prizes, and collected things. The only difference between me and the other boys was that I collected coins instead of stamps. The value of coins seemed less fictitious to me than stamp values. My first training as a gentleman was here.[58]

At home, Amy continued her own scheme of education. One morning in January 1904, for example, shortly before the end of the school holidays, she had reached down from the family bookcase the first volume of one of Robert Perceval Graves's massive biographies. Soon, as Amy wrote proudly to one of her sisters, the children 'were much interested in the early life of Sir William Rowan Hamilton, a great mathematical discoverer; particularly Robert was interested. He at once proceeded to copy the diagrams of the method of signalling invented by him & to practise it with Rosaleen.'[59]

In the early spring of 1904, when he was eight and three-quarters, Robert was unwell for a few weeks, and it was decided to send him into the country for a while to recuperate. So he spent the summer term boarding at Penrallt, a school in North Wales not far south of Harlech, up in the hills behind Llanbedr. Apart from his time in the fever hospital, this was the first time that Robert had been away from home. He coped with the situation by attaching himself to a hero figure, Ronny, 'the greatest thing that I had ever met'. Ronny 'had a house at the top of a pine tree that nobody else could climb, and a huge knife, made from the top of a scythe that he had stolen; and he killed pigeons with a catapult and cooked them up in the tree.'[60] This kind of attachment to someone whom he admired without reserve was to become a central feature of Robert's behaviour for much of the rest of his life.

Another happy experience at Penrallt was the discovery of 'a book that had the ballads of "Chevy Chace" and "Sir Andrew Barton" in it; they were the first two real poems that I remember reading.'[61]

On the other side of the coin were some frightening experiences which coloured Robert's attitude towards sexual matters. So sensitive was he that he was 'overcome by horror' at the sight of the older boys, who bathed naked in the open-air swimming-pool. 'I had not known', Robert wrote later, 'that hair grew on bodies.' And he 'was in a sweat of terror' whenever he met the headmaster's young daughter and her little girl-friend, because 'having no brothers, they once tried to find out about male anatomy from me by exploring down my shirt-neck when we were digging up pig-nuts in the garden.'[62]

Robert's absence in North Wales meant that he was away from home when in June 1904 Amy went abroad for a few weeks, travelling to a Swiss hospital for an operation on a persistent goitre. The operation was successful; but while she was still away from home she heard the news that her mother Luise had died at the age of seventy-two. Amy had visited Munich the previous autumn, when she had taken John out to Laufzorn to show him to her family, but now that she would never see her mother again – at least not in this life – Amy plunged into the deepest mourning. There were no children's parties at Red Branch House for the next sixteen months; though the family was so large and self-sufficient that this made comparatively little impact.

In November 1904, with Robert back at Rokeby again, there was another alarm when Clarissa caught scarlet fever, and had to go first into hospital and then into a convalescent home. She arrived back at Red Branch House in the third week of December looking 'terribly thin'. London was blanketed in a fog so thick that for some days 'all horse traffic had to be suspended in the streets',[63] and Amy, deciding that Clarissa needed some fresh sea air, spent the next three weeks shuttling by train between Red Branch House, where she left Susie, Charles and John; and Seaford, where she took Perceval, Clarissa, Rosaleen and Robert. At Seaford there was no fog, but gales 'blowing & making the most wonderful sight of big green waves breaking in mountains of piled foam on the shore'.[64]

The summer of 1905 began more cheerfully. It was a year since Luise had died, and Amy's profound sadness was replaced by sentimental nostalgia. In this mood she wrote to Heinrich: 'What a loving grandmama our dear Mother was! Johnny often talks of her & of you, as he sees your pictures in our bedroom.' Molly was staying with them at Red Branch House, together with her small daughter Janie, a year old, who sat in the nursery knocking down the brick towers which two-and-a-half-year-old John set up for her to demolish, 'getting his hair well pulled for his pains'.[65]

Elsewhere, Robert, rapidly approaching his tenth birthday, was showing a constructive streak which very much pleased his mother.

> He had built a pond [she wrote to her father], a pond with a moat & a bridge in the garden, so cleverly that I had not the heart to scold him for the mess it made on the lawn. He would like to be an architect or engineer he said 'because that would be the most scientific.' I have been thinking it all over, he said. Wouldn't you like to be a doctor, said Clarissa? Never, he said, I should live in terror of killing people. Or a clergyman? 'I should be so afraid of preaching the wrong thing.['] Or go to Oxford & get a degree & scholarship? I suppose one would have to try for that, he said. What pleases me was that he was thinking of other people in regard to being a clergyman or doctor, afraid of doing them harm. He is rather rough & naughty but I think he intends doing what is right. He is sweet with little Janie, & mentally very promising.[66]

From his earliest childhood, Robert and his brothers and sisters were brought up by Amy to be 'strong moralists ... [we] spent a great deal of our time on self-examination and good resolutions.'[67] Certainly they would intend 'doing what is right', and many of them led impressively unselfish lives thereafter; but Amy's efforts to make them 'pure and right-minded' allowed them,[68] as Robert later pointed out, 'no hint of [the world's] dirtiness and intrigue and lustfulness'.[69] The very words Robert chooses to describe this show the extent to which he had been affected by Amy's moralizing. It made it very hard for him to come to terms with the world as it really is; and his normal impulses in sexual matters were, in his own words, 'set back for years' because his upbringing made him overreact not only to the pig-nut incident the previous year, but to a new horror: he had to wait one day in the cloakroom of Wimbledon High School for Clarissa and Rosaleen, who were to go with him to be photographed:

> I was about ten years old, and hundreds and hundreds of girls went to and fro, and they all looked at me and giggled and whispered things to each other. I knew they hated me, because I was a boy sitting in the cloakroom of a girls' school, and when my sisters arrived they looked ashamed of me and quite different from the sisters I knew at home. I realized that I had blundered into a secret world, and for months and even years afterwards my worst nightmares were of this girls' school, which was always filled with coloured toy balloons.[70]

The latter part of the summer was spent at Harlech, and was enjoyable enough until five-year-old Charles caught 'what was thought to be a bilious attack and became very lethargic. This,' he wrote later,

> was probably a great relief to the household and I was put on a sofa in the garden to be out of the way and in the sunshine. I remember it particularly well because it was the first time I ever realised that the clouds moved about overhead. I had a favourite ball, dropped it unintentionally on the lawn, and called out to Emily Dykes to pick it up for me. She thought I was malingering and told me to get up and retrieve it myself. I said simply, 'I can't move.' She did not believe me at first. ... Yes, it was 'polio'.[71]

They visited a specialist in Harley Street, who recommended some electrical treatment to stimulate the muscles, but in those days there was no real cure. Charles would have been crippled for life but for Amy's determination that he should walk again. 'Day after day, night after night,' she massaged the wasting muscles of his legs; and by the New Year of 1906 she had him back on his feet. It was a major achievement.[72]

In the meantime, Amy had at last come out of mourning. Clarissa had been given a party to celebrate her thirteenth birthday in November; and the following month there had been a dance for Susan and Perceval. This was partly to celebrate Susan's success in passing some exams which qualified her to be a teacher; but it was soon realized that the effort had affected her nerves very badly, and her father had to insist that she did nothing for a year.

Alfred recognized as well as anyone that there is a nervous, oversensitive strain in the Graves family. In the 1840s one of the Bishop's sisters had a well-documented nervous breakdown from which she never recovered, and she wandered around Europe in a pathetic and probably schizophrenic condition for some years before her death. As recently as 1901, Alfred's own brother Charles had come very close to a major breakdown as the result of his unhappy marriage to Alice, the somewhat unbalanced sister of Sir Edward Grey; and subsequent generations of the family have had more than their fair share of mental troubles of one kind or another. Even Robert, with his good measure of Ranke strength, was sensitive enough to feel 'hot with resentment' for more than twenty years because of what was in those days a minor school punishment: two strokes on the hand with the cane, from a master at Rokeby, for forgetting to bring his gym-shoes to school. And where his sister Rosaleen, for example, found their religious life under Amy's supervision 'a happy one', Robert developed 'a superstitious conscience', and later wrote that he had been 'perpetually tortured by the fear of hell'.[73]

As the years passed, Wimbledon grew busier than ever. Lauriston Road was now lined with houses on both sides, and there was greatly increased traffic along the Ridgway. All carts and carriages at that time ran on wheels with metal rims, and as John recalled, the Ridgway,

> with its many tradesmen's vehicles, was a very noisy street. If anyone in the neighbourhood was seriously ill, all roads within, say, 50 yards were covered deep in straw, to deaden the sounds. In the afternoon the muffin man came round ringing a hand bell to draw attention to his wares stacked on a tray with green baize cloth carried on his head. At dusk the lamp-lighter came round with his ladder, which he propped against each lamp-post in turn while he lit the lamp by hand.[74]

The children sometimes wandered on to the Common, where they learned to skate on a long shallow pond which quickly iced over in frosty weather; but they brought few friends back with them to Red Branch House. Rose Gribble, who went to the High School with Clarissa and Rosaleen, was one of the exceptions; and she often played with the Graveses in their large garden with its massive chestnut tree.

In the autumn of 1906, when he was eleven, Robert was removed from Rokeby, 'because my father decided that the standard of work was not good enough to enable me to win a scholarship at a public school', and he was sent away to board at a preparatory school in Rugby. Despite some good teaching, especially in English, where he was instructed to eliminate 'all phrases that could be done without', and to use 'verbs and nouns instead of adjectives and adverbs wherever possible', Robert disliked his new school, and grew steadily unhappier for the next year and a half.[75]

In his unhappiness, he became for a while something of a bully. Indeed, Charles later wrote that he had been 'assiduously bullied' by Robert, who 'on one occasion threw me on the ground and twisted my arm with particular severity. I said, white-faced, "You are three years older now and so you're stronger. But when you are sixty and I am fifty-seven I will be stronger and I'll kill you." '[76] John was treated rather better; though, as he wrote in some verses addressed to Robert on his eightieth birthday, he was still 'victimised in some degree':

> As I grew up I'd hear your snarls
> At intermediate brother Charles:
> Your sympathy was more with me,
> Though victimised in some degree.
> If ever a four-syllable word
> From my young lips was overheard,
> You swung your right arm freely back
> And gave me a resounding smack.[77]

Robert's happiest times continued to be when the family was away in Wales or Bavaria. There were further visits to Laufzorn in the summers of 1906 and 1907, and Robert was now old enough to appreciate the strangeness of the experience, and its contrast with his usual English way of life. Bavarian food had

> a richness and spiciness about it that we missed in England. We liked the rye bread, the black honey (black, I believe, because it came from the combs of the previous year), the huge ice-cream puddings made with fresh raspberry juice, and the venison, and the honey cakes, and the pastries, and particularly the sauces made with different sorts of mushrooms.[78]

In the orchard, they ate as many pears, apples, greengages, gooseberries and blackcurrants as they liked. And sometimes, with Robert, Charles and John dressed in 'Bavarian peasant costume, very much embroidered, with footless stockings and a pair of ornamental braces',[79] they would drive out with their grandfather Heinrich, who 'was acclaimed with "Grüss Gott, Herr Professor!" by the principal personages of each village we went through'.

It was an enchanted world in which they jumped down from the rafters of a hay-barn at Laufzorn into the springy hay; visited uncles who kept a peacock farm; and stayed for a few nights at ancient Aufsess castle, where their Aunt Agnes was married to the Baron von Aufsess. But the best fairy-tales have their horrors as well as their enchantments, and to reach their bedrooms at Aufsess the children had to climb a turret staircase, past a 'terrifying portrait' of the gentleman who was said to be the resident ghost.

The children also found the farm servants, in Charles's words, 'rather frightening, talking a strange dialect and brutish in appearance. So was the colony of Italians imported by Grandfather for his brick factory [near Laufzorn].'[80] Moreover Robert, with his overdeveloped sensitivity, disliked their occasional visits to Munich, which he described as 'sinister – disgusting fumes of beer and cigar smoke and intense sounds of eating'; while his fears of hell were fuelled by 'the wayside crucifixes with the realistic blood and wounds, and the *ex-voto* pictures, like sign-boards, of naked souls in purgatory, grinning with anguish in the middle of high red and yellow flames'.[81]

Heinrich, who had become more and more formidable in his old age, was annoyed when Robert dreamily lingered behind on excursions; and once, as Alfred recalled, Robert 'was left behind altogether, when the rest of the family were taken for a drive. On our return, he showed us his first [real] poem, a charming lyric on the harvest.'[82]

By the spring of 1908, when Robert was twelve and a half, it became clear to his parents that his school in Rugby was making him more and more depressed. That summer Amy accompanied him from Rugby to Winchester, where he sat for a scholarship, but failed to win anything. As Alfred soon learned, she then

asked Dr. Montagu Rendall, the Headmaster, to recommend her a good Preparatory School from which to try next year. He suggested Copthorne, a school with an excellent scholarship record and of which his brother Bernard was Headmaster. We acted on his advice and Bernard Rendall, though reluctant to take a boy of Robert's age, generously accepted him.[83]

Robert had been taken back to Rugby after his examinations at Winchester, and expected to stay there for the remaining weeks of the summer term. However, he was suddenly removed by his father after some unexplained scandal. Apparently, the Headmaster 'came weeping into the classroom one day beating his head with his fists and groaning: "Would to God I hadn't done it! Would to God I hadn't done it!"' First he was said to be ill; later the story went round 'that he had been given twenty-four hours to leave the country'.[84] No wonder Robert had had such a depressing time: any institution with less than about four hundred inmates is soon dominated not only intellectually but morally and spiritually by the man or woman at its head.

For the next year, by contrast, Robert had the good fortune to attend Copthorne. Bernard Rendall, one of the great preparatory-school Headmasters of his day, was a small man with twinkling eyes, a determined jaw and an intellectual forehead. He was also a fine scholar, a keen sportsman, and a kindly Christian. Robert later wrote that 'the depressed state [he] had been in since the last school ended the moment [he] arrived':[85] and Alfred recognized that it was at Copthorne that Robert spent 'his happiest school year'.[86]

Here Robert made excellent progress with his school work; but as the summer of 1909 approached his parents began to worry about whether or not he would win his Winchester scholarship. Alfred, at the age of sixty-three, had decided that he would retire from his Inspectorship of Schools in the summer, and with a large family still to be educated he was very anxious about the expense involved.

He had no need to worry about Philip, who in 1908 had moved from Cairo to Constantinople, where he became the Turkish correspondent of *The Times*, and was entirely self-sufficient. Dick, after three years at Magdalen College, Oxford, had joined his uncle Robert Windham Graves in the Levant Consular Service, and was stationed in Armenia. He had continued to need occasional support from his father, because, as his uncle 'Bob' explained to Alfred, he had ideas on the subject of sports and games which were 'rather too lordly for his income, and he has got into a bad habit of regarding this scale of living and the running of bills with tailors and other tradesmen as an unavoidable necessity'. Alfred sent him a letter telling him plainly that 'he must now keep his head above water by his own unaided effort'.[87]

Molly was supported by her husband Arthur Preston in Egypt, though child-bearing had made her health frail, and she frequently came home to Red Branch House to avoid the worst of the Egyptian summer. Perceval still lived at home. A charming and warm-hearted character, he always had friends, and twirled his moustache engagingly as he described his latest excellent prospect; but he rarely stuck to a job for more than a few months, and was often being helped out by one of his Irish aunts, Grace Pontifex, whose especial favourite he had become. One of Perceval's friends was a young bank clerk called P.G. Wodehouse, with whom he once shared 'digs' for a fortnight. Wodehouse was then working on his first full-length story of school life; and there is a family tradition that he later modelled certain aspects of his rascally character 'Ukridge' on Perceval; though when they were both old men, and Perceval tackled him about this, he politely denied it.

Susan did occasional temporary teaching jobs, but was still effectively on her father's hands; while Clarissa and Rosaleen still had to be paid for at Wimbledon High School, Charles at Rokeby – from where he was soon transferred to Copthorne – and John in a mixed infants' class at his sisters' school. In the circumstances, Alfred Perceval Graves asked Rendall

if he could guarantee that Robert would secure a Winchester scholarship.
... It was really an unfair question, and Rendall could only answer that
though he hoped Robert would do well, no one could guarantee a scholarship at Winchester where the competition is so keen. We were afraid to
take the risk and sent him in for Charterhouse where he took first place.[88]

One advantage of the Charterhouse scholarship examination was that it contained no Greek grammar paper, and this was Robert's weakest subject. So
in after times he blamed his unhappy years at Charterhouse on his inability
to 'conjugate ἵστημι and ἵημι conventionally'.[89]

BOOK
THREE
CHARTERHOUSE
AND
FAMILY HOLIDAYS
1909–1914

CHAPTER
1
OPPRESSION
OF SPIRIT

The summer holidays of 1909 were spent at Harlech; Heinrich von Ranke had died earlier in the year, and there were to be no more visits to Laufzorn. Amy was proud of her eldest son's 'first scholarship',[1] and in the autumn of 1909, wearing the regulation dark-grey trousers and black jacket, Robert set out hopefully for Charterhouse. His train journey took him through the rolling hills of Surrey to the pleasant little country town of Godalming. Trunks were sent on 'in advance'; and from Godalming station most boys walked with their hand-luggage out of the town and up the long winding road which climbs up westward above the River Wey to the Charterhouse heights.

Unfortunately, in joining 'Gownboys', one of the eleven houses into which the school was divided, Robert was plunged into 'the reigning cess-pit of Charterhouse'.[2] He later wrote, 'From the moment I arrived at the school I suffered an oppression of spirit that I hesitate now to recall in its full intensity.'[3] He found himself in a world in which, as George Martineau, one of his contemporaries, confirms, school-work was generally despised, and the 'use of cribs ... swearing and "smutty" talk ... were ... general.'[4] Martineau adds that:

> Certain boys of girlish appearance, were known as 'tarts', and the wooing of their favour – sending notes, arranging secret meetings, and the like – was called 'tarting'.
>
> For some time, I believed that this was mere affectation, with nothing behind it. Various unpleasant scandals ... revealed that the ugly talk, of which I heard so much, had a foundation of ugly facts.[5]

These 'romantic friendships' appeared to Robert to be the chief interest in the school apart from games; and they came to him as a particular shock because, in his own words, he had remained 'as prudishly innocent as my mother had planned I should be. I knew nothing about simple sex, let alone the many refinements of sex constantly referred to in school conversation. My immediate reaction was one of disgust. I wanted to run away.' In addition,

Robert's clothes were of poor quality compared with those of many other Carthusians; and for this and other reasons he succeeded in irritating some of his fellow-Gownboys soon after his arrival.[6] One of them, H. L. Gandell, remembered

> chanting 'R von R' when we encountered him ... He began by being proud of the 'von' but soon wished it had never been. He was also proud of the fact that his father was the author of 'Father O'Flynn' and rubbing in these two pieces of information did not endear him to his contemporaries. He did not take ragging at all well and of course this led to his being baited all the more.
>
> Furthermore his appearance in those first quarters was unprepossessing and I think tended to make him rather uncompanionable. He was of course an individualist, and as such strongly suspect at a Public School, and his interests and pursuits tended to keep him rather apart.[7]

Robert later remembered being 'left alone more or less' during his first Oration Quarter (autumn term);[8] but during the Long Quarter (the short spring term) of 1910, the bullying became intense. He reacted to the attack upon his German origins by stressing his Irish background, but that only made matters worse, because a slightly older Irish boy resented the claim, and

> went out of his way to hurt me, not only by physical acts of spite, like throwing ink over my school-books, hiding my games-clothes, setting on me suddenly from behind corners, pouring water over me at night, but by continually forcing his bawdy humour on my prudishness and inviting everybody to laugh at my disgust; he also built up a sort of humorous legend of my hypocrisy and concealed depravity. I came near a nervous breakdown.[9]

This oppression of spirit is clearly revealed in a picture of Robert taken during the Cricket Quarter (summer term) of 1910. He had been allowed home for the day, to attend the wedding on 12 July of his sister Susan to Kenneth Macaulay, an official in the 'Delta Light Railways' of Egypt. Alfred had arranged for a family photograph to be taken in the garden of Red Branch House, and a carpet had been spread on the grass just outside the french windows. Perceval and Molly turned up too late to be photographed, but all the rest of the family were there. At the back, the aristocratic Dick, now known among his colleagues as 'Graves Supérieur', stands with his hands nonchalantly in his jacket pockets, flanked by Rosaleen and Clarissa in pretty white blouses and happy smiles. In the front, a mischievous-looking Charles and an elfin John sit cross-legged on the carpet; and in the middle row sit Alfred and

Amy looking genial and relaxed. On Amy's right sits Philip, who has put on weight since his illness, and looks fit and strong. On Alfred's left sits Susan, looking a little nervous and much younger than her twenty-five years; while Robert is perched on the arm of her chair, looking miserably tense, and unable to raise even the ghost of a smile.

CHAPTER
2
A PERSONAL
HARMONY

The long summer holidays of 1910 came as a substantial relief. Two years later, Clarissa and Robert recalled the start of that holiday, and their subsequent journey to Harlech. Clarissa begins the story with a dramatic flourish:

> A ring was heard at the front door. Rosaleen rushed to open it, carrying a sponge-bag and a pair of boots which she was in the process of packing. It was Robert returning from Charterhouse at the end of his first year. He was greeted hurriedly by the family and seemed rather bewildered in their presence. He talked in broken and inconsequent sentences and called his Mother 'Miss Farley' (his matron at Charterhouse and the only woman to whom he had spoken at all frequently for two and a half months). Luckily this mistake passed unnoticed but it was not till the evening that he slipped into his accustomed place in the family.

The next morning:

> The cook and the house-parlourmaid, flushed and panting from strapping trunks under a cross-fire of questions and advice, shook hands with all the family and wished them pleasant holidays. The door slammed, and as the two-horse omnibus lumbered off down the road, Mother sank into her seat with a breath of relief. 'We're off at last children, and this time I can think of nothing I have forgotten.'
>
> Father emerged from a corner murmuring 'glancing, prancing, dancing,' put the envelope on which he had been writing into his pocket, and said gravely, 'My dear, will you impress upon the boys that they must be nice to each other on the journey, I am sure that their quarrels are bad for your heart.'
>
> Clarissa ... looked up at this minute through the little window at the coachman's back, and realized that Charles and John were at it hammer and tongs already.

Later, there was a picnic lunch on the train. Clarissa 'would eat nothing but a lettuce leaf and a dry biscuit', and closed her eyes in fastidious horror after watching Charles, with filthy hands, crack a hard-boiled egg on the even filthier window. Their father, with Amy's consent, had already escaped to the restaurant car for a proper meal; and

> Rosaleen and Robert, too, had souls which rebelled against dinner in the train when it consisted of slices of bread cut by their mother from a large loaf, spread with butter from a cup, plastered with minced ham, and handed on the point of a knife to the greediest. Rosaleen's 'I do think, Mother' was answered by the harassed remark 'If, darling, instead of complaining now you had cut sandwiches for us all this morning, we might have been spared these disagreeables.' The sight of a tomato spreading its pips readily over Charles's collar was pronounced by Rosaleen to be the 'crowning straw'. She and Robert escaped into the corridor,

where before long they were 'signalling messages to some people they've made friends with at the other end of the train'.

Clarissa lays down her pen at this point, and Robert takes up the story with a conversation between his brothers and sisters:

> 'Mother's quite happy reading the Spectator,' [said Clarissa]. 'I believe she really enjoys journeys because of having time to read. Which window will you have? If you see a horse it counts 10, a cow 5, a donkey 2 (though we probably won't see any), a pig –'
>
> 'Urch! A tunnel,' [said Charles]. 'Shut the windows. Quick!'
>
> 'It's a tremendously long tunnel. I remember it from last time. It's just before the Black Country.'
>
> 'All right, Johnny,' [said Robert]. '"Tremendously" is more than three syllables. I'm going to come & smack you.'
>
> 'Ow! Mother, do you allow your son to hit me? Ow! Get out!'[10]

When at last they reached Harlech station, some of them took the short cut to Erinfa, striking across the fields and then climbing up through their own woodland to the Harlech–Talsarnau road. Crossing this road they came at once to the large stone pillars and wrought-iron gates at the foot of the Erinfa driveway; and opening the gates they ran cheerfully up to the front door. If they paused here, and looked about, they could enjoy the most magnificent views: northwards towards the Snowdon range, where mountain after mountain piled up against the horizon; westwards across a corner of the estuary towards Criccieth; or south-westwards towards Harlech Castle on its rocky promontory above the sea.

The peacefulness of this remote place was soon broken by their arrival. There was still, for example, a special hostility between Robert and Charles; and once, when Robert had been bullying him, Charles lost his temper and shouted:

> 'All right. I don't care. *Raca.*' I had not the slightest idea what it meant, and still have none, but the Bible threatened such awful punishment for anybody who used the phrase that I thought at least the fire and brimstone which would at once descend on me would also destroy Robert. Nothing happened, but at least my imprecation stopped him in his tracks and I can still see the expression on his face.[11]

Clarissa, as the eldest of the second family, tried to mediate between her siblings; and John, as the youngest, was usually prepared to fall in with what his elders had decided; but Robert, Charles and Rosaleen were children with strong ideas of their own, and when they clashed the argument was likely to be fierce.[12]

Expeditions involving the entire family were therefore difficult to arrange; but on days when they set out from Erinfa in their twos and threes, pursuing their own dreams and visions through that unspoiled landscape, all the pressures of school and family life could be forgotten. Robert's closest family friend at that time was Rosaleen; and the two of them, often in Clarissa's company, spent whole days wandering over the hills behind Erinfa, where 'one could easily walk fifteen or twenty miles without crossing a road or passing close to a farm'. Robert, whose liking for the ordinary world had been soured by his experiences at Charterhouse, felt increasingly drawn to this wild land which, with 'its independence of formal nature', seemed to be part of a world beyond the world. As Robert later wrote:

> The passage of the seasons was hardly noticed there; the wind always seemed to be blowing and the grass always seemed to be withered and the small streams were always cold and clear, running over black stones. Sheep were the only animals about, but they were not nature, except in the lambing season; they were too close to the granite boulders covered with grey lichen that lay about everywhere. There were few trees except a few nut bushes, rowans, stunted oaks and thorn bushes in the valleys. The winters were always mild, so that last year's bracken and last year's heather lasted in a faded way through to the next spring. There were almost no birds except an occasional buzzard and curlews crying in the distance; and wherever we went we felt that the rocky skeleton of the hill was only an inch or two under the turf.[13]

Since they came to regard these ancient hills as their own private world, they were irritated if an occasional sheep-farmer or fisherman intruded to remind them of normality, and for a long time they made no attempt to discover the real history of the area, or to involve themselves in Welsh mythology or folklore. Instead, Robert and his sisters invented their own local legends, deciding 'who was buried under the Standing Stone and who had lived in the ruined round-hut encampment and in the caves of the valley where the big rowans were'. It was here, on the hills behind Harlech, that Robert 'found a personal harmony independent of history or geography'.[14] This secret and timeless world was a foretaste of the world which he later came to inhabit as a poet, when Laura Riding taught him that in order to live life correctly, one must live in the presence of eternal truths, and as though history has come to an end.

CHAPTER
3
PROOF
OF INSANITY

Robert had been making great efforts to fit in with his contemporaries, but because of his strong moral convictions this was an almost impossible task. In his early days at Gownboys he had complained to his parents about the bad language which he heard, and he was still attempting to live on a moral plane which was far above the normal. In the circumstances this must have made him appear to be unbearably priggish. For example, a letter which he wrote to John in January 1911 contained the information that:

> Everyone here plays a game called pitch & toss where you gamble in pennies. I made a promise to myself that if I won any I would give it back & if I lost – well, I would lose. So I played it & lost 6d & then stopped it as being not worth playing. It is going on now but the monitors are pretty sure to stop it as it is Sunday. At work I am getting on very well. I got top marks by 20 in a Latin Unseen with max 85. I got 77. Our leagues (under football games) are absolutely rotten. They won't take the game seriously. I play centre-forward, have 3 new boys (no good) all round me, all muddled up & a very selfish outside right. I pass as much as possible, but everyone goes a few inches & loses it.[15]

Robert's feelings of moral outrage against his fellow Carthusians were heightened as the Long Quarter continued, and he spent hours preparing for his Confirmation, a religious coming-of-age which was due to take place in the school chapel on 28 March. Not long before that date Robert wrote to his parents, 'to tell them that I must leave Charterhouse, because I could not stand life there any longer.[16] I told them that the house was making it plain that I did not belong and that it did not want me.' To make them take his demand seriously, he added details of the bullying to which he was being subjected.

Nothing happened immediately; but when Alfred and Amy came down to Charterhouse for the Confirmation service a few days later, they had lunch with Robert's new but elderly housemaster, Mr Parry, and told him of Robert's complaints. He no doubt reassured them, and they went on to the chapel where, as Alfred noted in his diary that evening, they were 'in good position for service and saw the dear boy while the rite was administered. He seemed much impressed at the Bishop's address on the three Nos! to Bad Conversation, Bad Books, Bad Company & the Yes! to real prayer & the Communion both combined with positive good conduct.'[17] Afterwards, they told Robert that he must 'endure all', and gave him their own 'assurances of the power of prayer and faith'. That evening, Mr Parry denounced bullying to the house; but also made it clear that parents had complained, and that he disliked both informers and outside interference in the running of Gownboys. Although Robert's name was not mentioned, it was known that his parents had been there, as the Confirmation had taken place on a Tuesday, when visitors were not normally expected.

Robert was therefore obliged 'to stay on and be treated as an informer'. He now had a study, but there was no lock on the door, and:

It was always being wrecked. After my parents' visit to the house-master it was not even possible for me to use the ordinary house changing-room; I had to remove my games-clothes to a disused shower-bath. My heart went wrong then; the school doctor said that I was not to play football. This was low water. My last resource was to sham insanity. It succeeded unexpectedly well. Soon nobody troubled about me except to avoid any contact with me.[18]

Robert took the idea of shamming insanity from the Bible, where he had read in the First Book of Samuel how David, who was 'sore afraid of Achish the king of Gath ... changed his behaviour before them, and feigned himself mad in their hands, and scrabbled on the doors of the gate, and let his spittle fall down upon his beard'.[19]

There was a short respite from his misery in the Easter holidays, when the Graves family went to Harlech and Robert spent his time in golf, fishing, and searching with Rosaleen for birds' eggs; but all too soon it was time to return to Charterhouse for the Cricket Quarter. Robert was now 'thrown entirely on myself', but he found considerable relief from his unhappiness when he 'began to write poetry'. This was apparently considered by many of his contemporaries to be 'stronger proof of insanity than the formal straws I wore in my hair'.[20] But not everyone felt like this, and one of the first of his new poems was published in the June number of the school magazine, *The Carthusian*. In it, Robert wrote with undeniable power about the wild country above Erinfa:

THE MOUNTAIN SIDE AT EVENING

Now even falls
And fresh, cold breezes blow
Adown the grey-green mountain side
Strewn with rough boulders. Soft and low
Night speaks, her tongue untied
Darkness to Darkness calls.

'Tis now men say
From rugged piles of stones
Steal Shapes and Things that should be still;
Green terror ripples through our bones,
Our inmost heart-strings thrill
And yearn for careless day.[21]

R.G.

Robert was now nearly sixteen years old; and it was from this time, as he later recorded in *The White Goddess*, that poetry became his 'ruling passion'.[22]

CHAPTER
4
FRIENDSHIP

Towards the end of June 1911 there was a special 'Coronation Exeat' to celebrate the crowning of King George V, whose father, Edward VII, had died in May the previous year. Robert came home from Charterhouse, and Charles from Copthorne; and on 22 June, Coronation Day, the Graves family travelled into central London to join in the celebrations. Clarissa and Rosaleen went with their father to The Athenaeum, a London club to which both Alfred and his brother Charles belonged, and they had a magnificent view of the royal procession from the windows overlooking The Mall. Just below them they could see a contingent of cheering veterans of the Crimean War; and somewhere among the crowds were Amy, Robert, Charles and John. They managed to see the procession twice, both in The Mall and in St James's Street, and later said that they had 'greatly enjoyed it'.[23]

A few days later, as the exeat drew to a close, Alfred noted in his diary that although Robert was 'affectionate', he was still 'too absorbed in himself'.[24] This self-absorption, the outward mark of Robert's unhappiness and lack of school friends, shortly began to fade, as the second part of the Cricket Quarter saw a considerable improvement in the quality of Robert's life at school.

To begin with, the publication of Robert's poem in *The Carthusian* led to his being invited to become the seventh and youngest recruit to the school Poetry Society, whose members met once a month to read and criticize one another's work at the home of one of the masters, Guy Kendall. As an organization it was 'somewhat suspect',[25] because its members were of varying ages and from different houses, and this cut across the rigid school convention by which, in the interests of morality, pupils were normally allowed to associate only with fellows of their own age, and from their own house. In defiance of this convention, Robert very soon struck up a warm friendship with Raymond Rodakowski, who was not only a year his senior, but who belonged to Robinites, most distant of the eleven houses. Their friendship began as they were walking away from Guy Kendall's house after a Poetry Society meeting. Robert poured out his troubles to Raymond, and told him how the latest raid on his study had ended with one of his 'more personal' poems being seized, and then pinned up on a notice-board for public derision. Since the notice-board was in a room from which fellows of his seniority were excluded, he had been unable to retrieve it. Robert later recalled that:

> Raymond was the first person I had been able to talk to humanly. He was indignant, and took my arm in his in the gentlest way. 'They are bloody barbarians,' he said. He told me that I must pull myself together and do something about it, because I was a good poet, he said, and a good person. I loved him for that.[26]

Graves had become used to being called 'a dirty German' by fellows in Gownboys; and he learned that Rodakowski, as the son of an Austrian Pole, had also been tormented for his foreign origins. The difference was that Raymond had put an end to the trouble by taking up boxing; and he strongly advised Robert to follow his example. Robert agreed, and this meant that the two boys were able to meet not only at the Poetry Society, but in the boxing room over the school tuck-shop.

Robert now had a friend who believed in him, and the prospect that when he had learned to box he would be able to hold his own against the bullies. His self-esteem was further increased when, later in the Quarter, he won a Senior Scholarship worth 95 guineas a year. This in itself did little for Robert's standing in Gownboys; but at about the same time he had begun to make some impression as a cricketer, playing for Etceteras, the house second eleven. Towards the end of the Cricket Quarter Robert wrote a letter to his father telling him that he had taken part in a 'sport supper' which had been a great success; that the following day he had made 44 not out; and that he was now 'reconciled' to staying on at Charterhouse.[27]

As usual, the summer was spent at Harlech, where on this occasion the Graveses were joined by several of their German relatives. Amy's sister Lily brought with her not only her husband Frieduhelm von Ranke, but two of their daughters: Ruth, a great beauty with long fair hair and blue eyes, who was in the middle of a hopeless love affair; and Ermentrude, a plain but intelligent girl of eighteen. Another of Robert's cousins who came to stay at Erinfa was Maria von Faber du Faur, a lively and attractive seventeen-year-old, and the eldest daughter of Amy's sister Clara. Once they had all had a few days to settle down in Wales, there was a grand expedition to the Raven Falls, with, as Alfred Perceval Graves noted in his diary, '12 of us ... Fried, Lily, Ruth & Ermentrude, Maria, Claree, Ros, Robby, Charlie, Johnny, Amy & self.'[28]

Rosaleen had soon made a close friend of Maria, who was her own age; and they teamed up with the slightly older Ermentrude, and the slightly younger

Robert, to make a rather special foursome. Although Robert's voice had not yet broken, and for several years he had been very small for his age, he was at last beginning to grow; and when he went out walking with the three girls he cut something of dash with his handsome, open expression, his smart walking clothes, his elegant straw hat, and a cane which had replaced last year's walking-stick.

One day in mid-August the four of them climbed up to the top of Snowdon, and later alarmed Alfred with the story of their 'coming down in rather a risky manner'.[29] On another occasion, they slept in a barn at 'Fairy Farm', and returned the next day with 'a great weight of blackberries, and some mushrooms, but no Fairies heard'.[30] There were several moonlit walks; though occasionally the girls wanted to be on their own; and one night Robert was upset to discover that he had been unaccountably left behind. Nothing daunted, he set off to look for them in his carpet slippers; and Alfred, feeling sorry for his son, walked with him under the stars all the way to Llanbedr.

Robert also played golf with his father, went otter hunting with family friends and – when the German cousins had left – folk-song collecting with Rosaleen. This was their first excursion into genuine Welsh culture, and delighted Alfred, who had taken a keen interest in all things Welsh since Erinfa had first been built, and had actually been elected a Welsh Bard at the Bangor Eisteddfod of 1902.[31] Robert and Rosaleen learned a few Welsh phrases, which earned them a warm welcome in the lonely farms; and it was exciting to return to Erinfa to play on the piano their latest discoveries, which one day included 'The Old Grandmother by the Fire', 'The Red Robin', and 'Huw Huw's version of Lord Randall's song'.

In the autumn of 1911 the new academic year opened for several members of the family on a decidedly hopeful note. Clarissa and Rosaleen went to London: Clarissa to study at the Slade School of Art, and Rosaleen to begin at the Royal College of Music. Charles was joined at Copthorne by John, who was to spend a very happy five years at the school; while Robert set out on 28 September for a better year at Charterhouse. 'Robby much grown (my height),' commented Alfred in his diary, 'and the better for his holidays and companionship of his sisters and Maria and Ermentrude. His character has, however, not set. I am glad his uncle Bob [who had visited them towards the end of the holidays when they had returned to Red Branch House] has helped us to make him decide to go into his School Rifle Corps.'[32]

A new era had begun at Charterhouse with the arrival as Headmaster of the great Frank Fletcher, who won Robert's immediate respect as a man who would 'evidently keep the School in good order'.[33] Robert was also very much supported by his friendship with Raymond Rodakowski; and besides going boxing together, and meeting as members of the Poetry Society, they took up debating. On 11 November 1911 Robert made his maiden speech at a meeting of the Debating Society, on the motion 'That there is sufficient reason for believing in some kind of supernatural appearance'. Raymond had supported the motion, 'quoting the fearfulness of animals in haunted houses'; but Robert stood up and 'asserted that ghosts never appeared unless expected, and were usually the product of an overwrought mind'.[34]

Unless Robert was simply making a debating point, this comes strangely from the author of:

> 'Tis now men say
> From rugged piles of stones
> Steal Shapes and Things that should be still;

but Robert's own mind was certainly far less overwrought than it had been in the spring. Indeed, during the Christmas holidays of 1911–1912, besides learning to dance and playing endless games of a kind of table-bowls known as 'squails', Robert collaborated with Clarissa and Rosaleen on a collection of light verse which they called *The Bobbety Ballads*. The main component of this collection was a set of nonsense verses written by Robert and Rosaleen under the title 'Alpha Beta Pie'. Their father had already tried to get 'Alpha Beta Pie' into print, but although the literary advisers of two leading publishing firms were in favour of publication, 'in each case the business heads turned it down'.[35] Now Alfred was brought in again to discuss possible alterations; and one afternoon in January he and Robert 'rambled across the common ... and planned more humorous verses'.[36]

During the Long Quarter of 1912, when Robert was back at Charterhouse again, his father sent six of *The Bobbety Ballads* to *Punch*, including 'The Hushu Bird':

> The Hushu bird dejected stood
> Upon one leg;
> He was too old and weak to dig,
> Too proud to beg.
> And when a motor-car came by
> With dust and rush,
> He gently raised one skinny paw
> And murmured 'Hush!'
> Alas! Alas! The Hushu bird
> Is now no more.
> There lies a little lonely grave
> Upon the shore.[37]

Punch rejected these verses; but Alfred was as persistent as ever, and towards the end of February Arthur Mee, the distinguished editor of both *The Children's Newspaper* and *The Children's Encyclopaedia*, took not only twelve of *The Bobbety Ballads* but 'a railway song by Ros and a "Wind Song" by Claree'.

This was exciting news for Robert; and indeed the Long Quarter of 1912 was going very well except when in mid-March Robert was so badly hurt in a game of rugger, that he had to come home to Wimbledon to recuperate. One shoulder was excruciatingly painful, and his nose had been damaged to such an extent that for a while it was believed that an operation would be necessary. Robert managed to get back to Charterhouse after a few days, but continued to suffer from the after-effects of the accident for some time. When he joined the family at Harlech for the start of the Easter holidays, his father, who had been away lecturing in Ireland at the time of the accident, noted that Robert was still not looking well, and his nose was 'ridgy'; though he had 'got up five places this term', and was 'Improved in manner and taller'.[38]

CHAPTER
5
PILGRIMAGE
TO CANTERBURY

Although, like many people at the time of their Confirmation, Robert had felt a certain disappointment when 'nothing spectacular happened',[39] he was still a devout Christian. In November 1911 he and his sisters had begun planning a pilgrimage to Canterbury, on which they would 'tell tales like Chaucer's pilgrims did',[40] and now, on Easter Saturday 1912, Robert helped to gather primroses for Clarissa to arrange in Harlech church. The following day he went with his parents to Holy Communion, before taking part in the annual hunt for the Easter eggs which Amy and Alfred had hidden all round the garden.

The hiding of the Easter eggs was a happy custom, reflecting a generally happy marriage. Alfred still remembered his first wife with great love and sadness, noting in his diary on 24 March, the anniversary of her death, that 'there was an under key of feeling for dear Janie'.[41] Later in the year, however, he reminded himself that Amy 'is a very dear, good wife & I have much to be thankful for in her affection and wisdom'.[42] They played golf together, had shared interests not only in music and literature but also in their extensive family; they were both good Christians; and that May, at the age of sixty-five, Alfred was still enough of a romantic to propose walking out on a dark night 'to hear the nightingale at Queensmere', and Amy was still responsive enough to accept.[43]

Their only serious differences were in matters of morality, where Amy remained inclined to take a stronger line than her husband. For example, when he had been in Ireland he had met a niece who had behaved badly in the past, had forgiven her, and had then invited her to stay at Red Branch House. Amy was furious at this, and wrote to him: 'What a pity you invited her without reference to me, as it seems so unkind to take back an invitation.'[44] But even when she disagreed with Alfred, she was usually prepared, as a good wife, to let him have the last word; and would sometimes explain to her children, in a somewhat resigned tone of voice, that she would not hear any complaints against their father, because she had taken him as she found him.

Both Amy and Alfred wrote letters to their children in which they encouraged them to say their prayers, read their Bibles, and work hard; but Amy's were often so emotional and intense that as I read them more than seventy years later I cannot help feeling terribly sad that my father's generation of the family were subjected to such intense moral pressure. So often, Amy seems to be equating personal worth with the almost impossibly saintly behaviour and self-sacrifice which she was accustomed to demand of herself. Any falling short of the highest ideals is greeted with a terrible sorrow, all the more devastating for being couched in such loving language.

Clarissa, a tall, graceful and extremely moral nineteen-year-old, who taught in Sunday School as well as studying at the Slade, was the first to suffer from these unreasonably high expectations. One of her teachers began taking a very special interest in her work, and then declared that he loved her. Clarissa, who had been shown little enough affection when she was a small child, was deeply touched, and responded by falling passionately in love. It was only in the early summer of 1912, after they had enjoyed several secret meetings, and long conversations about their future together, that Clarissa discovered that the man she thought of as her future husband was already married. She had never slept with him; but the shock of finding that, as she saw it, her purity had been compromised by this relationship, was enough to unbalance her, and she had a serious nervous breakdown.

When Clarissa was well enough to travel, her parents hired one of Rosaleen's friends, a Miss Brownsword, as her paid companion, and sent both of them to live for a while at Whitstable, a sleepy little town on the Kentish coast only six miles from Canterbury. This proximity to Canterbury gave Rosaleen the idea of reviving the plan for a pilgrimage; Robert agreed that it would be 'great fun',[45] and by the time that he arrived home in June for his mid-quarter Exeat, everything had been arranged.

On the morning of the pilgrimage, Rosaleen felt too unwell to set out; and Robert and his parents had to catch their train for Whitstable without her. There they met Clarissa and Brownsword; and while Alfred went into the town to eat ham and eggs at an Italian restaurant, the others had a picnic lunch on the beach, and fell into an enjoyable conversation with some children whom they had heard singing one of Alfred's songs.

After lunch, Amy and Alfred were the first to begin walking towards Canterbury, eating cherries as they went. The others spent most of the afternoon on the beach, bathing and playing games, and then followed them. It was a pleasant walk, some of it through woodland, as they followed in the footsteps of the countless thousands who have made their pilgrimage to Canterbury since the murder there of St Thomas à Becket in the year 1170. After a while the Bell Harry Tower of the Cathedral became visible in the distance. Later, they crossed the River Stour by the mediaeval Westgate, and after making their way through some narrow lanes dominated by black-and-white sixteenth-century houses, they entered the walled Cathedral Close just as dusk was falling.

There they met Alfred, Amy, and also Rosaleen, who had recovered enough to travel down to Canterbury by a late train. It was the first time that any of them had visited the magnificent building which is the mother church of Anglican Christianity, and it must have been an emotional moment for them all. The following day Robert went to services both at the Cathedral and at a French Huguenot church elsewhere in the city; he and his sisters explored along the River Stour; and in the evening, back at their hotel, they listened while Alfred told them stories of his youth in Dublin Castle.

Family news was also exchanged: Robert heard that his half-brother Philip was shortly to be married to Millicent Gilchrist, the daughter of a Scots merchant whom he had met in Constantinople; that Dick was engaged to a Miss Eva Wilkinson, said by some to be too self-absorbed to be likely to make a good wife; and that Perceval, after many false starts, was trying to earn a living in Canada, and sent back optimistic letters about his prospects.[46] Robert himself, believing, as he wrote later, that 'Prose can be learnt and brought to perfection (honest homespun say-what-you-mean prose, not rhetoric like Macaulay or Pater or those blokes)', was trying to improve his prose style; 'every day ... [I] wrote a few notes in prose on any subject that came into my head, with the idea of being able to write with as much economy of words & simplicity of expression as poss.'[47]

CHAPTER
6
SONGS
AND POEMS

At the end of the Cricket Quarter of 1912, another happy summer was spent at Harlech with numerous friends and relations, including Susan and Kenneth, on holiday from Egypt; Uncle Bob, now working as a financial adviser to the Turkish Government; Dick and his fiancée Eva, who amused everyone by telling their fortunes; and Rosaleen's plain but agreeable friend from Lauriston Road, Rose Gribble. Robert spent his days in golf and hill-walking; and in the evenings he took part in occasional entertainments in the drawing-room at Erinfa. One Saturday evening, for example, as Alfred noted in his diary,

> Rose recited a passage from Stevenson – Clarissa a poem, both just learnt. Rob & Claree acted an absurd dialogue as Mr. and Mrs. Noah, & then they & Ros did Swiss Family Robinson, including the tamer of the 'Anagra' – Galloper! Kenneth told stories & sang. Susie accompanied. Amy sang, a German song, and I read 'The Dying Lover' & danced an Irish jig.[48]

On another occasion, they 'told ghost and dream stories', after which Robert sang several of his favourite songs. Foremost among these was the traditional folk-song 'Widdecombe Fair', which begins with the well-known lines:

> Tom Pearce, Tom Pearce, lend me your grey mare,
>> All along, down along, out along, lee.
> For I want for to go to Widdecombe Fair,
>> Wi' Bill Brewer, Jan Stewer, Peter Gurney, Peter Davy, Dan'l Whiddon,
> Harry Hawk, old Uncle Tom Cobley and all,
>> *Chorus:* Old Uncle Tom Cobley and all.

Robert had come across a variant of the chorus, and instead of 'Old Uncle Tom Cobley and all', twice repeated, 'he would sing "Bag Nigger, Bag Waller and Banty Baloo..." to a special tune, ending with an upward crescendo, with eyes popping out of his head'.[49] Robert particularly enjoyed singing humorous songs, and after 'Widdecombe Fair' came 'The Little Devils' which runs:

Have you seen the little devil
With his little spade and shovel
Digging 'taters in the garden
With his tail cocked up?

Have you seen his little wife
With her little wooden knife
Peeling 'taters in the garden
With her tail cocked up?

Have you seen his little son
With his little wooden gun
Potting bunnies in the garden
With his tail cocked up?

Have you seen his little daughter
With her little pail of water
Washing 'taters in the garden
With her tail cocked up?

So you take them by their tails
And you fill them full of snails
And you eat them in the garden
With their tails cocked up![50]

Next Robert sang 'The Whiskey Skin', a kind of black comedy which begins with an argument over a drink, and ends with a pile of corpses, and the 'mystery' of who finally gets the drink still unsolved. Rosaleen accompanied Robert 'in exactly the right spirit', and for some years 'The Whiskey Skin' was by far the most popular number in their repertoire.[51] It begins like this (and the final line of each verse was whistled again):

The strangest darkest mystery
I ever read or hear or see
Was long of a drink in Taggart's Hall,
Tom Taggart of Gilgal.

Then in came Colonel Blood of Pike
And old Judge Fynn, permiscuous-like,
And each as he meandered in
Remarked 'A Whiskey Skin.'

Tom mixed the measure full and fair
He slammed it smoking on the bar –
Some say three fingers, some say two,
I leave the choice to you.

Fynn to the bar stretched forth his hand,
Said Colonel Blood in accents bland,
'I'll axe your parden, Mr. Fynn,
'Jest drap that whiskey skin!'

No name high-toneder could be found
Than old Jedge Fynn the country round –
'I'll have you know, the tribe of Fynns
'Knows its own whiskey skins!'

He reached for his twelve-inch bowie knife –
'I tried to follow a Christian life,
'But I'll carve a slice of liver or two,
'My blooming shrub, from you!'

On a more serious note, the summer of 1912 saw the publication of Alfred Perceval Graves's *Welsh Poetry Old and New in English Verse*.[52] Alfred's installation as a Welsh Bard under the name of 'Canwr Cilarne', or 'Singer of Killarney', had brought him into contact with a number of Welsh poets, including Canon Edwards, whose Bardic name was Gwynedd; and in his Preface Alfred recalls a visit from Gwynedd, 'who threw much valuable light for me on Welsh Cynghanedd – verse harmony – and gave my son [Robert] and myself a delightful lesson on the construction of the *Englyn*'.[53] Later on, Alfred explains that 'The *englyn* is the Welsh epigram ... remarkable for the complexity of its structure', and he proudly introduced, for English readers,

an *englyn* in English wrought after the Welsh pattern by my son Robert. It will be observed that the first line is divided into two parts of seven and three syllables, respectively; that the second line consists of six, and the third and fourth of seven syllables, that the ends of the first division of the first line and of the second, third and fourth lines are rhymed or rather have the same termination, but that the last word of the third line is and indeed must be monosyllabic. The harmonic scheme is completed by the combined accentual and alliterative nexus, of *gleam*, *gloam*, ouT yoNDer iT waND'reth, Its FOrCE THa*t* is a FIeRCE THing, I*t dra*w*eth* men *to dro*w*ning*.

THE WILL O' THE WISP

SEE a gleam in the gloaming – out yonder
It wand'reth bright flaming;
Its force – that is a fierce thing!
It draweth men to drowning.[54]

To see one of his poems appear in a book must have pleased Robert; and Oration Quarter 1912 saw him moving into the Classical Upper VI, at the start of his fourth and happiest year at Charterhouse. This was despite the fact that he no longer had the refuge of the Poetry Society, which had come to grief after a scandal towards the end of the previous Quarter.

It had happened like this: *The Carthusian* had published unsigned poems by two of the VI-form members of the Poetry Society; and although at first sight the poems looked innocent enough, closer examination showed them to be acrostics of a most spiteful nature. The initial letters of the first spelled out 'Morrison and Mills', and of the second 'Stevens and Strachan'.[55] In this way the names of Morrison and Stevens, two 'bloods', or senior members of the sporting hierarchy, had their names linked romantically with two much younger boys. Another member of the Poetry Society, who was himself 'in love' with either Mills or Strachan, went 'in rage and jealousy' to report the matter to Frank Fletcher; and Robert, who had heard the poems read out at a Poetry Society meeting, and had 'incautiously told someone who the authors were ... was now dragged into the row as a witness against them'. The outcome was that the Poetry Society was 'dissolved in disgrace', and the two poets concerned 'were deprived of their monitorial privileges';[56] while the editor of *The Carthusian* lost both his editorship and his position as head of the school for lying to the headmaster about what had occurred.

The Poetry Society had sustained Graves during the period 'when things were at their worst for me';[57] but now he had no pressing need for it. He continued to write poems in his spare time, and during the Oration Quarter these included several more *englyns* which he sent home for his parents to admire. He also continued to see Rodakowski both at meetings of the Debating Society and at boxing;[58] and it was reported in *The Carthusian* that on 16 November 1912, in the 'Assault-at Arms', an annual display of boxing, gymnastics, fencing and the use of the bayonet, 'Rodakowski and Graves had a lively three rounds, which was obviously the best of the evening's boxing'.[59] Robert later wrote of this contest: 'I fought three rounds with Raymond. There is a lot of sex feeling in boxing – the dual play, the reciprocity, the pain not felt as pain. This exhibition match to me had something of the quality that Dr. Marie Stopes would call sacramental. We were out neither to hurt nor win though we hit each other hard.'[60] He added that 'This public appearance as a boxer improved my position in the house. And the doctor now allowed me to play football again and I played it fairly well.'[61]

In the wider school, Robert made an important friend in George Mallory, a young master in his twenties who had heard Robert speak at the Debating Society, and had taken a special interest in his development. Mallory was not popular in the school; and in 1919, writing to John Graves, then a pupil at Charterhouse,[62] Robert explained that Mallory was:

> ... always doomed to be ragged, because he's too good for the set ... who swell the Modern side at Ch'ouse, and who hate a gentleman and a man of enthusiasm because they can never understand him –
>
> But George, disliked and ragged though he may be has always been the champion of everything noble and downtrodden and enemy of everything that is base and uplifted, and has been the only friend to a succession of Carthusian Ugly Ducklings who but for him would have gone under altogether. I'd have burned off my hand for him my last year. Please do anything you can to help him, for he's a white man all through.[63]

A further ten years later, in 1929, Robert recalled with gratitude how Mallory had treated him as an equal from the first, 'and I used to spend my spare time reading in his room or going for walks with him in the country. He told me of the existence of modern authors. ... I had never heard of people like Shaw, Samuel Butler, Rupert Brooke, Wells, Flecker, or Masefield, and I was greatly interested in them.'[64] It was in Mallory's rooms that Robert began the most important part of his literary education.

CHAPTER
7
TWO
LOVE STORIES

Soon after the beginning of the Oration Quarter, Robert had enjoyed a day away from Charterhouse, when he attended Dick and Eva's wedding; and at that time Alfred was planning to spend the Christmas holidays of 1912–1913 visiting Dick, Philip, Molly and Susan in the Middle East. The outbreak of the Balkan Wars put a stop to his plans; and instead, after a busy autumn of writing and lecturing, Alfred decided to take his second family to Brussels, justifying the expense to Amy on the grounds that it would improve their children's French.

Apart from a brief holiday in an hotel near the boulder-strewn shore at Wimereux in northern France, this was the first time that Alfred and Amy had taken their children abroad since the visits to Laufzorn had come to an end. They arrived in Brussels without having arranged any accommodation in advance; but after being split up for a while, they all found rooms in a pension run by the 'ugly but hospitable' Madame Drapier.[65] She was delighted to earn some extra money by giving French lessons to the assembled Graves family each day. Charles later felt that these lessons had ruined the holiday; but Alfred, who could not resist the urge to compete with his children, noted proudly in his diary the occasion on which he came '1st in French verbs of the whole family tho' my dictée was only fg – compared to the girls & Amy'.[66]

When lessons were over they went shopping or ice-skating, and on one occasion visited the battlefield of Waterloo, where Robert bought a small cannon-ball as a souvenir. There was also the excitement of buying the Christmas number of the *Westminster Gazette*, which contained a short story written jointly by Robert and Rosaleen;[67] and Alfred, who had been a member of the pioneering 'Kinema Commission', and occasionally lectured on the educational opportunities offered by moving pictures, took Robert to see his first films. They watched 'a good clean show', which included 'scenes from Life of our Lord', and 'two love stories: Dr. who in the end wins his ward who nurses him through smallpox. Governess who fails to bottle a Widower'.[68]

Robert had been continuing to grow fast; and although it was another month before he began shaving,[69] he was now on the verge of manhood. His broken nose, far from spoiling his otherwise regular features, had given character to his appearance; and for the first time he began to attract serious attention from the opposite sex. Staying in the same Brussels pension there were 'two spirited Irish girls', Lola and Beth Irwin;[70] and it was soon obvious to everyone that Lola, who was 'very pretty', had fallen in love with him. Robert seemed to his family to be immensely embarrassed by Lola's attentions;[71] he himself put it more strongly, writing later: 'I was so frightened I could have killed her.'[72] This was not a surprising reaction from an adolescent who had been brought up to worship purity both of mind and body; who had led a cold and cloistered existence for much of each year since he was a small child; for whom all the girls of his acquaintance were either sisters, or honorary sisters, and therefore sexless; for whom other girls were 'despised and hated, treated as something obscene';[73] and who was suddenly faced with the extraordinary mystery of sexual attraction.

Robert avoided Lola as much as he could, but he was inevitably thrown into her company during the Christmas festivities. They all enjoyed 'a splendid Christmas dinner', with 'oysters, turkey, asparagus, snipe and a Christmas pudding flaming with brandy', after which they provided their own entertainment. First Lola and her sister danced an Irish jig, and performed a mime; then M. Koch, an eccentric Danish masseur, offered to sing a German song, but could not remember more than a few of the words. When he finally broke down, 'instead of apologising, he cried out "Ach! Zis horrid Madame Drapier!"' [and then, with 'an expressive high-water gesture',] '"I haf zee bifstek up to here!"' Another guest played the guitar, Robert sang 'The Whiskey Skin' accompanied by Rosaleen, and then everyone joined in a series of rounds.[74]

On Boxing Day they played charades, and there was an accident which might have been serious, because in the middle of one of the acts

> a huge picture of Job fell down on the players with a horrid crash. Robby and Lola were within the frame, Rosaleen outside. Madame Drapier looked ghastly, but luckily no-one was hurt. M. Koch muttered darkly that the same thing had happened at his Father's death, and remarked to his wife that he wished he were outside this horrible prison. He seemed really upset and sat glowering into the fire. Next day he came into the drawing-room with his dog. Robert stroked it and spoke to it. 'Monsieur' said Koch, 'you do not speak to me or my wife. You need not speak to my dog.'[75]

Lola and Beth stayed on at the pension until 10 January, when they left Brussels; and a few days later Robert and his family returned to London.

Robert went on to Charterhouse, where he was joined for the start of the Long Quarter 1913 by his cousin Gerald, Uncle Bob's son. Gerald entered Saunderites, one of the 'Block Houses' immediately adjacent to Gownboys, and run by the Headmaster, Frank Fletcher. However, Robert had now joined the school choir, as a bass; and he saw much less of his cousin than of another Saunderite, G.H.Johnstone, who was also in the choir, but who was three years younger than Robert, having entered Charterhouse at the start of the previous Quarter.

Johnstone was the first scholar of his year, as Robert had been; and besides having a fine treble voice he was 'strikingly handsome with dark hair and a clear, dead-white complexion'.[76] He was also interested in poetry, and Robert began having long conversations with him after choir practice. There was no fear or embarrassment, as there had been in his recent relationship with Lola; and it was not long before Robert fell idealistically and romantically in love with this 'exceptionally intelligent and fine-spirited' fellow.[77] Their relationship, which Robert later called 'pseudo-homosexual', was also described by him as 'chaste and sentimental'.[78] Robert affectionately nicknamed Johnstone 'Peter', a nickname which he had once given to his youngest brother John; and he was 'unconscious of sexual feeling' for the boy whom he loved. When their growing attachment was commented upon unfavourably by one of the masters who sang in the choir, Robert saw no reason to be ashamed; and later, in reply to questioning from Frank Fletcher, Robert 'lectured him on the advantage of friendship between elder and younger boys, citing Plato, the Greek poets, Shakespeare, Michael Angelo and others, who had felt the same way as I did. He let me go without taking any action.'[79]

When Robert's father came down to Charterhouse for a weekend in February, he found that Mr Parry, Robert's housemaster, 'spoke well of him and said he was to be next House Monitor; would have been before, but [Parry] prefers to put friends of good influence into such a position jointly, and there were such a set of Robert's friends coming on'.[80] Robert's reputation in the house, already good, was further improved when despite having been suffering badly from eye-strain, he 'won a boxing match for the Welters'.[81] Indeed Robert was enjoying school life so much that later in the term he wrote to his parents 'pleading' that Charles, still at Copthorne, should follow him to Gownboys.[82]

CHAPTER
8
'FALL NOT OUT
BY THE WAY'

George Mallory, as Robert had learned, was not only a kindly teacher with an interest in literature, but a very remarkable climber. Robert himself had always had a bad head for heights; but in his admiration for Mallory he had begun 'deliberately and painfully' training himself to conquer his fears. He began on:

> a quarry-face in the garden of our Harlech house. It provided one or two easy climbs, but gradually I invented more and more difficult ones for myself. After each new success I had to lie down, shaking with nervousness, in the safe meadow grass at the top. Once I lost my foothold on a ledge and should have been killed; but it seemed as though I improvised a foothold in the air and kicked myself up to safety from it.[83]

Mallory soon learned of Robert's new interest; and during the Easter holidays of 1913, while Robert was at Harlech, he received an invitation from Mallory to join him and a group of his friends for some climbing. They were staying not far from Harlech at the Snowdon Ranger Hotel, near Lake Cwellyn. Robert's father agreed that he should accept, and so between 19 and 21 April Robert spent what he described to Alfred as 'a pleasant time ... climbing Snowdon in 4 feet snow all roped together, singing folk-songs, telling tales, ragging, etc.'[84]

On returning to Harlech, Robert went back to his usual pursuits of walking and collecting folk-songs – which he and Rosaleen now recorded directly on to a phonograph; and, forgetting their 'scrimmage' earlier in the holidays, Robert also found time to help Charles to prepare for his Charterhouse scholarship exams by reading Cicero with him.

Charles was in a state of considerable anxiety, as he had been 'told that if I did not get a scholarship I would have to go to some dim, cheap, minor school, and this was my first and last chance'. When he took the exam in the summer, he came home to Red Branch House for a day or two to await the results, and had a nasty shock when Amy met him on the stairs one morning in her red dressing-gown, and said to him: '"Darling, I'm so sorry for you." I gulped audibly ... "Poor darling," she said, "we have just heard that you only got the *fifth* scholarship..." It was the only unkind thing Mother ever did to me.'[85]

When it was Robert's half-term exeat, he went down to Copthorne with his father to congratulate Charles and to visit both him and John, in whom Robert had taken a more kindly interest for some eighteen months, ever since John had survived a motor-car accident of which Robert had received telepathic information.[86] Bernard Rendall was most welcoming, gave Robert and Alfred lunch, and afterwards, over a cigar, 'spoke handsomely of both little boys'.[87] Robert was able to tell his former headmaster about his literary exploits, which ranged from serious criticism to light-hearted satire. In the Long Quarter, for example, Robert had contributed to a school magazine called *Greyfriar* an essay on 'Ragtime', which he attacked for 'wilfully abandoning grace and beauty for the sake of novelty', though he was pleased that it had 'ousted, temporarily at least, the objectionable "comic song"' and he eventually proposed 'Success to Ragtime till something more refined appears!'[88] And now, under George Mallory's guidance, Robert and Rodakowski, together with their mutual friend Cyril Hartmann, had been producing a humorous magazine called *Green Chartreuse*.[89] Robert's chief contribution was an article entitled 'My New Bug's Exam'[90] and the general level of humour in the magazine may be judged from the fact that on the inside of the front cover a notice declared, 'This space was reserved for THE BLOODS but they need no advertisement'. However, it was a great popular success when it appeared on O.C. (Old Carthusian) Day, and sold almost all its edition of 550 copies.

Before leaving Copthorne, Robert had promised Bernard Rendall that he would write an article about Charterhouse for the autumn edition of *The Copthorne School Chronicle*; and he later sent him some impressions of the 'Runabout', a form of football which was

> purely selfish in that each individual tries to dribble the football through the posts himself and is not allowed either to pass to one playing the same way or to shoot. There is no formal picking up of sides, everyone chooses his own goal, and without keeping any definite plan, manoeuvres all over the field, supposing, of course, that he enjoys the game and has evolved strategic principles.[91]

Robert described the game as a 'great leveller', in which old scores were settled, with the game resolving itself 'into a number of single combats, clique fighting clique, and each man his pet aversion', and he concluded that it had 'made the School famous for its dribbling'.

Although Alfred Perceval Graves joined Rendall in applauding Robert's literary endeavours, he was worried about the time which they were taking up. After their visit to Copthorne, as they were walking to the station at Three Bridges, Alfred had

> had a great confab with [Robert] on his future. He agreed to put more back into his work & try & recapture lost ground & get exhibition (leaving) as well as scholarship. Rodakowski to be asked to Harlech to read with him. Literature to be dropped awhile, but a literary career to be ultimately adopted after Oxford training.[92]

But this conversation had little immediate effect. Robert continued with his literary work, while Rodakowski was formally invited to Erinfa, but never came, since before the end of the Cricket Quarter he and Robert had quarrelled violently about religion. Raymond had begun boasting that he was an atheist, and asked Robert, 'What's the good of having a soul if you have a mind?' Robert was shocked, but found that in their arguments he was becoming less and less certain of his own ground: 'So in order not to prejudice religion (and I put religion and my chances of salvation before human love) I at first broke my friendship with Raymond entirely.'[93] Robert may also have given some thought to the extremely embarrassing situation which would have arisen had his parents discovered that he had introduced an atheist into Erinfa as one of his closest friends.

One of the problems about working at Erinfa was that there was virtually no peace and quiet; indeed, with so many relatives constantly visiting them at Harlech, Robert and his brothers and sisters had begun referring to a number of them by their initials: so that Uncle Charles became CLG, and even their father was often referred to as AP or (more usually) APG. Now, when Robert and his sisters declared that they needed somewhere more secluded to pursue their literary projects, Amy gave them some practical help. About a quarter of a mile from Erinfa, where the road to Harlech emerged from the trees, was the tiny hamlet of Llechwedd. It consisted, as John wrote, of

> one fair-sized house and about a dozen primitive cottages either side of the road. Those on the left backed straight onto the hillside, those on the right onto brambles and nettles at the edge of the wood. Mother had bought nearly all the cottages in Llechwedd, her aim being to help its poor inhabitants.

The first Llechwedd cottage on the right hand had, at one time, been a little school, 'Yscol Fach', but fell empty about 1911. It was in a poor state, and Mother [now] allowed her children to use it as a common workroom.[94]

Clarissa, helped by the Erinfa cook, Mrs Nelson, had begun putting the cottage in order and digging its garden in July. Over the door she painted the name 'Gwuthdy Bach', or 'Little Workshop'; and on 10 August, as she wrote in her diary:

> we had a housewarming. . . . The fire burnt brightly in my large wide grate. The wood was from rotten planks of the floor. Father gave us a little pink and white tea service, and Aunt Lily [who had looked after the Bishop], a basket-work chair. Uncle Bob [the diplomat], Uncle Charles [of the *Spectator* and *Punch*], Mr. Thornton [Gerald's tutor], Gerald [Uncle Bob's son], Father and Mother and all of us five were present. Tea was a great success, and afterwards we played 'Poet, Pudding, Painter'.[95]

Three days after the housewarming, Robert and a few others created a great stir in the village by dressing up to escort CLG to the station at the end of his holiday. Aunt Lily appeared as an old Galway woman, Clarissa as a nun, Rosaleen as a gypsy, their local friend Christopher Swayne as a tiger, and Robert as 'an awful bald man with crutches. . . . The cottage people', wrote Clarissa, 'really thought that we were a circus come to Harlech and did not recognize us at all.'[96]

Later in the summer Robert's half-brother Philip arrived with his wife Millicent, who was understandably 'nervous about meeting so many new relations',[97] but who had soon, in APG's words, 'won all our hearts'. Still later, Dick and Eva also arrived, and there was 'an enormous gathering of the clans'.[98] Philip was now a person of some importance: his articles in *The Times* on the Balkan Wars had established him as an authoritative source of information about the politics of Turkey and the Near East; and while Philip was staying at Erinfa he and his father were entertained to lunch at Criccieth by David Lloyd George, the future Prime Minister and already a leading member of a Liberal Government. After much talk with APG about Irish and Welsh literature, Lloyd George turned to Philip, and picked his brains as thoroughly as possible, telling him after a while that he was 'much obliged for interesting and valuable information which I shall hope to make use of before long'.[99]

Philip had been elected a Fellow of the Royal Entomological Society, and his chief recreation these days was studying natural history; but he had not forgotten his early love of fishing, and one day he and Robert set out to try the local streams. Philip found Robert the most interesting of his half-brothers, told him mildly scandalous stories about family history and, while admitting that he had put his own literary ambitions to one side (saying that '*Weltpolitik* is for the present imaginative work enough'), he took a keen interest in Robert's literary activities.[100]

Under George Mallory's tutelage, Robert had begun to feel much more sure of himself, almost too sure at times, Fletcher had begun to think, describing him to APG as 'not humble';[101] and the new poems which he was writing reflect this greater self-confidence. Here, for example, is his cheerful and vigorous:

THE JOLLY YELLOW MOON

Oh, now has faded from the West
    A sunset red as wine,
And beast and bird are hushed to rest
    When the Jolly Yellow Moon doth shine.

Come, comrades, roam we round the mead
    Where couch the sleeping kine.
The breath of night blows soft indeed,
    And the Jolly Yellow Moon doth shine.

And step we slowly, friend with friend,
    Let arm with arm entwine,
And voice with voice together blend,
    For the Jolly Yellow Moon doth shine.

And sing we loud, or sing we soft,
    The sound were wondrous fine.
Our chorus sure will float aloft
    Where the Jolly Yellow Moon doth shine.[102]

In other poems there is evidence of Robert's developing interest in the worlds of myth and magic. In 'Pan set at Nought'[103] he wrote of King Pan 'Weeping that such as we/His holy hill have trod'; while in 'Love and Black Magic', perhaps his most accomplished performance to date, his theme was that love is the most powerful magic in the world. A maiden who is assistant to a wizard scorns his powers for, as she declares:

    'To bring my lover to these my arms,
    What need have I of magical charms,
    Abracadabra and Reefy-rum?
    I have but to will and behold him come!

From bottomless depths he must rise and come!
My master pledged my hand to a wizard,
Transformed would I be to toad or lizard
If e'er he knew – but fiddle-de-dee
For a black-browed sorcerer now,' quo' she,
'Let Cupid smile and the Devil will flee,
　　　Come, love, come.'[104]

One Sunday right at the end of the holidays Alfred had to miss church after spraining his ankle while out picking blackberries. Robert and his brothers and sisters rallied to their father, and held what APG later described as 'a sweet service ... Charlie and Johnny read the lessons and Robbie and Claree preached excellent sermons. "Fall not out by the way" ([was] R's text) – advising brothers not to quarrel on the return journey to Wimbledon.'[105]

Robert was now on better terms than he had ever been with Charles, who accompanied him to Charterhouse in September for the start of the Oration Quarter; and before long Robert was also doing his best to patch up his tattered friendship with Rodakowski. But, as Philip had no doubt discussed with him, greater quarrels were brewing in the world, whose fury it would be beyond the power of any one man to contain.

CHAPTER
9
THE SHADOW
OF FAILURE

It was thirteen years since Philip Graves, lying on his sick-bed in Arosa, had decided that German militarism represented the greatest threat to European peace. That threat had become increasingly plain, and as early as the spring of 1913 Robert and Clarissa had been talking over what they would do in the event of a European war. Robert took a highly moral line: war was not something in which a civilized man should take part, and he himself would run away rather than fight.

Then at the start of the summer holidays in July 1913, Robert had spent a fortnight at the Corps camp at Tidworth on Salisbury Plain, and had been

> frightened by a special display of the latest military fortifications, barbed-wire entanglements, machine-guns, and field artillery in action. General ... Sir William Robertson, whose son was a member of the school, had visited the camp and impressed upon us that war against Germany was inevitable within two or three years, and that we must be prepared to take our part in it as leaders of the new forces that would assuredly be called into being.[106]

Sir William's militaristic views were generally supported at Charterhouse; but during the Oration Quarter Robert and a small group of his friends had a chance to put another point of view, in a debate on the motion:

> That this House, profoundly convinced that the safety of the country and the physical and moral well-being of the people demand the adoption of National Training, calls upon His Majesty's Government to complete the scheme of the Territorial Force by the legislative adoption of the principle of personal service in that force.

Most Carthusians believed that National Service was an essential part of preparing England to defend herself against the German threat, that, as one speaker in this debate declared, 'It was a question of submitting either to German militarism or to English militarism.' Raymond Rodakowski, however, one of the handful of speakers against the motion, argued that 'National Service would encourage the belligerent attitude so popular in Germany today. If you wish for peace, prepare for peace.' He was supporting Nevill Barbour, an old Copthorne friend of Robert's who was now President of the Debating Society, Editor of *The Carthusian*, and Head of the School. Barbour and Graves had already decided between themselves that war was a madness devised by politicians to further their own ends; and Barbour had declared that if a strong English army was created, 'our politicians would undoubtedly soon be employing it for aggressive schemes on the Continent'. Robert also spoke at some length against the motion, as reported in *The Carthusian*.

> R. von R. Graves protested against wasting educated men on war, when they could be of far greater value in other lines. He deprecated the pseudo-patriotism of the National Service League, and questioned the advantages that would accrue if their programme were carried out. Finally he asked the House not to be biassed in voting by politeness to Mr. Warner [the visiting speaker who had proposed the motion] or admiration of Lord Roberts [hero of the Boer War and President of the League].

However, Robert and his friends won little support for their opposition, and when the motion was put, it was 'carried by a triumphant majority of 104 votes to 15'.[107]

Such a massive defeat was galling. However, Robert could still escape to the protective atmosphere of Mallory's rooms; and it was here that one day in late October or early November he was called in after lunch to have coffee with Edward Marsh, a distinguished civil servant who was also a poet and a patron of the arts. Marsh had already published the first volume of *Georgian Poetry* which contained work by many of the 'new' poets; Robert was introduced to him as 'a senior boy of literary promise', and when Marsh left the school he carried away for further study some of Robert's contributions to *The Carthusian*.[108]

After his failure in the debate, it was encouraging to be taken seriously; but then later in the Quarter Robert once again faced the prospect of failure. In December he went up to Oxford to try for a Classical Scholarship or Exhibition, and heard before long that he had obtained nothing at all in the first group of colleges. Robert at first sent a cheerful telegram to Red Branch House, telling his parents not to worry; but no doubt he could not help comparing himself with his cousin Adrian, the younger of CLG's sons, who had just been awarded a History Scholarship by Balliol; and as the days went by and there was no news of any success in the second group of colleges, he became increasingly despondent. APG wrote as encouragingly as possible, telling Robert that he felt in his bones 'that the trial was for the best, that he would yet succeed';[109] and then on 15 December it was learned that Robert had been offered an Exhibition at St John's. Fletcher and his father both advised him to accept it, and he did so, saying that he hoped to raise it to a Scholarship the following year.

It had all been a considerable strain, especially in a family which set such a premium upon success. Robert's half-sister Susan later said that he had been under the most terrible pressure from Amy; and it was not long after this that Clarissa wrote in her diary:

Cleverness is worshipped in my family, so much so that I have begun to loathe it. If you are really clever, you will not be wicked. ... 'Aquila non captat muscas' [the family motto, meaning 'The eagle does not trouble itself with flies'] is the feeling breathing through nearly all the family.

My brothers are the sort of boys who take in the scholarships, ambitious boys anxious to do their things long before they are fitted for them. They would be ashamed if they did not keep up the reputation of the family. They are proud and keep away from vice because it is foolish, and unlikely to help anybody.

I have one brother, however [Perceval, at this time in Canada, making little progress with his legal work, and desperately trying to make his fortune with literary projects], who is just ordinary in the matter of brains. He took no scholarships. He has the warmest heart of anybody, but nobody gave him much credit for that. He felt himself to be the fool of the family and a failure, and gradually, because stability of character and honest effort had never been held up to him as more honourable than brains, he became a failure.

I have thought to myself that something must be vitally wrong with this mode of thought and I said to myself 'I will only live and learn. I will definitely choose no career.' I will ... wait till the Almighty needs an instrument like myself to express His thoughts, then He can tune me and use me.[110]

Robert's brush with failure had unsettled him, and when he arrived home on 22 December 1913, APG found him 'rather jumpy'.[111] The following day the family set out for a holiday at Champéry, a small skiing resort in the French-speaking part of Switzerland. Within hours of their arrival, Robert, Charles and John were out on the snow, sliding about on luges, the short raised toboggans popular in the Alps. The next few days were a cheerful round of luging sessions and skiing lessons, with hearty Christmas meals and sing-songs at their pension, the Chalet Soldanella. They also went to services in the local church, where on one occasion Robert and his father sang in the choir; and they saw in the New Year of 1914 by singing 'Auld Lang Syne' in what APG described as

> the approved fashion with crossed arms and hands and then [we] marched behind the Champéry band with lighted Chinese lanterns to Swiss and other march tunes; cheering ... and enjoying the beautiful effect of the coloured lamps round the Skating rink and of the limelight, rose, yellow and green upon the snow landscape.[112]

A few days later there was a family expedition by sleigh, skis and toboggan to the nearby valley of Trois Torrents, from which they walked up to the higher valley of Morgins in search of better snow. On the way, as their father recorded rather crossly, Robert and the others played word games 'as cleverly and contentiously as usual, Charlie's promise that the cold air of the Alps was to kill the quarrel germs not being at all fulfilled'.[113] Robert, despite the relaxing atmosphere of the last two weeks, was still on edge; and it was at Morgins that he took a terrible risk which might have led to his death. He had only been skiing for a week, but when he found an ice-run for luges,

> Without considering that skis have no purchase on ice at all, I launched myself down it. After a few yards my speed increased alarmingly and I suddenly realized what I was in for. There were several sharp turns in the run protected by high banks, and I had to trust entirely to body-balance in swerving round them. I reached the terminus still upright and had my eyes damned by a frightened sports-club official for having endangered my life on his territory.[114]

Robert had been saved by his remarkable natural balance. His parents were terrified by what had happened; but Robert himself, encouraged by his escape from death or serious injury, took up ski-jumping, and emerged unscathed from a short course of lessons.[115]

The family began a leisurely journey home on 14 January 1914; and on that day they lunched at Lausanne, and Robert wandered with his father along the shores of Lake Leman, and confided that 'he favours educational publishing for his bread and butter, literature for his jam'.[116] The others continued to England; but Robert spent a few days in Zurich, where his uncle Alexander von Faber du Faur was the German Consul-General. Robert went skiing and tobogganing with his cousin Konrad, a strange child who at one time kept mice in the attic 'like a deer farm. When he has enough he takes his gun up there and invites his friends and shoots them. When they are dead he skins them, and makes all sorts of things from the skins.'[117]

When Robert arrived back in London, he found that his father wanted to have a serious talk about his work. The hope was that Robert would win a leaving exhibition from Charterhouse to supplement the St John's award. Robert promised to work hard for this, on condition that APG wrote to Major Smart, the head of the O.T.C. at Charterhouse, exempting him from military drill.

This was Robert's answer to his defeat in the debate the previous Quarter. It made him very unpopular both with Major Smart and with a few other members of staff, who urged him to change his mind. Robert resisted them; indeed, the pressure which they put upon him was totally counter-productive, and made Robert feel more strongly than ever that the established authorities had got things badly wrong. His desire for reform, termed by his detractors as rebelliousness, became so strong that instead of using the extra time for work, as his parents had hoped, he threw himself into a still more time-consuming activity.

CHAPTER
10
PERPETUAL DISCORD
AND
'THE HERO
OF THE HOUR'

During the Oration Quarter of 1913, nine of Robert's poems had appeared in successive numbers of *The Carthusian*. These included not only 'The Jolly Yellow Moon',[118] 'Pan set at Nought'[119] and 'Love and Black Magic',[120] but the humorous ''Am and Advance. A Cockney Study';[121] and 'Rondeau: The Clouds',[122] a poem strongly influenced by Flecker, and beginning 'Word comes of a pursuing robber-band/From great Bokhara or from Samarkand.' Now, at the start of the Long Quarter of 1914, the Editor of *The Carthusian*, Robert's friend Nevill Barbour, persuaded him to accept the post of Assistant Editor.[123]

Almost at once, there was a marked change both of style and of emphasis in the magazine. In December, Barbour had penned an impassioned editorial defending the public school system from the attacks of Dr Cecil Reddie, the headmaster of Abbotsholme, a progressive school in Derbyshire. Barbour had concluded that 'our faith in the Public Schools and in the future of the British Empire remains unshaken'.[124] Three months later, in the editorial of February 1914, Barbour and Graves were themselves attacking Charterhouse for being

> very much cut up into little separate compartments: the House is a very self-contained and self-sufficient unit, and even within the House you have more or less hard and fast lines between the Monitors and Top Table, and between Top Table and Second Table, and so on. Anything that tends to break this barrier is, therefore, desirable.[125]

These sentiments, which sound so mild in the 1980s, were revolutionary in their day; and in the same issue there appeared an immensely long if rather woolly reply from Dr Reddie to the December editorial.

Since Dr Reddie would not make any specific demands, the editors decided that they must be more specific themselves, and they seized upon the fact that lawn tennis was not then played at Charterhouse. Traditionalists at the school were enraged to open their March issue of *The Carthusian* and find a letter from Anthony Wilding, the world lawn tennis champion, in which he suggested that tennis was a less selfish game than cricket. The *London Evening News* took up the story; and in the April issue of *The Carthusian* a number of extracts from *Evening News* interviews favouring tennis were set against a letter from an Old Carthusian who declared that tennis would encourage 'loafing'.[126]

The April issue also contained a shorter and more offensive letter from Dr Reddie, decrying 'absurd examination tests';[127] and the editorial was markedly anti-Christian in spirit, quoting approvingly from the philosophy of Marcus Aurelius, and looking forward to the day when man regains his natural dignity, and is 'as he was before the Fall'.[128] As if this were not enough, Robert and Nevill had composed a letter which they headed 'More Editorial Troubles'; although fictitious, it reads very much like a parody of a worried letter from Robert's father:

DEAR MR EDITOR, – Your last number seemed to me quite good and to display some originality. I fear therefore you have been wasting your time and instead of giving your whole mind to the study of dead languages and ideas, have been taking an intelligent interest in congenial work. It would be most regrettable if to gain some experience of life and a twopenny reputation for very indifferent verse and very inferior journalism, you were to neglect the study of the Classics on which your future bread and butter depends.[129]

The inevitable result was that Graves and Barbour were forced to resign; and at the end of the Long Quarter of 1914 they handed over *The Carthusian* to a new editor. In the June issue, there was an unusually abbreviated editorial, in which, by implication, Robert and Nevill were criticized for having wasted 'paper and patience in moralizing on things in general about which [they knew] nothing in particular'; and directly beneath the editorial was an ironic obituary notice which chronicled 'the sudden end of the last two *Carthusian* Editors. They were, like Keats, slain by criticism.'[130]

Robert later declared that at this period of his life 'Poetry and ['Peter' Johnstone] were now the only two things that really mattered,'[131] and while he was helping Nevill with *The Carthusian* they printed several more of Robert's poems. None of these is particularly memorable, but 'Youth and Folly', which appeared in the same issue as the anti-Christian editorial, shows how his growing independence of mind was now undermining his religious faith. Part of it runs:

> Often in Chapel when I bawl
> Louder than my fellows all,
> With bright eye and cheery voice
> Bidding Christian folk rejoice,
> Shame be it said, I've ne'er a thought
> Of that great Being whom we ought
> To worship: with unwitting roar
> Other godheads I adore.
> I celebrate the gods of Truth,
> Of Passionate Love, of Spring, of Youth.

Robert added that he never wanted to 'grow austere', or to feel 'Nervous about Judgment Day'. But he felt guilty about his change of attitude. The last lines of 'Youth and Folly' run:

> Then I realize and start:
> 'Down, thou bad rebellious heart!
> Child of evil, thou hast sung
> Praise to the folly of the young.
> Puffed with arrogance of youth,
> Who art thou to speak of Truth?'
>
> Then I with dismal drone confess
> The depth of my ungodliness.[132]

And instead of signing the poem with his usual RG, he signed it with the word PECCAVI, the Latin for 'I have sinned'.

Robert had not boxed at all frequently since his quarrel with Raymond Rodakowski the previous summer; but persuaded by a fellow house monitor he entered his name as a welterweight in the inter-house boxing competition. Before going into the ring he fortified himself with some cherry whisky.[133] It was the first time that Robert had drunk alcohol, having felt bound until now by the pledge card which Amy had persuaded him to sign when he was a little boy of seven, and which had been languishing for years among the family treasures which his mother stored away in a box-room at Red Branch House. The alcohol, combined with the knowledge that 'Peter' Johnstone was watching him fight, led Robert to abandon the 'ordinary school-boxing curriculum', and deliver some ferocious right and left swings.[134] The result was memorable, and Charles wrote home at once to inform the family that:

Robby is the hero of the hour! In the boxing competitions he not only won his own weight, but also the weight above. So he has won two silver cups. ... In doing so he knocked out (more or less) all the people against him, to the number of 5!!!

...Robby [also] led for nearly all the way (i.e. ¾ of a mile) in the steeple-chase, a mile long, but was just overhauled at the end & was 4th. ... He will be given his boxing colours today or tomorrow I suppose.[135]

Later on in the Quarter, Robert represented Charterhouse in the Public Schools Championship at Aldershot; but he was considerably handicapped by the fact that he had broken both thumbs in the course of his five successful fights at Charterhouse, and after 'a plucky fight' he was knocked out by 'a strong, hurricane fighter'.[136] When Robert returned home for the Easter holidays of 1914 he sported a distinctive black eye; but he assured his family 'that he had given his opponent a much better one';[137] and a few days later, when there was a fancy dress party at Erinfa, he appeared as 'a Boxer, the Pride of England'.

Robert was not then staying at Erinfa, but was spending a few days with the Swaynes, family friends who lived at Llys Bach, a substantial house situated above the road about two-thirds of the way from Erinfa to the village.[138] Erinfa itself was almost bursting at the seams, largely because of the unexpected arrival from Egypt of Molly, her daughters Janie and Roseen, and Roseen's Italian nanny Irma. At the age of thirty-five, Molly, who had been so beautiful, was looking prematurely middle-aged. Her husband's practice as a barrister was at a very low ebb, largely because he had done a great deal of work for poor people who had never paid him; and Molly, who had already borrowed substantial sums of money from Amy, was now depressed and 'in great dread of her future'.

Robert did not spend much time worrying about family problems, and indeed the slight distance from Erinfa was very much in tune with his current philosophy. George Mallory had introduced him some time ago to the work of the great satirist Samuel Butler; and since enduring such terrible family pressure in connection with his Oxford scholarship examinations, Robert had fallen increasingly under the influence of Butlerian ideas. When he had been visited at Charterhouse by Rosaleen, Clarissa and Konrad (all of whom were now at Erinfa) he had recommended to Rosaleen that she use some of her birthday money to buy 'a book called "Erewhon"', a satirical romance by Butler, which attacked hypocrisy, compromise, and a number of established institutions including the church and the family. Equally important was Butler's *The Way of All Flesh*, an autobiographical novel which contains a potent attack upon the values of middle-class Victorian society, and especially condemns the tyranny which both families and schools often exercise over the children in their care.

As a result of reading these books, Robert became determined to resist family pressure so far as was possible, and never himself to be the source of family pressure upon others. The closest relatives were to be treated no better and no worse than other people whom life threw in his way: nothing special was to be demanded of them, but nor were they to be given special treatment. Ideas of this kind were widely regarded as highly subversive, and Robert did not discuss them with his father. Instead, they talked about which poems to include in an anthology which Alfred was compiling; and then, two days after Easter, APG set off for a lecture tour in Ireland. While he was away, Robert spent ten days with George Mallory and

> a large number of climbers at the hotel at Pen-y-pass on Snowdon. ... This time it was real precipice-climbing ... the most honoured climber there was Geoffrey Young ... [an Eton master and] president of the Climber's Club. ... I was very proud to be on a rope with Geoffrey Young. He said once: 'Robert, you have the finest natural balance that I have ever seen in a climber.' This compliment pleased me far more than if the Poet Laureate had told me that I had the finest sense of rhythm that he had ever met in a young poet.[139]

After his recent clashes with the Charterhouse establishment over the editing of *The Carthusian* it was a relief for Robert to feel that he was among friends; and not just any friends, but 'a specially chosen band of people',[140] who were brave and honourable, and who enjoyed the informality of 'a leisurely breakfast and lie in the sun with a tankard of beer' before they set off to share the dangers of the day's climbing.[141] However, the conflict in Robert between old and new values was a painful one: fifteen years later, describing a climb on Lliwedd, 'the most formidable of the precipices', he recalled in precise detail how for a short while the shadow of a suicidal thought had circled in his mind, when:

> at a point that needed most concentration a raven circled round the party in great sweeps. This was curiously unsettling, because one climbs only up and down, or left and right, and the raven was suggesting all the diverse possibilities of movement, tempting us to let go our hold and join him.[142]

While Robert had been climbing with Mallory and his friends, Nevill Barbour had been staying at Abbotsholme as the guest of Dr Reddie; and at the start of the Cricket Quarter of 1914 their joint attack on the establishment was renewed. Robert's father hoped that he had persuaded Robert to settle down for his final Quarter, and to work hard for two of the school prizes;[143] but within a few days he heard that Robert was intending to publish an attack on the Carthusian Sixth Form in the *Morning Post*.[144] Nevill for his part wrote a letter to *The Carthusian* apologizing for his editorial attack on Dr Reddie the previous December, and making it clear that he now agreed with him in every respect.

Instead of returning home for the half-term exeat, Robert visited Abbotsholme, and was deeply impressed. His confidence in his own judgment was very much increased towards the end of June, when Edward Marsh, revisiting Charterhouse to give a dramatic reading, told Robert 'that his contributions to *The Carthusian* ... showed high promise of a future Georgian'.[145] And by 6 July Robert was writing to his brother John:

> I have been doing my best to get you sent to Abbotsholme School in Derbyshire where I went in the exeat & which is the most wonderful place I have ever seen. ... I would like to save you from Charterhouse which though better than most of the Public Schools is one of the vilest places on God's Earth tho' I have some splendid friends here: but then they all hate it.[146]

The previous day Robert had written an 'intimate letter' to Rosaleen which partly explains the strength of his feelings. He told her of 'an encounter with a master over whom he triumphed'.[147] What had happened was that Robert had been informed that one of the masters who sang in the choir had once been seen kissing 'Peter' Johnstone; and, as Robert later confessed:

> I went quite mad. I asked for no details or confirmation. I went to the master and told him he must resign or I would report the case to the headmaster. He already had a reputation for this sort of thing, I said. Kissing boys was a criminal offence. I was morally outraged. Probably my sense of outrage concealed a murderous jealousy.

Much to Robert's surprise, the master 'vigorously denied the charge', and sent for Johnstone, who arrived

> looking very frightened, and the house-master said menacingly: 'Graves tells me that I once kissed you. Is that true?' [Peter] said: 'Yes, it is true.' So [Peter] was dismissed and the master collapsed, and I felt miserable. He said he would resign at the end of the term, which was quite near, on grounds of ill-health.[148]

It was only much later that Robert found out from 'Peter' that 'he had not been kissed at all',[149] but had decided to help Robert out of an awkward situation. At the time, Robert felt elated by his 'triumph', and told Rosaleen, who retailed the news to their father, that in order to 'work off steam', he had rushed down to the school swimming-pool, and then 'jumped into water at full height from springboard – some 20 to 24 feet – fortunately,' commented APG, 'with no ill result.'[150]

A day later, Rosaleen received another disquieting letter from Robert. He and his friend Nevill Barbour had begun to look on Oxford as 'merely a more boisterous repetition of Charterhouse', and Nevill had said: 'Do you realize ... that we have spent fourteen years of our life principally at Latin and Greek, not even competently taught, and that we are going to start another three years of the same thing?'[151] In his letter to Rosaleen, Robert echoed these sentiments, declaring that he was now 'fed up with the Classics and not wishing to go to Oxford'.[152]

Once again, Rosaleen retailed the information to her father, who was very concerned about Robert's future, and went into London almost immediately to discuss the matter with his brother Charles. CLG wrote a serious letter to Robert that same day, but it had no effect. Indeed, Robert saw his uncle's letter as a prime example of the kind of moral blackmail in which families tend to indulge, and wrote the wounding reply which he felt that it deserved. Thanking CLG for the sovereign which had been enclosed with his letter, Robert announced that he was 'at last able to buy' a number of works by Samuel Butler, a name which he must have hoped would utterly infuriate his uncle. It did.[153]

By this time Robert was spoiling for a fight with anyone who opposed his views. Rosaleen visited him at Charterhouse on 14 July, and even she found him 'rather difficult and self-important'.[154] Life with his fellow house monitors, as he wrote later, had now become one of 'perpetual discord. I had grudges against them all except the house-captain and the head-monitor.'[155] He was continually teased for his attachment to Johnstone; and a few days after Rosaleen's visit he caught one of the monitors 'in the bathroom scratching up a pair of hearts conjoined, with [Johnstone's] initials and mine on them. I pushed him into the bath and turned the taps on.'[156] The next day the monitor took his revenge, and this led to further trouble, which Robert detailed in what APG described as a

> very trying letter from Robbie announcing his big row with his House monitors owing to their rummaging out his poems and documents and blue-pencilling and quoting them. He appears to have knocked out Thorpe

[the head-monitor] for not apologising. Then Parry [his housemaster] and finally Fletcher was called in and Robbie appears to have been far from wise in his interview, quoting Abbotsholme and Reddie (called a quack by Fletcher) v. Charterhouse. A very unfortunate finale for Robbie.[57]

Luckily, Fletcher realized that Robert had been considerably provoked. One of his manuscript notebooks, containing poems and essay notes, had been seized; and had been 'annotated ... critically in blue chalk'. Robert had demanded a signed apology, failing which he would knock down the first monitor he met; and that monitor had turned out to be the head-monitor. Parry had harangued Robert, 'clenching his fists and crying in his high falsetto voice: Do you realize you have done a very brutal action?' When Fletcher was brought in, he had 'reopened the question' of Robert's love for 'Peter' Johnstone. Robert 'refused to be ashamed', and 'heard afterwards that he had said that this was one of the rare cases of a friendship between boys of unequal ages which he felt was essentially moral'. As indeed it was. Fletcher therefore allowed Robert 'to finish my five years without ignominy';[58] though Robert chiefly remembered Fletcher's kindly meant but unthinkingly cruel comment on his cherished literary ambitions: 'Well, good-bye, Graves, and remember this, that your best friend is the waste-paper basket.'[59]

CHAPTER
11
BELGIUM
RAVISHED

Robert's final Quarter at Charterhouse came to an end on 28 July 1914, four days after his nineteenth birthday. As he walked down Charterhouse Hill, on his way to the station, he was still dreading the prospect of three years at Oxford, and still hoping ultimately to make his living as a writer. He had survived his years at Charterhouse, but had been wounded by them. After initial rejection by most of his contemporaries, he had gradually won a measure of acceptance and even popularity, only to find when he reached a position of authority and tried to be a reformer, that the establishment closed ranks against him; and his second rejection was even more painful than the first.

These experiences had taught him to value friends above institutions, and to trust in the ideals which he shared with his friends rather than in received wisdom. But however bravely he upheld his new beliefs, he could not simply shake off the lessons of his early upbringing. Although he was losing his religious faith, he remained loyal to the idea of Christ as a perfect man. Although he had begun to question the importance of the family, he remained a loving son and brother. These inner conflicts fuelled both his creativity and his occasionally violent temper. They also made him, at times, a prey to depression and even to near-suicidal thoughts; but Robert had too strong a will to drift into a state of romantic melancholy.

Already a rather eccentric, larger than life human being, he was intent on discovering the truth about things; and in the pursuit of truth he was relentless: a good friend, a fierce enemy, always prepared to modify his views when he heard a better argument than his own, but steadfast in his opinions when he did not; easy to please but quick to take offence; usually ready with a smile and a warm handshake, but occasionally just as ready with his clenched fists, Robert was very different from the naïve idealist who had left Copthorne five years earlier.

And yet that idealism was still at the heart of his character and at the core of his ambition. After catching his train at Godalming, Robert did not return at once to Wimbledon, but made his way to the poverty-stricken East End of London, where he spent a few days with 'a Mr. Embling ... who works among the criminal classes, to do them good'.[160]

On 30 July, while Robert was staying with Mr Embling, news reached London that Austria and Serbia were at war, and that Russia was mobilizing. It was little more than a month since the Archduke Franz Ferdinand of Habsburg had been shot dead by a Serbian conspirator; and his assassination had sparked off a conflict which already had two countries up in arms, and was soon to lead to a general European war.

Robert travelled at once to North Wales to join his mother. He found her looking desperately tired, and in charge of a dispirited household: Alfred was away in Dublin with Clarissa and Rosaleen, Charles and John were in bed with chesty colds, Aunt Lily, who was staying at Erinfa, was also ill; and Amy was trying to look after everyone, and all the time worrying about the absent members of her family. Alfred himself was heartily relieved when on Saturday 1 August he and his daughters recrossed the Irish Sea without incident, and returned safely to Harlech. Robert met them at the station, and together they walked up the woodland path to their home.

One by one, as the European powers honoured pledges and obligations which had been undertaken in order to preserve peace, they were drawn into the war. German militarism, as had been expected, was largely to blame; and on Tuesday 4 August, when Germany violated Belgian neutrality, England had no option but to declare war. She found herself fighting on the side of France and Russia against Germany and Austria. Later Turkey joined Germany; and still later Italy declared war on Austria. All this came as no surprise to most of the family at Erinfa: CLG, who was staying at Harlech, and whose wife Alice was the sister of the Foreign Secretary, had kept them fully informed about the likely course of events. But Amy, wringing her hands as she paced up and down the drawing-room at Erinfa, was deeply shocked, and declared again and again that her race had gone mad.

On Wednesday evening there was one cheerful item of family news: Philip had arrived safely back in England, after taking two days to cross Europe; and he announced in a telegram that his wife Millicent had given birth to a daughter, Elizabeth, and that both mother and child were doing well. By Thursday morning this news was overshadowed by the most dreadful accounts of German atrocities. Later these turned out to have been highly exaggerated; but people tend to believe what they read in the newspapers, and it was not long before Alfred and his brothers Charles and Bob – who had also joined them at Harlech – were agreeing that 'Germany will have to be bled white ... to have the Junker spirit crushed out of her.'[161]

Robert too was outraged to hear that the Belgians had been treated so badly. While Alfred busied himself with getting up a subscription to support the Harlech postman's wife, now that her husband, a reservist, had been 'called to the Colours', Robert went for a long walk over the hills with Rosaleen, picking blackberries while they discussed what he should do. In general terms Robert remained bitterly opposed to warfare, but he hated bullying in the larger world just as much as he had hated it at Charterhouse, and in the circumstances he began to feel that joining up was the only honourable course of action. There was the added incentive that joining the army would postpone Oxford for another year; and since Robert imagined, as most people did, that the war would be over by Christmas, he assumed that he would simply spend a few months on garrison duty in England, thereby releasing a professional soldier for overseas service. By Friday morning he had definitely decided to enlist, and he wrote a letter to the Old Carthusian Corps.[162]

However, before Robert could receive a reply from the O.C.C., More, the secretary of the Harlech golf club, had suggested that instead of merely enlisting he should take a commission. Telephoning the Adjutant of the Royal Welch Fusiliers at their regimental depot in Wrexham, More mentioned Robert's family connections, in particular the fact that one of his uncles-in-law, Admiral Sir Richard Poore, was now Commander-in-Chief on the east coast; and he also commended Robert on his own account, pointing out that he had served for several years in the Officer's Training Corps at Charterhouse. Not surprisingly, the Adjutant's immediate reaction was to say: 'Send him right along.'

The whole family were immensely proud of Robert's decision, and his uncle Charles was particularly delighted at what he saw as a profound change for the better. A year or two later he wrote some verses for *Punch* headed 'War's Surprises: The Poet', in which Robert appears as 'Eric':

> My gifted nephew Eric
>   Till just before the War
> Was steeped in esoteric
>   And antinomian lore,
> Now verging on the mystic
> Now darkly symbolistic
> Now frankly futuristic
>   And modern to the core ...
>
> In all its multiplicity
> He worshipped eccentricity,
> And found his chief felicity
>   In aping the insane.

And yet this freak ink-slinger,
   When England called for men
Straight ceased to be a singer
   And threw away his pen . . .

Transformed by contact hourly
   With heroes simple-souled
He looks no longer sourly
   On men of normal mould,
But, purged of mental vanity
And erudite inanity,
The clay of his humanity
   Is turning fast to gold.[163]

What really happened to Robert during the next four years was rather more complicated than CLG imagined, though after all this time the facts are sometimes hard to establish. We know, at least, when Robert's terrifying adventure began. On the morning of Wednesday 12 August the Graves family, as Alfred recorded in his diary, were 'Up at 6 a.m. to see Robbie off to join the Welch Fusiliers at Wrexham. He started in good spirits & was waving to us as long as possible from the carriage window.'[164]

BOOK
FOUR
MILITARY SERVICE
1914–1919

CHAPTER
1
'THE ONLY PLACE
FOR A GENTLEMAN'

Many Englishmen began the Great War of 1914–1918 in an exalted spirit of patriotism and self-sacrifice. In particular, a number of poets openly welcomed the war, and celebrated it in lines like these, by Edward Marsh's then relatively unknown young protégé Rupert Brooke:

> Now, God be thanked Who has matched us with His hour,
>   And caught our youth, and waken'd us from sleeping,[1]

or these, by the immensely popular poet Alice Meynell, who wrote in *The Times* in October 1914:

> Who said 'No man hath greater love than this,
>   To die to serve his friend'?
> So these have loved us all unto the end.
>   Chide thou no more, O thou unsacrificed!
> The soldier dying dies upon a kiss,
>   The very kiss of Christ.[2]

Robert could not see things quite so simply as this, though he wrote a moving poem about Christ's forty nights and forty days 'In the Wilderness';[3] and he also 'caught the regimental tradition', as he put it, during the earliest days of his service at the regimental depot of the Royal Welch Fusiliers in Wrexham. Opening a cupboard in the junior anteroom at the mess, he 'came across a big leather-bound ledger and pulled it out to see what it was about. It was the Daily Order-book of the First Battalion in the trenches before Sebastopol. I opened it at the page giving orders for the attack on the Redan Fort.'[4] The Royal Welch had no fewer than twenty-nine battle honours, and Robert felt immensely proud to be serving with them. Soon he was writing home full of enthusiasm for his work as a volunteer: though he found it embarrassing at first giving orders to the veterans of earlier wars.

In September 1914, after only three weeks of training, Robert was sent on detachment duty to an internment camp for enemy aliens at Lancaster. The commandant was a 'fatherly colonel', and Robert struck up a friendship with another officer who shared his literary interests, having at various times edited both *The Isis* and the *Oxford Magazine*. But although this was just the kind of job which Robert had originally anticipated, he thoroughly disliked it. Most of the fifty men of the Royal Welch detachment were Special Reservists with only six weeks' service who were constantly deserting, and whose chief interest appeared to be seducing the local girls. Robert, with his strongly puritanical streak, was disgusted by this. Nor did he admire the uninhibited manners of the warm-hearted Lancastrians, and unkindly compared their 'loathsome love' with the idealistic feelings which he himself had for 'Peter' Johnstone:

> The pale townsfolk
> Crawl and kiss and cuddle,
> In doorways hug and huddle;
> Loutish he
> And sluttish she
> In loathsome love together press
> And unbelievable ugliness.
> These spiders spin a loathly woof!
> I walk aloof,
> Head burning and heart snarling,
> Tread feverish quick;
> My love is sick;
> Far away lives my darling.[5]

Before long, Robert grew tired of his 'unheroic' duties at Lancaster, and began to want to join the fighting. Indeed, towards the end of September his news to his parents was 'that he hopes to go to the war before Xmas & that he has been chosen over the heads of many others, even the section commander at Charterhouse. He expects to go back to Wrexham shortly for hard drilling.'[6] But the expected recall from detachment duty did not arrive; and in mid-October, as Robert wrote to John, he was

> still in this horrid place guarding prisoners of war with no immediate prospect of relief, & so my men (as I am now – for this last fortnight – left in charge of the Fusilier detachment) are very restless & are always dashing out of barracks, which is a huge musty fusty dusty disused Wagon Works with a great stretch of bare fence where the active Tommy can easily climb in & out in the dark. This morning a fellow called Kirby who had just

been sentenced to 168 hrs cells slipped away from the military escort leaving the worthy police gaping after him. The German prisoners on the other hand are as quiet & peaceable as little bleating baa-lambs & give no trouble at all.[7]

Less than a week later Robert was at last given a date for reporting to Wrexham to complete his training. In the meantime, he was allowed a few days of leave, and on 20 October he arrived at Red Branch House, where his parents found him 'very flourishing & taller . . . full of his experiences'.[8]

The family news was that Erinfa was now full of Belgian refugees, and that until recently there had been six more at Red Branch House. APG, who had been trying to find a home for a patriotic poem of Robert's called 'Spoiled Salute',[9] had submitted his own 'Salute to the Belgian Flag' to the Duchesse de Vendôme, sister of the Belgian King. So pleased was she that she had thanked Alfred in her own hand; and just a few days ago she had come to Wimbledon Common for a Belgian Flag Day ceremony, at which a professional singer had sung Alfred's ode to the assembled crowds.

On the morning of 21 October Robert 'went to Charterhouse to say good-bye',[10] and came back the following evening after some pleasant hours in 'Peter' Johnstone's company. He had arrived at the school in uniform, and this was enough to sweep away all the unpleasantness of the previous Quarter. An observer noted that he 'seemed delighted to be back and was greeted with pleasure'.[11] Robert himself wrote to Cyril Hartmann, his collaborator on *Green Chartreuse*, that he had 'found . . . Ch'ouse is a grand place in spite of its efforts to cut its own throat & pollute its own cistern!' The fighting in France had already produced heavy casualties, and Robert added:

You have probably seen the Ch'ouse casualty list: awful! . . . I can't imagine why I joined: not for sentiment or patriotism certainly & I am violating all my most cherished anti-war principles but as D.N[evill].B[arbour]. says 'France is the only place for a gentleman now,' principles or no principles. The only grumble I have is that (seeing that the chance against returning whole-skinned if we go out now is about 2–1 & I have consequently resigned myself) I am renouncing far more than the majority of my fellow subalterns . . . who have never been at Ch'ouse, or understood the meaning of any art higher than that of – well let us say Peter Paul Rubens for old friendship's sake.[12]

The inner conflict between Robert's anti-war principles and his duty as a gentleman was so deep-seated that when he was a very old man it came back to haunt him; and while he remained intensely proud of having served with the Royal Welch Fusiliers, he talked with immense sadness and regret about having 'killed Germans'.[13]

However, it was some time before Robert was sent out to France. This was largely because he had never learned to take much care over his appearance, and this put him in the wrong with the adjutant at the depot, a keen regular soldier known as 'Tibs' Crawshay. It was not long since Robert had been writing proudly to John about his 'piles of new kit',[14] but Amy had been shocked by a 'gloomy and grimy' photograph of Robert in uniform, and Crawshay eventually summoned Robert to the Orderly Room,

> and threatened that he would not send me to France until I had entirely overhauled my wardrobe and looked more like a soldier. My company commander, he said, had reported me to him as 'unsoldierlike and a nuisance' ...
>
> I saw my contemporaries one by one being sent out to France to take the place of casualties in the First and Second battalions, while I remained despondently at the depot.[15]

In the meantime, Robert received regular letters from home. He had a special status in his parents' eyes, as he was the only member of the immediate family who was in uniform. John and Charles, of course, were still at school. Perceval had joined up in Canada, only to be invalided out within a month. Dick had wanted to enlist, but was not allowed to give up the semi-military appointment to which he had been seconded in the Egyptian Civil Service; while Philip, who was also in Egypt, was still working as a journalist, but was shortly to follow his uncle Bob into the world of diplomatic and military intelligence.

Numerous more distant relatives were fighting either for England or for Germany, and indeed Robert had told Cyril Hartmann that his own enlistment had 'put ... the family balance right, with ten members fighting on each side!'[16] Among those who had already seen active service were two of Robert's cousins: C.L. Graves's son Cecil, a captain in the Royal Scots, who was wounded and captured while fighting a brave rearguard action during the retreat from Mons; and Clara von Faber du Faur's son Konrad, who was serving with 'a crack Bavarian regiment', and was soon to win the coveted Iron Cross.

After a while, however, tales of heroic deeds gave way to more depressing news. John Cooper, the brother of Alfred's first wife, was lost at sea in November, when the *Monmouth* went down off the coast of Chile; and soon afterwards one of Amy's cousins died fighting for the Germans at Ypres. After Charles's fifteenth birthday on 1 December, Amy wrote gloomily that 'If the war lasts another 3 years I fear he will be old enought to fight also', and when she received a letter from Robert telling her that he might be posted to France at two hours' notice, she immediately arranged to travel to Wrexham to spend Sunday 6 December with her eldest son.[17]

Robert greeted his mother warmly: '"It was very jolly your coming," he said & kissed her repeatedly.'[18] Amy found him:

> looking well but not very brown. He was not in high spirits, but who can be in preparing for this dreadful business, war? Still I hope he is doing good work. ... The weather was very wet, but Robby cannot now do without exercise so we paddled about in the wet & I got rather rheumatic, but I am much less stiff now.[19]

Robert also introduced Amy to the very agreeable doctor's family with whom he was lodging in 'a beautiful old house'; and they went together to a military service. Amy sat at the back, the only woman among six hundred men, and was very shocked that the sermon contained 'no mention of God or salvation', but was simply an anti-German diatribe.[20]

The expected posting failed to materialize; and Robert, who had described his present companions to Amy as 'rather horsey young Welsh Squireens',[21] began to miss his peacetime friends badly. Towards the end of December he visited one of them, Ralph Rooper, another Old Carthusian volunteer, at Gresford; and a few days later he wrote to Rosaleen telling her 'that he would like to go to Snowdon with his friends before facing the German guns in the Low Countries', and comparing himself with a biblical character, 'Jephthah's daughter who went into the wilderness to bewail her virginity before going to her death.'[22]

But it was easier for Robert to meet his friends in London; and that was where he travelled when he was given a short leave at the beginning of January 1915. First he joined his family: Red Branch House had been let for six months, and they were staying at 18 Bina Gardens, just off the Brompton Road. This was the house owned by Robert's uncle Robert von Ranke, who had been the German Consul in London immediately before the outbreak of war. He had been compelled to leave the country in a hurry, and had placed the house in Amy's care. It was smaller than Red Branch House, and with Charles and John home from school, and Molly staying with her children, Robert had to sleep on the floor of his father's dressing-room. But it had the advantage of being much closer to central London, and Robert took full advantage of this.

On his first evening in London, Robert dined out with Ralph Rooper, who was also on leave; and then the two young soldiers went on to the theatre to watch a production of Shakespeare's *Henry V*, with its highly topical theme of an heroic war fought on French soil. The following day Robert's Carthusian cousin Gerald came to Bina Gardens for Sunday lunch, and afterwards they had a private walk during which they were able to talk about Gerald's contemporary 'Peter' Johnstone; and that evening Robert was given dinner by Sir Edward Marsh.

Marsh had long ago asked Robert to call on him when he was in London, and Robert had taken up this invitation in a letter written soon after Christmas. They had a stimulating talk about the state of modern poetry; and Robert left behind a number of his own poems for Marsh to read. Next morning, Robert was 'tired and late down'. His father found him very reserved about the nature of his discussions with Marsh, and commented in his diary: 'Thank God the boy is very affectionate and well disposed to us and is in excellent physical condition. May he only be preserved till his character, still much in the making, solidifies in the right direction.'[23]

On Tuesday, the last day of his leave, Robert was called for soon after ten o'clock in the morning by Devenish, another friend who, like Rooper, had recently left Charterhouse. He was half-Portuguese, and APG found something unpleasant in his manner, and took an instant dislike to him. Together Robert and Devenish travelled out to Crowborough, where they had decided to call on 'Peter' Johnstone. Finding him out, they lunched at a local hotel, before meeting Johnstone at four o'clock in the afternoon. They talked for three hours, by which time they had missed their train back to London, and so Robert returned to Bina Gardens much later than expected. He found an anxious family, disappointed not to have seen more of him, and worried that some accident had occurred which would cause him to overstay his leave. Amy seemed positively ill with strain.

However, there was still time for 'a happy hour together in the dining-room', and then they 'sallied out to see him off, Charlie nobly carrying his heavy haversack to Gloucester Road station, whither Molly and Amy also came and said the parting goodbyes'. Alfred went on with him to Paddington, where it was discovered that Robert had lost his ticket. They had just bought a new one, and reached the platform, when to Robert's embarrassment, and much to Alfred's surprise,

> Amy, though far from well, turned up ... with Robbie's sandwiches and drawers! ... We then had a farewell kiss and Robbie expressed the belief we should meet again all right. I gave him as my parting Maxim shot 'Sis sollers ac fortis in armis [May you be both crafty and brave in arms].' ... To bed rather tired after the long day's suspense, at 12.30.[24]

After two weeks back at Wrexham, Robert wrote to Marsh saying that he was 'suffering crushing boredom here as a reaction to the mental debauch of meeting you and others of my intelligent and humane friends', and asking for the poems which he had left with Marsh to be returned with critical comments, 'as cruel as you like'.[25] Marsh replied with a letter which has unfortunately been lost, but which, if not exactly cruel, was certainly extremely forceful. He told Robert that he was a prig – perhaps he had read Robert's poem about the 'pale townsfolk' of Lancaster – that his technique was obsolete, and that his poems 'were written in the poetic diction of fifty years ago'.[26]

This letter was a severe shock for Robert, but a very salutary one. He later declared that he had taken Marsh's criticisms 'deeply to heart', and that he had 'never used a *thee*, *thou*, or *where'er* since that day; or hardly ever'.[27] At the time he wrote a letter to Marsh in which he accepted his criticisms, while trying to explain exactly why his poems were so old-fashioned: his reading had been largely classical, and he had been too much influenced by the outworn poetic traditions of his father, 'a dear old fellow who in young and vinous days used to write with some spirit and very pleasantly; but now his inspiration has entirely petered out.' CLG was blamed for exerting 'a similar influence, which is made stronger by his great avuncular kindness and generosity'. As for Marsh's more personal criticism, Robert replied disarmingly: 'I know I am a prig but three years' misery at Charterhouse drove me into it, and I am as keen as you for the regeneration of poetry.'[28]

Robert's next leave, at the end of January, was spent at Harlech in the company of the Belgian refugees who were installed at Erinfa. They were naturally welcoming to a young soldier who was preparing to fight on their behalf, and whose family had given them a temporary refuge; and they told him vivid stories about their experiences in the early days of the German offensive. The Comte de Maulde, for example, told Robert that his father was lying dead under the ruins of his chateau, which had been destroyed by the Germans; that he himself had flown over the German lines in an aeroplane; that he had later been wounded twice, then captured; and that he had only escaped thanks to the inefficiency of a drunken German sentry. Robert was enthralled by these stories, and became more anxious than ever to get to the Front himself – especially as he was now the last of his group of subalterns who still remained at the depot.

In February Crawshay was ill, and in his absence Robert successfully marched eleven hundred men 'a good distance'.[29] News of this soon reached Crawshay's ears, and he promised Robert that he would send him out to France during the first week in April. Robert, in return, threw himself more wholeheartedly into the life of the regiment. St David is the patron saint of Wales, and St David's day, 1 March, was an occasion for special celebrations by the

Royal Welch. That night Robert ate raw leeks 'to the roll of the drum with one foot on a chair and one on the mess table enriched with spoils of the Summer Palace at Pekin'.[30] This conviviality came more easily because he liked his new fellow officers far more than the 'first drinking, rowdy lot' from whom he told his parents that he had kept deliberately aloof.[31]

Robert was also training harder than ever; and in mid-March, when he was entitled to six days of leave, he took only two, so that he could attend a course 'to learn the use of the machine-gun before his probable call to the front'.[32] He spent his shortened leave in the south, asking APG if he could find a publisher for some of his poems, and also visiting Charterhouse to see 'Peter' Johnstone.[33]

Despite Crawshay's promise, April and then the first week of May passed without Robert's being sent abroad. For some time he had been in favour, and had even been promoted to the rank of Lieutenant; but now it appeared that he had offended the adjutant again, and had been judged 'a poor sports-man', perhaps because he had shown no interest in going to watch the Grand National in which a horse of Crawshay's was running.

However, Robert soon had another chance to redeem himself in the adju-tant's eyes. Johnny Basham, a sergeant in the Royal Welch who was training for a welterweight championship fight, challenged all comers to fight three rounds with him. One young officer who took up the challenge was made to look utterly ridiculous in the ring; and then Robert 'asked Basham's Manager if [he] could have a go'. In three 'very brisk' rounds Robert held his own against Basham, and when Crawshay heard the story he was delighted. For an officer to box so well was, he said, 'a great encouragement to the men', and he promised that Robert would be drafted very soon.[34] Robert spent the next six evenings sparring with Basham; and on the seventh, Basham fought his title fight, and won the coveted Lonsdale Belt. The next morning, Wednes-day 12 May 1915, Robert sent a telegram to his parents which read simply: 'Starting France today, Don't worry, best love, Robbie.'[35]

Both Amy and Alfred were in fact desperately anxious; but Amy, in her husband's words, 'bore the news bravely, very'.[36] A week later Lloyd George, with whom APG was corresponding on the 'Ulster Question', wrote an optimis-tic letter 'with the hope which he sets before himself in the case of his two boys soon due at the front that even in the most sanguinary war the majority of the combatants get through the campaign either unscathed or with slight damage'.[37]

CHAPTER
2
BAPTISM
OF FIRE

Robert and six of his brother officers had a good passage from Liverpool to Le Havre, a massive port at the mouth of the River Seine.[38] The Base Headquarters were in the centre of the town in the Rue Thiers, just next to the Hôtel de Ville; but the Base Camp, with its long rows of tents, was on high ground to the north. That was where they proceeded, and for the next few days route marches were interspersed with periods of unloading stores in the Le Havre docks. Gradually the newcomers acclimatized themselves to wartime France, and Robert soon wrote home asking for £3 in gold, which was the most acceptable local currency. As 'the best French scholar' among his friends, Robert was chosen by them to be their interpreter;[39] but on his arrival he had been accosted by little boys 'pimping for their sisters', and he found Le Havre too licentious for his taste.

It was a relief to be ordered to the front; though Robert was 'disgusted' to find that instead of being sent to join one of the Royal Welch Battalions, he and four others were to be attached to the Second Welsh Regiment. On the morning of Monday 17 May, after wiring news of his departure to Alfred and Amy, Robert joined 'a great column', which, as he described in a subsequent letter home:

marched to the station and entrained. We took twenty-five hours to go about as many miles. ... When we arrived at the railhead [Béthune, within twenty-five miles of the Belgian border] ... we disembarked feeling a bit like the bottom of the proverbial parrot-cage, and were told by the guide who met us that we were to go straight into the trenches. Which we did after a five-mile march by cobbled road [eastward to Cambrin village] and a mile and a half down a muddy communication trench in the dark, lit by occasional star shells. I was posted to [C] Company and put in charge of No. — platoon. After a cup of tea, some cake, and an Egyptian [cigarette], I returned to ————'s dug-out where I slept like a top (broken only by the 'stand-to' for an hour before dawn). The trenches are palaces, dug by the French who occupied 'em for six months, wonderful places. I wish home was as tidy always. Clay walls, bomb-proof ceilings, pictures on the walls, straw-filled berths, stoves, tables, chairs, complete with a piebald cat.[40]

The German advance on the Western Front had been stemmed, and both sides were now 'dug in' along an enormous line of opposing trenches. The pressure of bombardment was terrible, and Robert had only been in the trenches for three days when he and his company were ordered out of the line for a rest. The landscape in this part of northern France is flat and dull, broken only by desolate heaps of spoil from the local coal-mines; and Robert's platoon was billeted in a barn full of straw in the mining village of Labourse, three and a half miles behind the lines. Robert himself, as an officer, stayed with 'a fatherly old man', and his 'three marriageable daughters'. One of the daughters took an interest in him, and uninvited, 'lifted up her skirt to show me a shell-wound on her thigh'.[41] Graves did not pursue this invitation, but wrote home asking for a collection of Keats's poems, and a copy of Samuel Butler's *Erewhon*. He also wrote to Marsh, commiserating with him upon the recent death of Rupert Brooke, and commenting that everything seemed unreal. 'I feel here,' he wrote, 'exactly like a man who has watched the "Movies" for a long evening and then suddenly finds himself thrown on the screen in the middle of scalp-hunting Sioux and runaway motor-cars: and rather surprised that I am not at all frightened, and that the noise doesn't disturb me at all yet.'[42] That night, Robert must have regretted his words. There was a colossal bombardment a few miles away, and although he was in no personal danger, he found that he 'couldn't sleep. [The noise] went on all night. Instead of dying away it grew and grew, till the whole air rocked and shook; the sky was lit up with huge flashes. I lay in my feather bed and sweated.'[43]

On Tuesday 25 May they returned to the trenches, but to the more dangerous area, about half a mile to the north of their previous position, the Cuinchy brick-fields, where there were great brick-stacks between twenty and thirty feet high. Here the Germans were 'very close: [they] have half the brick-stacks,' wrote Robert, 'and we have the other half. Each side snipes down from the top of its brick-stacks into the other's trenches. This is also a great place for rifle-grenades and trench-mortars.'[44] Robert survived these dangers, and even sent home a collection of rather gruesome mementoes from the trenches: a hand-grenade to be converted into a candlestick, bullets which had been fired by German snipers, a piece of shrapnel, and part of a shell which had killed a man.

On his next rest period, at the very beginning of June, Robert was billeted back at the railhead town of Béthune. From here he wrote home to say that he was with:

> a very nice French bourgeois family, the [Averlant Paul]'s. Today I have distinguished myself by writing out for the girl, who is in about the under-fifth of the local High School, an essay on the theory of Decimal Division. Now you didn't think I was as clever as all that, did you? It was of course a combined feat in French and Maths.[45]

But within a few days Robert was back in the trenches, 'in a nasty little salient, a little to the south of the brick-stacks, where casualties are always heavy'.[46] And when on 9 June he had a moment to write home, he described a particularly unpleasant experience which was still fresh in his mind, 'I can't stick those horrid fellows who write home to say war is adorable,' he began.

> Let me explain what I mean. Last night – we had seventeen casualties yesterday from bombs and grenades – I went round the fire-trench, which averages fifteen yards from the Germans' and at one point is only ten yards off, to see if all was correct, and turning a traverse sharply almost stepped on a Horrible Thing lying in the parados. We can afford to laugh at corpses, if we did not know them when alive, because with them it is a case of what the men call 'nappoo fineesh': we can joke with men badly wounded who are going to recover: but when a German bullet – and a reversed one at that – strikes a man on the head and takes the scalp and a lot of his brains clean away, and still lets him live for two hours, the joke is there no more.[47]

Alfred had been sending out a number of items which Robert had requested, including an expensive new periscope, and a copy of Drinkwater's poems. His efforts to find a home for some of Robert's war poems had so far been unsuccessful, but he had asked whether Robert would agree to his letters from the trenches being published; and in mid-June, when he was once more in billets, Robert willingly gave his permission, adding that his father could 'furbish up the style' if he pleased.[48] Robert also passed on the news that since he had conducted himself well under fire, he had been given an appointment reserved for 'the best of the senior lieutenants';[49] and he told his family that far from becoming a nervous wreck, he had actually put on three-quarters of a stone in weight since he went out to France.

Robert and his men were now billeted a few miles to the south of Cuinchy and Cambrin, in the cellars of Vermeilles, a medium-sized town which had been comprehensively damaged since the previous October when it had been 'taken and re-taken eight times'.[50] There was a startling contrast between the lovely gardens, full of flowers, and the houses, not one of which still had more than a few broken rafters for a roof. A few days later orders came for a return to Cuinchy, and Robert wrote home:

> We go back tomorrow into some rather sensational trenches, but I hope not for long: the first excitement of the baptism of fire soon wears off and the joys of sniping fat Germans, though sweet, are seldom long-lived. There is a ripple of machine-gun fire to and fro like a garden spray and the snippy sniper gets snapped.
>
> You can't imagine how dull everything is here; nothing but a perpetual field day, mostly aimless pottering. ... And when we leave the trenches and go back to billets there is always cursing at people who put their marmalade knife from the sardines into the ration jam. They have been dropping long-range shells quite near us ... and bag a few civilians every day, but, really, nobody troubles to cross the road to avoid them. London will be equally nonchalant after a short Zepp. course, I hope.[51]

Then the orders to move were countermanded; and Robert's generally cheerful mood was followed by one of extreme depression.

He did not tell his family exactly why; but on 29 June his parents received a letter in which Robert complained of the lack of correspondence from his family, and then spoke of some 'unimaginative idiots having given him bad news'....[52] 'Happiness out here', he declared, 'depends ever so much more on what is happening at home than on the immediate situation in which you find yourself.'[53] Alfred's first thought was that someone had written to Robert about Clarissa.

Uncertain about her own role in life, and acutely anxious about family and friends who were at the front, Clarissa had become increasingly restless and insomniac. Her state of mind had not been improved by a letter from Robert in which he had written very critically about her recent poems – though shortly afterwards he had written a second letter apologizing for his 'rather sharp attack'[54] – and now she was in the throes of a second major nervous breakdown.[55]

But after a moment's reflection Alfred realized that Robert 'Cd. not have heard abt. Claree', as she had only become seriously disturbed within the past forty-eight hours.[56] What else could have depressed Robert? It was unlikely to be news of the recent death of his cousin Charles Massie Blomfield, a thirty-five-year-old major in the Royal Warwickshires: they had hardly known each other, and had certainly never been friends. And the rest of the family news was far from alarming: Molly had gone out to France as a nurse; Rosaleen planned to follow her; and Dick had been sent as an interpreter to the Dardanelles. APG was baffled. He could only think that Robert might have been worried out of all proportion by news of a minor illness from which Amy had been suffering, and he wrote to reassure him on that score.

The truth was that Robert had received a letter from his cousin Gerald, who had written from Charterhouse to tell him that 'Peter' Johnstone 'was not at all the innocent sort of fellow I took him for. He was as bad as anyone could be.'[57] This was a severe shock for Robert, who for some months had found Johnstone's letters his 'greatest stand-by ... something solid and clean to set off against the impermanence of trench life and the uncleanness of sex-life in billets'. Much of the conversation in billets was about visits to the army brothels, and 'the peculiar bed-manners of the French women'; and Robert, who was teased for remaining celibate, had had to excuse himself 'not on moral grounds or on grounds of fastidiousness, but in the only way they could understand: I said that I didn't want a dose'.[58]

For a while Robert felt extremely bitter; and while that mood lasted he wrote his poem 'Over the Brazier', in which he describes a night when he and two other officers stand over a glowing brazier and ask each other:

> What life to lead and where to go
>   After the War, after the War?
>   We'd often talked this way before.
> But I still see the brazier glow
> That April night, still feel the smoke
> And stifling pungency of burning coke.
>
> I'd thought: 'A cottage in the hills,
>   North Wales, a cottage full of books,
>   Pictures and brass and cosy nooks
> And comfortable broad window sills,
> Flowers in the garden, walls all white.
> I'd live there peacefully and dream and write.'
>
> But Willie said: 'No, Home's played out:
>   Old England's quite a hopeless place,
>   I've lost all feeling for my race:
> The English stay-at-home's a tout
> A cad; I've done with him for life.
> I'm off to Canada with my wee wife.

'Come with us, Mac, old thing,' but Mac
    Drawled: 'No, a Coral Isle for me,
    A warm green jewel in the South Sea.
Of course you'll sneer, and call me slack,
And colonies are quite jolly . . . but –
Give me my hot beach and my coconut.'

So then we built and stocked for Willie
    A log hut, and for Mac a calm
    Rockabye cradle on a palm –
Idyllic dwellings – but this silly
Mad War has now wrecked both, and what
Better hopes has my little cottage got?[59]

However, in the absence of any definite proof about Johnstone's behaviour, Robert began telling himself that there was no truth in what he had heard. Possibly Gerald 'owed [him] a grudge'; it must all have been 'a very cruel act of spite'.[60]

When the flow of family letters began reaching him again, Robert replied more cheerfully. On 2 July he wrote from Vermeilles that he was: 'Still in the same ruined billets from which I wrote last time and in which I enjoy life thoroughly. No work to do, plenty of sunshine, food and drink and flowers, and drawing 12/9 a day pay and allowance the whole time!' They were playing cricket at that time with 'a rag ball, a stump of charred wood for bat and a parrot-cage for wicket'.[61] A few days later, when the officers of Robert's company were due to play tip-and-run against a team of sergeants, something better was needed. So, as Robert wrote home, they

got a couple of men to go about touting for wood to cut into stately stumps and beautiful bats and had a skin-covered ball sent up from the town. I got most of the wickets and made top score (27) which pleased me hugely.

A battery of our guns was firing at the end of our pitch & you heard 'How's that? Not Out! Over!' mingling with: '136–50 yards elevation – take the line over the haystack' & other snatches of gunner jargon & the roar of the guns. Last night my platoon & I went out with the Royal Engineers to lay a light wooden railway to bring the rations up to the reserve trenches in the dark.

The line makes a great horse-shoe all round us easily distinguished by the ring of flare lights. You could see great excitement over by the brickstack, flares going up one after another the whole time; but I suppose they had merely got the wind-up from the bombing and trench mortaring

that always goes on there &, as far away to the right as Souchez where
the French are fighting, red & green & white parachute lights showed
that the dear good people are still nibbling away at the Germans. We were
lying in the cornflowers & poppies waiting for an iron rail-curve to be
brought up on the trolleys as wood would not wear well enough, & talking
in low voices rather sleepily.[62]

By mid-July 1915, Robert was back at the front, but in the comparatively
safe trenches to which he had been assigned when he first came out to France.
For a while he commanded his company; and although to begin with he wrote
to his father describing his additional responsibilities as 'rather a nuisance',[63]
it was a proud moment when the famous Kitchener of Khartoum, who came
to inspect the Royal Welsh, passed on the message that he was 'pleased ...
with our soldierly appearance (what, what!) and our cheerfulness and good
discipline under arms'.[64]

A happy time followed, especially as a letter from Johnstone arrived admitting
that 'he had been ragging about in a silly way'; but adding that 'there was
not much harm to it', and promising that he 'would stop it for the sake of
our friendship'.[65] Robert was also spiritually sustained by a temporary renewal
of faith. At Vermeilles, for example, he had taken communion in the battery
square at a service attended by many of his brother officers. The altar had
been decorated with some of the madonna lilies which grew in such profusion
in the deserted gardens of the town; and Robert had written home to say
that services meant much more to him out in the war zone than they had
done at home.

CHAPTER
3
DANGEROUS
CLEAR LIGHT

Towards the end of July 1915, a few days after his twentieth birthday, Robert was ordered to report to the Second Battalion of his own Royal Welch Fusiliers, stationed at Laventie, in a flat and featureless landscape some sixteen miles north-east of Béthune. The Second Battalion had lost very few men, and therefore maintained a tiresome degree of snobbery towards any soldiers who were not regulars; but Robert admired their professionalism enormously, and very much wanted to be accepted by them. On his very first night he was sent out on patrol with a sergeant, and showed his courage by bringing back, from an unoccupied German listening post, a wicker basket containing a large, round and potentially dangerous object. This was the right way to proceed: Robert soon discovered that the Royal Welch had made it 'a point of honour to be masters of No Man's Land from dusk to dawn'; and when he also 'found that the only thing that the regiment respected in young officers was personal courage', he began to go out on patrol 'fairly often'.[66]

It was dangerous work; and early in August Robert wrote a letter to be sent to 'Peter' Johnstone in the event of his death:

Dearest Peter

This is in case I die. If I do, it'll be young & happy & in splendid company, without any fears of Hell or anxious hopes for Heaven: I leave all that to God: no good building on doubts. I should have liked to write something fine & lasting by which nice people hereafter might remember my name but childlessness loses its sting when I think that you who mean infinitely more to me than myself are going to be a greater poet than I could ever be & that perhaps I have sometimes helped you to understand & love, & so in a sense may live in you when my body is broken up, & have a share in all your doings.

I leave you all 'my friends & my books & wish you all the happiness from them that I have had. God bless you always. My favourite hope is to be remembered by the future as your friend – Really, old thing! –,

Robert Graves

Give my best love to Dev[enish]. George Mallory & Eddie Marsh if you can.[67]

In this letter, Robert 'leaves all that to God' in the manner of one who does not wholly believe, but who would like to do so, and who is not far from saying: 'Lord, I believe; help thou mine unbelief.'[68] At the same time, he was writing high-minded poetry about facing death; and less than two weeks after writing his farewell letter to 'Peter', Robert sent a poem to Rosaleen in which was to be found 'a very fine expression of his feelings showing he had conquered the fear of death by a religious spirit which had drawn him nearer to God'.[69]

However, on the Western Front in 1915 not even a return to religious faith could keep a man's nerves calm indefinitely, and towards the end of August came Robert's most dangerous and unsettling night patrol. He had volunteered to locate a German working-party who had been heard the previous night in No Man's Land; but when the sun went down, the moon 'shone so bright and full that it dazzled the eyes', and Robert's mission began to seem near-suicidal. Too proud to back down, he set out with a sergeant. Astonishingly they both came back alive, after making their way to within thirty yards of the working-party, and pin-pointing its position; but the experience disturbed Robert's mental balance. In a letter to APG he described 'the dangerous clear light of an evil-looking moon';[70] and he wrote a poem about a young child and his nanny entitled:

I HATE THE MOON

I hate the Moon, though it makes most people glad,
  And they giggle and talk of silvery beams – you know!
But *she* says the look of the Moon drives people mad,
  And that's the thing that always frightens me so.

I hate it worst when it's cruel and round and bright,
  And you can't make out the marks on its stupid face
Except when you shut your eyelashes, and all night
  The sky looks green, and the world's a horrible place.

I like the stars, and especially the Big Bear
  And the W star, and one like a diamond ring,
But I hate the Moon and its horrible stony stare,
  And I know one day it'll do me some dreadful thing.[71]

Fortunately it was only ten days or a fortnight later that Robert was given home leave, and was able to return to England.

CHAPTER
4
ALONG
THE SEA-SHORE

Robert reached Harlech on the afternoon of Thursday 9 September 1915,[72] and joined his parents who were holidaying at Erinfa with Rosaleen, Charles and John. Perceval was also present, having recently returned from his four unsuccessful years in Canada; and Clarissa, who was said to be making a good recovery from her breakdown, was expected to join them in a few days. With his family around him, and the familiar Harlech landscape looking quite unchanged by the war, everything seemed amazingly normal. That evening, there was even 'a great family sing-song', at which Robert was 'the chief Folk-Song singer'.[73]

Friday was spent in catching up on his sleep; but then on Saturday afternoon Robert set out with his father to call upon Dr James, the President of St John's College, Oxford, who was staying in the village. Before meeting him for tea, they walked down to the Morfa, and across the sand-dunes, and spent an hour wandering along the sea-shore. Robert and Alfred were closer than they had been for some time: Alfred had been delighted with Robert's increased spirituality, and had been assiduous in meeting all his requests from the trenches – chiefly for volumes of poetry such as Davidson's *Poems* or A.E. Housman's *A Shropshire Lad*; while Robert had written warmly in praise of APG's latest publication, *The Book of Irish Poetry*.[74]

For a while Robert talked about his brothers: Charles, for example, was deemed to be like their grandfather Heinrich von Ranke, and therefore inclined in Robert's view to be arrogant; while John was more like the Bishop, 'sensitive but with a very fine brain', and 'if he has his health,' said Robert, 'he should go far.' Then, as he and his father continued walking up and down the sands, Robert talked about his own plans. At present, he said, he favoured 'an open-air life – scientific agriculture with literature as his second string or schoolmastering on Abbotsholme lines'.[75]

Despite Robert's defensive remarks to Edward Marsh about his father and uncle having tried to mould him 'in an outworn tradition', he regularly asked for APG's critical advice on his poetry; and on Sunday morning there was great excitement when the postman arrived with the latest number of the *Spectator*, which thanks to the combined efforts of APG and CLG contained lengthy extracts from Robert's letters from the trenches.[76] These were clearly and directly written, and introduced readers to some of the 'weird war chants' then current on the Western Front, such as the curious:

> I shoved my finger in a woodpecker's hole
> And the woodpecker screamed GOD STRAFE YOUR SOUL.
> Take it out!
> Take it out!
> Take it out!
> REMOVE IT.

This was a vivid reminder of the reality of life in the trenches; and later on, after mattins in the local church, and a traditional Sunday lunch, Robert escaped into the countryside with Rosaleen. That afternoon they wandered through the Erwen nut-woods; and on Monday they spent almost the whole day walking over the hills. On Tuesday, after a brief glimpse of Clarissa, looking 'wonderfully better', Robert travelled back to London with his father. It had been a happy holiday for them both; and Alfred, very proud of his soldier-son, was deeply touched by 'Robby's dozing in the Railway carriage from Wales with his dear head on my shoulder'.[77]

Wednesday the 15th, the last full day of Robert's leave, was surprisingly warm for mid-September; and in the morning Robert and APG went into town. Together they visited the offices of the *Spectator*, where Robert made some corrections to the typescript of the next set of extracts from his letters. 'We then,' wrote Alfred,

> walked off down the Strand to Cox's Bank where Robby found £65 to his credit & got a cheque book, armed with which we stalked all the way down to the Army & Navy Stores where he bought French long boots, a new wrist watch, new cap & waterproof well-lined, & medicine re-fill.[78]

After completing his purchases, Robert travelled down to Charterhouse, where he had arranged to spend the night with the Mallorys. Term had not yet begun, so he could not see Johnstone; but he was greeted very warmly by his former Headmaster, Frank Fletcher, who subsequently wrote to APG congratulating him on the favourable impression that Robert had made.

On Thursday Robert's leave came to an end, and he returned to Red Branch House, packed up his kit, and set out for Victoria Station to catch the afternoon train for Folkestone. Amy, Alfred and Perceval were there to see him off – poor Perceval was about to make another unsuccessful attempt to enlist – and when the train was delayed for an hour, the four of them walked as far as Westminster Abbey, where they visited Poets' Corner and admired the banners of the Grand Cross Knights of the Order of the Bath, which hung in the Henry VII Chapel. Finally the train left, with Robert jumping in after it had started; and Alfred, waving goodbye, wondered apprehensively how many of the 'trainful of gallant young officers' would ever return from the battle-front.[79]

CHAPTER
5
THE BATTLE
OF LOOS

After being delayed for a day at Folkestone, Robert arrived back in France to find that preparations were well under way for a major offensive. On 19 September 1915 his battalion was sent to Cambrin, where he found himself back in the trenches which he had first experienced in May, and he was told that

> these were the trenches from which we were to attack. The preliminary bombardment had already begun, a week in advance. ... This was the first heavy bombardment that I had yet seen from our own guns. The trenches shook properly and a great cloud of drifting shell-smoke clouded the German trenches. The shells went over our heads in a steady stream; we had to shout to make our neighbours hear. Dying down a little at night, the noise began again every morning at dawn, a little louder each time.'[80]

The landscape was becoming pounded into a state of utter desolation, in which almost the only features were huge craters, spoil-heaps from the mines, and here and there the wreck of a pit-head winding tower. Survival seemed extremely unlikely; and on the 20th Robert wrote a letter to be sent to his family if he died. It is remarkably free from bitterness or self-pity, and the final sentence shows that Robert now had a definite expectation of being reunited with family and friends after death:

> Dearest Family,
>   This is just in case I get killed. You are a dear lot of people & I send you my very best love – I want Mother to dispose of my personal property as she thinks fit: it isn't much, but doubtless Father would like my sword & Mother my old school prizes & boxing cups & her signet ring back again & Ros my share in the old coin collection – My books I promised in an idle moment before the War to my friend Peter (G.H. Johnstone) who is still at Charterhouse. I would like an inventory taken when they've

been collected from Wimbledon Harlech & Oxford & Mother to write & ask when he'd like to take them over. If my verses are ever published I want the copyright held jointly between Claree Ros & Peter. They won't be much of a success of course, because even the melancholy interest of my early death will not make up for the immaturity of form & expression. If any good folk write & condole with you for my death, thank them from me & tell them that they're dears.

And now goodbye till we meet again

– Robbie[81]

On 23 September, Robert and his fellow officers were told that the attack would begin in two days' time, and that their first objectives were a heavily defended farmhouse, and then the town of Auchy, both clearly visible beyond the German trenches immediately opposite. But instead of being able to make sensible preparations for the attack, they were compelled to spend most of 24 September in exhausting marches. Higher authority had decreed that despite the cold, wet weather they should do without their packs, capes, greatcoats and blankets until the attack was over, and that all this 'spare kit' should be taken to the safety of the barracks at Béthune. The main road to Béthune was soon 'choked with troops, guns, and transport'; and having unloaded their kit, Robert and his men had to march many miles out of their way to get back to Cambrin. It was not until one o'clock in the morning that they arrived, 'cold, tired and sick', in the trenches sidings from which they would be moved up to the front line in a few hours' time.[82]

The great battle began at five-thirty in the morning of 25 September 1915, with the release of poison gas from the British lines. Robert was deeply ashamed that the British should be using so ungentlemanly a weapon; but, in any case, the gas did more harm to his own side than to the Germans. In his sector of the line, it hung in No Man's Land for a while, and then drifted back into the British lines, where the confusion which it caused was reinforced both by intense German shelling, and by the fact that some of the British bombardment fell short, killing survivors from the first near-suicidal British attack.

By the time Robert reached the front line with his men, who were part of 'A' Company, it was 'full of dead and dying', the air was still heavy with gas, and 'B' and 'C' Companies of the Royal Welch Fusiliers had been more or less destroyed. As Robert was waiting for the whistle which would send him and the rest of the other two companies over the top, the adjutant came up, and, horrified by the extent of the losses, refused to allow the attack to proceed. Instead, he sent a runner to ask for definite orders from Brigade.

For more than two hours Robert and his men continued to wait for the order to attack, an order which would lead to almost certain death. Like Frank Richards, a signaller in 'A' Company, they saw that they 'didn't have a dog's chance. The enemy trenches were about three hundred yards away and we knew that the men in front of us were good soldiers and excellent shots and could do without the aid of machine-guns to mow us down advancing from that distance.'[83] Shells continued to fall all around them, the noise they made interspersed with the groans of wounded and dying men. Robert found that his 'mouth was dry, my eyes out of focus, and my legs quaking under me. I found a water-bottle full of rum and drank about half a pint; it quieted me and my head remained clear.' At last the attack was called off. It had been a disaster in which most of Robert's fellow officers had been killed; and when it was over, Robert, now in command of the survivors of 'B' Company, was told that no one had expected it to succeed; their job had been to provide a diversion from the main attack at Loos some miles to the south.[84]

The night was spent in bringing in the wounded and dead; and, as Frank Richards recalled:

The enemy didn't fire a shot during the whole of the night. The dead that were too far out were left. Young Mr. Graves worked like a Trojan in this work and when I saw him late in the night he looked thoroughly exhausted. He was helping to get a stretcher down in the trench when a sentry near him forgot orders and fired a round. Mr. Graves called him a damned fool and wanted to know why he was starting the bloody war again. He told a few of us outside the signallers' dug-out in the trench how bravely Major Samson had died. He had found him with his two thumbs in his mouth which he had very nearly bitten through.[85]

To realize that so many men had been deliberately sacrificed simply 'to provide a diversion', and that he himself had come very close to death as a result, was a profound shock for Robert. Pressure of work carried him through the following day, which was spent in pouring rain trying to clean up the trenches, and carrying the dead down for burial; and then at night there was the task of carrying extremely heavy cast-iron gas cylinders to a new position in readiness for the next attack. But when Robert heard that this attack, planned for the morning of 27 September, would be another diversionary assault, he found that his nerves were near breaking-point: 'It was difficult for me to keep up appearances with the men; I felt like screaming'; and he began to drink 'about a bottle of whisky a day' to keep himself 'awake and alive'. This time the gas blew in the desired direction; but a patrol sent out to see whether it had been effective in clearing the German lines was cut to pieces; and although

Robert and his men waited for five hours with fixed bayonets, the order to attack never came.[86]

This prolonged nightmare continued until 3 October, when the remnant of the Royal Welch were withdrawn from the line. Robert reckoned that he had had no more than eight hours of sleep in the past ten days, and he wrote to his parents saying that it was a miracle he had survived. Bombs had burst near him, poison gas had drifted across his path and shrapnel was embedded in his boot; but the only physical injury he had suffered was a cut hand.

The battle went on around Loos; and from the cottage where Robert was lodging in Annezin, a little village just west of Béthune, he could hear the guns booming in the distance. Although he had been shocked by the loss of life, and it was impossible for anyone who had witnessed such hellish scenes not to begin to question the wisdom of those in command, Robert maintained a high-minded attitude towards the recent fighting, telling Edward Marsh that 'the men were splendid', and his parents that it had been 'a great experience'. He also told Marsh that he had had 'an inspiration ... of what the New Poetry is to be';[87] and he sent home two poems which APG thought 'very fine'.[88] The best surviving illustration of the tenor of Robert's thought at this time comes in a poem called 'The Face of the Heavens'. This was written at Annezin not long after seeing action in the battle of Loos;[89] and in it Robert declares without a trace of irony:

> By these signs and wonders
> You may tell God's mood:
> He shines, rains, thunders,
> But all his works are good.

CHAPTER
6
A STRAY
BULLET

Although Robert Graves could try to accept what was happening as being part of some divine plan, he very sensibly recognized that he could not fight effectively when his nerves were in such a bad state. For the time being, as he told Marsh, his 'chief solace' remained 'a fairly regular correspondence with Peter – or so the Gods call him, as Homer would say, though men call him George Johnstone – my best friend, a poet long before I'll ever be, a radiant and unusual creature whose age hovers between seven and seventy, and ... still wholesome-minded and clean-living'.[90] But Robert's dream was now 'for some high-souled General (if only I kept a pet General) to get me a transfer to a Reserve Battalion in England ... for tho' still loyal and willing I've ceased to feel aggressive and winter is hard at hand'.[91] Some easing of the pressure was needed; and after a false alarm on 13 October, when it seemed for several hours that he and his men were about to be recalled to the front line, Robert was delighted to be attached to the battalion sappers. He still had to be ready to take part in an attack, and there was the disadvantage of working by night and sleeping by day; but he lived in pleasant circumstances well behind the lines, sharing rooms above a butcher's shop with four officers, one drawn from his own, and the rest from other regiments.

At first this way of life seemed relaxed enough for Robert to cope; but then towards the end of October two of his men were killed when a trench mortar suddenly exploded. Soon after this, he wrote to his father – now working as a recruiting officer in Wimbledon[92] – saying that because his nerves were deteriorating he would not be much use after another month or two in France. But if he returned to England, he might do valuable work training fresh recruits in the art of trench warfare. Would APG put in a word for him with any high-ranking officer of his acquaintance?[93] Alfred immediately asked 'Brigadier General Thomas to befriend Robby in the way he desired';[94] but he received only a vague and unsatisfactory reply.

In the meantime, without any explanation, Robert was sent back to the trenches. This was a disappointment both for Robert[95] and for his father; but although Alfred had proved unable to help Robert in the military sphere, he was doing good work for him in literary circles. After agreeing with Rosaleen that they were 'a very good lot', he had recently had a selection of Robert's poems typed out; and on 11 November APG took copies of them to the Poetry Book Shop whose proprietor, Harold Monro, was the publisher of Eddie Marsh's volumes of *Georgian Poetry*.

Monro had probably heard from Marsh about the high quality of Robert's work; and to Alfred's great delight he not only agreed to look at the poems, but promised that if he liked them he would publish them at his own expense. Two days later, Alfred was given lunch by Marsh himself. Marsh had recently received six of Robert's more recent poems, including his 'I Hate the Moon', and he spoke warmly about them.[96] Then a week later he wrote to APG saying how much he had enjoyed their meeting, and adding that he 'had heard from Monro, who said he was delighted at his first look at Robby's poems'.[97] This news was particularly welcome to Alfred, because he and Amy had just received

> a beautiful letter from dear Robby, grateful for what his mother and I have done for him and regrets for misunderstandings of us both – apprecia- tion of the early teaching he has had and example set him at home – the help I have given him with his Poetry. Altogether a realisation of 'Cast thy bread upon the Waters and thou shalt find it after many days!'[98]
>
> Living so near to death is indeed a quickener of the Spirit.

In northern France, the rain and slush of the trenches now gave way to a hard frost; and after six days of considerable danger in the front line, Robert was moved back to the base camp. From here he wrote that he had been gazetted a captain in the Third Battalion (Special Reserve), that he hoped for leave early in December, and that he might then be allowed to remain in England training new recruits.[99] Returning to the Royal Welch had made Robert even more anxious to leave France: although he was respected by his men, he had become 'very much disliked'[100] by many of his fellow officers. For some time they had thought him a prig; and now, in the aftermath of Loos, as Robert began to question military decisions, and openly to defy conventions of which he disapproved, they described him among themselves as 'bumptious' and 'dep- lorably untidy'.[101]

However, there was a shortage of captains in the First Battalion; and towards the end of November Robert was ordered to join them in their billets at Locon, behind Festubert, which was a mile or two to the north of Cambrin. Each night working-parties were sent out to Festubert to dig new trenches, an almost impossible task in the deeply frozen marshland; but within eight or nine days of Robert's arrival the First Battalion was despatched for training to Montagne le Fayel, a village in Picardy some thirty miles away from the front line.

Robert's concern about remaining in France was soon submerged by the enormous admiration which he came to feel for the professionalism of his new comrades. He was attached to 'A' Company, which was given the main work of the move, and wrote home proudly about their 'wonderful piece of work', which included a 'March on empty stomachs from Station to Camp – 21 miles – without one man falling out, showing prime condition of troops'.[102] And although the older officers in the First Battalion disliked Robert, he found that the younger ones were 'an exceptionally nice lot', and on 10 December wrote to Eddie Marsh saying that he was 'very cheered with life'.[103]

Robert particularly liked Siegfried Sassoon, a twenty-nine-year-old poet and country gentleman, who had taken a commision with the Royal Welch Fusiliers earlier in the year. For some years before the war Sassoon had spent much of his time at his parents' home in Kent, 'hunting, playing cricket and writing poems, which he had privately printed in small editions'. Slim, wiry, dark-haired and elegantly dressed, Sassoon was a man of many contradictions. Longing for praise, he was also 'instinctively reclusive'; and in appearance his thoughtful eyes and sensitive mouth contrasted strangely with a firm chin, a nose which appeared rather too large for the rest of his face, and ears which stuck out awkwardly. Sassoon had only recently arrived in France, and had joined the First Battalion as an officer in 'C' Company.[104] Although he was nine years older than Robert, he was his junior in military experience, having as yet seen no front-line service; he found Robert 'overstrung and self-conscious', but 'interesting';[105] and the two men had in common their literary interests and their friendship with Edward Marsh.

Soon the two soldier-poets were reading each other's work. Sassoon liked some of Graves's poems, finding them 'full of promise and real beauty';[106] but he loathed others, including no doubt 'The Morning Before The Battle', which has lines such as: 'I looked, and ah! my wraith before me stood,/His head all battered in by violent blows'.[107] In his diary, Siegfried described poems of this kind as 'very bad, violent and repulsive', and stated, 'He oughtn't to publish yet.'[108] In conversation he was more restrained, telling Robert simply that some of his poems were 'too realistic'. Robert, with his first-hand experience of trench-warfare, could not accept this, and felt that it was Siegfried's poems which were too unrealistic;[109] however, he was a little alarmed by Siegfried's more detailed criticisms; which may account for his hostile reaction when a letter arrived from APG announcing that Monro intended to publish a thirty-two-page volume of his poems.

APG's letter also contained the news that Monro had sent on copies of the poems for Marsh to read; and instead of being grateful for what his father had achieved, Robert was overcome with embarrassment at the thought that Marsh would be looking critically at poems which their mutual friend Sassoon disliked so strongly. Writing to Marsh, he complained that his father had been far too hasty in showing the poems to anyone, even to Monro, as he had been 'charged and adjured ... to do nothing ... until I'd picked out what I wanted to keep and put these few to a thorough examination'. But having accused APG of 'again play[ing] me false', Robert ended his letter to Marsh with this curious tribute:

> I'm glad you liked my old father. He's a man who's never made an enemy in his life and I firmly believe hasn't committed the smallest peccadillo since he was my age, and has worked like a black in beastly surroundings for years and years though hopelessly dreamy and unpractical and absent-minded. I do admire him – even when he's most hopelessly and pathetically wrong-minded.[110]

Robert continued to be grateful for APG's constructive criticism of his poetry, and adopted many of his suggestions. He even dropped one poem, 'Francis', which Alfred had condemned as immoral, though he did not like giving way, and later complained to Marsh about having had 'an absolute *snorter* from Father' on the subject.[111]

The remainder of December 1915 and the first weeks of January 1916 were spent in training for the kind of 'open warfare' which it was hoped would follow a breakthrough on the Western Front. Field-days interspersed with days of drill and musketry practice were very far removed from the reality of the war, and Robert at last had a chance to recuperate from the strain of the previous year. At the same time, his friendship with Sassoon deepened, and the two of them became equally close with David Thomas, a second lieutenant in the Third Battalion. Thomas and Graves both played rugger for the battalion, and Robert later described his new friend as 'a simple, gentle fellow and fond of reading. Siegfried, he and I were together a lot.'[112]

Then in mid-January, when Robert was once again on the point of getting leave, he was selected to give instruction in trench warfare at Le Havre. This had the advantage of keeping him away from the trenches for a further seven weeks. He was also well housed and well fed,[113] and was soon lecturing 'all day to smaller or larger audiences, more or less appreciative as the weather varies'. Robert's experiences in the Debating Society at Charterhouse stood him in good stead: at a very early stage he found that he was 'able to hold 150 Ulstermen for 1½ hours';[114] later, he thought nothing of 'lecturing to 'eleven hundred men and fifty officers ... for a forty minutes on one of my favourite subjects: how to keep happy, though in the trenches;[115] and on one memorable occasion he spent an hour lecturing to three thousand Canadians about the disaster of Loos.

All this was good for Robert's self-confidence: 'I can't imagine myself facing an ordeal like that a year ago,' he wrote to Marsh after one lecture, 'but I've altered a bit – "C'est la guerre".'[116] His morale was further improved when towards the end of February he signed an agreement with Monro for the publication of his poems, not long after APG had arranged for some of them to appear in the *Westminster Gazette*.[117] On 1 March Robert confidently took the chair for a St David's Day dinner at which seven officers of the Royal Welch were present; and a few days later a family friend caught a glimpse of him 'reading Homer at 10.30 p.m. under a lamp post at Havre'.[118]

Robert was once again expecting to be given leave; and he planned to extend his time in England to at least three weeks by undergoing a minor but necessary operation. Ever since his nose had been broken in a game of rugger at Charterhouse, Robert had been unable to breathe properly except through his mouth. In normal circumstances this was not a serious handicap; but it made using a gas-mask awkward, and might therefore prove fatal in the event of a major gas attack by the enemy.

Once again, however, Robert's leave was delayed. Several of the Royal Welch officers were sick, and he was ordered to rejoin his regiment. By 10 March Robert was back with the First Battalion,[119] who were now in the front line again in the Fricourt trenches on the Somme, some forty miles south of the region in which they had previously been fighting.

Despite a plague of rats, constant German shelling, and an extremely unpleasant new type of trench mortar called a canister, which was packed with explosive and scrap metal, Graves remained for some days in excellent spirits. He and his fellow officers in 'A' Company cheerfully sang anthems when things were going well; and he thoroughly enjoyed the company of his friends Thomas and Sassoon. But then, on 18 March 1916, came a disastrous night in which a number of officers were killed.

One of them was Lieutenant David Thomas, who was hit by a stray bullet in the neck and choked to death a few minutes later. The following evening there was a burial service. Siegfried Sassoon was one of the mourners, and noted that Robert Graves stood beside him,

> with his white whimsical face twisted and grieving. Once we could not hear the solemn words for the noise of a machine-gun along the line; and when all was finished a canister fell a few hundred yards away to

burst with a crash. So Tommy left us, a gentle soldier, perfect and without stain.[120]

Robert himself recalled: 'I felt David's death worse than any other death since I had been in France ... It just made me feel empty and lost.'[121] The result was this sombre set of verses, which he entitled:

GOLIATH AND DAVID

'If I am Jesse's son,' said he,
'Where must that tall Goliath be?'
For once an earlier David took
Smooth pebbles from the brook:
Out between the lines he went
To that one-sided tournament,
A shepherd boy who stood out fine
And young to fight a Philistine
Clad all in brazen mail. He swears
That he's killed lions, he's killed bears,
And those that scorn the God of Zion
Shall perish so like bear or lion.
But ... the historian of that fight
Had not the heart to tell it right.

Striding within javelin range,
Goliath marvels at this strange
Goodly-faced boy so proud of strength.
David's clear eye measures the length;
With hand thrust back, he cramps one knee,
Poises a moment thoughtfully,
And hurls with a long vengeful swing.
The pebble, humming from the sling
Like a wild bee, flies a sure line
For the forehead of the Philistine;
Then ... but there comes a brazen clink,
And quicker than a man can think
Goliath's shield parries each cast,
Clang! clang! And clang! was David's last.

Scorn blazes in the Giant's eye,
Towering unhurt six cubits high.
Says foolish David, 'Damn your shield!
And damn my sling! But I'll not yield.'

He takes his staff of Mamre oak,
A knotted shepherd-staff that's broke
The skull of many a wolf and fox
Came filching lambs from Jesse's flocks.
Loud laughs Goliath, and that laugh
Can scatter chariots like blown chaff
To rout; but David, calm and brave,
Holds his ground, for God will save.
Steel crosses wood, a flash, and oh!
Shame for beauty's overthrow!
(God's eyes are dim, His ears are shut)
One cruel backhand sabre-cut –
'I'm hit! I'm killed!' young David cries,
Throws blindly forward, chokes ... and dies.
And look, spike-helmeted, grey, grim,
Goliath straddles over him.[122]

A single stray bullet, and the death of someone whom he had come to regard as one of his two closest friends, had undone in a moment all the months of recuperation, and Robert felt once again that his breaking-point was near. One of the anthems which he had grown used to singing with his brother officers, an anthem whose 'words repeated themselves in my head like a charm whenever things were bad', was 'He that shall endure to the end ... shall be saved.' First Robert began to wonder 'whether I could endure to the end with faith unto salvation'; and then, as 'David and Goliath' shows, with its line 'God's eyes are dim, His ears are shut', his newly-revived faith did rapidly weaken. At the time Robert feared 'a general nervous collapse'; but fortunately for his sanity he was almost immediately given leave; and he knew that he could stay in England for some time. A new gas helmet made it imperative that he should be able to breathe through his nose, and the battalion doctor advised him that the necessary operation should be carried out as soon as possible.[123]

CHAPTER
7
ON LEAVE

Robert arrived at Red Branch House on 27 March, and spent the next few days visiting family and friends,[124] including 'Peter' Johnstone, whom he found, as he wrote to Sassoon, 'exquisite as usual: I had tea in his study and went for a walk with him after, the longest time I have ever been in his society. It's very extraordinary though that if you add up all the times we've been together they would only total up a few hours, probably not a whole day yet.'[125] Meanwhile APG had been busy arranging for Robert's operation. On advice from Eddie Marsh, he had first of all written to Sir Alfred Keogh at the War Office, asking him whether the army would organize everything.[126] When this highly irregular approach failed to produce instant results, APG went to the War Office to discuss the matter in person with Keogh's private secretary. The secretary sent him on to the Millbank private hospital, where it was arranged that Robert should be admitted on 3 April.[127]

The operation was finally carried out on 6 April 1916, and seems to have been badly managed. Robert was left in considerable pain: his nose bled a great deal, he had a severe headache, and his back and side also hurt. One or other member of the family called on him every day, but for some time he was 'miserable and uncommunicative'.[128] A week after the operation he was still 'very weak', and it was not until 26 April that he was able to leave hospital, 'looking very pale'.[129]

Then, after two days at Red Branch House, Robert travelled up to North Wales to recuperate. To begin with he stayed with Clarissa at Erinfa, but he spent as much time as possible at the cottage; and early in May he bought it from Amy for just under thirty pounds.[130] After whitewashing his new acquisition, he described in a poem how:

> All the walls are white with lime,
> Big blue periwinkles climb
> And kiss the crumbling window-sill;
> Snug inside I sit and rhyme,
> Planning poem, book or fable,

At my darling beech-wood table
Fresh with bluebells from the hill.[131]

This was the 'cottage in the hills' which Robert had been thinking of when he wrote his poem 'Over the Brazier', and it meant, in Robert's own words, that he had 'something to look forward to when the guns stopped'.[132]

It was during this holiday in Harlech that Robert met for the first time the family of the artist William Nicholson, who had 'rented Llys Bach, a large stone house on the hill above the road from Erinfa to Harlech Castle for the duration of the war'. Robert's family had become acquainted with the Nicholsons while he was away in France; and Robert himself found a good friend in William's son Ben, another painter, whose asthma had kept him out of the war. Robert also met for the first time Ben's sister, sixteen-year-old Nancy, a spirited and independent girl with dark eyes and dark hair. There was more than four years' difference in experience between the battle-weary soldier of twenty, and the schoolgirl of sixteen, and at first Robert took little notice of her.[133]

He was more concerned with his male friends, and from Harlech he wrote two letters to 'Sassons', as he affectionately called Sassoon. In the first, he told Siegfried that he was 'really desolated at having deserted you and the battalion but I couldn't help it', and he unfairly suggested that the operation which had delayed his return to the front was all his parents' fault.[134] In the second, Robert said that if he survived the war he would like to spend at least a year in Oxford, 'with the view of finding out the nice people and consolidating them'; and he hoped that Siegfried would join him there. With this letter Robert enclosed an advance copy of his book of poems, which took their overall title from his 'Over the Brazier'. He also mentioned that he had been joined at Harlech by CLG, who intended to review *Over the Brazier* for the *Spectator*; and that he found him 'a yknarc [cranky] ... old scarecrow', but 'the best of company'; and Robert added that he would like CLG very much but for his hatred both of the Welsh and of Robert's idol, Samuel Butler.[135]

Robert returned to London with Clarissa and CLG on 15 May. Three days later, on Friday the 18th, Robert was his father's guest at a banquet held by a Welsh literary club, the Honourable Cymmrodorion Society, at the Trocadero. The main speaker was Lloyd George, who gave a marvellously eloquent speech. Robert felt that 'the substance of what he was saying was common-place, idle and false', and noted that his eyes 'were like those of a sleep-walker'; but he was fascinated when, after the speeches were over, APG introduced him both to Lloyd George and to the Australian Prime Minister, W.M. Hughes.[136]

The following Monday, after a pleasant weekend spent at Charterhouse, Robert returned to the Millbank hospital for a check-up. This was satisfactory,[137] and two days later, on Wednesday 24 May, an Army Medical Board passed him fit, and ordered him to report for duty. By the following evening[138] Robert was back with the Third Battalion of the Royal Welch Fusiliers, who were now stationed at Litherland, near Liverpool, where they formed part of the Mersey defence force.

At first Robert was pleased to find himself back among a number of old acquaintances, reported cheerfully to his parents that he expected to be 'actively employed',[139] and was soon hard at work both as a company commander and as the officer in charge of trained men. But within two days Robert was feeling both bored and depressed, and he wrote to 'Sassons' telling him that he wanted '"to go home" – to France'. Not only was Litherland 'squalid', but the subalterns were 'ridiculously respectful', and the only one with enough vitality to be interesting spent his time in drinking and womanizing.[140]

Far worse than this, Robert had suffered what he described to Siegfried as 'a great, a hardly bearable disaster'. 'Peter' Johnstone's mother had discovered some of Robert's letters to her son. So shocked was she both by the modern ideas which they contained, and 'at such signatures as "ever yours affectionately, Robert" and "best love, R"' that she had

> extracted a promise from the poor lad that he will have nothing to do with me till he leaves Ch'house. Complications too long to enumerate leave no loopholes of evasion for either of us, so I am now widowed, laid waste and desolate. However, Peter in his last letter said that he'd never forget me and after these few years all will be as before: and perhaps he'll be able to rebel sooner, and it's better than him being killed anyhow.[141]

For the next month Robert was so restless, and so impatient to escape from 'Bloody Litherland' to France, that he succeeded in offending almost everyone around him of any importance. The only good news was that after considerable delays *Over the Brazier* had at last been published, and the reviews were 'very affable, mostly'. Robert was particularly pleased that there had been more than a column in the *Spectator* written, at APG's request, by its editor and proprietor, John St Loe Strachey.[142]

At last, on the morning of Sunday 25 June, Robert heard the news for which he was waiting: he was ordered to France, where a major offensive was in preparation. First he was to have a short leave with his family; and that evening he arrived at Red Branch House, bringing with him another Fusilier whom he had discovered was an old friend: long ago they had attended the same dame's school in Wimbledon, and supper was enlivened by cheerful reminiscences of their childhood.

Robert spent most of Monday in town with his father. In the morning they called on Robert's aunt Ida, Lady Poore, whose recent volume of reminiscences had been a great success; they went on by hansom cab to the *Spectator* offices; and thence, as APG records,

> on by underground train to Poetry Book Shop & found from pretty Manager that Robert's book was going into a 2nd edition. ... Robby stood me lunch at Waldorf Hotel ... quite a banquet, winding up with strawberries & cream. On to Cox's where Robert found his account £123 – took out £7 in French money. Then he called on Eddie Marsh & was introduced to Mrs. Asquith who wished him all luck. ... We went on to Hotel York where Millicent and Philip were.[143]

After a while APG left, but Robert stayed on to have tea with Philip. His half-brother was on leave from Cairo, where he was working for military intelligence alongside an enthusiastic young second lieutenant called T.E. Lawrence, later to become famous as Lawrence of Arabia, and also to become one of Robert's most loyal friends.

The following morning Robert set out once more for France.[144]

CHAPTER
8
THE BATTLE
OF THE SOMME

The Somme offensive opened on the Western Front on 1 July 1916. The First Battalion of the Royal Welch Fusiliers were heavily involved in the fighting; but Robert was delayed in Rouen for a few days, and then found that instead of being allowed to rejoin the First Battalion, he was posted to the Second, who were then holding trenches at Givenchy, not far from the Cuinchy brick-stacks. On his way to join them, Robert began a letter to Eddie Marsh, asking him to be his literary executor, and adding: 'I hope to God that S.S. is all right.'[145] Siegfried Sassoon had become recklessly daring since David Thomas's death, and as a result of this had acquired the nickname 'Mad Jack'; but so far he was unwounded.

When Robert reached Givenchy, he received a very cool welcome. An officer who was jealous of Robert's captaincy revived 'the suspicion raised at Wrexham by my German name that I was a German spy ... the result was that I found myself treated with great reserve by all the officers who had not been with me in trenches before.'[146] However, within a few days of Robert's arrival the battalion were ordered to the Somme. They went by train to Amiens, and then marched by easy stages to the front.

By the time the Second Battalion reached Buire, on 11 or 12 July, the First had been temporarily withdrawn from the fighting, and Sassoon and some of his fellow officers were stationed not far away from Buire, 'in reserve at Transport Lines close to Méaulte'.[147] Hearing that the Second were in the area, Sassoon sent Graves a note asking him to call; and at the first opportunity, which came on the 13th, Robert borrowed a horse and rode over to see his friend. Unfortunately he was unable to find Siegfried, and instead sent him a very depressed letter saying that he was 'at last looking out for a cushy wound. ... I want to go home to a quiet hospital ward with green screens and no cracks in the ceiling to make me think of trenches.'[148]

On the following day the Second Battalion bivouacked less than three

hundred yards from the transport lines, and Robert had a long talk with Siegfried, who found him

> whimsical and queer and human as ever. We sat in the darkness with
> guns booming along the valleys, and dim stars of camp-fires burning all
> round in the dark countryside; and a grey cloudy sky overhead, and the
> moon hid. And there I left him, with his men sleeping a little way off.
> Tomorrow they'll be up in the battle...[149]

Sassoon was now convinced that in Graves, if they both survived the war,
he had found 'a life-long friend to work with'.[150] They had talked of travelling
to the East together; and Siegfried noted that 'whenever I am with him, I
want to do wild things, and get right away from the conventional silliness
of my old life'.[151]

On 15 July, the day after his conversation with Siegfried, Robert moved
up to the front with his men. They began their march through a pleasant
country landscape of small villages set amid fields and low wooded hills, which
had been dramatically altered but not destroyed by the war. The chief difference
was that hundreds of thousands of soldiers had been moved up towards the
battle area, and on all sides there were huge encampments, with row upon row
of tents, and enormous numbers of men. Horses were also much in evidence,
some of them being used to pull the smaller field-guns, others being ridden
by the officers, and still more tethered some distance behind the lines waiting
to be used for the rapid advance which it was hoped would follow a 'break-out'.

Indeed, apart from an occasional motor-bike or armoured car, the scene
was very like something from the Crimean War until they approached the
recent battle area. There the big guns had done their work, and the Fusiliers
entered a scene of terrible desolation. Corpses lay all around, and there were
also numbers of dead horses and mules. The ground was thickly pitted with
shell-holes, and the mist was heavy with shell-fumes. They bivouacked on
the edge of Mametz wood, which was full of the dead, and in which there
was not a single tree unbroken. From here Graves wrote a long verse letter
to Sassoon about their plans. After the war, he imagined, they would meet
at his Harlech cottage, where they could:

> ... stretch our legs,
> And live on bilberry tart and eggs,
> And store up solar energy,
> Basking in sunshine by the sea,
> Until we feel a match once more
> For *anything* but another war.

So then we'll kiss our families
And sail away across the seas
(The God of Song protecting us)
To the great hills of Caucasus.
Robert will learn the local *bat*
For billeting and things like that,
If Siegfried learns the piccolo
To charm the people as we go.
The simple peasants clad in furs
Will greet the foreign officers
With open arms, and ere they pass
Will make them tuneful with Kavasse.

. . .

Perhaps eventually we'll get
Among the Tartars of Thibet,
Hobnobbing with the Chungs and Mings,
And doing wild, tremendous things
In free adventure, quest and fight,
And God! what poetry we'll write![152]

This happy escapism did not blind Robert to the horror of what lay about him. In the same envelope, he enclosed a few lines about the terrible reality of the present:

. . . today I found in Mametz wood
A certain cure for lust of blood,
Where propped against a shattered trunk
In a great mess of things unclean
Sat a dead Boche: he scowled and stunk
With clothes and face a sodden green:
Big-bellied, spectacled, crop-haired,
Dribbling black blood from nose and beard.

For that day and the next there was 'nothing to do but sit about in shell holes and watch the artillery duel going on';[153] and then on the 17th they moved up to a position just to the north of the ruined village of Bazentin le Petit to relieve some Irish troops. 'D' Company, to which Robert had been posted,[154] at once began deepening the trenches. The following day there was some heavy shelling from the German lines some five hundred yards ahead, but it was not accurate enough to do any serious damage, and Robert later recalled that he was 'in a cheerful mood and only laughed. I had just had a parcel of kippers from home; they were far more important than the bombardment.'[155] That night there were strong-points to be dug ahead of the lines, but once again everything passed off safely.

Then on the evening of Wednesday 19 July the Second Battalion, now reduced by casualties to some four hundred men, was pulled out of the line in preparation for a major assault the following morning on the German position at High Wood. Although Colonel Crawshay tried to encourage his officers by telling them that they would be 'in reserve' for this attack, as the Cameronians and the Fifth Scottish Rifles were going over first, they must all have known that they were bound to be called upon sooner or later, and that to be involved in an attack of this kind was practically a sentence of death.

The Battle of the Somme, now almost twenty days old, was already a major Allied defeat. On the first day of the fighting alone there had been 60,000 casualties, including 20,000 deaths, as lines of brave and well-disciplined men walked uphill towards the German barbed wire and machine-guns, and were cut down in great swathes. Casualties had continued to average some 10,000 killed or seriously wounded every day. News of the battle was at first totally distorted by the British press, so that Alfred Perceval Graves's diary for the first fortnight of July contains frequent comments about the good news from the front. Even when the mounting losses could no longer be hidden, as a generation of young men was pointlessly slaughtered, the politicians continued to allow Sir Douglas Haig, the British Commander-in-Chief, to carry on with his plans for a 'break-out' in what was one of the best defended sectors of the German line.

Crawshay, whom Robert had come to admire, managed to make a joke of the fact that "if we are called for, that means it will be the end of us." He said this with a laugh, and we all laughed,'[156] though the noise of gunfire was so great that it was only just possible to hear his voice.

The following morning, the Cameronians and the Scottish Rifles succeeded in getting into High Wood; so the Royal Welch were not needed for a while. However, the Germans put down a barrage on the ridge where they were lying in reserve, and, as Robert wrote later:

It was heavy stuff, six and eight inch. There was so much of it that we decided to move back fifty yards; it was when I was running [downhill through a small cemetery on the edge of a shattered wood] that an eight-inch shell burst about three paces behind me. I was able to work that out afterwards by the line of my wounds. I heard the explosion and felt as though I had been punched rather hard between the shoulder-blades, but had no sensation of pain. I thought that the punch was merely the shock of the explosion; then blood started trickling into my eye and I felt faint and called to Moodie [the company commander]: 'I've been hit.' Then I fell down.[57]

Besides several minor wounds, Robert had two that were serious: one piece of shell had travelled through his left thigh, 'high up near the groin'; while the main wound had been 'made by a piece of shell that went in two inches below the point of my right shoulder and came out through my chest two inches above my right nipple, in a line between it and the base of my neck'.[58]

Robert lapsed rapidly into semi-consciousness. Captain Dunn, the battalion doctor, reached him quickly and dressed his main wound, but reported to Crawshay later that day that there was 'no chance' of Graves surviving. Robert himself was aware of 'being put on a stretcher and winking at the stretcher-bearer sergeant who was looking at me and saying: "Old Gravy's got it, all right."' Then he became unconscious. Taken down to 'the old German dressing station at the north end of Mametz wood', he received no further attention, but was left quietly in a corner to die. From here, too, a message was sent to the Colonel saying that there was no hope.[59]

But Robert had inherited the enormous strength and resilience of the von Rankes, a gift which had seen more than one of Amy's descendants confound medical opinion with a near-miraculous recovery. On the morning of Friday 21 July, when orderlies were clearing away the dead, they were astonished to find that Captain Graves was still breathing. Robert was put in an ambulance, and began bumping along the shell-pitted road which led westwards, and away from the War.

CHAPTER
9
'BUT I WAS DEAD,
AN HOUR OR MORE'

Robert was jolted for a brief while into screaming consciousness; but soon he was silent again; and although he was still alive when the ambulance reached Heilly, the nearest field hospital, he was deeply unconscious, and a report reached Colonel Crawshay 'saying he died of wounds on the way down'.[160] The Colonel made out the official casualty list, in which he reported Robert's death; and on the next day, Saturday 22 July 1916, he sent a letter to Amy which began: 'Dear Mrs. Graves, I very much regret to have to write and tell you your son has died of wounds. He was very gallant, and was doing so well and is a great loss.'[161]

As Robert gradually regained consciousness, he became aware of 'little bubbles of blood, like red soap-bubbles, that my breath made when it escaped through the hole of the wound'.[162] Refusing tea and boiled water, he managed to eat 'two rather unripe greengages' brought to him by a sympathetic doctor; but it was hot inside the tented dressing-station, and on Sunday morning he begged to be moved somewhere cooler. The reply was that his best chance of recovery was to lie still, and that if he was moved he could not hope to reach the Base alive. But very shortly afterwards orders arrived that the hospital must be evacuated to make room for a further wave of casualties; and Robert, still lying on the stretcher upon which he had been carried from the battlefield, was lifted on to a bunk in a hospital train bound for Rouen.

The journey was, in Robert's words, 'a nightmare'. Amazingly, when an orderly gave him a pencil and paper, he was able to write home 'in a bold hand', saying that he was 'very uncomfortable', but hoped to be home before his letter.[163] He reached Rouen alive, though so badly shaken that for many years afterwards he found that train-travelling brought on terrible attacks of nervous anxiety.

Robert's letter arrived at Red Branch House on Monday 24 July, his twenty-first birthday and coming-of-age. Alfred at once went into town, where he tried 'in vain to get particulars from 41 Parliament Street [the Officers' Casualty Office], or [the] War Office'.[164] At last, on Tuesday afternoon, the following telegram arrived from the War Office:

> Report now received states that Captain R von R Graves Welch Fusiliers was admitted to General Hospital Rouen with gunshot wound penetrating chest seriously ill will report any further.[165]

Later that day three more communications arrived: Crawshay's letter regretting that Robert had died of wounds; a letter from the Matron of the Rouen hospital saying that Robert's condition was serious but that everything possible was being done for him; and a letter from Robert himself saying that his temperature was normal, that he was losing very little blood, that he was recovering his appetite, that he was sleeping better, and that he was being well looked after.

It seemed impossible to make sense of these contradictory reports, and on Wednesday Alfred again travelled into London, and called at 10 Downing Street, where he found that Marsh too was 'dreadfully concerned'. By Friday morning there was still no definite news. Alfred visited Marsh again, and found him with 'a distracted letter about R. from Sassoon'. That evening there was 'an alarming wire about R. [confirming his death] which after great sorrow we hoped might be a mistake'; and at 10.30 p.m. Alfred and Amy set off together to 41 Parliament Street, where they learned that the telegram had not come from the hospital, but from the General Staff.[166]

On Saturday 29 July things began to look more hopeful: there was a letter from Robert, written on Wednesday, saying that his heart, which had been forced from its place, was becoming normal and absorbing the blood from his lungs; and that he was eating and sleeping well. Later that day the War Office assured APG that the reports of Robert's death must have been a mistake, and he went home 'and informed Amy and Claree of this much to their rejoicement'.

But their ordeal was not quite over. On Sunday morning there was a large bundle of post, from which Amy picked up a letter from Robert's batman. She opened it to find the news that Robert was dead and that his personal belongings were being sent home. This seemed as final as any news could be, and both parents broke down and wept. But then, among the rest of the post, Alfred discovered a fresh letter from Robert; and when they re-examined the batman's letter, they realized that it had been sent not from Rouen, but from the front. 'When we found out our mistake,' Alfred wrote in his diary, 'Amy fairly jumped for joy. Then came a wire saying: "Captain Graves progressing favourably, transferred England shortly." '[167]

Robert had arrived at Rouen on the 23rd in very bad shape. Once he had been briefly aware of a doctor examining him and saying 'hopeless case'; and on another occasion, disliking the way in which the Last Post had been sounded, Robert had 'told an orderly to put the bugler under arrest and jump to it or I'd report him to the senior medical officer'.[168] But gradually his mind had cleared; and by Sunday 30 July he was able to read and appreciate an apologetic letter from Colonel Crawshay, which began: 'Dear von Runicke, I cannot tell you how pleased I am you are alive.'[169] On the following day Robert's chest wound was successfully drained,[170] and he was at last out of danger. Three days later, on Thursday 3 August 1916, APG received a wire from Robert telling him that he would be arriving at Waterloo on the 1.38 hospital train.

It was impossible to gain admission to the platform, where each new stretcher case from the train was greeted by 'a new roar' of approbation from the crowd; but Alfred sent in some fruit to his son; and then, 'by rushing out to look in each ambulance, I at last succeeded in seeing [Robert] and gaining his attention. He waved to me and I signalled with my brolly.' Robert found the sight of his father 'hopping about on one leg, waving an umbrella and cheering with the best of them' embarrassing, and assumed as the ambulance pulled away that it would be some while before he saw him again. He had underestimated his father's persistence. APG was determined to talk to his son as soon as possible, and having found where Robert was being taken, he

> tubed via Charing X to Kentish Town and trammed thence to Parliament
> Hill Fields and on West Hill was stopped by Robby's ambulance. The
> good nurse stopped it for me to get in and we drove up to Queen Alexandra's
> Hospital [Highgate] for wounded officers. After he had washed & changed
> I had 1½ hours with Robert who told me all about the first 3 terrible days.[171]

On Friday afternoon Amy and Rosaleen visited Robert, who pointed out with some amusement that Thursday's *Times* had published his name among a long list of those who had died of wounds. 'The joke', he later wrote, 'contributed greatly to my recovery. The people with whom I had been on the worst terms during my life wrote the most enthusiastic condolences to my parents: my housemaster, for instance.' On Saturday 5 August *The Times* made good their mistake, by publishing a free announcement in their 'Court Circular' to the effect that:

> Captain Robert Graves, Royal Welch Fusiliers, officially reported died of
> wounds, wishes to inform his friends that he is recovering from his wounds
> at Queen Alexandra's Hospital, Highgate, N.

This led to a flood of friendly and encouraging letters, and Robert was particularly pleased by those which he received from his old friend Ralph Rooper, from Eddie Marsh, and from Siegfried Sassoon, who was now back in England himself with suspected lung trouble.

Replying to Marsh's letter, Robert joked: 'As a matter of fact, I did die on my way down to the Field Ambulance and found myself just crossing Lethe by ferry',[72] and later in the year he turned this fantasy into the following poem

ESCAPE

... But I was dead, an hour or more.
I woke when I'd already passed the door
That Cerberus guards, and half-way down the road
To Lethe, as an old Greek signpost showed.
Above me, on my stretcher swinging by,
I saw new stars in the subterrene sky:
A Cross, a Rose in bloom, a Cage with bars,
And a barbed arrow feathered in fine stars.
I felt the vapours of forgetfulness
Float in my nostrils. Oh, may Heaven bless
Dear Lady Proserpine, who saw me wake,
And, stooping over me, for Henna's sake
Cleared my poor buzzing head and sent me back
Breathless, with leaping heart along the track.
After me roared and clattered angry hosts
Of demons, heroes, and policemen-ghosts.
'Life! life! I can't be dead! I won't be dead!
Damned if I'll die for anyone!' I said. . . .
Cerberus stands and grins above me now,
Wearing three heads, lion, and lynx, and sow.
Quick, a revolver! But my Webley's gone,
Stolen . . . No bombs . . . no knife . . . The crowd swarms on,
Bellows, hurls stones. . . . Not even a honeyed sop . . .
Nothing. . . . Good Cerberus! . . . Good dog! . . . but stop!
Stay! . . . A great luminous thought . . . I do believe
There's still some morphia that I bought on leave.
Then swiftly Cerberus' wide mouths I cram
With Army biscuit smeared with Tickler's jam;
And Sleep lurks in the luscious plum and apple.
He crunches, swallows, stiffens, seems to grapple

With the all-powerful poppy ... then a snore,
A crash; the beast blocks up the corridor
With monstrous hairy carcase, red and dun –
Too late! for I've sped through.
               O Life! O Sun![173]

Robert used his obituary in *The Times* to try to improve his position with 'Peter' Johnstone's mother: through his brother Charles, who like Johnstone was still at Charterhouse, he 'instructed Peter ... to employ all his literary skill in a letter of pathetic reproach to his mother about my death and the way she's treated me and him'. Charles soon reported that Johnstone had agreed to this; and to cheer up his brother still further, Charles enclosed a punishment which he himself had been set: a master had asked him to write a hundred lines 'to the effect that he mustn't be a baby', and Charles had written a hilarious piece containing sentences like: 'I must not be a baby. Oh God, save me from shrinking smaller and smaller, from boyhood to babydom and finally from vanishing completely away.' Reading this made Robert 'laugh ... till I was nearly ill'.[174]

Although Robert seems to have been reasonably cheerful, he made a slower recovery than expected. On 7 August the doctor had said that he would be fit to travel 'in a week or ten days', and Robert was making plans to 'lug [Sassoon] up to Harlech';[175] but it was not till the 20th that he was able to leave his bed; and then, as Rosaleen reported to the rest of the family, who had gone on to Harlech, he was still very weak, and could only sit in an armchair on the hospital balcony. Two days later, however, Robert was walking again; and on Saturday 26 August he was strong enough to leave hospital and to catch a train, although he later recalled 'crying all the way up to Wales'.[176]

CHAPTER
10
ROBERT
AND SIEGFRIED

When Robert arrived at Harlech station, many of his family were waiting on the platform to give him a hero's welcome. Amy had ordered a motor so that he could be driven up to Erinfa, and Robert was embarrassed to find that it had been covered with flags, which he pulled down while being driven up Harlech hill. Alfred Perceval Graves was now an old man of seventy, and had been lying ill in bed with gout and neuralgia; but he hobbled downstairs to greet 'dear wounded Robby'; and later the whole family enjoyed 'a happy evening very' with the son and brother who had more than once been given up for dead.

Robert spent a quiet Sunday recovering from his journey; and on Monday he felt well enough to join Clarissa and APG when they motored over to Llanbedr to watch an open-air play being staged by some of their friends.[77] The following day, after lunching at the Golf Club with Charles, Robert went on with his brother to the station, where Siegfried Sassoon was expected by the afternoon train.

Siegfried duly arrived, bringing with him Topper, a charming and extremely affectionate little terrier of whom he was clearly extremely fond. The three men and Topper made their way up to Erinfa, where Sassoon made an extremely favourable impression on APG, who described him in his diary that evening as a 'fine tall manly, modest fellow'. Sassoon was particularly interested in talking to Robert's father about Tennyson, Rossetti, and the other writers whom APG had known long ago;[78] while at table he impressed John, who had just left Copthorne, with his

> wonderful store of amusing stories which he told in a nervous but entrancing way. He seemed particularly to enjoy amusing situations. One story concerned a Hunt that pursued carted stags. The stag on one occasion arrived at the railway station in a special truck ... somehow he escaped along the platform and went to ground in the map room, where he did enormous

damage before he was finally cornered and lassoed. Finally, with much
Tally-hoing the Hunt moved off down the main street.[79]

On Wednesday evening Robert and Siegfried attended a village concert
at which it was hoped to raise money for a war charity. APG took the chair,
and later recorded that 'to us the most touching incident was Robby's practically
impromptu speech of thanks on behalf of the Welsh soldiers – manly, modest,
simply eloquent. It brought down the house. Amy was very proud of it &
so were we all. We had a happy little supper after of sardines & blackberries
& junket.'[80] But despite this public appearance, Robert and Siegfried had
both begun to have serious doubts about 'whether it was right for the war
to be continued ... its continuance seemed merely a sacrifice of the idealistic
younger generation to the stupidity and self-protective alarm of the elder'.[81]
They also thoroughly disliked the feeling that some men back in England
were making money out of the war, and one of Sassoon's favourite stories,
as John recalled,

> reached its climax when someone, I think Sassoon himself, hurled an over-
> ripe pear, which burst full in the face of a particularly odious man of
> the Profiteer type sitting in an enormous motor-car. In telling the story,
> [Sassoon] somehow managed to impart to his hearers the extreme joy he
> had felt as the pear landed full on target.[82]

During the next two weeks Sassoon did a great deal of golfing, mainly
with Charles;[83] and also joined in several family outings, such as a picnic
lunch on Shell Island, where he and Robert amused themselves by setting
the grass on fire, and then smothering the flames with sand. But Siegfried
had come to Harlech intending to work, and he and Robert also spent much
time on their poetry.[84]

The two men worked closely together, amicably accepting amendments
to each other's poems; and towards the end of Sassoon's visit, when they
felt that they were ready to be judged by a friendly outsider, APG was called
in to have tea and to listen to 'a good selection'. Siegfried had been working
on his 'Old Huntsman' collection, a series of poems in which he distanced
himself from the war by writing about hunting and pastoral scenes; while
Robert had written this moving tribute to David Thomas:

NOT DEAD

Walking through trees to cool my heat and pain,
I know that David's with me here again.
All that is simple, happy, strong, he is.

> Caressingly I stroke
> Rough bark of the friendly oak.
> A brook goes bubbling by: the voice is his.
> Turf burns with pleasant smoke:
> I laugh at chaffinch and at primroses.
> All that is simple, happy, strong, he is.
> Over the whole wood in a little while
> Breaks his slow smile.

Robert was also turning from the war to write poems about childhood. These included the haunting 'Babylon', which begins:

> The child alone a poet is,
> Spring and fairyland are his.
> Truth and reason show but dim,
> And all's poetry with him.[185]

Two days later, on 11 September, Robert and Siegfried set out together for London, where they both visited a lung specialist. Then they travelled on to Kent, where Graves was to stay at Weirleigh, Sassoon's country home.

There was one aspect of this return visit which Robert found very displeasing: Sassoon's elder brother had been killed in the war, and his mother held private seances at night in a despairing effort to contact him again. Robert's nerves were in a poor condition; and to be 'continually awakened' on his first night in a new house 'by sudden rapping noises' followed later by 'a diabolic yell and a succession of laughing, sobbing shrieks that sent me flying to the door' was highly disturbing. In the morning he told Siegfried that he was leaving, as it was 'worse than France';[186] but when Siegfried explained the situation, and said that he too was irritated by his mother's behaviour, Robert made light of it, and settled down to a stay of more than a week.[187]

Graves and Sassoon continued to discuss their attitude to the war; and at length Sassoon arranged for them both to be invited to Garsington Manor near Oxford. This was the home of Lady Ottoline Morrell, a remarkable lady whom Siegfried had met for the first time earlier in the year. Lady Ottoline and her husband Philip, a Liberal politician, were pacifists and the friends of pacifists; and she conceived a particular liking for Siegfried, writing after this visit that she found him 'very sympathetic and attractive, and my instinct goes out to him'. She and Robert were therefore rivals for Sassoon's attention, and this partly accounts for Lady Ottoline's unkind description of Robert as 'an odd fellow with the face of a prize-fighter'. She added: 'He is very possessive of Siegfried, and I think he resents any friendship between us.'[188]

After a night or two at Garsington, Robert went on alone to Llandrindod Wells, where his father and his uncle Charles were playing golf and taking the waters. They had 'a quiet, healthy time'; and Robert passed on the news that the lung specialist whom he had seen in London had advised him to winter abroad.[189] Robert and Sassoon had already discussed with APG 'their idea of going to Egypt', and now Robert wrote to his uncle Bob to see if anything could be arranged. While he waited for a reply he went on to Harlech, where he stayed for some weeks, eating well and working on a novel based upon his war experiences.[190]

When Robert travelled down to Red Branch House at the end of October, his parents thought that he looked 'much better';[191] but as they very soon realized, he had by no means made a full recovery. The first of November was All Saints' Day, and Robert found that Amy and Alfred, not realizing the profound change in his religious views since David Thomas's death, expected him to accompany them to church. Not wanting to spoil the day for his mother, he reluctantly agreed to go; though he discovered that he was also expected to wheel APG to the church in a bath chair, as his gout made it too painful for him to walk.[192] Robert then had to sit through what even his father described as 'a longish service'; and he also had to listen to an over-zealous sermon about 'Divine Sacrifice' and 'the Glurious Perfurmances of our surns and brethren in Frurnce today', which was particularly displeasing to someone who had endured the horrors of both Loos and the Somme. The ordeal stretched out still further when Alfred insisted on staying on for communion; and then on the return journey to Red Branch House Robert found that pushing the bath chair was 'rather too much for him, & he owned his lungs are not yet all right'. Alfred was extremely worried about Robert's health after this incident, and when he wrote about it in his diary that evening, he added the words: 'I do hope he will get to Egypt with Bob.'[193]

However, the next twenty-four hours saw a major shift in Robert's opinions. On Thursday 2 November he lunched in town with Siegfried Sassoon, and they were joined by Robert Ross, the literary journalist who had once been a friend of Oscar Wilde.[194] In the course of their conversation Siegfried declared 'that we had to "keep up the good reputation of the poets", as men of courage, he meant. The best place for us was back in France away from the more shameful madness of home service. Our function there was not to kill Germans, though that might happen, but to make things easier for the men under our command.'[195] Robert was immediately converted to this point of view, though some of his family took a more cautious view. On Saturday he travelled up to Warwickshire to spend a weekend discussing his poems with his sister Clarissa, who was teaching in Nuneaton; and no doubt she repeated her recent admonition that it was important for the Medical Board to 'examine you properly and [not] just take your word for it that you are fit'.[196]

It was therefore particularly pleasing for Robert to find that his new sentiments were precisely echoed by Raymond Rodakowski, who wrote to him out of the blue from a military hospital in Oxford. 'Personally,' declared Rodakowski, 'I am longing to be back with my Battn., as I hate the unsettled feeling one has in this country, and though wounded in an attack ... I was hit too early in the day to see all I wanted to see.'[197] Robert and his father had already planned to spend a night at Oxford on 13 November: Robert was to meet his future tutor at St John's, while Alfred was trying to interest the Vice-Chancellor in a scheme for sending books to the troops. Now it was also possible for Robert to have a long talk with Rodakowski, whose atheism no longer seemed a bar to close friendship.[198]

Later that week, on Friday 17 November 1916, Robert attended a Medical Board at Caxton Hall. He was found fit to rejoin his regiment, and was told to report to Litherland, where a month's light duties could well be followed by a return to France.

CHAPTER
11
BLACK
VELVET DRESS

Robert had never liked Litherland, and soon after his arrival he was disappointed to find that he was likely to be stationed there for some time: there were as many as one hundred officers waiting to go out to France, and the fact that he had been absent on sick leave for so long meant that his name would be very low on the list. In the meantime, he was overworked at his so-called 'light duties', so that he later complained to his parents of becoming 'a military automaton';[199] and the bitter cold kept him awake at nights; though when Amy heard of this, she at once lent him an eiderdown, telling him: 'It cannot be right to lie awake from the cold, and is against your efficiency on the day after.... Think of me when you feel comfortable, dear Robby!'[200]

Litherland began to seem slightly less disagreeable when on 4 December Sassoon also rejoined the regiment, and moved into Robert's hut; while the following week the normal routine was broken by a visit from Rosaleen and APG, who was due to give a lecture in Liverpool. On this occasion the farcical vein which seems to run very close to the surface in the lives of certain members of the Graves family was more evident than usual.

First Amy sent a telegram to Robert announcing when Alfred and Rosaleen would be arriving at Lime Street Station in Liverpool. Unfortunately, she told him the wrong time. Nor had she mentioned to Alfred or Rosaleen that she intended asking Robert to meet them. When Robert arrived at the station, hoping to bring them back to the camp in a taxi, they had already begun an extraordinarily complicated journey through the Liverpool suburbs. At one point, they had a 'near shave' when the seventy-year-old APG, 'encumbered as I was by goloshes, top coat and umbrella', had to jump on to a moving tram. Later, they became completely lost. When they finally reached the camp, they were surprised to learn that Robert 'had gone into Liverpool in answer to a wire'. Sassoon, who took charge of them until Robert's return, then proceeded to dose them with formalin, 'to prevent us being flued'; and when that evening Robert, Rosaleen and APG went back into Liverpool for the lecture, the evening began with what Alfred later described as 'a momentary panic owing to the mislaying of my bag & MS'.[201]

The rest of the evening went more smoothly. Lord Ashbourne, who was in the chair, gave Alfred Perceval Graves a warm welcome in Irish; the lecture itself was a huge success; another speaker dubbed Alfred 'The Irish Burns'; and when by popular demand Alfred recited one or two of his poems, they were rapturously received. Afterwards, he was touched when 'one poor lady [came] to ask me to write my name in the prayer bk. found on the body of her boy killed at the front whose portrait she was wearing'.[202] For Robert, seeing his elderly and gout-ridden and often comically impractical and forgetful father at the centre of such adulation, was a forcible reminder not merely that his father was highly respected in his own field; but that ideas and sentiments and modes of expression which Robert felt were hopelessly out-of-date were still extremely popular.

Within the family, Robert tried to be a counter-balancing influence on his younger brothers. Sixteen-year-old Charles had recently turned to Robert for support when he felt that a master at school was marking his work unfairly; but as the tone of his letter suggests, he was not very biddable. 'It's simply not good enough,' Charles ended his letter angrily. 'I'm not going to do another stroke of hash this quarter ... if he plays the shit with [my next Greek prose] I shan't do another bally stroke. ... "Up his bloody crack" say I, your loving brother, Carolus.'[203] On this occasion Robert persuaded him to settle down to his studies; but in the long run he found that Charles was unpromising material for his more 'advanced' ideas.

Robert had greater hopes for thirteen-year-old John, a quieter and more serious character; and in December he decided that it was time for John to be introduced into the circle of his closest friends. Ruth Mallory was asked to invite John to tea, and Robert explained to John:

> I asked her to because I wanted you to meet my friend Peter Johnstone whom she was to invite at the same time: I hope it all came off ... & that you met Peter & liked him.
>
> Because he's a person I want you to know: if ever things get wrong & you can't put them right through people in the house because you're Charles's brother, Peter would jump at the chance of doing anything for you, for my sake.
>
> And a person like Peter can pull a lot of strings in a quiet way. Well, what do you think of Ch'ouse? I'd awfully like to know, before I go back to France & get killed.

He added, in a postscript, that he had a Medical Board very soon, and that he was 'going to persuade the doctors to send me back as soon as poss. Next spring we'll be fighting for our lives.'[204]

John had duly attended the luncheon party, and thought well of the handsome and brilliant Johnstone, who was now editor of *The Carthusian*, in which he had been publishing some more of Robert's poems. But since Johnstone was now such a senior member of the school, and John such a junior one, John 'was not surprisingly rather shy of him. He also seemed rather embarrassed ... and we did not exchange more than a few words ... [and we] did not meet again.'[205]

At Robert's Medical Board on 18 December, his wish to be passed fit for overseas service was granted. A few days later he arrived at Red Branch House for a week's leave, announcing that he expected to be going to the front soon after Christmas. He was still not very fit, and his family were disconcerted when he spent most of Christmas Day in bed – though this may have been partly to avoid the otherwise inevitable church services; and on Boxing Day he felt well enough to join his family in a long walk over Wimbledon Common.[206]

Robert had already travelled down to Godalming, presumably to see the Mallorys; and now he went into town, once to meet Devenish and Rooper, and on another occasion to buy himself a new revolver. But the call to arms came less rapidly than Robert had expected, and when his leave was over he spent nearly three more weeks at Litherland with Sassoon.

Occasionally the two men played golf together; but their friendship was clouded for a while, and on at least one occasion Robert 'rather annoyed' Siegfried by 'play[ing] the fool' on the golf links.[207] To Robert's chagrin, while Siegfried's new volume of poems was to be published in March by Heinemann, his own hopes in that direction had come to nothing. Robert wrote to the young poet Robert Nichols, a new protégé of Edward Marsh, explaining that 'Heinemann wanted too big a book';[208] but it was a considerable disappointment; and eventually Robert decided that he would pay to have the nine best of his recent poems privately printed, under the *Goliath and David* title. Siegfried welcomed this plan, and on 18 January 1917 he posted the poems to the Chiswick Press on Robert's behalf.[209] The following day, Robert was told that he had seventy-two hours of leave, and would then be going overseas again for his fourth tour of duty in France.

After spending the night of Friday the 19th at Red Branch House,[210] Robert went on to Charterhouse. There, as he wrote to Sassoon, he had 'a long talk with [Johnstone]: he was extraordinarily intelligent and seems now to have read about four times as much poetry as myself – makes me rather afraid of him.'[211] By Saturday evening Robert was back in Wimbledon; and then on Sunday he travelled into London to call on Robert Nichols,[212] who was

lying in a private hospital suffering from syphilis. He had served for three
weeks in France, with the Gunners, and had seen no major battle; but, as
Graves later wrote, 'he was highly strung and the three weeks affected him
more than twelve months affected some people'.[213]

It was their first meeting and one might have expected Graves to be sympathetic to his fellow poet. Instead, he gave him 'a hell of a lecture on his ways,
and finding he took it well, made friends with him. It was the usual story
– shellshock, friends all killed, too much champagne, sex, desperate fornication,
syphilis.'[214] Nichols evidently respected him and was prepared to accept his
advice; and in the circumstances Graves adopted a protective attitude towards
him, began to treat him as a close friend, and rated his poems rather more
highly than they deserved.

While he was in town, Robert also called on the Nicholsons in their Apple
Tree Yard property. He had gone there chiefly to say goodbye to his friend
Ben Nicholson, who had been using Robert's cottage in North Wales, in return
for making some improvements to it;[215] but when Robert left their house, the
last person to say goodbye to him was Ben's sister Nancy. Robert was hardly
aware of it at the time, but something in Nancy's appearance as she stood
in the doorway, pretty and appealing in her black velvet dress, made a profound
impression upon him.[216]

The following day Robert's leave came to an end, and he was accompanied
to Waterloo Station by his parents. On the platform they were joined by his
uncle Charles and by Uncle Charles's friend Lidgett, the editor of the *Contemporary Review*. Lidgett told Robert that he would be glad of a poem for publication. This was encouraging news; but Robert was unable to enjoy it for long.
He and his parents were about to be involved in yet another mildly farcical
incident. Just as Robert's train was about to pull out, he discovered that he
had left all 'his money and his regimental list in a pocket of the tunic he
had changed before starting'. Amy, who despite a badly inflamed eye had not
only done Robert's packing, but had been 'sewing his name on his khaki
handkerchiefs up to the very last moment', immediately left to retrieve the
missing items. Then, as Robert had asked, she followed him all the way down
to Southampton by the next possible train. She was rewarded for this devotion
by having another hour with her son before he sailed.[217]

CHAPTER
12
HOPE AND
WET MATCHES

After a few days at the Infantry Base Depot at Rouen,[218] Robert was posted to the Second Battalion of the Royal Welch Fusiliers, who were in the line near Bouchavesnes on the River Somme. Reaching them on 26 January 1917, Robert found that Crawshay was in hospital after being badly wounded by one of his own men in a shooting accident. But Doctor Dunn was still with the battalion; and he insisted, knowing Robert's recent medical history, that Robert was unfit for service in the trenches. The acting Colonel therefore placed Robert in temporary command of the Headquarter Company,[219] which was stationed by a bend of the Somme at Frise, some six miles behind the lines.

Robert at first enjoyed the challenge of his new appointment, and even took personal command of the daily expedition which took rations and other supplies up to the trenches. But it was bitterly cold, with twenty degrees of frost; the Somme was almost completely frozen over; and Robert lived for some weeks in an utterly desolate landscape. 'In all this area', he later wrote, 'there were no French civilians, no unshelled houses, no signs of cultivation. The only living creatures that I saw except soldiers and horses and mules were a few moorhen and duck in the narrow unfrozen part of the river.'[220]

There was one friendly meeting with Raymond Rodakowski, who had recovered from his wounds and was back on active service with the Irish Guards; but correspondence was Robert's chief consolation, and in one letter he found time to give Robert Nichols a memorable definition of what a poet should be. Not just a 'mere craftsman', but

> a woman suffering all the hardships of a man; hardening her weak softnesses; healthy and clean, loving the elements, loving friends more than life itself, proud, whimsical, wise, simple. But appreciating the refinements of Life as much as the harshnesses – warm sun on the bare chest, comfortable armchairs, a good fire, a jolly red Burgundy or claret, music above all

and colour and sleep, and mountains seen from a distance as well as from the precipice face of Lliwedd.[221]

One of Robert's most regular correspondents was his sister Clarissa, who was now working as a private tutor. One night the house in which she lived was burned to the ground, and it was largely thanks to her presence of mind that anyone escaped alive. Her letters on the subject made exciting reading for Robert, whose dull routine remained unbroken until mid-February. Then he began suffering from a toothache so painful that eventually he had to ride twenty miles to the nearest army dental station: only to be treated by a dentist so incompetent that he spent half an hour removing the offending tooth 'in sections'.

A few days after this unpleasant experience, the Second Battalion nearly became involved in another offensive; and since the acting Colonel was ill, and Robert was the next senior officer available, he had the opportunity, unusual for a young captain, of representing his battalion at a Commanding Officers' Conference at Brigade Headquarters. The plan was to 'bite off' a German salient; and, as the most junior officer present, Robert showed considerable courage by openly declaring that the attack was impossible. It was in any case postponed because of a thaw, which left No Man's Land a morass of mud; but when Robert took the rations up to the front that night, the other officers were pleased to hear of his uncompromising stand.[222] The authorities at Brigade H.Q. may have been less impressed: when a new Colonel was appointed to the Second Battalion, one of his first tasks was to relieve Robert of his temporary command.

One afternoon shortly afterwards, it was discovered that two of the supply horses had broken away during some shelling, and Robert spent the next eight hours with the transport sergeant looking for them with 'hope and wet matches'. They were unsuccessful; and the strain of this immensely long search, which did not end until 12.30 in the morning,[223] was too great for Robert's health. Within twenty-four hours he went down with severe bronchitis, and soon he was back in the Rouen hospital to which he had first been admitted the previous July. The major of the Royal Army Medical Corps, astonished to see Robert again, asked him: 'What on earth are *you* doing out in France, young man?' Then he added, very severely, 'If I find you in my hospital again with those lungs of yours I'll have you court-martialled.'[224] Later Robert was asked to say where in England he would like to go to hospital. He recalled that he had liked the look of the military hospital in Somerville College, which he had visited the previous year when looking for Rodakowski; and so he chose Oxford.

Robert's parents, Alfred Perceval Graves and Amy von Ranke, at the time of their wedding in Munich in December 1891.

Alfred Perceval Graves with his first family, Robert's half-brothers and sisters.
From left to right, Perceval and Dick stand at the back; Molly, APG and Philip sit
on chairs; and Susan sits on the rug in front.

George Mallory, described by Robert as 'the champion of everything noble and downtrodden and enemy of everything that is base and uplifted'.

G. H. ('Peter') Johnstone who became a close friend of Robert's at Charterhouse and who was described as 'Dick' in Robert's autobiography, photographed in 1913 at Charterhouse.

Robert Graves in his early days at Charterhouse.

Robert in uniform. Robert sent this photograph to his parents with the inscription 'Ever your loving son, Robbie'.

Siegfried Sassoon, 1915.

T. E. Lawrence drawn by Augustus John in 1919.

Edward Marsh, editor of *Georgian Poetry*, in fancy dress.

Edmund Blunden who became a friend of Robert's when they were both living on Boar's Hill.

Above: The Graves family on 22 November 1917. Back row (left to right): Rosaleen, Charles, Alfred and John. Front row: Robert, Amy and Clarissa. Robert was about to hurry off to St Ives to meet Nancy Nicholson. Rosaleen was to be a nurse in France.

Below: Robert and Nancy at Maesyneuardd, near Harlech in June 1918, five months after their wedding.

Robert's first wife, Nancy Nicholson.

Robert, Nancy, Catherine, David and Jenny at Islip.

Robert's children, Catherine, Jenny, Sam and David, photographed in Oxford probably in the summer of 1925 when they were three, six, one and five years old.

CHAPTER
13
SHELL-SHOCK
AND MARJORIE

Robert did not take long to recover from his bronchitis; but his nerves had been desperately overstrained by his military service, and he had developed a number of phobias. These did not yet prevent him from carrying on apparently as normal, but they were becoming an increasing handicap. The first of them dated from his earliest days in the army, when he was guarding prisoners at Lancaster. One night he was answering an official telephone call, when 'the line was, I suppose, struck by lightning somewhere. I got a bad electric shock, and was unable to use a telephone properly again until some twelve years later.'[225] Travelling by train also made Robert feel nervously ill, as he relived his nightmarish train journey to Rouen after his near-fatal wound in 1916; while from about the same time the fear of gas had become 'an obsession; in any unusual smell that I met I smelt gas – even a sudden strong scent of flowers in a garden was enough to set me trembling'.[226]

While Robert was still in hospital at Somerville, he also became subject to rapid and not wholly rational swings of mood. One day, for example, he felt that he could not cope with a visit from his family, and wrote to put them off; the next, when they did not arrive, he sent a postcard complaining of their absence. However, he enjoyed corresponding with those to whom he had sent copies of *Goliath and David*. Edmund Gosse wrote him an especially encouraging letter; and when Robert was able to leave his bed, he began to circulate among the Oxford intellectuals, renewing his acquaintance with Lady Ottoline Morrell, and meeting Aldous Huxley and other young poets. Robert felt that he was among reasonably congenial people, and he also realized that neither his lungs nor his nerves could stand any more active service in France. So when on Saturday 17 March he arrived back at Red Branch House for a short visit, he mentioned that he was hoping to secure a staff appointment in Oxford for the rest of the War.

After spending a long weekend at home and looking, his father thought, 'rather low in spirits',[227] Robert set off to Liverpool on Tuesday morning to ask his Commanding Officer if he might become an instructor in an Officer Cadet Battalion stationed in Wadham College. There was some difficulty as the C.O., knowing of Robert's literary skills, had planned that he should remain at Litherland and edit the regimental magazine. But by Tuesday evening Robert had obtained the necessary permission, and so elated was he that he travelled down to London through the night to tell his parents of his success.[228]

For the next few days Robert went frequently into town, where he saw much of Robert Ross and his friends; and then he set out for a short holiday at Harlech. He remained thoroughly opposed to the continuation of the war, and from Erinfa he wrote to 'Dear old Sassons' rejoicing that 'The pacifists are putting up at the next election not a measly and pathetic conscientious objector but a soldier called Armstrong with only one leg, a DSO and an MC. What a score!'[229]

Then at the beginning of April Robert's staff appointment at Wadham was confirmed, and, as he informed Sassoon, he was soon 'comfortably settled' in the college,[230] where he was 'a member of the senior common-room and had access to the famous brown sherry'.[231] The platoon assigned to his charge was largely composed of New Zealanders, South Africans and Canadians, and Robert enjoyed their company. One of them, Lester Pearson, a future Prime Minister of Canada, later recalled that Robert was clearly suffering to some extent from shell-shock, and was therefore 'an unlikely choice to manage our unruly and high-spirited "colonial" platoon. He had, however, enough good sense to give us our heads and to accept our somewhat unconventional ideas of spit and polish and military discipline, so we got along well together.'[232]

At weekends, Robert went regularly to Garsington. In Sassoon's absence he and 'Lady Utterly Immoral' found it easier to like each other; and Robert was soon on very friendly terms with Ottoline's eleven-year-old daughter Julian. He also had tea with the great Edmund Gosse, who gave him an introduction to John Masefield; he contributed to at least one undergraduate magazine, the *Palatine Review*, which was edited by Aldous Huxley and others; and he corresponded with such men as John Drinkwater and Duncan Grant about his *Goliath and David*.

Old friends were not forgotten; and Graves was eagerly awaiting the publication of Sassoon's *The Old Huntsman*, when he heard from Robert Ross that Siegfried had been wounded while leading an attack. He had been shot through the shoulder and neck, but fortunately the shrapnel bullet had missed his spine and his jugular vein by a fraction of an inch, and he was now recovering at Denmark Hill, the London hospital where Rosaleen was nursing. APG, calling on Sassoon at Robert's request, found him 'in some pain but very cheerful', and 'promised to do what I could for his book of poems ... in

Observer and *Morning Post*';[233] while Robert wrote to Siegfried asking to be told when he was fit for light duty, so that 'I could get you a job in a cadet Battalion . . . through my Colonel.'[234]

Before that could be arranged, Robert was back in hospital himself. At the beginning of May he had written home cheerfully enough about his work; but his nerves were not up to it. Soon he was dosing himself with 'a strychnine tonic' in a desperate effort to keep himself going. There was an unpleasant incident in which a pleasure-trip ended with a boat plunging over a weir and depositing Robert and some of his friends in the Isis; and at last, in mid-June, he fainted, fell down a staircase in the dark, cut his head, and was sent back to Somerville.

It was while Robert was in hospital that he fell in love with 'Marjorie, a probationer nurse'.[235] Men often fall in love with their nurses; but for Robert, now a month short of his twenty-second birthday, this represented a major change of emotional direction. In a prolonged adolescence of a kind not uncommon in the Graves family, and made more stressful by the monastic conditions of boarding-school life, Robert had been notably ill-at-ease with women outside the circle of his immediate family. The intense idealism of his soul had been poured into masculine friendships which, while they lasted, involved (on his side at least) complete trust and loyalty, and the readiness to accept direction. Ruth Mallory once observed, perhaps a little unkindly, that while he was at Charterhouse Robert always appeared to want other people such as Rodakowski or Barbour to make decisions for him; and Robert's deepest friendships invariably included a strong element of hero-worship.

For several years Johnstone and Sassoon had been the human beings who meant most to him; but Robert's immeasurably greater experience of life since he became a soldier must have been weakening imperceptibly the bonds between himself and Johnstone; while his friendship with Sassoon was complicated by occasional feelings of jealousy, and by the fact that, for once, more of the warmth in the relationship came from the other side. Although Robert recognized that he was in love with Marjorie, he

> did not tell her so at the time. ... I felt difficulty in adjusting myself to the experience of woman love. I used to meet Marjorie, who was a professional pianist, when I visited a friend in another ward; but we had little talk together, except once when she confided in me how beastly a time the other nurses gave her – for having a naturalized German father.[236]

Robert's head-wound was not a serious one; but he had clearly suffered from some kind of nervous collapse, the delayed effect of shell-shock, and he was in need of at least a month's rest. By 7 June it had been settled that as soon as he was well enough to travel, Captain Graves should go to Osborne Palace on the Isle of Wight, once one of Queen Victoria's favourite haunts, and now a convalescent home for officers.[237]

When Robert first arrived at Osborne, he began writing to Marjorie; but when he 'found that she was engaged to a subaltern in France', he decided that the only honourable course of action was to break off their correspondence. As he commented later: 'I had seen what it felt like to be in France and have somebody else playing about with one's girl.' He was consoled a little by a final letter from Marjorie 'reproving me for not writing', which suggested to Robert that she might have been as fond of him as she was of her fiancé.[238]

While he was convalescing at Osborne, Robert was not confined to the grounds, and he found much relief from his private troubles and anxieties in the company of some French Benedictines who lived nearby in their Abbey at Quarr. 'Hearing the Fathers at their plain-song', he wrote later, 'made us for the moment forget the war completely.' After the roar of the trenches, and the untimely end of his affair with Marjorie, 'almost before it started', Robert found that he 'half-envied the Fathers their abbey on the hill, finished with wars and love affairs. I liked their kindness and seriousness; the clean whitewashed cells and the meals eaten in silence at the long oaken tables, while a novice read the *Lives of the Saints*.' Meeting the Benedictines ended the antipathy which Robert had previously felt towards Roman Catholics; but when the Father Superior asked why he did not join 'the true religion', Robert temporized.[239]

Robert's true dedication was now to his poetry. Encouraged by the reception given to *Goliath and David*, he was working steadily on a new collection of poems to be called *Fairies and Fusiliers*. This included 'The Assault Heroic', a poem which shows something of Robert's fierce determination to survive the worst that might befall him; and not only to survive, but to 'alchemize' the worst of his experiences into literary 'lumps of gold'. Utterly worn out, he finds himself in a place where the 'dungeon of Despair' threatens him as it 'looms over Desolate Sea'. From within the walls of this 'most malignant keep', his enemies call out that his friends have been murdered, that his health and happiness have been undermined, and that he has nothing to hope for. Despite this, he has faith in himself; and

> . . . with my spear of faith,
> Stout as an oaken rafter,
> With my round shield of laughter,
> With my sharp, tongue-like sword
> That speaks a bitter word,

> I stood beneath the wall
> And there defied them all.
> The stones they cast I caught
> And alchemized with thought
> Into such lumps of gold
> As dreaming misers hold.
> The boiling oil they threw
> Fell in a shower of dew,
> Refreshing me; the spears
> Flew harmless by my ears,
> Struck quivering in the sod;
> There, like the prophet's rod
> Put leaves out, took firm root
> And bore me instant fruit.[240]

Osborne itself was a restful place, but somewhat gloomy, since many of the patients were so badly shell-shocked that, as Robert commented, they 'should have been in a special neurasthenic hospital'.[241] Despite his own nervous troubles, Robert retained a sense of humour; and after a while he decided that everyone else wanted cheering up. Towards the end of June he wrote to Rosaleen telling her not only that he was 'much better, of rest, sea air, and good food', but also that he and another inmate had founded 'the Albert Edward Society' in mock honour of Queen Victoria's Prince Consort.[242] It was, as he explained more fully in a letter to Nichols, 'a rag society; now very strong and hilarious after two meetings. We affect Albert chains and side-whiskers and invent monstrous yarns about our hero.'[243]

Robert's good humour was of some comfort to Charles, who had been unable to take the Charterhouse O.T.C. seriously since his brother had told him that its drill was hopelessly out of date. Charles had been allowed to resign from his house platoon, and become corporal in charge of the band; but when some of the 'men' under his command were found to have deserted their post during a Field Day, and to have made their way to a village sweetshop, the corporal's stripes were torn from Charles's shoulders in front of the entire Corps.[244] This was humiliating; but Robert soothed Charles's wounded pride with this sympathetic parody of 'The Private of the Buffs', which appeared in *The Carthusian*:

AMBASSADOR OF ENGLAND'S PRIDE

> They've sent me back, no word of thanks;
> They've sent me back, back to the ranks.
> Lance-jack I was, and now, O, pain!

A beery private once again.
Poor sweating Tommy, once lance-jack,
No marshal's baton in my pack,
No soap, no hope, no blatant shoutings
On annual Arthur Webster outings;
No eulogy in a major key,
And little left but privacy.
I stand among my fellow roughs,
Like the old private of the Buffs;
My trusty rifle at my side,
Ambassador of England's pride.

GREGARIUS[245]

These light-hearted verses suggest that Robert was making a good recovery from his nervous breakdown. But then in the first weeks of July 1917 he was 'upset thoroughly' by separate items of news about Sassoon and Johnstone.

For some time it had been evident that Sassoon was in a very much worse mental state than Robert. Convalescing down in Kent, he had written weeks ago to tell Robert that:

> the thought of all that happened in France nearly drove him dotty sometimes ... he could hear the guns thudding all the time across the Channel, on and on, until he didn't know whether he wanted to rush back and die with the First Battalion or stay in England and do what he could to prevent the war going on. But both courses were hopeless.[246]

Sassoon had returned to London early in June, but was then suffering from terrifying inner visions or even hallucinations, so that 'often when he went out he saw corpses lying about on the pavement'.[247] By 15 June however, encouraged by Bertrand Russell and others of Lady Ottoline Morrell's pacifist friends, he had decided on a course of action. First he composed a statement which he described as 'an act of wilful defiance of military authority', in which he declared that 'this war, upon which I entered as a war of defence and liberation, has now become a war of aggression and conquest',[248] and that it was morally wrong for it to be prolonged. Then he circulated his statement to leading journalists, politicians and writers.

Surprisingly enough, this had no immediate effect. So at the beginning of July Sassoon took things a stage further, by deliberately over-staying his leave. When he was asked to report to Litherland, he sent a copy of his statement to the Commanding Officer of the Third Battalion, together with an accompanying letter in which he stated that 'it is my intention to refuse to perform any further military duties ... as a protest against the policy of the Government in prolonging the War by failing to state their conditions of peace.'[249] Sassoon added that he was aware of the possible consequences of his actions; and that he would now come up to Litherland if requested to do so.

Robert was sent a copy of Sassoon's statement on 10 July,[250] and he read it with horror. He had recently quoted to a Benedictine monk the old proverb that one should not change horses in mid-stream; and although Robert thoroughly approved of Siegfried's sentiments, he also felt that Siegfried was acting in a disloyal and dishonourable manner. Loyalty to one's comrades was of the first importance; and however much one disapproved of the continuation of the war, one must see it through to the end in their company. On 12 July, while he was still wondering how to save Sassoon from himself, Graves wrote to Marsh:

> It's an awful thing – completely mad – that he's done. Such rotten luck on you and me and his friends, especially in the Regiment. They all think he's mad. ... I don't know what on earth to do now. ... I think he's quite right in his views but absolutely wrong in his action. ... I'm a sound militarist in action however much of a pacifist in thought. ... 'Better no world than a world ruled by Prussia!' (there speaks my old Danish grandmother!)

Robert added that 'This SS business' had taken him at a very bad time. He had just received 'the worst possible news about my friend Peter, who appears to have taken a very wrong turning and to have had a mental breakdown'.[251]

Robert had just been sent a press cutting from *John Bull* containing information about a recent court case. Apparently a boy had been found guilty of making 'a certain proposal' to a corporal in a Canadian Regiment stationed near Charterhouse. If he had been a commoner he would have been given three months in prison 'without the option'; but because he was the grandson of an earl he had merely been bound over and put in a doctor's care. The boy, to Robert's great shock, was 'Peter' Johnstone. 'This news,' Robert recalled twelve years later, 'was nearly the end of me. I decided that [Johnstone] had been driven out of his mind by the war. There was madness in the family, I knew; he had once showed me a letter from his grandfather scrawled in circles all over the page. It would be easy to think of him as dead.'[252] Once before, when there had been some question of Johnstone's behaviour, Robert had given him the benefit of the doubt, finding it impossible to believe for long that the friend whom he loved could have given way to such 'low' homosexual impulses; but then it had been hearsay, and now he had before him a newspaper cutting with the solid 'evidence' of a conviction.

It was a conviction from which Robert was determined to distance himself as far and as fast as possible, and in doing so he played the part of a stern Victorian moralist not only with 'Peter', but with himself. If high-minded feelings of the kind which he had entertained for Johnstone could lead to bad behaviour followed by a humiliating public disgrace, then such feelings must be immediately renounced, as must the company of anyone likely to inspire them.

To think of Johnstone 'as dead' was a very harsh judgment on a close friend, but Robert was so shocked that he appears to have made no effort to hear the other side of the story. And there may be one. My father heard years later, from someone whom he regarded as 'a reliable source', that

> Peter had, it seems, been staying with the Headmaster ... and one evening went for a walk in the woods. Here he came upon the Canadian Corporal having intercourse with a girl. Being naturally curious, he stopped to watch. But when the Corporal noticed him and invited him to have a turn, he refused. The Corporal became angry and in revenge handed him over to the police and secured his conviction on a trumped-up charge.[253]

Whatever the truth of this story, Johnstone was placed for some months in the care of a doctor; he was then pronounced cured; and in November 1917 he joined the army as a signaller in the 14th London Regiment.

Meanwhile Robert was relieved to recall his fleeting love affair with Marjorie. It proved to him that although, like many young men, he had gone through what he now described as a 'pseudo-homosexual' phase,[254] his natural instincts were heterosexual.

CHAPTER
14
SAVING SASSOON

One of Robert's great strengths was always the whole-hearted way in which he threw himself into whatever he was doing; but this meant that he was sometimes a man of extremes; and his 'all-or-nothing' approach to friendship is vividly highlighted by the contrast between his sudden and complete abandonment of Johnstone, and the heroic efforts which he made to save Sassoon.

On Thursday 12 July 1917, the day that Robert wrote his worried letter to Eddie Marsh, Sassoon had received a telegram ordering him to report at once to Litherland.[255] When he did so, on Friday the 13th,[256] he received a surprisingly warm welcome. The Colonel was away on leave, but had left his senior major as acting C.O. with clear instructions. Sassoon should be asked to withdraw his ultimatum and told that if he did so, the whole incident would be forgotten.

Sassoon refused. His aim was to gain maximum publicity for his stand against the war by forcing the army to court-martial him, and when he refused, he did so fully expecting and indeed hoping to be placed under arrest. Instead, he was told to stay quietly at an hotel in Liverpool until higher authority had been consulted.

In the meantime, Robert had decided on a course of action. First he wrote to the senior major – not knowing that he was acting C.O. – asking him to persuade the Colonel to see things 'in a reasonable light'. Sassoon was clearly ill, and must be protected from himself. Robert received in reply 'a most kind sympathetic letter ... saying that Siegfried would be ordered a Medical Board and the best would be done to treat the whole thing as a medical case'.[257]

Robert's next step was 'to get out of Osborne' so that he could 'attend to things'. He knew that he was by no means well enough to leave the convalescent home, but he persuaded a Medical Board to pass him as fit for home service. They allowed him to leave Osborne on the morning of Monday 16 July, and Robert wired the news to APG, who met his cab coming up Wimbledon Hill.

On Tuesday morning Robert went into town to discuss Siegfried's case with some of those who knew him best. First he lunched with Eddie Marsh – now intending to use six of Robert's poems in his next volume of *Georgian Poetry* – and then he kept an appointment to meet Robert Ross. Graves had to tell Ross that he had no up-to-date news. He had not yet received a letter written to him by Siegfried on Sunday night, which had arrived at Osborne after his departure; nor could he have known that Sassoon had now been ordered to appear before a Medical Board, but had torn up the order, and had then spent the rest of the day learning poems by heart so that he would have something to recite in prison.

On Wednesday 18 July Robert arrived at Litherland, where the situation was serious. The Colonel was now back from leave, and had already told Sassoon that his failure to appear before a Medical Board meant that matters would soon be beyond his control. A court-martial seemed inevitable. Robert immediately went to call on Sassoon, whom he found looking 'very ill; he told me that he had just been down to the Formby links and thrown his Military Cross into the sea.'[258]

The two men talked together for a long time. Robert made it clear that he agreed with Siegfried about the futility of the war, but tried to persuade him not to persist with his defiance: it would do nothing to end the war, and would be regarded as a betrayal by his comrades-in-arms. This line of argument made no impact upon Sassoon, and Graves began to realize that it would be impossible to sway him from his self-destructive course of action so long as he believed that he could compel the army to court-martial him. Graves knew that Ross had obtained a 'promise of powerful help if necessary at the War Office';[259] and in what he did next he felt perfectly justified by the overriding necessity of rescuing Sassoon from a further ordeal which might permanently unbalance him.

First Robert declared that Siegfried would be locked in a lunatic asylum if he persisted, and that 'nothing would induce them to court-martial [him]. It had all been arranged with some big bug at the War Office in the last day or two.' Then, when Siegfried pressed him on this point, Robert swore on an imaginary Bible that what he had said was true. Sassoon saw that in the circumstances his struggle was futile. He immediately gave way, and agreed to go before a Medical Board. The strain on his nerves had already been enormous, and now he felt 'a sense of exquisite relief' that it was all over.[260]

The very next day a Medical Board was convened and Robert, giving evidence as a friend of the patient, helped to convince its members that Sassoon was in a state of mental collapse. Robert's own nerves had been affected by his efforts to help Sassoon, and he burst into tears three times in the course of his statement. As he left the room the psychologist who was present said to him: 'Young man, you ought to be before this board yourself.'[261] But that evening Graves could write triumphantly to Marsh:

> My dear Eddie,
>
> It's all right about Siegfried. After awful struggling with everybody (I arrived at 59 minutes past the eleventh hour) I've smoothed it all down and he's going away cheerfully to a home at Edinboro'. I've written to the pacifists who were to support him telling them that the evidence as to his mental condition given at his Medical Board is quite enough to make them look damned silly if they go on with the game and ask questions in the House about his defiance. I'm quite knocked up. . . .[262]
>
> R.

A further letter went to the Hon. Evan Morgan, who was private secretary to a Government Minister. He was also a poet, and had been one of the friends who had been with Robert in the boat which had gone over the weir into the Isis earlier in the year. Robert outlined the story of Sassoon's revolt, and asked Morgan to use whatever influence he possessed to keep the 'defiance letter' hushed up.

Within the next few days, Robert was one of two officers[263] detailed to escort Siegfried up to a convalescent home at Craiglockhart, near Edinburgh; though Robert and the other escort both missed the train, and actually arrived at Craiglockhart four hours later than their 'prisoner'. Sassoon was placed in the care of Dr W.H.R. Rivers, a psychologist and a Fellow of St John's College, Cambridge, who was now a temporary captain in the Royal Army Medical Corps. Sassoon liked him from the first; and although it seemed strange being among '160 officers, most of them half-dotty', Sassoon wrote in a relaxed mood to Robert Ross, telling him that it was 'very jolly seeing Robert Graves up here', and adding that on 24 July, Robert's twenty-second birthday, 'We had great fun . . . and ate enormously.'[264]

When Robert arrived back at Litherland, it was to find that his efforts to hush up Sassoon's 'defiance letter' had failed. A pacifist M.P. read it out in the House of Commons; and although he was personally silenced by a Government Under-Secretary, who pointed out the state of Sassoon's mental health, the press took up the story, and the letter was published in dozens of newspapers, from *The Times* to the *Bradford Pioneer*. But by this time Sassoon was out of harm's way at Craiglockhart, and Robert wrote to him affectionately and almost a little jealously: 'Well, you are notorious throughout England now you silly old thing!'[265]

CHAPTER
15
'THE FAIRY
AND THE FUSILIER'

Robert's success in averting a court-martial had made him a far more respected figure in the senior echelons of the Royal Welch Fusiliers. Earlier he had complained about the prospect of spending August in 'that horrid hole Lither-land';[266] but now he was 'having a good time ... amongst good friends, with 325 men and 35 officers to drill, squash rackets and tennis, and the hope of being sent to Egypt'.[267] Robert's spirits improved still further when he learned not only that Heinemann would publish *Fairies and Fusiliers* in the autumn, but also that there would be an American edition by Knopf the following year; and on Thursday 30 August 1917 he arrived at Erinfa for a few days of leave looking 'right well'.[268]

It was to be a memorable long weekend. Robert heard that some of the Nicholsons were in Harlech; and on Friday evening, after an early supper, he walked over to Llys Bach to call on them. It was a pleasant walk along the country path which meandered from the gate at the back of Erinfa towards the village. The road was down to the right, but invisible beyond the trees; and to the left there was a little stretch of wooded ground, and then the hills. Robert had almost reached the outskirts of the village when he pushed open a gate to his right; and there, with views across the sea just as magnificent as those from Erinfa, stood Llys Bach.

Ever since January, when he had last seen the Nicholsons, Robert had been curiously haunted by his last memory of Nancy in her black velvet dress; and now he found her transformed from a schoolgirl into a cheerful, rosy-cheeked and highly independent young woman, within a fortnight of her eighteenth birthday.[269] Boyishly dressed as a bandit, Nancy was just about to set out for a fancy dress dance in a private house; and Robert, suddenly feeling that he wanted to stay with her, went along uninvited. That evening was the first occasion upon which Robert and Nancy spent much time talking to each other; and Robert was so elated by the experience that he stayed up half the night. He escorted Nancy back from the dance at two in the morning; and then, not feeling like sleep, he persuaded Ben Nicholson to drive him all the way to Talsarnau, where they called on some other friends of theirs.

Later on Saturday, after snatching a few hours of sleep back at Erinfa, Robert paid another visit to Llys Bach. He was away for some time, and when he returned he said nothing to his family about Nancy, but told them that he had been playing with Nancy's younger brother Kit, and then having supper with Ben. Whatever Robert's feelings for Nancy, he kept them to himself at this stage: wisely, perhaps, in such a large and sharp-tongued family. But it is interesting to notice that when Nancy's birthday came on 13 September Robert, who was back at Litherland, decided to write a letter to Sassoon saying that he was no longer going to dedicate *Fairies and Fusiliers* to him, as he had promised. Instead there would be a general dedication to the Royal Welch Fusiliers. This, Robert explained, would avoid jealousy from any individual among his 'friends and lovers'.

In the meantime, winter was approaching and Robert was still hoping to leave Litherland, where the cold damp weather with 'the mist coming up from the Mersey and hanging about the camp full of T.N.T. fumes' would be very bad for his lungs. France was out of the question in his present state of health, but he believed that he might be able to stand active service in Palestine, 'where gas was not known and shell-fire said to be inconsiderable in comparison with France';[270] and as he had indicated back in August, he certainly hoped to get as far as garrison duty in Egypt, where the dry climate would do him a great deal of good. By the end of September Robert felt that he had things well in hand. He wrote home to say that he had been passed 'fit for garrison service at home', and was shortly to join the Third Garrison Battalion at Oswestry. With the Third he would move to their new quarters at Kinmel Camp, near Rhyl on the North Welsh coast; and after that he hoped to go abroad.[271]

Robert duly went to Oswestry and then to Rhyl, where he trained young officers fresh from their cadet battalions; but thereafter nothing went according to plan. For a while it seemed that he would be sent on garrison duty to Gibraltar rather than Egypt, and early in October he was given eight days' leave preparatory to going overseas. This gave him a chance to see Nancy Nicholson again Robert travelled down to Wimbledon; and one Thursday, after going into town, he simply failed to return. It was not until Friday lunchtime that a telegram arrived announcing that he had unfortunately missed the last train back to Wimbledon, and had had to spend the night at Apple Tree Yard with the Nicholsons.

Nancy was pretty rather than beautiful; but she combined the attractive youthfulness of an eighteen-year-old with the wistful expression of one who appears to be haunted by a different reality, and Robert found this enormously appealing. We have already quoted the first lines of 'Babylon', in which Robert declares that 'The child alone a poet is:/Spring and Fairyland are his'; and he goes on to lament the fact that by the time they reach adulthood most people have entirely forgotten all the magical figures of their childhood:

> Jack the Giant-killer's gone,
> Mother Goose and Oberon,
> Bluebeard and King Solomon.
> Robin and Red Riding Hood
> Take together to the wood,
> And Sir Galahad lies hid
> In a cave with Captain Kidd.
> None of all the magic hosts,
> None remain but a few ghosts
> Of timorous heart, to linger on
> Weeping for lost Babylon.[272]

In Nancy, Robert had discovered a woman who shared his growing conviction that there was something better and more true in the myths and legends of childhood than in the terrible 'reality' of the adult world. When Nancy showed Robert some of her paintings, which included illustrations to Robert Louis Stevenson's *A Child's Garden of Verses*, he found that 'my child-sentiment and hers – she had a happy childhood to look back on – answered each other.'[273]

Their new plan, that Nancy should illustrate some of Robert's verses for children, was the symbol of a shared commitment to the arts which was the cornerstone of their relationship. At the age of fifteen or sixteen Nancy had designed a cover for *Vogue*; and although she had never had a formal training, she had been brought up among artists, and she was just as much set on becoming a great painter as Robert was set on becoming a great poet. Indeed, Nancy was unfashionably determined that any partnership upon which she embarked must be a partnership of equals. This ardent, and in 1917 scandalous feminism had nothing to do with an interest in the suffragette movement or in politics, but sprang from Nancy's close observation of her mother's life: Mabel Nicholson, although a very fine artist, had totally sacrificed her career in order to make a home for her husband and children; Nancy was determined never to make the same mistake.

Nancy was also, to Robert's great relief, 'as sensible about the war as anybody at home could be'.[274] While she could not fully appreciate the appalling conditions of the trenches, she believed that the war was insane, and she was in a state of considerable anxiety over the fact that her much-loved brother Tony, only a little older than she, was about to be sent out to France as a gunner. At the same time, like Robert, she was determined to play her part; and she had volunteered to be one of the 'land-girls' who worked on farms to replace men who had joined the forces.

By the morning of Friday 12 October, Robert had only a few hours left in London, because he had previously arranged to spend the last part of his leave visiting Sassoon at Craiglockhart. Much of the time was taken up with such tedious matters as going to the dentist and doing some essential shopping; but he also managed to see Edmund Gosse, whom he 'converted to a more human view of Sassoon'; and in the evening, after his father had kindly offered to take his kit-bag to Euston and leave it there for him, Robert went off to dinner with the Nicholsons.[275] Afterwards Nancy and her family broadened Robert's outlook a little by taking him 'to a revue, the first revue I had been to in my life. It was *Cheep*; Lee White was in it, singing of Black-eyed Susans, and how [like Nancy] "Girls must all be Farmers' Boys, off with skirts, wear corduroys".'[276]

After this invigorating taste of the kind of light-hearted entertainment which had played too small a part in the lives of the younger Graveses, all of whom had been destined by Amy to be 'if not great, then at least good',[277] Robert caught the night train for Scotland. At Craiglockhart he found Sassoon in a restless mood, still profoundly unhappy about the continuation of the war, and wanting to be sent back to fight among his comrades in France. Robert had expressed his own point of view in a recent poem, when he wrote:

> It doesn't matter what's the cause,
>   What wrong they say we're righting,
> A curse for treaties, bonds and laws,
>   When we're to do the fighting!
> And since we lads are proud and true,
>   What else remains to do?[278]

But Sassoon was no longer satisfied with Robert's talk about being 'proud and true', or 'acting like a gentleman'. Perhaps he was also irritated by some hint of Robert's increasing attachment to Nancy; in any case, a few days later he wrote a letter with a quarrelsome paragraph in which he told Robert that such talk as his was 'a very estimable form of suicidal stupidity and credulity', and that 'If you had real courage you wouldn't acquiesce as you do [in the continuation of the war].'[279]

Robert wrote a perfectly amiable reply to this bitter attack. He knew that Siegfried still had a high regard for his poetry; he was also grateful for a recent loan of £20; and he was prepared to make considerable allowances for the state of Siegfried's nerves, but from now on the relationship between the two men became increasingly awkward and uncomfortable.

The best thing to come out of Graves's journey to Scotland was his meeting with another patient at Craiglockhart, the young soldier poet from Shropshire, Wilfred Owen. Sassoon, who had recognized Owen's outstanding talent, brought the two men together by asking Owen to meet Graves when he arrived, and then to bring him over to the golf course where Sassoon would be enjoying his morning round. Owen was not very impressed with his first sight of Graves, describing him in a letter to his mother the following day as 'a big, rather plain fellow, the last man on earth apparently capable of the extraordinary, delicate fancies in his books'. Sassoon had apparently showed Graves some of Owen's work when they were alone together, and Owen was irritated to hear that 'Graves was mightily impressed, and considers me a kind of Find!! No thanks, Captain Graves! I'll find myself in due time.'[280] However, Owen's resentment rapidly faded when some days later Graves returned the draft of one of his poems with some constructive critical advice;[281] and Sassoon encouraged Graves in this valuable work, writing to him: 'I am so glad you like Owen's poem. I will tell him to send you on any decent stuff he does. His work is very unequal, and you can help him a great deal.'[282]

Robert had arrived back at Rhyl at the end of his leave fully expecting that he would shortly be sent out to Gibraltar, which he regarded as a 'dead-end'; but at the last moment he persuaded a friend in the War Office to cancel the order posting him abroad, until something could be found for him in Egypt. In the meantime, Robert had fallen in love with Nancy, and was corresponding with her about her proposed illustrations for his verses. In some ways this new attachment was an awkward one. None of Robert's friends knew about his feelings for Marjorie earlier in the year; but they were well acquainted with his long-standing friendship with Johnstone, and in the circumstances he felt that some explanations were in order. To Robert Nichols, for example, he wrote:

> It's only fair to tell you that since the cataclysm of my friend Peter, my affections are running in the more normal channels and I correspond regularly and warmly with Nancy Nicholson, who is great fun. I only tell you this so that you should get out of your head any misconceptions about my temperament. I should hate you to think I was a confirmed homosexual even if it were only in thought and went no farther.[283]

Graves's posting abroad continued to be delayed; and in early November the delay became an indefinite one. The Colonel of the Third Garrison Battalion received orders that all the fit men under his command should move at twenty-four hours' notice to Cork in Ireland. He told Robert that he was 'the only officer he could trust to look after the remainder of the Battalion', and Robert suddenly found himself 'in charge of a detachment of 600 fusiliers and 80 officers'.[284]

This was Robert's most important command of the war, and he thoroughly enjoyed it. Indeed, the combination of successfully running his own show, and of carrying on an increasingly loving correspondence with Nancy, put Robert into a frame of mind which Sassoon found offensively cheerful. 'Robert Graves writes that he is "very happy",' he told Lady Ottoline Morrell crossly. 'I don't think RG feels things as deeply as some ... with all his egotism.'[285]

By the third week in November Robert had things running so smoothly at Rhyl that he felt able to award himself a few days of leave. His sister Rosaleen, now a fully qualified nurse, was about to set out for France, where she had volunteered to work in an army hospital, and APG had arranged a family gathering at Red Branch House on the eve of her departure. Robert made the journey from Rhyl; Charles and John were given an exeat from Charterhouse; Clarissa travelled down from Cheshire where she was still working as a private tutor; and by late on the evening of Wednesday 21 November 1917 all five of Amy's children were once again under the same roof. The following morning, after 'a good family breakfast', Alfred had decided to commemorate the occasion in true Victorian fashion by taking everyone for what he hoped would be a leisurely and enjoyable session at the local photographer's, before they all accompanied Rosaleen to the station to bid her farewell.

But APG's plans were thwarted when Robert declared that he himself wanted to catch a train for Cambridge almost immediately, and that he would wait for only two photographs to be taken before setting off.[286] The tension which this produced is evident in the final prints. The whole family looks uncomfortable. Alfred, dreadfully disappointed, stands and scowls at the camera. Amy, sitting beside him, is trying to smile, but wears her most martyred expression; while Robert, smartly dressed in his army uniform, looks both impatient and rebellious.

Later on, when Alfred and Amy returned to Red Branch House, everything became clear. A telegram arrived for Robert with the words: 'Hurrah! meet me at St. Ives, Nancy.' This did nothing to lessen Amy's fury; but APG, his annoyance largely forgotten, was both amused and pleased. Evidently Cambridge was only the first stop on Robert's journey. He was really 'on the way ... sly dog! to see Nancy Nicholson.'[287]

Nancy was now working as a land-girl on a farm at Hilton, just to the south of St Ives. Except for her black poodle, Smuts, Nancy was 'alone ... among farmers, farm-labourers, and wounded soldiers who had been put on

land-service'.[288] But this small village has a surprising charm. From the dull
flat fields which surround Hilton, Robert entered a wooded area deeply criss-
crossed with streams and ditches. Here and there he could see thatched houses
with shuttered windows nestling under the trees, a large farmhouse or two,
in one of which Nancy was living; and, to the north of the village hall, the
famous Hilton maze or labyrinth, one of the very few earth-cut mazes in England, and almost certainly connected with ancient fertility and marriage rites.

It was in this strangely appropriate setting that Robert conducted his courtship. First Nancy showed him something of her work, and together they
'chopped mangold wurzels & groomed carthorses'.[289] Then they talked; and
in the course of their conversation Nancy expressed her feminist views very
plainly, warning Robert that he must be 'very careful what [he] said about
women; the attitude of the Huntingdon farmers to their wives and daughters
kept her in a continual state of anger'.[290] Robert was already in love with
Nancy, and he listened to what she had to say with growing admiration. His
deep attachment to his mother had predisposed him to think well of women
with strong convictions; as a follower of Samuel Butler he applauded Nancy's
spirited attacks upon convention; and as a romantic Robert wished to adopt
Nancy's ideals as his own. Nancy, deeply flattered by the adoration of this
handsome young soldier, was also falling in love; and when Robert returned
to Rhyl, after 'an immense 1913 tea ... about fifteen different cakes', their
correspondence 'became more intimate'.[291]

Robert was more concerned than ever that his friends should not be hostile
either to him or to Nancy in view of his change in emotional direction; and
having heard that Robert Ross 'doesn't like the idea of [Nancy]' he wrote
begging Sassoon to

> quiet him down, *if he mentions her.* She's doing a children's book with
> me. Otherwise leave her out of the conversation. I don't want to have any
> unfriendliness and I'll not even allow dear Robbie to bully Nancy. I'll
> parade her one day for your approval. She's an unusual person, young,
> kind, strong, nice-looking and a consummate painter as well as a capable
> farmer's boy. I know you'd like her.[292]

Three weeks later, in the early hours of Saturday 15 December, Amy and
Alfred were woken by pebbles being thrown at their bedroom window. It was
Robert, who had turned up unexpectedly at Red Branch House for another
short leave. *Fairies and Fusiliers* had now been published, to generally good
reviews; and he had brought with him a number of friendly letters from 'Birrell,
Mrs. Masefield and others', but his principal aim in coming south was to
see Nancy; and later that day Robert went into town to meet her, returning

home very late. On Sunday, after an early lunch, he went into town again, and did not arrive back in Wimbledon until three in the morning, after walking the last part of the journey, all the way from Putney, in a driving blizzard.

Robert and Nancy were deeply in love with each other; and, as Robert wrote later, they 'decided to get married at once'. Nancy evidently 'attached no importance to the ceremony', and Robert was bound to agree with her. Luckily for him, however, Nancy also said that 'she did not want to disappoint her father'.[293] At that stage in his life Robert very much desired the approval both of his family and of his friends; and it is highly unlikely that the man who talked to Sassoon about 'acting like a gentleman' could have seriously contemplated 'living in sin' with this girl of eighteen, an act which in the late 1910s would have created a terrible scandal and utterly destroyed his reputation.

The lovers decided to keep their plans to themselves for a day or two; and on Monday the great family news was that Charles, following in Robert's footsteps, had won a Classical Exhibition to St John's College, Oxford. Then on Tuesday the 18th, Nancy, her parents, and her brother Kit all came to lunch at Red Branch House. Nancy had defied convention by arriving not in a skirt but in the trousers of her land-girl's 'uniform', of which she was immensely proud; but Alfred accepted this tolerantly, and wrote in his diary that evening that 'Nancy grows on one', and that it had been 'a delightful party. Mr. N. most witty and charming, Mrs. N. a very capable and wise woman'. When the other Nicholsons had departed, Nancy stayed on for tea, 'and then went off with Robby into town carrying part of his baggages. Before this John came in and announced their engagement as Cupid. Robby threw the family ring, the ancient Eagle, with "Catch" and she caught on and caught it.'[294]

Later that day, Robert and Nancy broke the news of their engagement to her parents; and on Wednesday, when the Graveses were attending Kit Nicholson's birthday party at Apple Tree Yard, Alfred was taken aside by William to discuss the proposed marriage. Since Nancy, at eighteen, was three years under age, her father's consent was vital. He was in a highly emotional state, and told Alfred that 'he had been in love with N[ancy] for 18 years and not slept a wink the night before, when he heard of the engagement, but felt they were intended for each other and both he and his wife were greatly pleased as both had high ideals which he believed they would realise together'.[295] Nicholson also promised to consider illustrating a novel which Clarissa had just finished writing; and APG commented happily in his diary that it had been 'Altogether a red-letter day in the Family annals'.[296]

Within two days Robert was back at Rhyl, where in due course he received a letter from his father approving his choice, but reminding him that 'his was a great responsibility considering what [Nancy] was to her people'.[297] Sassoon's reaction was less enthusiastic. He was now back with the Royal Welch Fusiliers at Litherland; and on Christmas Day he noted in his diary, without comment: 'Last Friday went to Rhyl to see Robert Graves, and received his apologies for his engagement to Miss Nicholson.'[298]

Robert spent Christmas at Harlech with Nancy and her family, and afterwards wrote to his parents telling them that the wedding was provisionally fixed for 23 January 1918. He could not be more definite, because at any moment he might be sent out to Egypt; besides, Mabel Nicholson had now made it clear that she would only 'permit the marriage on one condition: that I should go to a London lung specialist to see whether I was fit for eventual service in Palestine'.[299]

On 8 January Robert therefore travelled down to London to be vetted by Sir James Fowler who told him, to his great relief, that his lungs were 'soundish', despite the fact that he had bronchial adhesions, and that his wounded lung had only a third of its proper expansion. This was good enough to satisfy Nancy's mother; though Sir James had also noted that Robert's nerves were still in a very poor state. Indeed, it was only recently that Robert had been badly upset by news of Raymond Rodakowski's death at the battle of Cambrai. Replying to a letter from Cyril Hartmann on the subject, Robert had written bitterly:

> It's been a bad war hasn't it for us lads. All our contemporaries gone West with very few exceptions, those the maimed the blind & the insane. God bless our Politicians & Press. ... Poor old Raymond: I felt that very nearly. Can't talk about that. ... Evans's poem was good & honest & in fact one of his best but it would have to be a bloody fine poem to do justice to Raymond.[300]

Now Sir James told Robert firmly that active service in any theatre of war would lead to another breakdown. 'So I stay back I suppose,' Robert reported forlornly to Sassoon, who was now with the Third Battalion in Ireland; 'it seems rather silly after all my sabre rattling: still, I suppose it's good news for Nancy.'[301]

The day after Robert's examination, he and Nancy ('still in male garments', as APG noted rather less tolerantly) turned up unannounced to lunch at Red Branch House; and while Robert was in London he also took Nancy to see Robert Ross. This seemed likely to be a difficult meeting, as Ross was so opposed to the marriage that he had hinted to Graves 'that there was negro blood in the Nicholson family', and that one of his and Nancy's children 'might revert to coal-black'.[302] However, when faced with Nancy in person,

Ross was perfectly civilized, and Robert persuaded himself that 'they liked each other though R was ill and Nancy shy'.[303]

Soon invitations were being sent out for the wedding, which was now definitely fixed for Wednesday the 23rd. Alfred Perceval Graves wired the news to Alexandria, and spent many hours writing a poem for Nancy and Robert which, in honour of Robert's latest volume, he entitled 'The Fairy and the Fusilier'. George Mallory had already agreed to be best man, and Robert wrote a personal letter asking Sassoon to be present, and telling him that it 'should be rather a rag as all the best sort of people will be there: no relations bar a very few will be allowed to come on after the ceremony [at St James's Piccadilly] to drink champagne at the studio in Appletree Yard, only the elect of God will be there'.[304] But although Sassoon still greatly admired Graves's poetry, news of the wedding did not please him. He declined to ask for leave, excusing himself on the grounds that the wedding coincided with the start of an Anti-Gas Instruction course which he was expected to attend at Cork.

The day before the wedding there was great excitement at Red Branch House. Susan and Clarissa arrived after tea; then came Robert with Ruth and George Mallory, described by APG as 'such a beautiful-looking pair'; in the middle of dinner, Charles and John arrived from Charterhouse; and afterwards they 'had a great time looking over the presents, [and] making best man arrangements'.[305]

On the morning of the 23rd, Robert and his best man set off early; and then came:

Amy in her wedding war paint, a fine green velvet with gold trimmings and a suitable hat ... then [wrote APG] the rest of us ... we taxied, 5 inside, to Apple Tree Yard and thence walked to Church. I had a new suit (grey morning) admired of all but Amy and neat bowler and gloves, and a trimmed head and beard. We were almost the first arrivals, but the Church filled up. Family (Amy, I and six children, including Perceval and Susie but dear Roz had failed to get leave) CLG, Lily, Rosy ... Miss North ... and no end of others –

Robby looked fine and said his responses firmly and clearly, as did Nancy. She was in a beautiful blue check dress with veil and had a wonderful bouquet arranged by her good father. The choir boys sang beautifully and the Parson was in earnest.[306]

Nancy and Robert looked very fine: she in her blue dress, and he in his uniform, with field-boots, spurs and sword; but behind the scenes there had been an awkward meeting. As Robert later recalled: 'Nancy had read the marriage-service for the first time that morning and had been horrified by it. She all but refused to go through the ceremony at all, though I had arranged for it to be modified and reduced to the shortest possible form.'[307] Although Robert realized that Nancy was still 'utterly furious' when she met him in the aisle ('How the poor Nancy-bird hated the marriage-service!' he wrote indulgently a few months later),[308] she had her feelings well enough under control for no one else to notice anything amiss. Wilfred Owen, who was present, did describe Robert himself as 'pretty worked up, but calm';[309] but that is hardly an unusual state of affairs at a wedding. Robert's Carthusian friends George Devenish and Nevill Barbour were also present; as were Robbie Ross and Eddie Marsh, together with a large number of Nicholson family friends, including such celebrities as Lutyens and Beerbohm.[310]

Afterwards there was what APG described as 'a great gathering of the clans' at Apple Tree Yard, where 'champagne flowed', and 'everyone was jolly'.[311] Not quite everyone: because Robert loved Nancy, he could not help feeling hurt when she grabbed a bottle of champagne with the words 'Well, I'm going to get something out of this wedding, at any rate!' Amy too was upset by Nancy's practically obsessive determination to be unconventional. After leaving to change into her 'going-away' clothes, Nancy reappeared wearing 'her land-girl's uniform of breeches and smock ... "Oh dear, I wish she had not done that,"' Amy exclaimed.[312] However, by now most of the guests were too merry for Nancy's unusual attire to cause much of a sensation. Instead they all gathered round, 'A slap-bang photo was taken and bride and groom went off in Lady Sackville's motor with gas bag on top, and old shoe behind.'[313]

CHAPTER
16
ANOTHER WORLD

Robert and Nancy were both virgins at the time of their wedding; and the story has been passed down within the family that Nancy (like Amy before her) was not at all prepared for the sexual side of married life, and that this led to some early difficulties. However, they were very much in love with each other;[314] and, as Robert later recalled, the embarrassments of the wedding-night itself 'were somewhat eased by an air-raid; bombs were dropping not far off and the hotel was in an uproar'.[315]

On the morning after their wedding, Robert and Nancy travelled up to Harlech, where they honeymooned for eight days at Llys Bach. 'We are up here on the hills having a simply splendid time,' Robert wrote to one of his friends, 'I recommend matrimony thoroughly.'[316] And in a joint letter to Rosaleen, whom she had yet to meet, Nancy wrote of their wedding: 'It was a great day and these are great days that follow.'[317] Then on 1 February 1918 Robert returned to Rhyl; while Nancy, as they had agreed, went back for a month to Hilton and her duties as a land-girl.[318]

After all the excitement of the past weeks Robert felt Nancy's absence keenly; and early in February, as he wrote to his mother, he suffered from 'a very bad cough & a nervous attack of sleeplessness that comes with hideous recollections of France every two months'.[319] However, he told Rosaleen that he had kept busy even while he was ill, and had

> written on an average ten letters a day & compiled an address book & pasted in my press cuttings & got my mind clear again & written some good new poems. ... I have also made out a list of people I have to write to: Mother once a week, Nancy once a day, Charles once a month, Bones once a year, M. Koch once a century & so on, so you can reckon on getting a letter at least once a fortnight & oftener in special cases.[320]

Then, as he had successfully arranged, Robert was appointed as an instructor to the 16th Officer Cadet Battalion at Kinmel Park, Rhyl. Since he was now assured of home service for the remainder of the war, he was able to send for Nancy, for whom he had found work with a local market-gardener.[321]

To begin with they lodged at Terfyn Bungalow with a retired old Welsh farmer 'touched in the head', his 'motherly' wife and 'superior' piano-playing daughter,[322] in rooms which were 'tiny & v. expensive but with a bath [and] quite close to my camp'.[323] Unfortunately, Nancy's 'trousers and dog [Smuts] gave offence'; as, most probably, did Nancy's feminist resolve not to take Robert's name, but to insist on being known as 'Miss Nicholson'. So in the third week of March they moved into new lodgings in Bryn-y-pin, a farmhouse on a hill above the camp.[324]

Like most lovers, Robert and Nancy had soon created a world of their own at a tangent to the normal world. One day they talked fancifully of emigrating: 'Not necessarily [to] California,' Robert told Rosaleen, 'but thereabouts, that is Cuba or the Caribees or Kentucky or Barking Creek';[325] another day, Robert planned to compile 'a map of Harlech ... putting in all the special places, for the use of our children when they live there';[326] and all the time they busied themselves collecting toys, 'soldiers and wooden animals & ivory men & silver Buddhas and coloured boxes of plaited straw'.[327] The war continued, and could not be altogether forgotten; but Robert was no longer in the mood for writing bitter poems about death and destruction. Instead, there began to flow from his pen a number of nursery rhymes, songs and ballads such as:

> Lady, lovely lady, careless & gay!
> Once when a beggar called, she gave her child away:
> The beggar took the baby & wrapped it in a shawl
> 'Bring him back,' the lady said, 'Next time you call.'[328]

Or the much anthologized:

> *Allie, call the birds in,*
>   *The birds from the sky.*
> Allie calls, Allie sings,
>   Down they all fly.
> First there came
> Two white doves
>   Then a sparrow from his nest,
> Then a clucking bantam hen,
>   Then a robin red-breast.[329]

Some of Robert's songs almost made him a great deal of money: early in May 1918, on one of his visits to London,[330] Robert met Ivor Novello, who promised to set some of them to music. But neither Robert's happiness with Nancy nor the prospect of financial success could heal in a moment the nervous damage of the past three years. It was at about this time that Robert was introduced to the artist Eric Kennington, who drew a pastel head of Robert which shows him tense and strained. Amy found Robert looking 'thin' and 'not ... at all well';[331] and there were periods when alongside his pastoral idylls Robert was writing more sombre lines, such as these from 'Haunted' about his fallen comrades:

> I meet you suddenly down the street,
> Strangers assume your phantom faces,
> You grin at me from daylight places,
> Dead, long dead, I'm ashamed to greet
> Dead men down the morning street.[332]

Luckily Nancy was used to dealing kindly and sensibly with highly-strung men. William Nicholson was extremely emotional; and years later Nancy commented wryly about father and husband: 'I never knew two men who cried so much!'[333] But she was less practical in her ideas for the life which she and Robert would lead when the war was over, and on one occasion wrote with childish enthusiasm to Rosaleen telling her that:

After the War we're going to have a farm on the Downs & have everybody nice such as you (do come), Tony [Nicholson] & Bob Nichols & Sassoon, Johnny (not Charles because he slacks) etc. to work it. What's your speciality? I've bagged the cart horses (awfully rude sorry – you can have them if you like) Sassoon [can have] the Race horses: we're going to make Bob Nichols the Shepherd. Great fun what? Do you like pigs? or not?[334]

When in mid-May Nancy became pregnant, she and Robert continued to think along these highly unrealistic lines; and Robert told Sassoon:

When Nance and I get our home going (and you can be assured old poet that it's going to be a real good place) we want you to make it your HQ for as long as you can bear it. ... I do want you to be properly looked after. You wouldn't recognise me these days, the way Nance has smartened me up. I wash my eyes and neck and ears every morning and evening and brush my teeth inside and out. And my clothes! I'm an awful toff now.

... I have no doubt at all that you'll like Nancy: she gets better and better on acquaintance. I didn't know a great deal about her when we got married except what I saw at once by instinct, but, my goodness, instinct is nearly always right.[335]

Sassoon was not in the mood for this kind of cheerful paternalism, and after reading Robert's letter he noted in his diary in a bitter and somewhat bemused fashion that it came 'from another world, talking of "leave" and all that is life'.³³⁶

At the beginning of June Robert wrote to John, another possible member of their 'commune', telling him that Nancy was in London seeing the dentist, and that he was feeling lonely. 'Isn't she a nice person?' he added. 'I hope you agree because she's very fond of you & (but this is a secret written very small) of no-one else in the family though she hasn't met Ros of course & she likes Mother in a way & Charles in a way.'³³⁷

Robert had been impressed by the fact that Ivor Novello could make a living from popular music, while maintaining the high standards of his more serious work; and, as he told John, he and Nancy were hoping 'to make our fortune now from a set of six china plates for the Nursery which I designed & [Nancy] executed. It's these simple sort of things that make the money.'³³⁸

Much to Amy's disgust, farming remained their long-term plan. On 14 June, after reading Robert's 'really beautiful' introduction to the catalogue for an exhibition of Kennington's war pictures, she wrote to John: 'I am quite elated about [the introduction] & regret to hear that [Robert] wants to turn farmer as soon as possible after the war. It will be like cutting blocks with a razor.'³³⁹

Rosaleen's first chance to meet Nancy came at the end of June, when various leaves coincided, and a great house-party was arranged at Maesyneuadd, an old family manor-house a few miles to the north-east of Harlech. Robert later described it as 'the most haunted house that I have ever been in, though the ghosts were invisible except in the mirrors. They would open and shut doors, rap on the oak panels, knock the shades off lamps, and drink the wine from the glasses at our elbows when we were not looking.'³⁴⁰ Here Rosaleen joined Robert, Nancy, Tony, Clarissa, Mabel Nicholson, and Mabel's friend Mrs Stuart-Wortley, for 'three lovely dream-like days'. She was soon writing to Amy that she 'liked Nancy & all the Nicholsons very much'. The feeling was mutual: Rosaleen was once again invited to join them on the Sussex farm which Robert and Nancy intended to buy; and she even consented to having her beautiful long tresses cut short in the 'modern' style by her new sister-in-law.³⁴¹

Not long afterwards, Robert had two letters from Sassoon. The first attacked Robert for no longer 'writing deeply', and declared that if he were killed, he would haunt Robert and Nancy in their 'beastly old house'. The second, written on 5 July, contained a generous early birthday present: £1 for each of Robert's twenty-three years. Robert thanked him for the money, after declaring with robust good humour:

As for my not 'writing deeply' blast you, you old croaking corbie, aren't I allowed for the honour of the Regiment to balance your abysmal groanings with my feather top rhymes and songs? And I have written croakingly too lately but I haven't sent you specimens because I think it's bad taste and most ungrateful when God's so nice to me.[342]

Robert was a religious man both by upbringing and by temperament; and since the appalling shock of David Thomas's death he had once again been edging his way back towards belief in a personal God. However, Nancy was a most determined atheist, and in one of her first letters to Rosaleen had written:

By the by, I'm not religeous [*sic*]. Robert says you're not so now we know each other all right what? Your father seems to have been worrying mightily about my not having been confirmed so my Father wrote to yours & told him not to worry any more because it wasn't any good: it was 'like chucking a hymn book at a Zeppelin'. Rude but funny.[343]

For a while the question of Nancy's confirmation had caused something of a breach between the two families, and when Robert had first given Rosaleen instructions for calling on the Nicholsons he had told her: 'Ring 3 times to show you belong to the family. But Don't bring any of the Graves family with you. Especially Father's arrival is always a signal for every Nicholson to hide. He talks religion & poetry at them & they get frightened.'[344]

Nancy's atheism did not prevent Robert from becoming friendly with the Bishop of St Asaph;[345] and he also wrote to Sassoon asking him to be the unborn child's godfather. But Nancy's influence was already making itself felt, and he added that Sassoon's chief duties would be 'to stop the child becoming dirty or too religious, and to send it a copy of your collected works at Confirmation, which should prevent it taking the ceremony seriously'.[346]

While Robert and Nancy were still staying in haunted Maesyneuadd, Nancy, despite her declared disbelief in other-worldly experiences, saw the ghost of a small dog. It was said to appear as a harbinger of death; and during the next few months a series of deaths and near-deaths reminded the young lovers very forcibly of the normal world from which they had temporarily escaped.

CHAPTER
17
A TIME TO DIE

Death among one's family or friends is a safe enough prophecy in wartime. Robert had already lost many of his friends, and indeed it was only a few weeks since he had heard that Ralph Rooper had been killed while driving an ambulance, but it was Nancy who had seen the dog; and the next death in her intimate circle could hardly have been foretold.

The Nicholsons had returned to London when Nancy's mother caught influenza. Not wishing to spoil Tony's leave, she hid her illness from him, secretly taking aspirin and refusing to go to bed. Pneumonia set in, and within a few days, on 13 July 1918, she died. So devoted was Mabel to her son that apparently 'while she was dying her chief feeling was one of pleasure that Tony had got his leave prolonged on her account'.[347]

Robert and Nancy were still feeling shocked by Mabel's death when they heard from Siegfried Sassoon that he had narrowly escaped death himself. Returning from a daylight patrol in No Man's Land, he had been mistaken for a German, and shot in the head by one of his own sergeants. In the circumstances Robert's reply was less sympathetic than the occasion demanded: 'How clever of you,' he wrote, 'to get a bullet thro' your napper and write me a saner letter than you have sent me for some time past.' Then, after asking bluntly whether Sassoon was 'bent on getting killed', Robert turned to his own concerns, and outlined his plans for dairy-farming in Sussex. 'The only drawback to this scheme', he explained, 'is one concerned with the dibs. ... I think you'll have to promise to help us out if we get into a hole, with some of your Persian gold.'[348]

Sassoon retaliated with an understandably angry verse-letter which contained the line: 'Why keep a Jewish friend unless you bleed him?'[349] Robert realized that he had gone too far, and tried to patch up their relationship by asking Sassoon to look over some recent poems, as 'I like this ceremony of friendship and you generally know where my work is bad'.[350]

However, there was clearly no longer any chance that Sassoon would provide them with financial backing; so while Robert 'went on mechanically'[351] at his cadet battalion work, he and Nancy modified their plans. The price of land was far lower in North Wales than in Sussex, and by the end of the summer it had been decided that Nancy and Rosaleen, after training, should take a small farm near St Asaph, while Robert remained in the army 'till he can afford to go forward'.[352]

In the meantime Sassoon had looked over Robert's poems, and condemned most of them as too sentimental. Robert was at first inclined to ignore this advice, asking in some exasperation, 'Old boy do you want me to stop writing altogether? I can't write otherwise than I am now except with hypocrisy for I am bloody happy and bloody young (with only very occasional lapses).'[353] But when Robert Ross appeared to agree with Sassoon, Graves took the criticisms to heart, and wrote to Sassoon: 'Don't worry about me: I am going to write you a heavy epic soon; I am not entirely swamped by the approaching family.'[354]

Nancy was five and a half months pregnant when towards the end of September she and Robert moved from the lodgings at Bryn-y-Pin to their first real home, Rose Cottage in Rhuddlan. Here they had four rooms to themselves; though Amy felt that life would be very hard for them, explaining to John that they had 'no servant ... [so] Robby helps!'[355]

Not long after their move Robert and Nancy were holidaying at Apple Tree Yard when one of the dreaded orange telegrams arrived from the War Office with the news that Tony Nicholson had died of wounds.[356] Robert accompanied Nancy and William Nicholson on a melancholy journey into the country, where they went to the school at which Kit boarded, and broke the news to him. Nancy spent most of the following day in bed, feeling utterly miserable; but she received a comforting visit from Amy, and this kindly act made a great impression upon her. Soon Nancy was confiding in Robert that Amy was no longer just a mother-in-law, but 'a real person'.[357] Robert was equally grateful for Amy's calming influence: he had been seriously alarmed that the shock of Tony's death might damage Nancy's unborn child, and he remained anxious until reassured by a doctor that all was well.

Robert himself had been much affected by another recent death, that of Robbie Ross, and he wrote sadly to Sassoon: 'There'll never be another Robbie, cynical, kind-hearted, witty, champion of lost causes, feeder of the fatherless and widowed and oppressed. I felt his loss more than people could suppose.'[358] However, when he and Nancy returned to Rose Cottage, they tried to be positive. Their current plan was to 'settle down at Harlech next September for farming or gardening and literary and art work';[359] and in the meantime, Robert and his father-in-law had decided to launch a miscellany to be known as the *Owl*, for which they had promises of contributions from Max Beerbohm, John Masefield, and a number of other distinguished figures.

Then more bad news arrived. Robert's brother Charles, who had spent the summer of 1918 with an Officer Cadet Battalion in Oxford, was lying on a hospital bed in Somerville, seriously ill with influenza. It was a deadly virus, and had soon killed several of his comrades. Charles's own temperature shot up to 104.8 degrees, and his death was hourly expected. The turning-point was a strange one: it came when 'Uncle Charles . . . sat beside me and angered me so much that I broke into the desired sweat and my temperature dropped with a bump.'[360]

On 11 November 1918, not long after Charles's unexpected reprieve, came the Armistice, and the end of 'The Great War'. With American aid, Germany had at last been defeated; but it was difficult to believe that the slaughter was over. Tragically, Wilfred Owen had been one of the final casualties; and Robert's first reaction to news of the Armistice was one of bitterness. The end of the war had come too late for so many of his comrades-in-arms; and he went out 'walking alone along the dyke above the marshes of Rhuddlan . . . cursing and sobbing and thinking of the dead'.[361]

CHAPTER
18
DEMOBILIZATION

Robert's initially bitter reaction to the end of the war was soon succeeded by a mixture of relief and patriotic delight. 'Oh Bob,' he wrote to Robert Nichols, 'isn't it extraordinary to feel that the War's won at last: I keep a small silk Union Jack at the stairhead to remind me of it so that I shan't grouse at the petty annoyances of peace.' Many fine poets had died in the war; but Graves gladly accepted his enlarged share of the literary burden, exclaiming to Nichols: 'Thank God that there are still living four or five poets ... to do something with the language of the conquering races of the world.'[362]

Poetry would be Graves's principal calling; but a subsidiary occupation would be necessary. So as soon as he could get demobilized, he planned 'to go up for a month or two to Oxford to learn a bit about agriculture', before retreating to Wales to 'grow cabbages like old thingummy the Roman Emperor – Galba wasn't it?'[363]

But although the idea of farming still sounded attractive, Nancy's baby was due in the New Year, so she would be unable to take any active part in such a venture for some while; and in any case Robert was still short of capital. When he discovered that if he took up his Classics exhibition at St John's College, Oxford, he would also qualify for a Government grant of £200 a year while he remained a student, it seemed too good an opportunity to turn down. Having decided this, Robert wished to begin as soon as possible; and he learned that St John's would ask for him to be demobilized once he had obtained a signed release from the Colonel of his Officer Cadet Battalion.[364]

On 12 December 1918 Mrs Stuart-Wortley accompanied Nancy down to London, where she could relax in comfortable surroundings at Apple Tree Yard during the final days of her pregnancy; and on the 17th Robert followed her south. But first he secured his signed release; and at Oxford he handed it over to the St John's authorities, who made out an application for his demobilization, and forwarded both documents to the War Office for clearance.

A few days later Robert accompanied his wife, his father-in-law and Mrs Stuart-Wortley down to Hove on the Sussex coast, where William Nicholson had taken a villa at the sea's edge so that Nancy's child could be born in the healthiest possible circumstances. Mrs Stuart-Wortley was devoted in her attentions to the expectant mother; a maid was also engaged; and Robert decided that if necessary he would overstay his leave until the baby was born so that he too could minister to his wife.

On Monday 6 January 1919, to the sound of gulls crying, and waves breaking on the shingle beach just beyond her window, Nancy gave birth to a daughter. Nancy was slightly built, and the experience was far more painful than she had expected;[365] but on Tuesday a telegram reached Wimbledon announcing that mother and child were both doing well.

Some days later Amy arrived at Hove to visit her first grandchild. It was an anxious walk 'thru wet rubble between wave and lagoon' to reach the villa; but, as she told Alfred later that day, she was welcomed very warmly. Amy decided that the little girl, who had been named Jenny, was 'a dear'; she was also pleased to see that Nancy was already 'sitting up at glasswork'; and still more pleased when Robert, who walked back to the bus with her, declared that he was 'determined to give Jenny the good home training he had got'.[366]

Robert now discovered that for him to be officially released from the army, it was not enough for the St John's application to be cleared by the War Office. He would have to receive demobilization papers in person from his battalion, now stationed at Limerick in Ireland; and he would then have to report to a 'dispersal centre' which, curiously enough, was on Wimbledon Common not far from Red Branch House. It all seemed very tiresome; but he made plans to set out for Ireland on the 15th, and wrote asking Sassoon to accompany him, 'so that we can spend our last days of "soldiering" together'.[367] To Sassoon this smacked too much of the kind of naïvely 'heroic' attitude which he particularly deplored. He wrote an unfriendly reply, and Robert crossed the Irish Sea and travelled to Limerick alone.

This was the first time that Robert had visited Ireland since he was a baby, and he was considerably moved by the experience of being in the 'town of my ancestors'.[368] This was understandable. The Graves family had put down few roots in England; and in Wales they were comparative newcomers; but the whole of southern Ireland from the Ring of Kerry in the west to Dublin in the east is full of Graves associations and Graves memorials. More than half a century later, Ireland feels more like home to me than any other place in the world; and Robert in his day wrote a touching letter to his father 'describing his feelings that Limerick was native air'.[369]

However, these nostalgic sentiments did not prevent Robert from writing to Eddie Marsh asking him to do what he could to speed up his demobilization. Limerick was a Sinn Fein stronghold, and Robert was soon tired of having 'mud and stones thrown at my back in O'Connell Street by my fellow countrymen who mistake me for the brutal invader'.³⁷⁰ In the meantime he wrote loving verses for Nancy and Jenny; and continued to immerse himself in the family past. He was conducted round Limerick Cathedral by the current Bishop; and one of Janie Cooper's brothers invited him to spend a night at Cooper's Hill on 2 February. This latter visit nearly proved disastrous. The sheets on the bed were damp, and Robert 'woke up with a chill. I knew that it was the beginning of influenza.'³⁷¹

With his lungs in their present state, there was a high risk that influenza would kill him; and Robert, who had seen enough of the inside of military hospitals, began desperately wanting to return to Nancy's care and protection. When he arrived back at the barracks he found that all demobilization was about to be stopped because of the political troubles; but by a lucky chance his own demobilization telegram had finally come through from the War Office, and provided he was on the 6:15 train that evening, he would be able to leave Ireland just in time. His papers had already been made out; and all that he needed was the Colonel's signature to a statement that he had handled no company moneys for the last six months; together with the secret code-marks which could only be supplied by the battalion demobilization officer.³⁷²

But then the Adjutant, reckoned by Robert to be 'hand-in-glove' with the demobilization officer, reminded him of a promise to help with some battalion theatricals, and made it clear that he would prevent Robert from leaving. In the circumstances, Robert 'decided to make a run for it'. Obtaining the code-marks was clearly impossible; but he managed at the last moment to secure the Colonel's signature – something which would be enough to save him from a charge of outright desertion – and he 'tumbled into' the 6:15 train as it was moving out of Limerick station.³⁷³

When Robert reached London he managed to commandeer the only available taxi at Paddington – there was a strike on the underground, and so taxis were in short supply – and he very kindly shared it with another officer and his wife. They were delighted, and the officer asked Robert whether he could return the favour in any way? He certainly could! By an amazing coincidence he turned out to be the Cork District Demobilization Officer, and he was able to complete Robert's papers for him.

Robert arrived at Red Branch House just as his parents were finishing lunch. He told them that he had caught cold at Cooper's Hill, spent an hour with them, and was then accompanied by Alfred to Wimbledon Common to be demobilized.³⁷⁴ Immediately afterwards he travelled down to Hove, and went straight to bed. After four and a half years, Robert's military service was over; but it was soon obvious that he was dangerously ill.

BOOK
FIVE
HARLECH AND
BOAR'S HILL
1919–1921

CHAPTER
1
'THE TROLL'S NOSEGAY'

Robert Graves had reached Hove on the evening of Tuesday 4 February 1919. So feverish was he, that his thinking had become confused. He got it into his head that it was St Valentine's Day (14 February), and before stumbling into bed he told William Nicholson that he had just been demobilized at Brighton.[1] On first entering the villa Robert had suffered a severe shock which had helped to throw him off balance: he thought that he saw the ghost of Nancy's mother sitting at the table. 'It was like a bad dream,' he wrote later. 'I did not know what to say or do. I knew I was ill, but this was worse than illness,' but then the familiar-looking woman was introduced as 'Nancy's Aunt Dora, just over from Canada'.[2]

By Wednesday evening Nancy and Mrs Stuart-Wortley were also in bed with influenza; but luckily neither William Nicholson nor Jenny nor their maid caught the disease, and Nicholson managed to procure 'two good nurses ... and an excellent doctor'.[3] Nancy and her maid were comparatively mild cases; but Robert developed septic pneumonia. Both lungs were affected; and at one point, as APG was told a few weeks later, 'the doctors had practically given him up'.[4] Later Robert was to deride his nurses, describing one of them as 'competent, but frequently drunk', and the other as 'sober but incompetent'.[5] But according to William Nicholson it was his anger with one of them that saved his life: she 'riled him, so that it prevented his sinking'.[6]

By Sunday 16 February Nancy was 'up and about again';[7] while Robert, though still in bed, was on the mend. Indeed, he was working his way through some thirty-five drafts of a new poem, 'The Troll's Nosegay', in which he describes what it can mean to give one's partner the thing which is apparently desired:

THE TROLL'S NOSEGAY

A simple nosegay! was that much to ask?
  (Winter still gloomed, with scarce a bud yet showing.)
He loved her ill, if he resigned the task.
  'Somewhere,' she cried, 'there must be blossom blowing.'
It seems my lady wept and the troll swore
  By Heaven he hated tears: he'd cure her spleen;
Where she had begged one flower, he'd shower fourscore,
  A haystack bunch to amaze a China Queen.

Cold fog-drawn Lily, pale mist-magic Rose
  He conjured, and in a glassy cauldron set
  With elvish unsubstantial Mignonette
And such vague bloom as wandering dreams enclose.
  But she?
    Awed,
      Charmed to tears,
        Distracted,
          Yet –
Even yet, perhaps, a trifle piqued – who knows?[8]

Although still very much in love with Nancy, Robert had become aware of a strongly capricious streak in her nature. Not that he resisted this: indeed Robert catered so lovingly for Nancy's whims that she was encouraged in her capriciousness; and her independence developed into something rather spoilt and stubborn. It had long been clear that Robert was touchingly ready to accept ideas simply because they were Nancy's; but this attempt to be intellectually subservient to a woman whose ideas were dogmatic rather than carefully thought out, inevitably created conflict in Robert's mind. It also placed an unfair burden of responsibility upon his wife.

Nancy's ideas could in any case be unintentionally cruel: she had begun to say to the man who loved her so devotedly that marriage was such a bad institution that she would like to be 'dismarried – not by divorce, which was as bad as marriage – and able to live together without any legal or religious obligation to live together'. Robert accepted the general principle easily enough;[9] but the particular application must have wounded him. It is true that many of the poems which he wrote during the next two years present a picture of domestic happiness. 'The Patchwork Bonnet', for example, begins:

Across the room my silent love I throw,
  Where you sit sewing in bed by candlelight,

> Your young stern profile and industrious fingers
> Displayed against the blind in a shadow show
> To Dinda's grave delight.[10]

But even in this poem the wife is characterized as 'stern' (not perhaps because Nancy was by nature a tyrant – she seems to be anything but stern – but because Robert subconsciously craved for direction); and Robert was also writing a number of poems about the unhappiness which a man of his fundamentally loving and unselfish temperament must occasionally endure if he places himself entirely at the mercy of a mother, wife or mistress. In the last verse of 'A Lover Since Childhood', for example, he writes memorably:

> Give then a thought for me
> Walking so miserably,
> Wanting relief in the friendship of flower or tree:
> Do but remember, we
> Once could in love agree.
> Swallow your pride, let us be as we used to be.[11]

By 1 March Robert was more or less back to normal, and he told Sassoon cheerfully enough that he had been 'busy dying with no prospect of a military funeral at the end: better now. Going to Harlech on Friday next to get really well.' He added that in spite of his influenza he had written 'some perfect poetry, nearly all of which you'll hate. Oxford next term, I hope: shall invite you up to Harlech if I find there's any food or lodging available: but don't expect you'll come.'[12] This offer of hospitality was rather lukewarm. Sassoon had been living in Oxford for a short while, and in his plans for a debating society and a dining club he had disconcerted Robert by suggesting that Trotsky should be made an honorary member. Robert, under the separate influences of both Nancy and Sassoon, had begun to think of himself as a socialist; but he felt that this was going too far. He had made it clear that while he respected Lenin and Trotsky 'for their thorough-going idealism', he believed that their extreme methods were unnecessarily harsh, and that it would be possible to 'save Western Europe from so deep an operation and at any rate leave the bourgeoisie alive: being a bourgeois myself,' he had added, not unreasonably, 'I feel I want to remain alive.'[13]

On their way to Harlech, Robert and Nancy spent a few days in London;[14] and on 7 March they joined John and Perceval for lunch at the Sesame club with Alfred and Amy – for whom Nancy brought along a bunch of anemones. Perceval talked enthusiastically about his latest (temporary) job; and they heard that Philip, now back in Constantinople, had been promised the French Legion of Honour for his work as an Intelligence Officer during the war. But the main talking-point was that Red Branch House was up for sale. The Graves parents intended to retire permanently to Erinfa, and they were now hard at work trying to clear out the accumulated rubbish of more than twenty years.

CHAPTER
2
THE
MUTUAL IMPROVEMENT
SOCIETY

When Robert Graves and his family arrived in Harlech, they did not try living in Robert's cottage, which needed some attention before it was habitable, but instead moved into Llys Bach, (sometimes called 'Slip Back') which Nancy's father was still renting from the Swaynes. This was to be their home for the next seven months;[15] and although Robert's nerves had deteriorated again after his recent illness, and there were times when 'shells used to come bursting on my bed at midnight', and 'strangers in day-time would assume the faces of friends who had been killed',[16] those seven months also included some of the happiest and most carefree periods of Robert and Nancy's married life.

As Robert recovered his strength, he and Nancy could appreciate their good luck in having survived the war; and they embarked on this new stage of their lives with a useful capital sum of £400, £150 of which Robert had saved from his pay, and the rest of which was his 'war bonus'. Used cautiously, and eked out by Robert's disability pension of £60 per annum, and the occasional small sums which he could expect to earn from his poetry, this might have lasted them for a couple of years or more.

However, they were too full of hope for the future to think about living economically in the present; and, in Robert's words, they 'engaged a nurse and a general servant and lived as though we had an income of about a thousand a year'.[17] They were soon busy writing and drawing; and despite the extremely cold weather – there were icicles a foot long on the water-spout at Erinfa – it was not long before they were surrounded at Harlech by a cluster of family and friends.

Charles arrived first with his great friend Richard Hughes. The two of them had been demobilized back in January, and had just completed their first term at Oxford: Charles at St John's, and 'Diccon' at Oriel. After spending a night at Llys Bach on 20 March 1919 ('Did Charles talk?' wrote Robert, 'Ask the gramophone which positively blushed'), they moved into Erinfa.[18] Rosaleen was next on the scene, arriving on the 24th. Instead of going to Erinfa to look after her brother and his guest, as Amy had hoped, Rosaleen went to Llys Bach, explaining to Amy that Robert and Nancy had 'pressed her terribly to go to them first'. At times she may have regretted her decision, since Nancy was determined that she should wear a 'modern' woman's outfit of trousers, smock and red tie. Rosaleen eventually agreed to do so at Llys Bach, but declined to walk through the village dressed so oddly.[19]

While Nancy took driving lessons, Robert had been busy writing 'a short play for [John] Masefield who wanted one for his village people to act'; but now they both enjoyed a holiday, and one day, as Charles wrote, there was 'a huge snow-ball fight. By myself I fought Roz, Robert, Nancy & Diccon. It was open Warfare & started above the Quarry and ended near Scraggy Owen and lasted for about 2 hours.'[20]

The five of them turned to calmer pursuits after the arrival on 31 March of William and Kit Nicholson. Rosaleen moved on to Erinfa; and before long had helped to found what she described in a letter to her parents as a 'Mutual Improvement Society', in which they all had their roles to play. Rosaleen was teaching Nancy music, in return for which Nancy was teaching her gardening; Nancy was also teaching Robert 'home duties and gardening'; Charles was teaching Rosaleen golf, and 'being instructed by her in domestic work'; while Diccon Hughes was 'getting singing lessons and instructing the rest in considerateness'.[21]

Hearing of this new 'society' considerably mollified Amy, who had been highly displeased with Charles for inviting Diccon to Erinfa, and thereby incurring extra expense. Now she forwarded Rosaleen's letter to Charterhouse for John to read, with the comment: 'Are they not a happy party? It is a good thing that they are happy & so useful to each other as it cost me a lot to keep a second household going for them at this time.'[22] To Robert, as a token of her approval for his part in the Mutual Improvement Society, Amy sent a gift of some of the double red daisies which had been his favourite flowers as a child.[23]

By 16 April Amy, Alfred and John had joined the others at Harlech. The next three weeks were a delightful round of walks, musical evenings, and mutual hospitality between the Graveses, the Nicholsons, and Mrs Stuart-Wortley, who had followed William to Harlech; and when Diccon Hughes moved out of Erinfa on the 18th, Amy found him a cottage in the hills which became yet another focus for social activity.[24]

Robert's relations with his parents were not entirely easy at this time. In some things they saw eye to eye: for example, Alfred and Amy very much approved of 'the excellent Margaret',[25] a Scottish nanny who was employed to look after Jenny, and who with her warm heart and her fund of common sense was able to temper Nancy's rigid adherence to the latest set of up-to-date methods for bringing up children. They were also interested to see that Robert was having some work done to improve his cottage;[26] and Alfred was as ready as ever to give advice on Robert's latest poems, when asked to do so.[27] But they found some of Robert's new socialist ideas extremely strange. It seemed odd (though they were too tactful to comment upon it) to find that Robert and Nancy treated their general servant, a local girl called Barbara Morrison, more or less as an equal, and included her in the great family picnic on 6 May, which was followed by an elaborate game of hide-and-seek in the woodland below Erinfa. Two days later APG and Robert did have an argument over an otherwise pleasant lunch on 'the labour question'; but no bones were broken, and Nancy, whom APG declared in his diary to be 'a real good sort', was even prepared to take Alfred's side against that of her husband.[28]

In any case, Robert and Nancy were so cheerful and optimistic that it was difficult to find fault with either of them for long. A few days earlier they had been suggesting that APG should 'bring out the cream' of his lyrics, 'say 30', chosen by Robert and Rosaleen, with a cover design by Nancy;[29] and indeed for some weeks they were positively bubbling over with money-spinning ideas. Even setbacks hardly troubled them: so that when Ivor Novello decided not to continue with his plans for setting some of Robert's songs to music, they simply found a local musician, Dr Heath of Barmouth, who promised to take Novello's place.[30]

At the end of the Easter holidays the Mutual Improvement Society was partially dispersed, when Charles and Diccon returned to Oxford.[31] John also left for Charterhouse, where he was about to become a house monitor; and Amy and Alfred returned to what Robert called their 'impossible task' of clearing out the rubbish at Red Branch House.[32] However, Rosaleen lingered on at Harlech for another month. Looking at events in her usual clear-sighted manner, she had begun to realize the real difficulties which faced her brother and sister-in-law. There was a great deal of talk, but little was emerging of any practical value. May 1919 saw the publication of the first number of the *Owl*; but this was unlikely to earn much money; and in the meantime the dream of a shared farm was rapidly fading away. In the circumstances, Rosaleen very sensibly decided to strike out on her own. Strongly influenced both by the strong sense of duty which she had inherited from Amy, and by Nancy's conviction that women must fight for their own hand in what was still a man's world, Rosaleen decided to become a doctor. 'Her mind is quite made up,'

Amy wrote to John, '& we have agreed to help her. She does not think she would be in the first rank for music & she can do more in the world as a doctor.'[33]

CHAPTER
3
FRESH IDEAS

Robert remained optimistic, and in June 1919 he began talking about giving up the idea of Oxford altogether, and earning his own living at once. Alfred was as helpful and constructive as possible, and wrote on Robert's behalf to a lecture agent who might be able to find work in America;[34] but CLG was thoroughly annoyed to hear that Robert was giving up the prospect of a good degree and secure employment thereafter.

Annoyance became shock later in the month when it was discovered that Robert was writing book reviews for Sassoon, who had now left Oxford, and had been appointed literary editor of the socialist *Daily Herald*. APG was so worried by this new development that he went to see Marsh about it; and Marsh told him that Sassoon had 'apparently Bolshevized or tried to Bolshevize Robert ... and others'; and promised to write to Robert about his involvement with a paper which he himself regarded as 'a very fishy try-on'.[35]

Left-wing extremism seemed a real threat in the light of events in Europe, and was brought very close to home when Alfred and Amy learned that rioting mobs from Munich had sacked Laufzorn. So when at the end of June Robert and Nancy stayed for a while at Apple Tree Yard,[36] APG 'tried to talk [Robert] over, reminding [him] that [his] brother Philip had once been a pro-Boer and a Fenian, but had recovered from his youthful revolutionary idealism and come out all right in the end'.[37] As this savagely ironic sentence by Robert suggests, it would have been wiser for APG to have held his peace.

Certainly Robert had learned from Sassoon to be deeply concerned about the plight of the working man or woman. He showed his concern in practical ways, treating not only servants but all members of the working class as people who were worthy of his interest; and for a while, with its news of strikes and unemployment, the *Daily Herald* spoilt his and Nancy's breakfast every morning. But Robert was no revolutionary; while Nancy herself was chiefly concerned about achieving 'judicial equality of the sexes';[38] and Rosaleen, who was probably their closest confidante during this period, recalls that she 'never once heard [Robert] talking about politics or socialism of any sort'.[39]

215

Socialism presented Robert with a further conflict between the way of life in which he had been brought up, and the way of life in which he now believed. But some of Nancy's ideas came as a great relief to him. Although Robert kept being drawn back towards the religious beliefs of his childhood, to be a good Christian was for him too painful a road to the truth, as this poem perhaps makes clear:

REPROACH

Your grieving moonlight face looks down
    Through the forest of my fears,
Crowned with a spiny bramble-crown
    Dew-dropped with evening tears.

Why do you spell 'untrue, unkind,'
    Reproachful eyes plaguing my sleep?
I am not guilty in my mind
    Of aught would make you weep.

Untrue? but how, what broken oath?
    Unkind? I know not even your name.
Unkind, untrue, you charge me both,
    Scalding my heart with shame.

The black trees shudder, dropping snow,
    The stars tumble and spin.
Speak, speak, or how may a child know
    His ancestral sin?[40]

The closer Robert drew to Christianity, the more he was tormented by fear and guilt. Nancy, who saw his suffering at close quarters, later took some pride in having finally persuaded Robert to turn his back upon conventional religion; while Robert himself commented that: 'Nancy's crude summary of the Christian religion: "God is a man, so it must be all rot," took a load off my shoulders.'[41]

But for the time being Robert was far more concerned with his own financial future than with either politics or religion; and on 10 July 1919 he wrote enthusiastically to Rosaleen: 'Have the best idea ever for a children's play: founded on our rhymes. Heath is going to do the music. A fortune to be made, but don't tell Father.' Another scheme, mentioned in the same letter, involved marketing a black gollywog doll of Nancy's design. Examples of these dolls 'went everywhere with them' at that time; and Robert asked Rosaleen to tell their father that he and Nancy were in the process of having their design patented.

Two days later, writing a letter to thank the young poet Edmund Blunden for some possible contributions to the next number of the *Owl*, Robert sounded a still more aggressively businesslike note, when he declared: 'War-poetry is played out I'm afraid, commercially, for another five or ten years. Rotten thing for us, but it's no good blinking at it. Country Sentiment is the most acceptable dope now, and this is the name I've given my new poems.'[42]

Sadly, by the beginning of August, Robert's cheerful and self-confident mood had evaporated. Money was running out. None of his schemes seemed likely to earn anything in the near future, and Nancy had conceived another child. Alfred, back in Harlech after another lecture tour in Ireland, found his son 'looking older and careworn'.

Somewhat ironically, in view of Nancy's latest and possibly ill-timed pregnancy, she and Robert had only recently become members of the 'Constructive Birth Control Society'. Robert later regarded circulating its literature among the village women of Harlech as an act of rebellion against the established order; but at the time it caused little offence. The villagers themselves could tolerate eccentricity in a respected war hero, and on 12 August Robert was loudly cheered when he attended a local Soldiers' Dinner and made a speech about the glorious dead. Nor were his family upset: indeed, Alfred was a friend of Marie Stopes, the pioneer advocate of birth control, and had attended her wedding.[43] They were much more concerned by Nancy's refusal to have Jenny baptized;[44] and Amy, who was proud to have become a Graves, was considerably saddened by Nancy's determination to retain the Nicholson surname both for herself and for any daughters of her marriage.

However, there was no open breach between the families. Robert went bilberrying with John or mushrooming with his father, and joined in family parties with his usual relish. Indeed the only major family row at this time was about Rosaleen's unconventional behaviour. Her half-sister Susan was staying in the village, and was shocked to learn that Rosaleen planned to dine unchaperoned with Leonard Morgan, an Oxford friend of Charles's who was staying at Erinfa. Despite the fact that the dinner was to take place in the thoroughly respectable surroundings of the St David's Hotel, the morning of 21 August was spent in a family 'imbroglio' over this plan. Much to APG's relief, Robert acted as a peacemaker, 'argu[ing] as to new set of conventions while not regarding the old as foul and nasty-minded as R[osaleen] calls them'.[45]

Robert and Nancy were still full of money-spinning ideas: the latest being for Nancy to do a set of twelve posters for 'Vanity Fair', for each of which she hoped to be paid £50. But fine words, as they used to say, butter no parsnips; and financial pressures finally compelled Robert to take up his place at St

John's, where at least he could be certain of his government grant. APG was told by the president of St John's, who came to tea at Erinfa on 28 August, that Robert had made up his mind just in time. Oxford had never been so full, and he had 'refused 50 or 60 men anxious to enter his college'.[46]

CHAPTER
4
MOVING TO
OXFORD

Although Robert now had a secure place at St John's, the prospect of being subjected once again to the kind of examination pressures which had unsettled him so much back in his Carthusian days was not a happy one, and he began hoping for a last-minute reprieve. But what else could he do? Amy had recently had to make Robert a present of £100, finding that he and Nancy were financially 'at the pin of their collars',[47] and they were still living far beyond their means. For a while, in some desperation, Robert considered earning his living as a schoolmaster. He enlisted his father's help, and by mid-September 1919 APG had procured for him the offer of an assistant mastership at a school called St Ninian's.

But by this time Robert had found that his plans for going up to Oxford had been generally welcomed by his friends. Sassoon had come to stay for a fortnight at the end of August and the beginning of September, and he approved;[48] so did Marsh, who also came up to Harlech;[49] and so did Edmund Gosse, whom Robert and Nancy called on at Llandudno.[50] In the circumstances Robert reverted to his Oxford plans, and turned down the St Ninian's post twice.[51]

The next problem was finding somewhere to live. The Oxford authorities normally insisted that undergraduates must reside within three miles of Carfax, the crossroads at the centre of the city; but low-lying Oxford can be bitterly cold and damp, and as far back as January Robert had realized that the poor state of his lungs meant that he would need to live in some healthier place on the hills nearby. He was then hoping to find a house in the village of Garsington, on high ground to the east; but nothing had come of a letter which he had written to Lady Ottoline Morrell; and in the third week of September Robert heard that there was the possibility of renting a cottage in the garden of John Masefield's house on Boar's Hill, some five miles to the south-west of Carfax.

When Robert and Nancy arrived at Boar's Hill to be interviewed for the cottage they began with several advantages over the many other applicants: Graves and Masefield had several mutual friends, they admired each other's poetry, and they had been conducting an occasional correspondence ever since the summer or autumn of 1917.[52] Masefield, grey-haired but still looking healthy and vigorous, greeted them in his 'deep rich voice' at the door of his own home,[53] a substantial red-brick mansion which stands beside the Ridgway Road on the north-east corner of Boar's Hill, and has magnificent views towards Oxford. Masefield was a wonderfully kind man, especially to other writers; and he found it easy to like the young couple who were so obviously devoted to each other. Indeed, it was only recently that Robert had written to Edmund Blunden declaring that marriage to Nancy had entirely altered his writing, and altered it for the better: 'One gets a surer touch', he had written, 'and doesn't kick one's heels quite so high.'[54] After introducing them to his wife Constance,[55] a shrewd, protective woman who was helping him to 'vet' applicants, John Masefield took Robert and Nancy along his garden to show them the 'cottage'. Though much smaller than the main building this was a fair-sized dwelling, solidly built and with at least three good bedrooms. Robert and Nancy both liked it very much, which was just as well as they 'could not hear of another suitable house of any kind';[56] and although the Masefields explained that it would be unfair to promise them the cottage before interviewing the rest of the applicants, Robert and Nancy returned to Harlech feeling extremely hopeful.

Before long they heard that the cottage was theirs, at a rent of £3 a month. Nancy had already made a 'lovely little fitted dress basket which is for Jenny for her travels';[57] and as soon as the Oxford authorities had agreed to Robert's living at Boar's Hill, they began the work of packing up and planning for their move. The lease of Llys Bach was almost up, and William Nicholson very generously told Robert and Nancy that they could take as much of the furniture as they required for their new home.[58] William could afford to be generous, as his own fortunes were changing for the better: on 7 October he and 'Edie' Stuart-Wortley were married at Portmadoc – Robert was best man – and then set off to honeymoon in France.

Nancy, who was said by Charles to be 'a little hurt at the soonness of it all', did not attend the wedding;[59] but there was no serious rift in the family; and on Thursday, two days after the ceremony, Nancy set out for London with Margaret and Jenny, who were to stay in Apple Tree Yard until the Boar's Hill cottage was ready for them. Before leaving Harlech, Nancy asked Susan to 'help [Robert] and see he d[oes]n't get too tired'. Susan records that she and Nancy now got on 'rather well.' 'I think she's a pet,' Susan told Amy, 'but not to be taken too seriously and her age has to be often remembered.'[60]

Susan and Charles spent the rest of Thursday helping Robert to do the final packing: Charles 'carted things about & saved Robert a lot of heavy work', while Susan

> packed among other things 50 lbs of jam a 4 poster bed aided by Mrs. Jones who came to fetch back the borrowed coal – & 3 lots of china – in a large bath tub & a wicker basket – it was slow work because each bit of china seemed to be a special treaure in Robert's eyes! He was very sweet & so grateful for any little thing one could do, that it was a great pleasure helping him.[61]

Then on Friday morning Robert and Charles set out for Oxford with a lorry-load of furniture. It was a bitterly cold day, but they reached Oxford without mishap by eight o'clock in the evening. Charles was dropped off in the city, and went to call on Rosaleen, who was about to begin her medical training, and was lodging in Polstead Road.[62] Robert travelled on to Boar's Hill, where he was joined later than evening by his wife, who had seen APG only a few hours previously, and brought with her some good news about their financial situation.

It was less than a month since Amy had given Robert £100, but he and Nancy had continued to live beyond their means, and Robert had recently written to his father 'disclosing debts of £100 and asking for (a loan of) £140'.[63] He had also made it clear that he was very keen to make a success of his time at Oxford; and he had explained that he and Nancy intended to live more economically, and that although they would keep Margaret, Barbara was to be let go. Luckily, Amy had at last managed to sell Red Branch House. It did not sell as well as she had hoped, but at least it would no longer be a drain upon the family resources; and when she and Alfred had discussed Robert's letter, Alfred had been despatched to Apple Tree Yard to tell Nancy that it was 'all right re the money'.[64]

When CLG heard from Alfred about this new loan, he was 'very severe on Robby', whom he was beginning to regard as a bloodsucker. APG, considerably shaken by the ferocity of his brother's comments, was reassured when a few days later he received 'a touching letter from Robby about his Oxford prospects'.[65] Their loan had evidently been received in the right spirit; and now Robert had the chance to make a fresh start, unencumbered by financial worries and with something positive to work for.

CHAPTER
5
'AWFULLY HAPPY
IN SPITE OF IT ALL'

Robert, following Charles's example, had managed to change his course from Classics to English Language and Literature, while retaining his £60 Classical Exhibition; and to begin with he took his academic work extremely seriously. Each morning he was up early, and then cycled along the tree-lined Ridgway, down Boar's Hill, and through the little village of South Hinksey, a cluster of stone-built houses with a church and a public house, The General Elliot. From here he rode along a footpath, carried his bike over a footbridge across the Hinksey stream and the railway line, and then cycled up the Abingdon road into the centre of Oxford. Crossing over Carfax, he soon arrived at St John's, where to begin with he breakfasted and lunched each day with his brother Charles.

Apart from one or two tutorials a week, the mornings and afternoons were spent either at lectures, or studying in the college library or the Bodleian; and Robert found himself in generally congenial company. It is true that he was a little irritated or, as he put it later, 'amused' by the difference in manner displayed towards him by some of the elder dons. During the war they had 'regarded all soldiers, myself included, as their noble saviours'; but they now appeared to have 'recovered their pre-war self-possession'.[66] However, Robert was enjoying his new studies; and during the course of the term Powell, the Senior Tutor of St John's, spoke very highly of Robert's work to CLG.

One of Robert's fellow undergraduates was the poet Edmund Blunden, with whom he had been corresponding earlier in the year. Blunden, like Graves, had permission to live on Boar's Hill, in his case 'on account of gassed lungs', and he was sharing rooms there with his wife Mary. Before long the two men became close friends, with Robert often calling for Edmund on his way in to Oxford in the mornings. Other poets living on Boar's Hill included Robert Bridges, the Poet Laureate; Gilbert Murray, then well known for his verse translations of classical Greek drama; and Robert's friend Bob Nichols, with 'his flame-opal ring, [and] his wide-brimmed hat'. Nichols's *Ardours and*

Endurances had been immensely popular during the war, and great things were still expected of him.[67]

This miniature Parnassus also attracted visiting poets. In November 1919 Alfred and Amy decided to visit Oxford, where they put up at the Roebuck Hotel; and when they had bussed out to the foot of Boar's Hill, the first man they met was their old friend W.B. Yeats accompanied by his wife; and the four of them 'talked and walked' to the top of the hill together. APG and Amy then made their way along the Ridgway, where Masefield showed them over his garden before taking them across to Dingle Cottage. Here they found that Robert and Nancy, who had been joined some time earlier by Margaret and Jenny, were comfortably settled in.[68]

On the evening of the following day, Sunday 16 November, Alfred Perceval Graves had an invitation to dinner at All Souls, the famous graduate college in the centre of Oxford. He had asked his host, Professor Edgeworth, if Robert might be included in the invitation; and father and son were given places of honour on the High Table. During the dinner, Robert talked to Edgeworth about the proper scientific training of soldiers; and afterwards, in the coffee room, Robert and his father met for the first time the famous Colonel T.E.Lawrence.[69]

During the past few months Lawrence had been popularized as 'Lawrence of Arabia' in a series of hugely successful illustrated lectures in London; and this slight-looking man with piercing blue eyes was now one of the most famous men in England. He 'spoke affectionately' to APG about 'Philip and Uncle Bob',[70] with whom he had worked in military intelligence; and then he made an immediate hit with Robert by praising his poetry, which he said that he had read while he was in Egypt, 'during one of his flying visits from Arabia'.[71] Lawrence was working at All Souls on *Seven Pillars of Wisdom*, his account of the remarkable role which he had played in the Arab revolt during the war; and he was passionately interested in writers and writing. At this time he was thinking seriously about reverting to an old undergraduate plan of his for setting up a printing press; and he also saw Robert as a useful link with the younger poets, of whom he knew little. Robert in his turn, as APG noted in his diary that evening, was evidently 'delighted to meet a man who had become a "legendary hero" in his life time'.[72] This was the start of a friendship which was to have important consequences for Robert's subsequent career.

But despite the enjoyment which Robert took both in his work and in his circle of friends and acquaintances, ill health and financial worries constantly overshadow the period. Robert had still not recovered from his wartime experiences, and he and Nancy still tended to live beyond their means. When his brother John sent him an encouraging letter from Charterhouse, Robert's reply veered wildly between happiness and misery:

> In a day or so a bright streak might appear in the gloomy sky of my mind and I might throw off a ruse or two. I am pleased by your touching faith in Robert Graves but he expects in the end to suffer the fate of a greater poet than himself John Clare of Helpston who was shut up for 22 years in Nottingham Asylum for having spent
> 'A life addicted to poetical prosings.'
> This is a heavenly life on Boar's Hill and we are all ill well. Jenny spends the day as I am reminded by bumps upstairs standing up in her cot and pulling the Caldecotts off the wall. We are in deep debt and very happy. We see Ros & Morgan every Sunday – don't tell Mother – we always ask them to lunch: they are sweet.
> I don't know if we'll be able to afford Harlech this winter and it's a glubshious place here, a double view from the top of the garden, as wide as the Slip Back one. One way over Ox[fordshi]re the other over Berks – The Masefields are angels.[73]

Despite the constant pressure of his academic work, and despite feeling, as he described it, 'ill well', Robert did not allow his literary interests to fall into abeyance for a time. Perhaps he should have done. But at the start of the term he was busy with the final proofs of *Country Sentiment*, which was to be published the following spring by Secker in London and by Knopf in New York; in November came the publication of some of his poems in *Georgian Poetry 1918–1919*; and there was also a new edition of the *Owl* to be seen through the press. Besides all this, he and Nancy were hoping, as he told Edward Marsh, that by the New Year they would 'have a tiny book of new poems to send you, privately printed by the Chiswick press with a Nancy illustration'.[74]

This 'tiny book', which they called *The Treasure Box*,[75] contained ten of Robert's poems, and two small illustrations by Nancy. On the whole the poems continue in the pastoral vein of *Country Sentiment*, and one or two are charming, such as 'The Gifts', which runs:

> Henry was a worthy king
> Mary was his queen,
> He gave to her a lily
> Upon a stalk of green,
> Then for all his kindness
> And for all his care
> She gave him a new laid egg
> In the garden there.

There is also 'The Kiss', in which Robert describes what it feels like to be 'spell-bound' by 'a whisper of love', so that Time itself ceases to move. But by far the most powerful poem in the collection is 'Lost Love', a searing description of grief which is so evidently based upon personal experience that although it may relate back in part to the death of David Thomas, it probably draws most strongly upon the emotions which Robert had felt at the time of his break with 'Peter' Johnstone – who incidentally had survived the war and was now up at Oxford writing poems and reading Modern Languages. Robert's poem runs:

> His eyes are quickened so with grief,
> He can watch a grass or leaf
> Every instant grow; he can
> Clearly through a flint wall see,
> Or watch the startled spirit flee
> From the throat of a dead man.
>   Across two counties he can hear,
> And catch your words before you speak.
> The woodlouse or the maggot's weak
> Clamour rings in his sad ear;
> And noise so slight it would surpass
> Credence :- drinking sound of grass,
> Worm talk, clashing jaws of moth
> Chumbling holes in cloth:
> The groan of ants who undertake
> Gigantic loads for honour's sake,
> Their sinews creak, their breath comes thin:
> Whir of spiders when they spin,
> And minute whispering, mumbling, sighs
> Of idle grubs and flies.
>   This man is quickened so with grief,
> He wanders god-like or like thief
> Inside and out, below, above,
> Without relief seeking lost love.[76]

It was not many months after writing this poem that Robert once again met Johnstone, who had made a considerable mark in Oxford literary circles, and in the spring of 1920 was to win the coveted Newdigate Prize with a poem on 'The Lake of Garda'. Although the mutual attraction between the two men had vanished, and although Johnstone had 'changed so much' that in some ways 'it seemed absurd to have ever suffered on his account', there was still 'a caricature likeness' to the boy whom he had loved; and Robert found the meeting extremely upsetting.[77]

In the meantime, on 8 December 1919, soon after the Michaelmas term at Oxford had ended, Robert received another letter from John, and began his reply:

> Dearest John Wingle,
>
> Your welcome and distinguished blather came opportunely to a house suffering from overwork and the weather – We come (sweemy – walkee) to stay with the Mallories on the 18th and hope to see your lovely-ugly face again –
>
> We have just broken up: I won't say 'come down' as it would give a false idea of our geographical situagger.
>
> Am writing hard: Nancy's drawing ditto – afraid we won't see you in the Christmas holidays: are too poor to leave here, you see.[78]

Nancy was now six months pregnant, and financial needs were pressing; but Robert was hoping to clear his debts by selling, to a man named Holbrooke, the Harlech cottage which Robert had bought from Amy during the war. Holbrooke soon made it a condition of purchase that Amy should sell him an acre of her land to go with the property. She was agreeable to this, and by mid-December the deal appeared to be going ahead, but then ran into difficulties, as Holbrooke began asking Amy for a great deal more land, which she did not wish to sell.

By the end of January 1920 everything was still very uncertain, and Robert was feeling too poor to pay John for some ivory chessmen which he had asked his brother to purchase on his behalf. Some money was saved by sending Margaret and Jenny to Erinfa for a short holiday at Amy's expense; but in their absence Robert and Nancy entertained their former maid Barbara Morrison, who had been working at a nunnery in Slough and was shortly to emigrate to Canada. It had been one of Robert's grievances in the autumn that Barbara, despite writing 'charmingly' to Nancy, had answered neither of the two letters which he himself had written to her: 'They open all her letters, the bloody Nuns,' he had declared to John, adding sentimentally: 'I love old Barbaree.'[79] Now Robert wrote again to John, explaining that he and Nancy were 'mucking about at our own work with Barb's help, who by recent discoveries I have come to think of as not only a good girl but one of the best I know; but I don't tell her so or she'd slack off a bit & get meditative'.[80] Besides entertaining Barbara, Robert and Nancy had gone ahead with an expensive scheme to have 'a glorious shed put up in our garden which gives us a studio & a spare bedroom'. This was humorously justified on the grounds that 'if we ever get as poor as all that we can live in it altogether & be completely uncomfortable'; while their increasing burden of debt was blamed entirely upon the fact that they were still 'waiting for that ass Holbrooke to stump up'.[81]

Margaret and Jenny returned to Dingle Cottage on 4 February; six days later Barbara Morrison left for Canada, and Nancy, now eight months pregnant, sank into a state of depression. Towards the end of the month Robert, 'much distressed' to learn that Amy had refused to allow John to join Mallory on a Snowdon climbing party, wrote to his brother:

> Snowdon is not as expensive as all that: oh I wish to hell I could come instead of you, but we are expecting this baby any day next week & Nancy's mind, as is usually the case in these businesses, gets so mazed and wingle that I can't leave her for more than an hour or two – which is b—y bad for my Oxford work.
>
> However, she'll be all right – We want you to be godfather (if a boy, to be called John) together with John Masefield.[82]

Robert added that the failure of 'that four-letter-man Holbrooke' to buy the cottage had left them 'in a hopeless financial state curse his soul'. He had been lecturing on Modern Poetry to raise a little more money; and Sunday was a happy day, when Leonard Morgan, 'an angel of the highest and brightest variety' came up for lunch and then helped with the housework for a few hours. But on other days, while Margaret looked after Jenny, Nancy lay in bed, and Robert was left with the cooking and washing up. 'What a charming life!' Robert concluded. 'But I'm awfully happy in spite of it all.'[83]

On 7 March 1920 Nancy gave birth to a son, John David; and soon afterwards she received an excited telegram from Erinfa: 'God bless the first Graves grandson!'[84] Amy, writing to John, remarked with pride that Robert had 'overtaken' all his much older half-brothers, who had fathered only girls. However, her pleasure was a little diluted by memories of her unsuccessful efforts to have Jenny baptized, and she asked John sharply: 'How can you be a godfather, if there is to be no christening?'[85]

A few days later Robert wrote to his parents 'in good spirits' with the excellent news that William Nicholson had generously offered to clear all his and Nancy's outstanding debts; and Robert's cheerful mood persisted into early April, when Martin Secker at last published *Country Sentiment*. The Blundens were away in Northamptonshire engaged in their important work of copying out unpublished poems by John Clare, whose work they were rediscovering;

and on 5 April Robert sent them a letter full of what was intended to be good-humoured banter:

> Dear Mary and Edmund
>
> Curse you to Hell for not having written. Why not remember your living friends instead of grubbing in Museums after the Dead? All well here; Nancy has been up for some time now and swaggers about in her breeches and smocks as of old. John David is a great little lad and treats us well.[86]

He added that Jenny and Margaret were staying for a while with Nancy's Aunt Fanny, but 'thank God we have a maid in here every day who is very capable and trustworthy and has a Scottish Mother, so we're well away'. Robert also passed on the news that '*Country Sentiment* is selling like anything and the reviews are good.'[87] Unfortunately this was to a large extent wishful thinking. Robert's campaign to be happy in spite of everything was to be put severely to the test.

CHAPTER
6
'LET US BE
AS WE USED TO BE'

In the first week of April 1920 Alfred Perceval Graves noticed that in a *Spectator* review, Robert's poems were 'praised for fancy [but] blamed for slightness';[88] and before long Robert had to accept that *Country Sentiment* was not after all 'the most acceptable dope', as it appeared to please few of his critics or his readers. In May, while his father was being honoured and 'sumptuously' entertained at a Celtic Congress in Edinburgh,[89] Robert seemed to be sliding downhill into debt and obscurity.

However, the commercial failure of *Country Sentiment* helped to prevent Robert from becoming too facile a poet. Never again did he boast that his poems would cater for the public taste; instead he began to consider that he should write poems only when they forced themselves upon him – something which happened, he came to believe, when he was oppressed by an inner conflict which poetry alone could resolve.[90]

The immediate problem of debt was solved in mid-June by an application to Eddie Marsh, who put to one side all the royalties which he received for his popular *Memoir* about Rupert Brooke, and used them to help writers in distress. 'Ever so many thanks,' Graves wrote to Marsh when the necessary money had arrived. 'We are now firmly established for some time, and can breathe again.' He added that he would send Marsh some new poems as soon as he had had them typed: 'I hope it won't be too much of a shock. I seem to have travelled a long way in the past three years.'[91]

A few days later Robert and Nancy went up to Harlech with Margaret and the two children for a summer holiday.[92] They stayed at Erinfa, where Robert found that his parents were already well-entrenched in village society. APG was organizing a grand 'Harlech Pageant',[93] and was about to be inducted as a lay reader in the local church; while Amy was busy with girl guides, sewing classes and jumble sales. Robert was especially amiable towards his father, making it clear one lunchtime how much he appreciated APG's 'life work'; but tensions between mother and daughter-in-law made it an uneasy

229

holiday, as is clear from a letter which Amy wrote to John on 12 July: 'The children are very sweet, but my nerves get much frayed by the baby's loud & continual crying, which is not attended to on principle. I got a stare from Nancy when I one day took him up during one of these fits of crying to have him changed, which he needed, & Margaret says nothing makes the Mother more furious.'[94] Amy added that Robert's nerves were 'still very much upset' from shell-shock, but that he found it 'very soothing' to play bridge in the evenings; and that, in her eyes, Robert had 'become wonderfully unselfish in many ways & does everything he possibly can to save Nancy trouble or to please her'.[95]

Nancy was well enough to go out walking or collecting wild fruit with Robert on several occasions, and once they attended a concert which was part of the Harlech Music Festival;[96] but Nancy was often tired. In the evenings she would retire early to her bedroom; and Robert either had to miss the parties and social events of the summer, or to go out without her. Usually he stayed in; but one evening in mid-July he accompanied Charles and Rosaleen to a fancy-dress ball; and towards the end of that month, not long after his twenty-fifth birthday, he was drawn into a bizarre experience.

John had now joined the family at Erinfa; and he and Robert had gone out to play bridge with a Canadian colonel and a young ex-airman. After some indifferent play, the colonel suggested that they go bathing instead. The others agreed, though it was a cold night. Afterwards, when they were drying themselves, Robert felt irritated with the colonel and challenged him to a climb. First he took him 'up the castle rock from the railway station in the dark', which was quite difficult enough; and then, with John and the ex-airman looking on in horror:

> We climbed into the castle and walked through the chapel into the north-western tower. It was pitch dark. I took them left into the turret which adjoined the tower but rose some twenty feet higher. The sky showed above, about the size of an orange. The turret had once had a spiral staircase, but ... only an edging of stones remained on the walls. This edging did not become continuous until about the second spiral. We struck matches and I started up. The colonel swore and sweated, but followed. I showed him the trick of getting over the worst gap in the stones, which was too wide to bridge with one's stride, by crouching, throwing one's body forward and catching the next stone with one's hands; a scramble and he was there. ... I was glad when we reached the second spiral. We climbed perhaps a hundred and twenty feet to the top.[97]

This risky adventure, combined with the experience of meeting new people, excited Robert's shell-shock for some days.[98]

Earlier in the year (1920), Robert had suffered from a far more severe recurrence of shell-shock, and, 'in a most agonized condition of mind for which I was quite unable to account' (but which he later believed to be fear of another war) he wrote his gruesome poem 'The Gnat', in which a shepherd, fearing imminent death from a 'busy Gnat, swollen to giant size,/Pent-up within the skull', murders his sheepdog to save him from falling into anyone else's hands. But then the gnat escapes; and the shepherd with no sheepdog is reduced to being a common labourer. Three years later Robert explained the poem by saying that at the time he had been 'under the impression that if I allowed myself to be treated by a professor of the New Psychology (believing then in Freud & Jung as I no longer do) I could get cured by having my dreams interpreted'. However, he also feared that if he became too completely cured, he would no longer be able to write poetry. How could this dilemma be resolved?

> In waking life [wrote Robert] I decided that at all costs I must get cured; in the dream-life, or rather the mood of poetic inspiration, the beaten side asserted itself. The Gnat is an assertion that to be rid of the gnat (shell-shock) means killing the sheep-dog (poetry) ... in fact I would have to give up being a poet and become a schoolmaster or a bank-clerk ... I had made several approaches to various doctors but never took treatment.[99]

While suffering from shell-shock Robert also wrote 'The Pier-Glass',[100] in which a woman servant is racked with guilt for having killed the employer who seduced her, and is continually troubled both by day and by night with nightmarish memories of the room in which she murdered him. Perhaps she even visits the room; but this is deliberately left ambiguous; and in reality or in nightmare she stares into 'A sullen pier-glass cracked from side to side', and asks desperately:

> Ah, mirror, for Christ's love
> Give me one token that there still abides
> Remote, beyond this island mystery,
> So be it only this side Hope, somewhere,
> In streams, on sun-warm mountain pasturage,
> True life, natural breath; not this phantasma:

But then she realizes, from seeing a colony of bees at work, that she has a duty to the present. According to Christian morality, she should have forgiven her employer; but she sees that to preserve her sanity in the present, she must challenge that judgment and accept what she has done in the past:

Kill or forgive? Still does the bed ooze blood?
Let it drip down till every floor-plank rot!
Yet shall I answer, challenging the judgment:-
'Kill, strike the blow again, spite what shall come.'
'Kill, strike, again, again,' the bees in chorus hum.

The speaker's dilemma is now clearly resolved; and perhaps this was the way in which the 'woman', or the sensitive and poetic side of Robert's nature, sought to come to terms with having fought in the Great War. If so, it was not wholly successful. Robert had realized for some time that he could only find peace of mind by challenging the Christian judgment of his upbringing, but he could never entirely shake it off.

Fortunately Nancy, however difficult she was at times, remained extremely sympathetic to Robert's mental sufferings; and sometimes, when she proposed a sudden 'burst for freedom', it was not just to satisfy a private whim, but to distract Robert from one of his gloomy moods by providing a change of scenery.

One evening towards the end of August, for example, feeling perhaps that she and Robert needed some time alone, Nancy suddenly told him: 'I must get away somewhere out of this for a change. Let's go off on bicycles somewhere.' Leaving Margaret to look after the children, they 'packed a few things and rode off in the general direction of Devonshire. The nights were coldish and we had not brought blankets. We found that the best way was to bicycle by night and sleep by day. We went over Salisbury Plain past several deserted army camps; they had a ghostly look.'[101] Finding themselves near Dorchester, they turned in to visit Thomas Hardy, whom they had met not long ago when he had come up to Oxford to be awarded an honorary doctorate. Hardy gave them tea and dinner and put them up for a night. It was a memorable visit, and Robert kept a record of their conversation, which ranged from Nancy's keeping her own name ('Why, you *are* old-fashioned,' said Hardy. 'I knew a couple here sixty years ago that did the same') to the future of free verse, which Hardy felt could come to nothing in England, adding humbly: 'All we can do is to write on the old themes in the old styles, but try to do a little better than those who went before us.'[102]

It was a happy time for Robert and Nancy, and they bicycled on to Tiverton in Devonshire, where they stayed for a few days with Nancy's old nurse. Nancy was very fond of her, but unfortunately this visit brought a great deal of trouble in its wake. For the nurse kept a fancy-goods shop, and Nancy 'helped her dress the shop-window and advised her about framing the prints that she was selling. She also gave the shop a good turn-out, dusted the stock, and took her turn behind the counter.' When Nancy learned that as a result of her work the takings had gone up for a few weeks, she began to think that she had found an easy way of making money. Why should she not start her own shop on Boar's Hill?[103]

CHAPTER
7
THE SHOP
ON PARNASSUS

Robert was soon as enthusiastic as Nancy about her new idea. At the time, there was no shop within several miles of Boar's Hill; and a traditional village shop, serving a large and wealthy residential district, should have every chance of success. A steady income from such a venture had obvious attractions: no more running into debt, and having to be bailed out by family or friends; and no reason for Robert, once he had completed his degree, to find any other profession to supplement his income from writing. In addition, running a shop would satisfy Nancy's desire to be independent, though married.

For it was to be Nancy's business; and she went into partnership not with Robert but with a near neighbour, the Hon. Mrs Michael Howard, who 'undertook to keep the books while Nancy did most of the other work'. Another neighbour rented them the corner of a field not far away; and they employed a carpenter to build a wooden shop there to Nancy's design, at a cost of £50.[104]

However, Robert had undertaken to help Nancy while the summer vacation lasted; and even while the new business was at the planning stage, it occupied a great deal of his time and energy, so that in mid-September, when John, newly-appointed editor of *The Carthusian*, wrote asking Robert for a contribution, he replied:

> I'll send ... what I can, when I can – but have nothing at all, & written nothing for weeks ... Margaret has been away on her holidays (first for two years) & as we have no servants, no gas, no taps, no shops within 4 miles in fact no bloody anything (except me who has the toothache & no dentists because it's the weekend) we are having a busy time.[105]

Towards the end of September 1920 Robert managed a brief visit to London, where he met Sassoon, and also took to Secker his *Pier-Glass* collection of poems, which Secker told him that he wanted to publish 'at once'.[106] But this short literary excursion was followed by still more work on the shop, which opened early in October. On the 7th of that month Robert wrote to Eddie

Marsh, thanking him for a 'large and timely' royalty cheque from his contributions to one of the *Georgian Poetry* volumes; and telling him that he was 'worn out from much work, chiefly in the last few weeks, helping Nancy with her shop she has sportingly started up here'.[107]

A week and a half later news about the shop reached Erinfa, from where Amy reported anxiously to John: 'I hear that Nancy & David look radiant but Robby looks pale & worried & says he's overworked & Jenny is actually smaller than David now & not placid.' However, the shop was doing extremely well. In the first week they had turned-over £37 worth of goods; which, allowing for a profit of twopence halfpenny in the shilling, gave them a net profit of approximately seven pounds and fourteen shillings: in those days a very respectable weekly income.[108]

In an attempt to increase sales still further, Robert's brother Charles was called upon for help. Charles was now editor of *Isis*, an Oxford undergraduate magazine which appeared weekly during term time; and he included the following item in his 20 October number:

> I understand that under the auspices of the wives of the major and minor poets on Boar's Hill (*alias* O.P., *alias* the Oxford Parnassus) a shop has just been started there. Though it is underselling Oxford considerably, it is nevertheless paying well, and as light refreshment is provided, minor versifiers might do worse than go there and 'sometimes counsel take, and sometimes tea.' It is certainly a surer way to get to know these celebrities than frequenting their hairdressers.[109]

Charles also contacted the national press, so that within a few days of his own article appearing there were pictures of 'Miss Nicholson' and her shop in both the *Daily Mirror* and the *Daily Mail*.[110] However, the bantering tone of Charles's writing had thoroughly irritated Robert,[111] and he was still more annoyed by the light-hearted manner in which, in the same number of the *Isis*, Charles reported on a poetry-reading given by the American poet Vachel Lindsay.

Robert was very proud of the fact that it was he who had persuaded Sir Walter Raleigh, the Professor of English at Oxford University, 'to get Lindsay a hearing'. Robert had been looking forward to the poetry-reading as 'a unique event',[112] and afterwards wrote home to say that it had been a great success. Charles however printed a story in which he made fun of Lindsay. One of Lindsay's poems had apparently been recited 'in a kind of moan'; another, entitled 'The Congo', had been introduced as 'a study of the Negro Race', and had been divided into three parts – 1) Their Basic Savagery, 2) Their Irrepressible High Spirits and 3) Their Hope of Religion. This poem most certainly achieved its objective. Never have I seen Basic Savagery or Irrepressible High Spirits so truthfully expressed. Mr. Lindsay did a kind of jazz dance while reciting this poem, which was very effective.

I noticed a number of our younger poets listening with great interest. Let us hope that the howl and dance habit won't spread. Just fancy Mr. Austin reciting his poems while dancing a minuet, or the Poet Laureate howling his hexameters to a lively fox-trot.[113]

Robert was thoroughly irritated by this article; and he was still more annoyed when a week later, on 27 October 1920, Charles published an extremely teasing article about T.E. Lawrence. The 'Isis Idol' feature, usually used to give a highly favourable portrayal of a leading figure in Oxford, was headed 'Mr. T.E. LAWRENCE (Arabia and All Souls)' and described how the *Isis* correspondent (almost certainly Charles himself) had found Lawrence 'sound asleep in bed at eleven-thirty in the morning'.[114] Three days later Robert wrote to John telling him angrily that 'Charles as Editor of the *Isis* has reached his final goal of utter Carolosity: he'll end up as a Lord Northcliffe, and be as rich, powerful, and unhappy as anyone can wish.'[115]

Robert was angry because, as he explained to John, he now spent 'most of my time at Oxford with Col. Lawrence the man who smashed the Turks in Arabia & Palestine: he is at All Souls & a great man on poetry, pictures, music & everything else in the world.'[116] At their first meeting the previous November Robert had 'felt a sudden extraordinary sympathy' with Lawrence; and this feeling persisted, although Robert was later told that everyone was fascinated by Lawrence, and therefore 'tried to dismiss [it] . . . as extravagant'.[117] The truth is that Lawrence had a great gift for reflecting back to people the best of which they were capable; and he sustained Robert's sense of his worth both as a poet and as a human being at a time when he was increasingly full of self-doubt.

In return, Robert drew Lawrence into the literary world: after the Vachel Lindsay poetry-reading, for example, it had been arranged that Lawrence should give lunch in his rooms not only to Robert and Nancy, but also to Lindsay and Lindsay's mother; and in due course Robert gave Lawrence introductions to Hardy, Blunden and Sassoon. Between lectures Graves often visited All Souls where Lawrence, who never drank himself, 'used always to send his scout for a silver goblet of audit ale for me . . . it was as soft as barley-water but of great strength.' The two men 'talked most about poetry'.[118] For a while Lawrence acted as chief critic, so that Graves's poem 'The Pier-Glass' was dedicated 'To T.E. Lawrence, who helped me with it';[119] and he may even have provided Graves with themes: 'Children of Darkness', for example, reflects Lawrence's odd views on procreation:

> We spurred our parents to the kiss,
> Though doubtfully they shrank from this –
> Day had no courage to review
> What lusty dark alone might do –
> Then were we joined from their caress
> In heat of midnight, one from two.[120]

Robert's anger with Charles for his mocking article about Lawrence was balanced by a greater regard than ever for John, whose first *Carthusian* contained an innovative literary supplement including one of a cycle of poems which Robert had written about the Blundens' landlady Delilah Becker, a Boar's Hill cottager who had reputedly murdered her husband.[121] If the story was true, she had done so under extreme provocation, like the woman in 'The Pier-Glass'; and Robert had taken a great liking to her. Now he was pleased to see 'Delilah's Parrot' in print, and wrote to John: 'You are a great lad & I only wish we saw more of you.'[122]

Robert also had much time for Edmund Blunden. In June, Graves had written to Marsh asking him to accept the Blundens 'as a sacred charge', and describing Edmund as 'the "intrinsically" (whatever that means) best fellow I've met since I left school (Siegfried only excluded)'. Blunden was 'going to beat the lot of us as a poet if he goes on at the present rate';[123] and in October Graves was 'awfully glad Blunden has had such a success' with his new collection of poems, *The Waggoner*.[124]

Graves's estimate of Blunden's worth seems a fair one; but in general his critical judgments had remained not only forceful, but highly independent, and this was beginning to alarm his less imaginative tutors. When in mid-November APG spent a few days in Oxford, he was allowed to attend a tutorial at which Robert read out an essay on Wordsworth and Coleridge. Robert's tutor, Simpson, listened with interest but then commented that although it was quite acceptable for Robert to put his own views forward, he must do so discreetly, 'under cover of other people's criticisms'.[125] These efforts to keep Robert in check were unsuccessful, and a few months later, in a private interview, Simpson confided to APG that although he had a very high opinion of Robert's talent, he was 'greatly wanting in literary perspective, e.g. his attack on Burke, for which he was forced to call him a silly young ass, and Pope'.[126]

Alfred had spent a night at Boar's Hill, where he was shown over the shop, and where he enjoyed watching Nancy, Rosaleen and Robert playing together in a local hockey match. The next family visitors were John and Amy, who stayed with Robert and Nancy for a few days in December. John was waiting to hear whether he had won an award to Oxford, where he was hoping to read Classics.[127] Like Robert before him, he was disappointed to learn that he had won nothing in the first group of colleges; but on 20 December there was a great celebration at Dingle Cottage when it was learned that he had been given a scholarship worth £80 per annum by St John's.

Robert and Nancy then spent a quiet Christmas at home with Margaret and their children. Amy had taken Rosaleen, Charles and John winter-sporting in Austria, while APG, who was very sad not to have all his family round him at Christmas, visited Clarissa at her place of work in Cheshire. Then, early in January 1921, despite both the appalling weather and his advancing age – he was now well into his 75th year – Alfred Perceval Graves set out for Oxford, arriving there

> in a storm of rain ... [I] had to go to Boar's Hill in a hansom. It took 1¼ hours against the driving rain and wind which blew out one of our lights. Finally I reached Dingle Cottage when John Masefield most kindly lent me a lantern to go down in the dark to Dingle Cottage and helped down my heavy box with his powerful arm. Diccon Hughes who was staying there also helped. I gave the man 10/6 to his complete satisfaction and then had a warm welcome and hot supper from Robert and Nancy, both looking very well: and so rather tired to bed.[128]

Alfred stayed with Robert and Nancy for ten days. In many ways it was an enjoyable and relaxing holiday: he was given breakfast in bed every day, and then had a leisurely time visiting friends in Oxford or on Boar's Hill.[129] But one morning, when there was heavy rain, APG was given some of Robert's poems to read, including a revised version of 'The Pier-Glass', from which it was easy to see the mental burdens under which Robert was labouring.[130] That afternoon, the weather cleared, and Robert and Nancy went off to play hockey against Abingdon. They returned flushed with success (they had won 6–2 and Robert had scored four of the winning goals) to find that Alfred, worried by his son's state of mind, had spent almost the whole afternoon working on the text of a treatise which Robert was writing *On English Poetry*; and after supper, when his son and daughter-in-law had gone to bed, the old man toiled on into the night.[131]

On the morning of Monday 17 January, when APG had been staying at Dingle Cottage for a week, Robert decided that it was a good moment to begin a long talk about business. Alfred now learned for the first time that

Robert was 'in some difficulties about the shop'. Exactly what had been going wrong with the business remains obscure. Probably it had been under-capitalized from the start; certainly, there had been an expensive and ill-judged expansion after the initial success. Now Mrs Howard had announced that she wanted to withdraw her capital and to cease being a partner. No doubt her bookkeeping had shown her that all was not well, and she wanted to get out while there was still time. Robert and Nancy still had hopes for the business, and APG was told that '£170 in addition to the £30 already advanced would enable [them] to settle bills with the wholesale people and buy Mrs. Howard out'.[132]

Alfred did not feel that he could give an immediate answer. The winter sports holiday for which Amy had budgeted so carefully had meant withdrawing £180 from the bank; there was no more spare cash; and therefore sufficient money to meet Robert's needs could only be raised by digging into capital. To begin with APG talked instead about ways in which Robert and Nancy might become more self-sufficient.[133]

Their conversation was not a great success. For reasons which at the time were totally obscure to APG, Robert had already turned down an amazingly generous offer. Sir Walter Raleigh, who clearly appreciated Robert's intelligence and his independent spirit, had suggested that he should become the Sandhurst Professor of English Literature.[134] But this had not been acceptable to Robert, who now proceeded to turn down two ideas which APG had been discussing on his behalf with Blackwell: a book on Skelton, Robert's favourite poet; and the editing of a 'Library of Satire'. All that came out of the conversation was an agreement that father and son should collaborate on The Hobby Horse, an idea for a popular musical play to include a large number of folk-songs; and in his diary that evening Alfred noted: 'Altogether [Robert] seems depressed & I feel monetary help at this crisis w[oul]d mean a great deal to him.'[135]

Robert spent Tuesday afternoon in Oxford doing 'an exam on his vacation exercises', while his wife and father walked over to Gilbert Murray's open-air theatre, where they watched Diccon Hughes playing Theseus in a production of Murray's translation of the *Hippolytus*. That evening Alfred 'had great talks about the Play & other matters' with Nancy;[136] and before long he decided to tell her that he would definitely give Robert the money which was needed.

Two days later Alfred left Dingle Cottage after a particularly affectionate parting from Robert and Nancy, and travelled straight to Wimbledon. There, despite the lack of money in his account, he persuaded Barclays Bank to allow him to send his son a cheque for £170. Amy returned from Austria that evening,[137] and was not at all pleased when she learned that her first duty the next day would be to go to Wimbledon herself, 'to sell out stock to meet Robert and Nancy's £200'.[138] Indeed, she made her displeasure widely felt, and one result was that increased pressure was placed on John to gain a leaving exhibition from Charterhouse. Robert and Nancy themselves sent a grateful thank-you letter for the cheque, and mentioned that they were also receiving practical help from one of Nancy's aunts, who was actually working at the shop.

Unfortunately this improvement in Robert's affairs was only temporary; and it did nothing to ease the domestic tension which indirectly contributed to the collapse of the business. Artists rarely make good shopkeepers; and both for Robert and for his family the shop on Parnassus was an expensive and time-wasting mistake.

CHAPTER
8
FINANCIAL WRECKAGE
AND
'THE LOWEST
OF SPIRITS'

While Alfred Perceval Graves was staying at Dingle Cottage in January 1921, he had learned from Margaret that she and Nancy took 'a different view of looking after children', and that Robert was 'evidently exercised about their divergent views'.[139] Nancy had begun to feel that Jenny and David were seriously at risk from Margaret's kindly but 'old-fashioned' methods of child care, and the tension between the two women became so unbearable that by the end of January Margaret became ill with nerves.[140] A doctor advised a complete rest, and on 1 February Robert sent a reply-paid wire to Erinfa asking if his parents would have Margaret for three weeks, 'and if possible at once'.

This request came at a difficult moment: Alfred's sister Lily was about to descend upon Erinfa after 'a very bad time' in London, and, as Amy explained to John, it would be 'very awkward to have [Margaret] with Aunt Lily, as M expects to sit at table & of course Aunt L. is a Tory and would hate it'. However, Amy felt that it was her duty to wire: 'Immediately. Will do our best, Mother.' She only showed her displeasure by avoiding the use of 'the word welcome as I really did not feel it'.[141]

Margaret arrived at Erinfa on Thursday 3 February; and the following Sunday APG was walking with her to church when, under the influence of his sympathetic interest, she began telling him how difficult her life had become. Although devoted to Robert and the children, she was very much upset by their lack of religion, and by having been forbidden to teach Jenny any prayers; she also considered that Nancy, though 'more social' than before, had been 'spoilt by father and mother; is all for her own views and Robert does not care to differ with her'.[142]

There was news too about the Sandhurst Professorship. From what Margaret said, APG concluded that Robert had probably turned it down because it had been 'coupled with some requirement about Nancy's falling in more with the "convenances" in a place where her calling herself Mrs. Nicholson and wearing the breeches would be much canvassed'.[143] In other respects the professorship would have suited Robert very well: he had gained extensive lecturing experience during the war, and had followed it up since: on the very evening of APG's conversation with Margaret, Robert was lecturing, in Sassoon's presence, to the Oxford Labour Club.[144]

Once Margaret had left Dingle Cottage, Nancy announced to Robert that she would not have her back again under any circumstances. Before long Robert was equally concerned about Margaret's 'bad influence', and he wrote to Sassoon a few weeks later explaining that Margaret had been 'unbearable and ... dishonest (not financial but [she] was spoiling Jenny's health without our knowledge)'.[145] Amy was informed of the decision to sack Margaret, and was given a letter of dismissal to pass on to her, together with the instruction that Margaret must never return to Dingle Cottage, and must never again see the children.[146]

Poor Margaret! To be turned away so abruptly when, as Amy wrote to John, she had been 'almost the mistress of the house, having charge of the money & giving R and N pocket-money weekly out of their own money'. Amy did her best to see Nancy's point of view, and recalled that she herself had considered Margaret to be too emotional in her dealings with the children. Yet she recognized that Margaret 'loved Jenny like her own child & the break was terribly painful'.[147] Margaret was working at a doll's dress for Jenny when told of her dismissal; and she cried out: '"Oh my Jenny! My darling Jenny!" in floods of tears.' APG, who witnessed this miserable scene, wrote in his diary that evening: 'I hope Nancy will get as faithful a servant in her place.'[148]

Margaret's sudden departure came as a severe shock for Jenny, a highly-strung little girl who later attempted to secure her own position in the family by telling her apparently capricious parents exactly what they wanted to hear, whether it was true or not.

It had been agreed that Margaret should work out her month's notice at Erinfa, with Robert paying her wages; but he sent no money, so Amy paid what was due and then, early in March, she wrote to Robert asking for reimbursement.[149] When Robert replied, he said nothing about the money he owed, but explained his long silence. He and Nancy had been on the way to Rottingdean, where they intended to have a few days by the sea, when the children fell ill with influenza and had to be nursed in lodgings. Robert himself had been suffering from a 'touch of shell shock', and Nancy was also unwell. Robert added that Nancy intended not to replace Margaret, but to do without a nurse and to look after the children herself. Recording this news in his diary, APG followed it with the single despairing word: 'How?'[150] And then a week later, to add to the increasing gloom at Erinfa, Charles wrote to say that there seemed little chance of Robert's taking a degree, because 'he is not really working'.

What had happened was that the 'touch of shell-shock' was far worse than Robert had indicated; indeed, he later recalled that 'War horror overcame me again'.[151] It was a desperate time both for him and for Nancy, relieved only by two things: the publication by Secker of *The Pier-Glass*, and the generosity of T.E. Lawrence, who made Robert 'a present of four articles to publish in America', for three of which he was subsequently paid £200. The unhappy state of Robert's mind can be seen from his reply to Edmund Blunden's letter congratulating him on *The Pier-Glass*. He began by telling Blunden that Mrs Howard was 'intent on ruining us', went on to attack Constance Masefield (who had eventually found Nancy a rather tiresome neighbour), and said that he was 'tired of Boars Hill, too many BB's (chiefly female) about. Show me a nice healthy hill in Suffolk and a cottage, and we'll come like a shot.'[152]

Since Robert was not well enough to deal with customers, and Nancy was spending the whole of each day with Jenny and David, they had to put a manager into the shop. But by this time the business was beyond saving. Robert had retained a personal following, but latterly this had been based as much upon his unorthodox business methods as upon his celebrity. To his amusement he had found that if he charged two different prices for the same quality of vegetable, and placed them side by side on his counter, the wealthier residents of Boar's Hill would automatically select the ones at an artificially inflated price. This meant that impoverished cottagers like old Mrs Becker could buy their vegetables on the cheap. Once this experiment in practical socialism came to an end or, as Robert wrote to Eddie Marsh, 'once the personal touch was removed', trade slumped.[153] Before long the weekly receipts were down to £20 and falling, and the moment came when the manager's salary was more than the profits.

The strain on both Robert and Nancy increased day by day. By mid-March, realizing that he was becoming too ill to cope with anything, Robert very sensibly changed his mind about the dangers of seeking professional help,[154] and went to Cambridge to consult Dr Rivers. Rivers immediately sent him on to McDowell, a London nerve specialist who told Robert that if he wanted to avoid a total breakdown he must stop all work at once, and must postpone his degree for at least a year.

Announcing all this in a letter which reached Erinfa on 4 April, Robert added that he would probably be favourably reassessed for his Army Pension, that his father-in-law had promised him a small allowance, and that he hoped to secure work reading poetry for a small publisher. But there was no chance at all of continuing to run the shop: not only was he unwell, but 'Nancy has broken down too'. Amy became dreadfully anxious, and during the next few days she first wrote to Robert, and then wired to Nancy, asking her to bring the children to Erinfa, and sending the railway fare. However, nothing more was heard from Boar's Hill for ten days.

During that time, Robert was desperately trying to salvage something from the financial wreckage. He might at least have recovered his original expenditure if he had been allowed to sell the shop as a going concern to an interested firm of grocers from Oxford; but Mrs Masefield prevailed upon their landlord 'not to let any ordinary business firm take over the shop from us and spoil the local amenities',[155] and so, as Robert wrote to Eddie Marsh on 13 April, thanking him for some *Georgian Poetry* royalties:

> The long and short is that we have to quit and sell up almost at once. ... We can't afford to live on the hill, our cottage is unhealthy and our neighbours are not neighbourly so we are hoping to move to WORLD'S END, ISLIP with the money from Lawrence's articles he gave me before he went off [on a diplomatic mission to the Middle East], if we can get the lawyer to raise the remaining purchase money on mortgage; and there live in true country sentiment, not this suburban squalor. But it's a baddish outlook at the moment, especially as Nancy is feeling the strain even more than I.[156]

Later Robert told Virginia Woolf that Nancy had said to him that she 'must have a house for nothing; on a river; in a village with a square church tower; near but not on a railway'.[157] There was indeed a house on the edge of the village of Islip, about five miles to the north-east of Oxford, which almost exactly fitted this description. The only problem was that instead of being available for nothing, it was on the market for over £500. It seemed a hopeless task to raise this amount of money, and Nancy's next actions might be unkindly construed as an attempt to 'soften-up' her long-suffering in-laws, whose outstanding grievances, chiefly that they were owed money, and that Nancy would not bring the children to stay at Erinfa, were rapidly dealt with. On 14 April Alfred and Amy received 'a very welcome letter from Nancy enclosing £9 odd and asking for full particulars of what they owe';[158] and then on the 23rd a wire arrived with the news that Robert and Nancy would come in two days' time 'with a nurse and the two children'.[159]

They arrived at Harlech station, at the foot of the great Castle Rock, on Monday 25 April, and found Alfred and Amy waiting for them on the platform.

APG walked home with Robert by the short cut, across the flat land and then steeply up through the woods below Erinfa; while Amy took the women and children home in a carriage. To begin with, there was no hint of the trouble that they were in, and APG noted how well Nancy and the children were looking. That evening, Robert showed his father some of his latest poems, which were much admired; and then they played two rubbers of bridge against Amy and John, who was also holidaying at Erinfa.[160] The following day, the weather was wonderfully fine, and Robert and his father went for a walk in the Talsarnau direction, with Robert merrily singing 'Kennst du das Land?' on the way.

Robert's cheerfulness was genuine: Harlech always improved his spirits; and Nancy was making a special effort to be agreeable. On Wednesday morning she helped Amy to collect some eggs from Talsarnau; later that day she had her first lessons in bridge, Alfred and Amy's favourite card-game; and it was only that evening that she and Robert began talking about their difficulties, saying that they were very keen on the house at Islip, but that it was doubtful whether they had enough money to take on a mortgage. In his diary Alfred wrote gloomily: 'We have not yet got to the bottom of their troubles';[161] and the next day he and Amy

> had a heart to heart talk with Robert & Nancy ab[ou]t their affairs which are in a very serious state & indeed they owe nearly £500 in connection with the shop: the man they put in charge cannot spare more time & has put things into the hands of a sol[icito]r who asks for an immediate sale. Nor will the B[ui]lding Society advance money for Islip. We have persuaded Nancy to ask her father to save them & to get the manager of the shop to go on for a week, pending the result of her interview with him.[162]

It was arranged that Nancy should travel down to London to see her father on 2 May, the following Monday; and in the meantime Amy had 'a straight talk' with Nancy, and was astonished to find that she appeared not to mind very much about the threat of bankruptcy.

After visiting William Nicholson, who promised to send what money he could, Nancy made her way back to Boar's Hill. From there she reported to Robert that Mrs Masefield had kindly agreed to pay £50 for the shed which they had put up in her garden; and that there was a chance that a Mrs O'Connor would take on the shop if allowed to do so by their landlord. In addition, the lawyers had offered better mortgage terms through the owners of the Islip house.

This was encouraging news for Robert, who had just received another £10 of *Georgian Poetry* royalties, and had also heard that he had been awarded a small government grant. In the meantime his literary work was going well, and on Saturday 7 May he completed a draft of his book *On English Poetry* before going for a long walk and then having a swim in the sea. The following day he was feeling companionable enough to go to church with his father, and after the service the two men jointly wrote a poem called 'The Table and the Pack' which they sent off to *Life* magazine.

Monday morning, however, brought a dreadfully depressing letter from Nancy about their prospects. Even after her father's generous contribution, which took the form of a £100 note sent in a matchbox, they were still desperately short of money. Robert was plunged into a state of misery; and the next day, Tuesday 10 May 1921, was described by Alfred as

one of the most anxious days in our lives; for it was evident that Robert was in the lowest of spirits and he had a summons from Nancy to go and help her out of her difficulties, so he hastily made up his mind to go by the 11.30 train [leaving Jenny and David to be looked after by their new nurse, Dorothy], and he and Amy took his traps down the hill while I sent off a telegram announcing his going to Nancy. Sitting talking to him after Amy had said goodbye and gone to see about the draining operations at her cottages below the Station, I determined to help him with the Islip House, and I said I would talk it over with his Mother and wire. He went off ... and I then had a great talk with Amy and finally she agreed to a letter to the owner of the house to be forwarded to Robert – and to a telegram to him. The affair coming at lunch-time upset Amy's digestion and she was quite ill till bed-time.[163]

Alfred's idea was that Amy should buy 'The World's End', and that Robert should become her tenant. This was an inspired plan. It is most unlikely that Amy would have agreed to the outright gift of another substantial sum of money. The Boar's Hill shop had recently swallowed up another £200; and she was too shrewd not to realize that more money might very easily go the same way. Alfred's scheme meant that she would retain control of her capital; and if Robert paid a proper rent, then the rescue operation need not impose any additional strain upon their own finances.

Robert was delighted with the proposed arrangement, and wrote to APG saying how glad he was to be his tenant at Islip and placing his debts outside the capital ones at about £15. For the next few weeks, Dorothy and the children remained at Erinfa while Alfred negotiated the purchase of the Islip house. To begin with the vendors held out for more money than seemed reasonable, and time began to run short, as Robert and Nancy had given in their notice to the Masefields, and promised to be out of Dingle Cottage by the end of the June Quarter. On 20 May Amy wrote to John telling him: 'It is all very worrying & lies like a blight upon us.'[164]

However by 25 May the vendors had accepted an offer of £525 for The World's End;[165] and meanwhile a solicitor was dealing with the shop on Boar's Hill. Since it could not be sold as a going concern, the stock was disposed of at bankrupt prices. For the time being no one could be found to buy the building, which in any case would have to be broken up and sold for the value of its timber; but the sale of the stock, the sale of the garden shed to Mrs Masefield, and the gift from Nancy's father, enabled them to reduce their debts to the wholesalers and others to around £200; and that would be covered by the sale of the Lawrence articles.[166]

The huge burden of debt was gradually being lifted, and there was also the prospect of a fresh start at Islip. Robert, as he completed a revised version of his book *On English Poetry*, soared out of his depression into a state of great excitement. On 29 May he wrote to Sassoon, enclosing a typescript of his new work, and telling him: 'I am feeling very conceited and want taking down; I dare say when domestic troubles vanish and I no longer feel the necessity of cheering myself up with self-praise about my writing I will be all right. But at present, as you may gather, I am insufferable.'[167] The chasm had appeared to yawn wide just a footstep ahead of him; and in his near-miraculous escape from total ruin Robert began to feel that he had been pre-served by destiny for some great achievement. The very name of 'Islip' became somehow symbolic of this feeling. For many months Robert had felt 'a curious affinity' with the poet John Skelton,[168] of whom he wrote a few years later:

> Skelton has had a stronger influence on my work than any other poet alive or dead: particularly I have admired in him the mixture of scholarship and extravaganza, his honest outspokenness and unconventionality in life and writing, his humour, his poetic craftsmanship, and, in spite of appear-ance, his deep religious sense.[169]

And in the story of Skelton's life there had been an Abbot Islip who had befriended him when he was compelled to take sanctuary in Westminster Abbey. It was in this exalted mood, feeling that some higher power was protecting and guiding him, that Robert had completed *On English Poetry*, which turned out to be a highly autobiographical tract about the poetic life.

CHAPTER
9
ON ENGLISH POETRY

Robert Graves's book *On English Poetry* was dedicated to his friends and mentors Lawrence and Rivers, and was offered as 'notebook reflections ... based on the rules which regulate my own work at present'.[170] It was a brave act to expose his working practices to the public eye, and his book is full of interesting ideas. In one section, for example, he seems to anticipate Professor Housman's famous pronouncement in his 1922 lecture 'The Name and Nature of Poetry', that poetry finds its way 'to something in man which is obscure and latent, something older than the present organisation of his nature, like the patches of fen which still linger here and there in the drained lands of Cambridgeshire'.[171] Graves also believes that poetry is set apart from the normal run of things, a mysterious survivor from a forgotten past; it is, he declares, 'a modified descendant of primitive Magic'.[172]

The emotional landscape of much of the best in Graves's own poetry had been set down very clearly in his *Country Sentiment* poem 'Rocky Acres'. Like his earliest *Carthusian* poem,[173] it describes the apparently timeless lands to the east of Erinfa:

> Time has never journeyed to this lost land,
>   Crakeberries and heather bloom out of date,
> The rocks jut, the streams flow singing on either hand,
>   Careless if the season be early or late.
> The skies wander overhead, now blue, now slate:
> Winter would be known by his cold cutting snow
> If June did not borrow his armour also.[174]

It is a land of beauty, legend and alarming power, described in another verse of the same poem as:

> Bold immortal country whose hill-tops have stood
> Strongholds for the proud gods when on earth they go,
> Terror for fat burghers in far plains below.

In another poem, 'Unicorn and the White Doe', written for the *Country Sentiment* collection, but then set aside and used several years later in *Whipperginny*,[175] Graves had written a striking parable about the poetic life. The poet is seen as a Unicorn, and his muse is described as the White Doe: perhaps the first description by Graves of the magical source of inspiration to which he later referred as the 'White Goddess'. First the Doe introduces herself:

> 'Alone
> Through forests evergreen,
> By legend known,
> By no eye seen,
> Unmated,
> Unbaited,
> Untrembling between
> The shifting shadows,
> The sudden echoes,
> Deathless I go
> Unheard, unseen,'
> Says the White Doe.

Then comes the Unicorn, and he pursues the White Doe without success, asking despairingly:

> 'Where are you fled from me?
>   I pursue, you fade;
> I run, you hide from me
>   In the dark glade.'

To which the White Doe replies:

> 'Seek me not here
> Lodged among mortal deer,'
> Says the White Doe;
> Keeping one place,
> Held by the ties of Space,'
> Says the White Doe.

Instead, she is to be found:

> 'Under shadow of myrtle
> With Phoenix and his Turtle
> For all time true;
> With Gryphons at grass

> Under the Upas
> Sipping warm dew
> That falls hourly new;
> I, unattainable
> Complete, incomprehensible,
> No mate for you.
> In sun's beam
> Or star-gleam
> No mate for you,
> No mate for you,'
> Says the White Doe.

This source of inspiration, which Robert had once glimpsed, appeared to be unattainable now that he was a married man, and his poetic relations with Nancy were complicated by domesticity. For the time being, therefore, his ideas about poetry had taken another turning, and he was seeking to explain it in terms of psychology. So he declares in his book *On English Poetry* that 'an emotional conflict is necessary for the birth of true poetry', because he has come to see the principal function of poetry as the resolution of conflicts within the mind of the poet.

Poetry can therefore be written only by a particular type of suffering individual, for whom poetry, or 'the unforeseen fusion in the mind of apparently contradictory ideas', might be described as 'a form of psycho-therapy'. In Robert's own case, he is prepared to say, like the biblical character inhabited by a host of devils: 'My name is Legion: for we are many.' As he explains:

> Two or three poets of my acquaintance have admitted (I can confirm it from my own experience) that they are frequently conscious of their own divided personalities; that is, they adopt an entirely different view of life, a different vocabulary, gesture, intonation, according as they happen to find themselves, for instance, in clerical society, in sporting circles, or among labourers in inns.

This leads to a tremendous difficulty in remaining loyal; but the poet, described elsewhere in the book as 'the outsider who sees most of the game', is able to find 'a certain compensation in the excitement of doing the quick change'. Analysing his own sudden shifts of mood, Robert states that a poet may well be liable 'to sudden excitement, delight or disgust with ideas for which mature consideration entirely alters the values, or with people who change from mere acquaintances to intimate friends and back again in a flash'. As their values change, Robert tells us, poets 'of good family' might well find that their relatives are 'scandalized by their subsequent adoption of unusual social habits'. And he adds the warning: 'Poets who modify the general ethical principles first taught them at home and at school, can only afford to purchase the right to do so at a great price of mental suffering and difficult thinking.'

Describing the actual process of composing a poem, Graves compares the mind of a poet to 'an international conference', with delegates and a chairman. After much debate, they 'contrive to sign a report [which] reconciles the aparently hopeless disagreements of all factions ... [factions which may be described as] the poet's sub-personalities'.

But poetry is not something of merely private significance. As the chairman, or the 'controlling personality' within the poet's mind becomes stronger, so the poet may develop into 'a more or less capable spokesman of that larger group-mind of his culture. ... [And the result is that] men of smaller scope ... hear at times in his utterances what seems to them the direct voice of God.' This is a large claim for poetry, which some might find arrogant; but Graves rightly insists upon arrogance, for without it no artist is likely to attempt any great work; and he qualifies his insistence by explaining of himself and his fellow poets: 'They have most arrogance before writing their poem of the moment, most humility when they know that they have once more failed.'

CHAPTER
10
A LETTER
FROM CHARLES

Towards the end of May 1921 Nancy travelled alone to Erinfa, where she stayed for three or four days before returning to Boar's Hill with Jenny, David and their nurse Dorothy. She was no longer on her best behaviour, and APG noted crossly in his diary:

> She is very frank about how they call and accept or refuse invites, making excuses when they don't care to go. She still wears a land-girl's dress and had to tell [two Harlech ladies] yesterday that she was not working on the land, nor does she wear a wedding ring and [she] is very crude in her political views. I had some difficulty in proving to her that Lloyd George was not a swine.[76]

Then on Saturday 4 June, just as a period of unusual calm seemed to be descending upon the Graves family, APG received a 'very tumultuous' letter from Charles. His Finals were imminent; and he had suddenly been informed that besides the Literature papers which he was expecting, he was also required to pass a Divinity examination of which he had never even heard. In the circumstances he 'begged & begged ... to be let off & said it would drive him silly & he did not need a degree.'[77] Immediate action was clearly necessary; and Alfred decided that 'a personal interview with Charles after ascertaining the difficulty of "Divvers" was the only way of saving the situation and that this would also give us a chance of seeing [The World's End at] Islip, the "pig" which we had bought "in a poke" to save R. and N., so we got ready in hot haste.'[78] They arrived in Oxford that very day, discovered that 'Divvers' could be postponed until September, called Charles down, persuaded him to go ahead with his Finals; and finally went to bed 'much relieved in mind'.[79]

On Sunday, much to Robert and Nancy's surprise, Alfred, Amy, Charles and Rosaleen all arrived at Dingle Cottage for afternoon tea; and the following day Robert showed his parents over The World's End. Amy was impressed by Islip, which seemed to her to be 'forgotten by time and progress; it is very peaceful & old world & picturesque'. The house did not please her quite so much, as it had very low ceilings, and 'the most awkward stairs and steps'; but she hoped that 'they will get used to it', and noted that 'the little walled garden looks safe for the children'.[180]

After inspecting Robert's new home, all three of them had tea with the local vicar and his wife. He was a psychologist and she an artist, which pleased Alfred, who thought that they would make good friends for his son and daughter-in-law; and indeed Robert and the vicar seemed to get on extremely well. Amy felt less cheerful, as she could not help wondering what on earth the vicar's wife would have to say to 'ringless Mrs. Nicholson as Robby's wife'; and she wrote to John: 'It is such a pity for Nancy to have such awkward & misleading fads, while she is a good wife & mother.'[181]

When on 15 June 1921 Robert and Nancy finally moved into The World's End with Jenny and David, they were on their own. Dorothy, the nanny, had been let go;[182] and although the Boar's Hill shop had not yet been sold, there was no one in Islip who knew anything about their difficulties during the past ten months. It was a fresh beginning.

BOOK
SIX
THE WORLD'S END
1921–1925

CHAPTER
1
AN ISLIP SUMMER

To alight at Islip station after a journey of only ten minutes from Oxford was, as Robert and Nancy had discovered, to leave the modern world behind, and to find oneself on the northern edge of a peaceful and picturesque old village. It was also a flourishing community, and in the streets and lanes which clustered round St Nicholas's church were to be found a post office, a school, four public houses, two blacksmiths, and eight or nine shops, including two butchers, two bakers, and a general store. Walking southwards past the church and down King's Head Lane took them to a meeting of four roads, where the Swan public house overlooks the stone bridge which crosses the River Ray.

To the south of the Ray (a tributary of the River Cherwell) there was a stretch of what appeared at first sight to be open countryside; but thirty yards or so beyond the bridge Robert and Nancy could take a right turn into a narrow street running westward from the main road. This was Collice Street: on the northern side, a low stone wall with trees between it and the river; on the southern, a dozen or more terraced cottages; and then the street swung sharply round to the left.

On the outside of the bend, there was a large barn, and then a builder's yard; and round the corner they came to a cul-de-sac, on the right-hand side of which two stone cottages had been knocked together into a long, low house. This was 'The World's End, Collice Street, Islip', where Robert and Nancy were to spend the next four and a half years. They had come to the most peaceful corner of a traditional English village, far removed from the artificial writers' and artists' colony on Boar's Hill; and Robert's first reaction was to describe Islip to Edmund Blunden as 'Heaven', with its

Stone Houses. Cricket. An old stone bridge where there was a Civil War skirmish. Flowers. River. 4 Publics. A famous molecatcher. A square church. Gossips. ... The quarry from which Westminster Abbey came. Cows and other rustic birds including the whirry-dor and the piffle. ... A retired serjeant-major and a postman who was butler to My Lord the fifteenth Lord Valentia. A village schoolmaster with ambitions. Nip-cats playing at tip-cat but I have patented that rhyme and if you pinch it you shan't play on my lawn.[1]

There was no shop to worry about, and so Nancy, in the intervals of looking after Jenny and David, was very happily painting the stairs 'all colours, in semi darkness'.[2] Nor was there any great academic pressure: after consultations with Sir Walter Raleigh it had been agreed that instead of Robert's Finals being postponed for twelve months, he should altogether abandon his plans for a B.A. degree. Instead he should write at his leisure a thesis on 'The Illogical Element in English Poetry, with a study of its modification by Classical, and its exploitation by Romantic writers'. This, Sir Walter assured Robert, would lead to an honorary B.Litt., 'as certain[ly] as a cat having kittens'.[3]

While starting work on this thesis Robert also spent some of his time selecting poems for an edition of *Oxford Poetry* which Blackwell was to publish in the autumn;[4] and as he was doing work which he enjoyed, his mind remained tranquil. In the circumstances his preoccupation with Skelton became less obsessive; and he wrote an amusing letter in which he gently teased Blunden for a similar obsession of his, that he was a reincarnation of John Clare. 'Mr. Clare', Robert wrote to Edmund,

> Mr. Clare,
> 　Dear Sir,
> 　　or shall we say
> 　　　　　　Mr. Shakespere
> 　　　　　　　　　Most honoured sir,
> For indeed if Clare confidently thought he was Shakespere and you are Clare as I have no reason to doubt, therefore, etc., QED. It is quite possible on the other hand that I am Skelton, and your senior by a good many years. Let us only hope that Shakespere was not Skelton, or we get a 'which is absurd, therefore.'
> 　Anyhow, as I have also no doubt that we are goodish poets without any necessary preincarnation let's start all over again.
> 　With
> 　　'Robert Graves
> 　　　to Edmund Blunden greeting.'[5]

Robert was also corresponding with Robert Bridges, who had only become a friend towards the end of Robert's time on Boar's Hill. Graves had contributed a letter to a tract *On Hyphens, & Shall & Will* which had been published by 'The Society for Pure English' which Bridges had founded just before the war, and had now revived.⁶ After a meeting between the two men Bridges had arranged for Graves to be sent copies of all the tracts published so far; and on 20 June 1921 Robert wrote in reply:

> Very many thanks for the SPE tracts which have been forwarded here, & make me want very much to join the Society & help it as much as I can. ... What I meant when we were talking the other day was that the principle of purifying the language by the example of a more or less informal group of writers, and by the more indirect methods of propaganda is admirable; but that it would be far better for the language to remain slipshod & cloudy than to become hag-ridden by an Official Academy. ... But the purification is essential if, as I expect & hope, English is to become the World-Language; it has the pull over all competitors at present by being the language of trade.⁷

It is a peaceful kind of summer in which one has time to worry about the purification of the language; and Robert and Nancy had only one guest from the outside world at Islip: the Franciscan friar Father Giles, who came to stay with them during the third week of July.⁸ His philosophical calm may have helped them to come to terms with the fact, only recently discovered, that Nancy was once again pregnant.

CHAPTER
2
THE ARRIVAL
OF JOHN

After taking Third Class Honours, Robert's brother Charles had now left the university, and was working for Lord Beaverbrook on the *Daily Express* in London.[9] His place at St John's College was taken in the autumn of 1921 by my father, whom Robert found far more to his taste; though John, like Charles before him, reacted strongly against having been made to work so hard at Charterhouse, and despite being a scholar, he plunged almost at once into a life of sport and sociability. On Friday 14 October, three days after the start of the Michaelmas term, John was invited to lunch at The World's End; and so he cycled out to Islip, where, in his own words, he was

> introduced to Edmund Blunden and his nice wife – He seems very nervous and jumpy. Chopped wood and talked to Robert a bit – Ros arrived soon after on foot. We had a chicken for lunch – I went out to get some beer from the Swan … Jenny & David are delightful – Jenny a trifle shy & pensive perhaps … David toddles about on his immense, fat legs, and laughs loudly at everything – He and J[enny] play with one 'Jimmy', a small youth aged two & a half from the cottage opposite.[10]

From then on, Robert saw John on an informal but fairly regular basis once every week or ten days. On Monday 24 October, for example, Robert called in at St John's, talked pleasantly to his brother about 'playing a lot of football' for the Islip team; and then wandered through Oxford with him, chatting and doing a little desultory shopping. Six days later John cycled out to Islip for another Sunday lunch; and the following Friday afternoon Robert arrived unexpectedly at John's rooms with Nancy and the children, hoping to be given tea.

John was working on some Latin verses which had to be completed in time for a tutorial later in the day, so he suggested that Robert and his family should wander in the college gardens for half an hour while he completed his work; and he ordered tea at four o'clock. When they returned, John noticed that: 'They all ate largely, saying quite frankly that they hadn't eaten anything for close on a week (in the meat line, they meant); and I think they enjoyed themselves.' Before they left, John introduced Robert to a graduate from Toronto who had the rooms immediately opposite his own: it was Lester Pearson, who had already told John that he recalled being drilled by Robert at Wadham five years earlier.[11]

It was a successful meeting; and on Sunday, when John cycled out to Islip again for lunch, Pearson went with him. Rosaleen was also there; and soon they were eating 'an excellent lunch, with many vegetables, sausages, cherries & apples which I had brought, washed down with good cider.' It was a happy occasion, and Robert was in a cheerful mood as one of his most recent poems, 'The Sewing Basket', had been published in the latest *Spectator*.[12]

Despite his cheerfulness, Robert was once again short of money.[13] Unable to pay Amy the £4 rent due in September, he wore clothes which were beginning to look 'dilapidated', and he had started asking John for small sums of money. John himself had spent more than he meant to during his first few weeks in college; and by mid-November, finding himself with an overdraft, he wrote home enclosing his accounts and asking for more money. Amy was furious. She sent the necessary cheque, but pointed out that John had spent money on inessential items such as hot chocolate in the Cadena. He must learn to deny himself; and must not think, 'like dear Molly used to think, that if you put a thing down in your accounts it was therefore all right'.[14] Amy followed up this letter with another one telling John not to take any more visitors out to Islip for lunch: it was 'too much for our poor dear little people at present'; and she forbade him to lend Robert money, as 'it only means you have to come upon me for more. ... He must come to me or Mr. N if he cannot get on.'[15]

Some days later Robert arrived at St John's one morning 'rather swollen-faced', and suffering from an excruciatingly painful toothache. He helped John for a few minutes with some Latin verses, went to see his dentist, and returned for a late lunch 'in very bad spirits & all befuddled by the gas – and very cold. He ate his fish & pudding standing by the fire in a dazed way & then went to sleep on my sofa with a rug over him while I finished my verses.'[16] It was depressing seeing Robert not only unwell, but increasingly down at heel; and the very next day, as if to highlight the contrast between his two brothers, John was walking through Oxford when he 'ran straight into Charles of all people – very smart in a 12 guinea overcoat & blue suiting to match, bowler hat, and spats'.[17]

CHAPTER
3
CLARISSA
HELPS OUT

Robert and Nancy were in need of help; and since the beginning of November 1921 they had been pressing Amy to visit them, no doubt hoping that if she could see their circumstances for herself she would be inclined to feel more generously disposed towards them. Amy eventually agreed to stay at Islip, and she arrived at The World's End on the afternoon of 21 November.[18] She found Robert very hard-worked; while Nancy, now seven months pregnant, was 'low and restless and wants to go to her old nurse at Devon'.[19] There were a few happy hours on the 26th when John came for lunch, and then joined Robert in a memorable game of football against Stanton. Twenty minutes from the end, Stanton were leading 1–0; but then John scored two goals, Robert another, and the game ended in an Islip victory. However, as soon as the game was over Robert hurried away to Cambridge to consult Rivers, and a few days later Amy returned to Erinfa. She had failed to offer Robert and Nancy any more assistance, though she privately told John: 'I wish I could help them more';[20] and she reported to Alfred that although she had had 'a very trying time indeed' at 'The World's End', she felt it right to praise 'Robert for his unselfishness and Nancy for her devotion to him and the children. The young couple are having a hard time but they are bearing up well and if their health is maintained should have their characters strengthened by their hard trial.'[21] Something more than noble sentiments was required; and on 5 December, less than a week after Amy's return to North Wales, a telegram came from Robert 'begging Claree to go to them as the Doctor had forbidden Nancy to go on working'.[22]

Clarissa had been working at Erinfa for some months as APG's secretary, having found her previous employment too taxing; and both her parents were worried about exposing her to the strains of life in Robert's household. As an alternative, they proposed paying for Dorothy to return to help Nancy; but Robert sent a further wire saying that this could not be managed; and the next day Clarissa took matters into her own hands, saying that she would be more than happy to go to Islip for the next two and a half months. Amy and Alfred reluctantly agreed, though they had strong reservations about the wisdom of this course of action; and APG recorded gloomily in his diary: 'It was determined that Claree should be sacrificed, but I wrote very strongly to R. imploring him to safeguard her from such a nervous breakdown as she had in 1915.'[23] In the event Clarissa was soon writing very cheerfully about her new work. She found 'Nancy's temper "exquisite" etc. etc. I hope', wrote APG, 'that all may go well.'[24]

Oxford Poetry 1921, of which Robert was joint editor, had just been published; and the day after Clarissa's arrival it was reviewed in *Isis*. The volume as a whole received only qualified praise; but besides the work of numerous minor figures (including Robert's sister Rosaleen) there were also poems by Robert himself, by his co-editors Diccon Hughes and Alan Porter, and by Edmund Blunden. In such company Robert must have been well pleased when the reviewer declared that 'Mr. Graves is in a class by himself both in promise and achievement.' The 'best poem of the book' was said to be Robert's 'Unicorn and White Doe', that haunting poem which Robert had written much earlier, but which he had now revived; and in which he comments upon the fact that romantic love cannot easily survive domesticity, but is to be found, in his view, in some magical and timeless realm beyond the bounds of ordinary experience. Attention was also drawn to the memorable last verse of Robert's 'A Lover Since Childhood', which concludes with the line: 'Swallow your pride, let us be as we used to be.'[25]

The difficulties of domestic life appeared frequently as a theme of Robert's more recent work. 'Sullen Moods', for example, is a simple and touching set of verses clearly addressed to Nancy:

> Love, do not count your labour lost
>   Though I turn sullen, grim, retired
> Even at your side; my thought is crossed
>   With fancies by old longings fired.
>
> And when I answer you, some days,
>   Vaguely and wildly, do not fear
> That my love walks forbidden ways,
>   Breaking the ties that hold it here.
>
> If I speak gruffly, this mood is
>   Mere indignation at my own
> Shortcomings, plagues, uncertainties:
>   I forget the gentler tone.

You, now that you have come to be
  My one beginning, prime and end,
I count at last as wholly me,
  Lover no longer nor yet friend.

Friendship is flattery, though close hid:
  Must I then flatter my own mind?
And must (which laws of shame forbid)
  Blind love of you make self-love blind?

Do not repay me my own coin,
  The sharp rebuke, the frown, the groan;
Remind me, rather, to disjoin
  Your emanation from my own.

Help me to see you as before
  When overwhelmed and dead, almost,
I stumbled on the secret door
  Which saves the live man from the ghost.

Be once again the distant light,
  Promise of glory, not yet known
In full perfection – wasted quite
  When on my imperfection thrown.[26]

It is difficult for a wife to remain as a 'distant light'; and it would be fair to deduce from these and other verses that Robert had discovered that both as an artist and as a romantic he wanted more from Nancy than she could possibly provide. However, he was still very devoted both to her and to their children, was quite prepared to take his share (and perhaps more than his share) of the blame for their occasional quarrels and disagreements, and did his best to make their marriage as happy and successful as possible. Indeed in December 1921, writing to thank Gilbert Murray's wife for some Christmas presents, he told her:

We are awfully happy here at Islip too busy to worry & a pleasantly relaxing atmosphere which makes children sleep & keeps parents from getting too brilliant.

Nancy is all right really the Dr thinks so & she thinks so herself which is really more important – I have never felt better & have a good year to look back on, two books (both good, I think) & getting to know the children intimately & seeing them grow up happy & strong.[27]

Clarissa, living at close quarters with Nancy for the first time, became extremely fond of her; and noted approvingly that when Nancy left on 5 January 1922 for Brighton (where it was expected that her third child would be born on or around the 18th), she and Robert corresponded daily. This was the act of two people who, whatever their differences, remained deeply attached to each other; and later in the year Siegfried Sassoon was asked by Robert to accept the fact that he and Nancy were 'that physical monstrosity the Phoenix-and-Turtle',[28] of whom Shakespeare had written:

> So they lov'd, as love in twain
> Had the essence but in one;
> Two distincts, division none:
> Number there in love was slain.[29]

During her weeks at The World's End Clarissa certainly came to think of it as 'a place of love and hard work and a magic sense of home'.[30]

CHAPTER
4
'THE LANDS
OF WHIPPERGINNY'

In December 1921 Robert had sent Edward Marsh the manuscript of a new collection of his poems; and 'Sullen Moods' and 'A Lover since Childhood' were both included. But the volume, as Robert later remarked, also 'showed the first signs of my new psychological studies'.[31] In his *On English Poetry*, in which he was heavily influenced by his visits to Dr Rivers at Cambridge, he had declared that poetry was a form of psycho-therapy;[32] and now he said much the same thing in 'Whipperginny', the title poem of his new collection. Whipperginny is the name of an obsolete card-game; and men play cards:

> When Time with cruelty runs,
> To courtly Bridge for stress of love,
> To Nap for noise of guns.

Card-games allow one to escape to a 'fairy earth', where:

> No present problems vex
> Where Man's four humours fade to suits
> With red and black for sex.[33]

Whipperginny, says Robert, is the right 'game to play apart/When all but crushed with care'; and it is therefore an appropriate 'Namesake' or symbol for his poetry, which is written under similar pressure.

It was a pressure under which Robert had become fascinated by the subconscious world with its dream-like and sometimes nightmarish images; and this is evident in some of his new poems. Here, for example, is 'The Lands of Whipperginny':

> Come closer yet, sweet honeysuckle, my coney, O my Jinny,
> With a low sun gilding the bloom of the wood.
> Be this Heaven, be it Hell, or the Lands of Whipperginny,
> It lies in a fairy lustre, it savours most good.

Then stern proud psalms from the chapel on the moors
  Waver in the night wind, their firm rhythm broken,
Lugubriously twisted to a howling of whores
  Or lent an airy glory too strange to be spoken.[34]

This fragmentary glimpse of Robert's inner world is both strange and sinister. It is also somewhat obscure; and, much to Robert's chagrin, Marsh took a dislike to this new work, and told Robert that although he acknowledged the passion and spirit of his poems, he could not always catch their drift; Robert's style was a wonderful instrument, but he did not appear to be putting it to its best use.

Marsh had particularly disliked two long poems, one of which, 'The Feather Bed',[35] concerns Rachel, who kisses a young man, and then runs away to a convent. Her lover pursues Rachel; and it appears that the Mother Superior, after first compelling Rachel to reveal the secret of the kiss, goes to the guest bedroom where the young man is staying for the night, and attempts to seduce him. Robert had tried to explain the poem to Marsh, telling him that the Mother Superior was no more than a 'synthetic spook' of the young man's fancy, and that the poem had been 'written on the whole for ten years hence when knowledge of morbid psychology will be commoner than now'.[36] In the event Robert decided to remove 'The Feather Bed' from his 'Whipperginny' collection, and to arrange for it to appear as a separate publication. It is a curious fantasy which may contain an echo of Robert's warm feelings for Barbara Morrison, who had left his household to work in a convent before departing for Canada; and, like Robert's still more obscure poem 'The Snake and the Bull',[37] it suggests that Robert faced a serious personal problem in trying to reconcile his sexual desires with traditional ideas of virtue.

CHAPTER
5
THE BIRTH
OF CATHERINE

While Nancy was away in Brighton, Robert continued to write daily letters to her; and by the beginning of February 1922, when her baby seemed to be long overdue, he was 'on the rack with anxiety'. There were a few distractions: one afternoon, for example, he and John had tea with George Mallory, who had come to Oxford to lecture about mountain-climbing; and Robert was also occupied with running the Islip football team. On 2 February he wrote asking John to play in a match, 'as we are badly off'; and he added, with an irritable dig at their sister's Victorian turn of speech, 'Clarissa can spare you.' Then, the following day, came the news for which he had been waiting: Nancy had given birth to a daughter,[38] whom they had already decided to call Catherine, and mother and child were both in the best of health.

Believing that it was unwise to leave Clarissa in sole charge of Jenny and David, Robert had to arrange for Nancy's Aunt Fanny to take his place at The World's End, and so was unable to set out for Brighton until some eight or nine days after Catherine's birth. He found that Nancy was quite extraordinarily well; and within a few days of Robert's arrival she was writing very cheerfully to Clarissa to tell her that she was looking forward to coming home, and that:

Catherine is sweet and beautifully behaved.

I am awfully well. .... What I'd like you to do is to stay on for a bit & do nothing except your own stunts. In fact be a guest & have a rest & see Cathy. But I expect you're rather keen to burst out on some job or go to Palestine....

Robert's coat is beautifully made though I'm not quite reconciled to the colour. He's looking awfully well.

I am longing to see the children again. You have saved our lives by being clever as well as kind.[39]

Nancy was to remain at Brighton until the end of the month, to ensure that she was entirely fit before rejoining her other children; but Robert had promised to be back at Islip within a week, and so he set out alone on the first stage of his journey home. On the way he spent a night in London, where he had asked to be present at a very special family occasion.[40]

It was fifty years since Alfred Perceval Graves had published his first volume of poetry, *Songs of Killarney*, and on 19 February the Irish Literary Society celebrated this jubilee by giving him a complimentary dinner at Pinoli's. A hundred and twenty people were present; the speakers included T.P. O'Connor and Plunket Greene; a number of Alfred's songs were sung, including of course 'Father O'Flynn'; and the event was widely reported in the press. Robert, for once, was not entirely overshadowed: he had the satisfaction of hearing his own work being highly praised by one of the speakers;[41] and Amy was immensely proud of the whole affair, writing afterwards to John: 'I am glad you know a little more what a father you have got.'[42]

Alfred and Amy stayed for a night in Oxford on their way back to Harlech on 28 February,[43] and went out to Islip where they 'had a good time with John, Claree, and Jenny and David', and Amy paid some of Robert's outstanding bills before watching him bath the children.[44] The following day Clarissa left to begin a tutoring job in Ireland;[45] and Nancy, accompanied by her Aunt Fanny, brought Catherine home to The World's End.

Nancy was so remarkably fit that she and Robert began wondering whether Clarissa's prayers had been instrumental in giving her such a painless delivery. The doctor had said that from the medical point of view it had been a difficult birth; but apparently Nancy had no after-pains, and 'thought herself she'd had an easy time. .... The most strange thing of all', wrote Robert to Clarissa a week or two later,

is the complete disappearance of her enlarged thyroid which has been the cause (i.e. from a medical standpoint shall we say 'symbol'?) of all her irritability hitherto; it has, after Jenny & David's birth, been particularly obnoxious. ... I am (that is we are) too full of gratitude for your help to be able to frame a suitable letter to meet the case but the best thing to do is to change the formula of signature & become again after many years
    your loving brother
    Rob.[46]

While Aunt Fanny remained with them, Robert and Nancy enjoyed a comparatively rare period of calm; and in early March Robert even managed to repay £9 of 'rent loan' to his mother, which she found 'a pleasant surprise'. But the only fundamental change in their situation was that they now had a third child to feed. Before long they were once again feeling anxious and unsettled, and this had unfortunate consequences.

CHAPTER
6
LOSING FRIENDS

By the beginning of April 1922 knowledge of the deteriorating state of affairs at The World's End had reached Erinfa; and APG wrote to Robert repeating an earlier suggestion that he should consider increasing his income by giving University Extension lectures.[47] Robert's only reply was a letter full of misery 'about Nancy's influenza and over-anxiety'.[48] Further proposals were made, all of them to be at Amy's expense: the whole family should come to Erinfa for a while; or Nancy should holiday in Brighton with the children, while Robert spent a few days in London renewing some of his literary contacts; or a maid should be hired from the village to ease some of the pressure of work.

Not one of these proposals was taken up. Nancy wanted to remain at home, but she had developed a positive hatred of having anyone else in the house; and she remained in such low spirits that Robert was placed under an increasing strain. Later in the year he described to Marsh how:

> My trouble here is that Nancy isn't strong and we have no servants, so I am largely nurse to the children, gardener, allotment tiller, housemaid and cook. I get about an hour a day of writing, including letters, and can only escape in the evening to see anyone after the children are in bed. [He added bravely] I am not complaining, for I am completely happy in spite of debts and all; but that's how it is.[49]

As April went slowly by, and Nancy remained depressed, Robert wrote to Siegfried Sassoon explaining that he would have to decline an interesting invitation from Edith Sitwell. Apparently Edith had asked him to come up to London on 29 April to read some of his poems at a meeting of the Anglo-French Poetry Society, of which she was the secretary. Sassoon received the news with mixed feelings. He had recently quarrelled with Edith's brothers Osbert and Sacheverell Sitwell, who had published a vicious satirical attack upon Robert and some of Sassoon's other friends; and in the circumstances he felt that it would be undignified for Robert to have anything to do with Edith. On the other hand, Siegfried was irritated to learn that Nancy was keeping Robert at home. For several months he had felt 'vaguely resentful of Nancy for monopolizing him';[50] and this resentment had been fuelled by reports from his Garsington friends, who told Sassoon that Nancy prevented Robert from seeing them.

Then shortly before the Poetry Society meeting, Nancy suddenly revived; and Robert decided to go up to London after all. The meeting was a success; but when Graves called upon Sassoon the following day, and mentioned that he had seen Edith Sitwell, Sassoon felt betrayed. As he later admitted, he spoke to Robert very bitterly; and when,

> in the middle of vituperations, I actually suggested lunching with him, he (tactlessly) said that he was lunching with T.E. Lawrence, who 'never sees anyone except a few people' [he was living in obscurity in London and working on *Seven Pillars of Wisdom*]. Of course this made me worse than ever. It was a rebuff to my vanity ... we parted in mutual huffiness.

After lunch, quite by chance, the two men collided with each other in Piccadilly; and, in Sassoon's words: 'My spontaneous feeling was reconciliatory. But R. drew my attention to a little man in a long, ready-made-looking, rough brown "ulster"; it was T.E.L. Immediately I became self-conscious and nasty-tempered.' There was a ridiculous scene in which Sassoon was unnecessarily rude to Lawrence. Later he apologized for this to Graves, but added that the trouble was 'that he had always been passionately attached to Graves and in return was continually treated with half-pitying disapproval'.[51]

Some weeks went by before on 29 May Robert replied to Siegfried's letter. Unfortunately his own feelings were now hurt, and after a half-hearted attempt at reconciliation he continued the quarrel, sneering at 'the odours of Garsington', and ending his letter on exactly the note of half-pitying disapproval which had already given so much offence: 'I want to ask you about a lot of things', he wrote, 'and I wish you wouldn't rhyme Bach with Hark instead of coming to see us.'[52]

Two more letters were exchanged: in the first, Sassoon defended his bad rhyme as intentional, made 'several sarcastic references to Graves's understanding of psycho-analysis', and asked what he meant by writing so offensively against Garsington.[53] In the second, Graves told Sassoon that it was no good writing to him as though he were the Robert Graves of the war years. He was now, he said, so closely identified with Nancy, in a Phoenix-and-Turtle manner, that he was no more than the 'son and heir' of his former self; and it was 'as an old friend of my father that I want to meet you; my father had a sort of hero-worship of you and I have heard him talk of you with great awe even'. For good measure, Robert declared that Siegfried's friend Lady

Ottoline Morrell had been 'very bad to my friends', that Nancy 'has very real reasons for wanting to have nothing more to do with her', and that he had recently met Ottoline and had 'kindly but rudely' refused to visit her again at Garsington.[54] All this was utterly infuriating to Sassoon. He could see from some passages in the letter that Graves wanted to be reconciled to him: but only on his own terms. For Sassoon, these were too demanding; and their correspondence and friendship both lapsed for a while.

The following month Robert realized that there was also a lack of sympathy between himself and Edmund Blunden, and he wrote a letter asking what had gone wrong between them. 'I think of you', wrote Robert, 'with great friendship and having lost most of my literary friends lately I would not like to lose you without an attempt at reconciliation. I am certainly as much to blame as you are in this case.'[55] Blunden replied frankly that he resented Robert's 'ethical guidance', and that although he realized that he owed much to Robert, he had felt 'pained and isolated' after being told of a conversation at Islip in which Robert had apparently 'referred to him as morally feeble and by heredity liable to lapses with the bottle'.[56] Robert denied the conversation; and although he qualified the denial with what amounted to more 'ethical guidance', beginning: 'All I have ever said is that you have an "inferiority complex" (excuse technicality) concerned with your father's shortcomings'. The rest of the letter made it so clear that he valued Blunden's friendship that the offence, if any, was forgiven.[57]

Meanwhile Robert's *On English Poetry* had been published in America, and was due to be published in England at the beginning of July. He knew that he would make little money from it, partly because he had incurred considerable costs by making extensive alterations when the book was already in proof; but he was working as hard as he could on his B.Litt. thesis, 'The Illogical Element in English Poetry', which he hoped would also find a publisher as soon as it was complete. The thesis was to be dedicated to Sir Walter Raleigh, his official supervisor, who had advised him on the literary side of the work; and to Dr Rivers, who had advised him on the psychological side. It therefore came as a severe shock to Robert when both men died prematurely, and within a few weeks of each other: Raleigh on 13 May and Rivers on 4 June. This deprived Robert of two of his closest friends and working colleagues, and had other consequences: after Raleigh's death he 'felt [his] connection with Oxford University was broken';[58] and after Rivers's death he made a much more determined effort to restore good relations with Sassoon, writing to him: 'Bless you Sassons and if you don't buck up a bit I'll die really this time just to spite you. 1916 was a threat only.'[59]

Some compensation for his loss of friends in the world beyond Islip came from the close links which Robert established locally. Known respectfully as 'the Captain', Robert had soon impressed villagers with his energy and his determination both on and off the football field. The strength of his anger when he was roused was also something to be reckoned with. For example, Robert could not bear to hear the sound of gunfire, because it excited his shell-shock. So he was furious when one morning Wilf Stopp, then a seventeen-year-old boy, began firing a muzzle-loaded gun at some tin cans in his back garden, which was just across the river from Robert's property. Bicycling round to the Stopps's cottage in Mill Street at top speed, Robert barged in through the front door, tore into the back garden, and gave Wilf Stopp a lecture which Wilf remembered vividly for more than sixty years.

The strength of Robert's socialist convictions was also impressive; and although he gradually alienated some of the 'village gentry', he soon became a respected local figure in this largely working-class community. His closest friend in the village was William Beckley, an agricultural labourer who was on the Parish Council; and together they set up a local branch of the Labour Party, which met at The World's End each week during the winter months.[60] Robert's evident poverty must have made it easier for him to be accepted: the villagers could see that his clothes, like theirs, were usually far from new; even his football boots were really old army boots with the heels cut down, and studs added. Like the villagers, he joined the local working men's insurance club, and like them he attended its annual dinners, at which there was much singing and feasting. Like them, he usually ate very simply, and hunger was often close at hand. One evening the Wilkinsons, who lived opposite, were startled when Robert came in while they were eating, and inquired: 'What's for supper, Dick?' He was told there was bread, cheese and pickles. 'That's fine', said Robert, pulling up a chair and starting to help himself. When asked what on earth he was playing at, he explained that he had brought two kippers back from Oxford for his evening meal; but the Wilkinsons' cat Felix had found its way into the Graves's larder and eaten them. This had left Robert without anything to eat, and coming round had seemed the fairest solution to his problem.

Holidays were definitely a luxury; but in early July 1922 Robert and Nancy decided that they needed a 'burst for freedom'; and so the following month they hitched up an ancient horse to the shafts of a derelict baker's van which they had commandeered; and then they set off for the south coast. Unfortunately it rained almost continuously during the month that they were away; and keeping three children under the age of four clean, dry and well fed was a formidable task. There were accidents, too: once the shafts dropped off, and once the back of the cart flew open and a young child rolled out on to the road. However, the children 'grew fat and strong', and they finally reached Rottingdean, a lovely little seaside village in a fold of the South Downs not far from Brighton.[61] On the way home they called in at Charterhouse to see the Mallorys;[62] and Robert returned to The World's End feeling mentally refreshed and alert, with an elaborate theory about the real meaning of Shakespeare's *The Tempest* forming in his mind.

One of Graves's first tasks when he arrived home was to send his *Whipperginny* poems to be typed. He had made great efforts to improve the collection since Marsh's hostile criticisms the previous December; and several of the revised poems had already found a home in the fifth volume of *Georgian Poetry* which Marsh was to publish later in 1922. Graves had loyally told Marsh that he was 'very proud to serve again in the old ship in spite of storms, squalls and barnacles'; though the disappointing reception given to the fourth volume had meant that Sassoon and Nichols, among others, had refused Marsh permission to use any more of their work.[63]

Graves had already made a powerful attack upon 'poets with floppy hats, long hair, extravagant clothes and inverted tendencies'[64] in his *On English Poetry*; and Nichols's defection from *Georgian Poetry*, together with a marriage of which Graves strongly disapproved, marked the final breach in their friendship. At about the same time Robert broke for a time with Diccon Hughes, telling him that he should 'get finally independent of my literary influence of which you have grown conscious and find a hindrance to your development'.[65] This was kindly meant; but in a relatively short space of time Robert had now lost, irritated or temporarily alienated many of his closest friends; and without their guidance and support he had begun to fall under the spell of a Bengali philosopher, Basanta Mallik of Balliol.

CHAPTER
7
MALLIK AND
MOCKBEGGAR HALL

During the spring and summer of 1922 Robert had spent some time in making substantial alterations to his long poem 'The Feather Bed';[66] and towards the end of August he sent it to Leonard and Virginia Woolf at the Hogarth Press, and succeeded in capturing their interest.[67] The original 'plot' of the poem was still there; but besides the psychological allegories there were now a number of philosophical musings. These may safely be attributed to the influence of Basanta Mallik, a perpetual student on the grand scale.

After graduating from Calcutta University, and finding favour with the Maharajah of Nepal, Mallik had arrived at Oxford in about 1912. He had been there ever since, first taking a degree in law at Exeter, and then studying the nebulous subject of 'British Political Psychology'. Mallik had a strong personality, and he had made a great impression upon Robert, who had met him when reading a paper to an undergraduate society.[68]

Robert's earliest mention of Mallik comes in a letter written to Edmund Blunden in August 1922; and since Robert enjoyed passing on news about any new discoveries in the intellectual or artistic field, it is unlikely that he had seen much of Mallik before the early summer of that year. During those summer months it was Mallik who gradually turned Graves's interests away from the Freudian psychology, largely derived from his sessions with Rivers, which informed *On English Poetry* and *Whipperginny*. The final version of 'The Feather Bed' was a turning point, and from then on, in Robert's own words,

Metaphysics ... made psychology of secondary interest for me: it threatened almost to displace poetry. Basanta ... believed in no hierarchy of ultimate values or the possibility of any unifying religion or ideology. But at the same time he insisted on the necessity of strict self-discipline in the individual in meeting every possible demand upon him from whatever quarter, and he recommended strict self-watchfulness against either dominating or being dominated by any other individual. This view of strict personal morality consistent with scepticism of social morality agreed very well with my practice.[69]

It was this 'scepticism of social morality' which led Robert to make the social experiment of answering no letters from his family, 'even', as he later made clear to his parents, 'when pressing'.[70] Invitations to Erinfa in the summer and early autumn therefore went unanswered; and Amy and Alfred were relieved when the autumn term began, and John, at the start of his second year at St John's, was able to write to them with first-hand news of Robert and his family: they were happy, he reported; their garden looked attractive, and Catherine appeared to be a highly intelligent baby.

It was not until mid-November that Robert wrote to his parents himself, enclosing £4 of rent, and telling them of a pleasant visit to the Mallorys. A generous present by Marsh from his Rupert Brooke royalties had restored Robert's credit; and the Mallorys had kindly agreed to look after the children for a few days while he and Nancy enjoyed a short holiday on their own.

During his long silence, Robert had been working hard on a number of projects. These included a new number of the *Owl*, for which Lawrence had supplied a further extract from his unpublished *Seven Pillars of Wisdom*; there were also contributions from Beerbohm and Blunden; and an article by Mallik in which, as Robert reported to Blunden, he presented 'a new philosophic system in brief which is (by the way) going to have a shattering effect on the philosophic dove cotes'. Robert had also visited London, where he had dined with Marsh, had effected something of a reconciliation with Sassoon, and had been used by Kennington as one of his models for a war-memorial sculpture due to be set up in a London park.[71]

In the meantime Robert had acquired a new admirer: the American poet John Crowe Ransom, who taught English at Vanderbilt University in Nashville, and, as one of the editors of the *Fugitive* poetry magazine was at the centre of a new literary group which included such names as Allen Tate and Merrill Moore. Ransom had written to Graves asking if he might dedicate a volume of poetry to him, 'because you represent as I see it the best tendency extant in modern poetry'; and Graves responded to this flattering interest by trying to find Ransom an English publisher.[72]

The new *Owl* and *Georgian Poetry V* both appeared towards Christmas; but they were completely overshadowed by the literary event of the season, the publication of A.E. Housman's widely reviewed and immensely popular *Last Poems*.[73] Housman had produced no volume of poetry since *A Shropshire Lad* in 1896, and nothing more had been expected of him. Yet here was a new collection of poems which were haunting, romantic, doomed, heroic. It was as though Housman had returned from beyond the grave to remind a younger generation how poems should be written. By comparison much of the new volume of *Georgian Poetry* seemed insipid and third-rate, and Marsh wisely brought the series to an end.

Robert, with his new philosophical interests added to his psychological studies, was not unduly worried by this turn of events. Nor had the 'strict self-watchfulness against ... being dominated' which Mallik advocated, prevented him from becoming Mallik's disciple: so much was clear to Alfred and Amy on 14 December, when they spent a night at Islip *en route* for a dinner in London, though APG liked Mallik's face, and enjoyed the 'great talk on dreams' which went on for much of the evening.[74]

The following morning Amy left Robert an early Christmas present of £15; and in the New Year of 1923 she received a thank-you letter from Robert, who had used the money 'to put up all sorts of useful contraptions' at The World's End.[75] The rest of Robert's news was less good: Nancy had lumbago, Jenny and David had whooping cough, Robert himself 'was suffering badly from his teeth', and, as Amy reported to Clarissa, 'they all have bad nights & there is much extra washing'.[76]

Difficult times of this kind are common in families with three children under school age; but they tend to last days or weeks rather than months, and if the family is reasonably well-balanced they are patiently endured and rapidly forgotten. However, Robert's family was clearly out of balance. Nancy, after a pampered childhood, had rushed into an early marriage and had then had too many children too quickly. There was little or no time for the art which meant so much to her; and although she herself used to point out that she and Robert had more money than the Islip farm-labourers, she was mentally unprepared for the comparative privations to which their low income reduced them. Within the family her word remained law; but she had become increasingly dependent upon Robert's constant presence and moral support. Meanwhile Robert, still suffering from the after-effects of the war, had to lavish upon Nancy the support of which he himself was desperately in need; and although looking after his wife and family was something positive for him to do at a time when his literary career was at a depressingly low ebb, it was only an inner determination to 'get by somehow' which enabled him to survive.[77]

Fortunately Robert recognized the moments when determination alone was not enough: in the spring of 1921 he had been driven to seek professional advice about his mental troubles; and now, almost two years later, when those troubles once again threatened to overwhelm him, he embarked upon a course of psycho-analysis.[78] In the short term this raised a host of sleeping demons;

and it is hardly surprising that many of Robert's new poems had a haunted air, or that he later published them as *Mockbeggar Hall*, the name of a former leper-house which he had dreamed was full of quarrelling ghosts.[79]

The most vigorous and memorable of these new poems, none the worse for its reminiscence of Coleridge in the last verse, takes up an earlier theme about the baleful influence of the moon:

FULL MOON

As I walked out one harvest night
  About the stroke of One,
The Moon attained to her full height
  Stood beaming like the Sun.
She exorcised the ghostly wheat
To mute assent in Love's defeat
  Whose tryst had now begun.

The fields lay sick beneath my tread,
  A tedious owlet cried;
A nightingale above my head
  With this or that replied,
Like man and wife who nightly keep
Inconsequent debate in sleep
  As they dream side by side.

Your phantom wore the moon's cold mask,
  My phantom wore the same,
Forgetful of the feverish task
  In hope of which they came,
Each image held the other's eyes
And watched a grey distraction rise
  To cloud the eager flame.

To cloud the eager flame of love,
  To fog the shining gate:
They held the tyrannous queen above
  Sole mover of their fate;
They glared as marble statues glare
Across the tessellated stair,
  Or down the Halls of State.

And now cold earth was Arctic sea,
    Each breath came dagger keen;
Two bergs of glinting ice were we,
    The broad moon sailed between;
There swam the mermaids, tailed and finned,
And Love went by upon the wind
    As though it had not been.[80]

Other poems show the extent to which Graves had fallen under Mallik's influence: in 'Knowledge of God', for example, he declared that God is so far beyond human knowledge or understanding that it is blasphemous to attempt to define Him in terms of a particular religious cult, and then to be bound by the dictates of that cult, rather than by one's own inner convictions.[81]

For the most part the new poems are artistically disappointing, and Graves later came to regard them as a side-track in his poetic career. Nevertheless they mark an important stage in his thought. In 'Attercop: the all-wise Spider', for example, Robert makes it clear that he regards not only religious cults, but any coherent philosophical systems as being suspect: freedom lies elsewhere.[82] And in 'The Witches', Robert shows that abandoning formal religion has not converted him to the sunny rationalism of a Llewelyn Powys. He still believes that the world is a stranger and more magical place than is at first apparent; and the narrator, after describing the flight of a coven of witches, is made to add:

Such feats on oath we testify
    To whom like powers have long been known,
But we for love the cold heavens fly
    Which other whiles for lust are flown,
We walk the swellings of the sea
    Dryshod and free, for love alone.

Do you, my crabbed empiricist,
    Judge these things false, then false they'll be
For all who never swooped and kissed
    Above the moon, below the sea;
Yet set no tangles in their place
    Of Time and Space and Gravity.

For Space and Time have only sense
    Where these are flattered and adored;
And there sit many parliaments
    Where clock and compass have no word,

Where gravity makes levity,
Where reason snaps her blunted sword.[83]

Robert had now become so bound up in his course of psycho-analysis that he felt increasingly alienated not only from many of his friends, but also from his close family, and especially from Rosaleen and from John. A death in the family therefore passed him by almost unnoticed. Nineteen-year-old Janie Preston, daughter of his half-sister Molly, died of pneumonia towards the end of January; and Molly returned to England in a state of shock. A few days later Robert wrote to APG accepting an invitation to stay at Harlech in the spring; but his main concern appeared to be whether he might bring Mallik with him as part of his household: an idea which was vetoed by Alfred as being 'too much of a good thing'.

APG was still trying to secure an appointment for Robert as a University Extension lecturer; and on his way to Janie's funeral he spent a night at Oxford, where he had arranged to meet Robert on the morning of 27 January for a discussion about his future. The two men enjoyed 'a long & very friendly but straight talk'. Robert's interest in psychology had side-tracked him into a study of 'Conflict and Poetry'; but he said that he hoped to complete his B.Litt. thesis in the spring. And what then? They discussed a letter which APG had just received from the Oxford Delegacy, which contained the news that there was an opening for an Extension Lecturer, and, in APG's words, 'this promised at first'. But then Robert made a crucial reservation: he would have to consult Nancy, 'in whose hand', Alfred reported sadly to Amy, 'I fear he is wax. After all putting his name down for [an interview on] Feb 3rd is only provisional.' In his diary that evening APG added: 'I felt anxious about [Robert's] very hesitant manner and fear effect of psycho-analysis.'[84]

Alfred had guessed correctly that Nancy's attitude would be hostile towards anything which took Robert away from home. On 29 January, the day of Janie's funeral, he was having tea with Molly at Susan's home in Ewell, just south of Wimbledon, when a wire from Robert arrived 'refusing Oxford Extension post because of Nancy's opposition and his health. All of us', noted Alfred, 'were much upset.'[85] Never one to give up easily, Alfred went into London the following day and enlisted the help of Robert's half-brother Philip, who had achieved a measure of fame 17 months ago for exposing as a forgery the *Protocols of the Elders of Sion*,[86] and was now back in England enjoying an extended leave. Philip promised to write to Robert, but his letter clearly had little effect: the following week Nancy wrote at some length to her parents-in-law explaining exactly why she felt that Robert must remain at home. APG and Amy both wrote diplomatic letters in an effort to calm her down, and then, as a last resort, they asked Molly to see what she could do.

Molly was equally unsuccessful; but she elicited from Robert some information which disturbed her. Apparently Basanta Mallik's years as a student were finally drawing to a close, and he had asked Robert and Nancy to follow him out to Nepal.

CHAPTER
8
HARLECH INTERLUDE

Early in February 1923, while Robert was tryng to make up his mind about whether he and his family should leave England, all of them but Nancy went down with whooping cough. What with sickness, trying to decide about Nepal, and putting up with well-meaning but relentless pressure from various members of the Graves family for Robert to take up lecturing, it was an exhausting time. Robert and Nancy were soon feeling 'done in', and towards the end of the month they decided that they needed a holiday.[87] Before leaving Islip, Robert wrote to Siegfried Sassoon sending the uncorrected proofs of *Whipperginny* for him to read over, and apologizing for what he described as his 'recent bloodiness'. Then Robert and Nancy took their children to spend a week on a farm under canvas.[88]

Despite the cold, the children enjoyed themselves; but it was not at all restful for Robert and Nancy, and when they returned to Islip they realized that they were now too unwell to cope without outside help, so they hired 'Nurse Engel', and took her with them when it was time for their holiday in Harlech. They arrived at Erinfa on 23 March, and Alfred was alarmed to see that Nancy appeared worn, and had lost so much hair that she was wearing a wig; while Robert had a bad cough and looked positively haggard.

Erinfa was more peaceful than usual, except when Smuts barked furiously at some casual visitor or other. John, waiting to hear how he had done in Mods, his first major Oxford examination, was the only other guest for the time being; and he, like his parents, did his best to give Robert and Nancy a relaxing holiday. While Nurse Engel kept an eye on Catherine, John and APG took turns looking after Jenny and David; John lit fires for them in the woods, and APG took them out for long walks, and helped them to gather gorse and hawthorn blossom, and bunches of celandines, daisies, and primroses to give to their mother.

Meanwhile Robert and Nancy rested, or went out together for walks and drives. They had been reconciled to Diccon Hughes, who was now living with his mother in a little hillside cottage at Garreg Fawr, a few miles to the north of Harlech; and one Wednesday they accepted an invitation to spend the night there.[89] Diccon, who had seen a play of his performed on the London stage while he was still an undergraduate, told Robert and Nancy that his latest play, *The Man Born to be Hanged*, was due to be premièred the following week by a local group known as 'The Portmadoc Players'. Diccon's play would form part of a double bill with another new play, *The Cloud Break*, by A.O. Roberts; and it had already been arranged that APG would review both plays for the *Liverpool Post*.

Soon it was being suggested that Robert too should try his hand as a reviewer, and the *Manchester Guardian* was persuaded to call upon his services. Charles had now arrived at Erinfa for a short holiday; and on the evening of Wednesday 4 April a large party, including Robert, Nancy, Nurse Engel, Charles and APG drove over to Portmadoc. APG, like a true professional, had already done some background research for his article: he telegraphed his first five hundred words to Liverpool before the curtain went up, and added a further five hundred words of kindly criticism as soon as the performances were over. By contrast Robert, quite unused to play-reviewing, ran into difficulties and turned to Charles for help. It was therefore Charles who wrote most of what appeared in the *Guardian* on Friday morning.

Unfortunately Charles had written with more honesty than tact; worse still, although it was the author of *The Cloud Break* who had arranged for the *Guardian* review, Charles had not even mentioned the play, but had devoted all his space to *The Man Born to be Hanged*. The result was an extremely angry telegram from Diccon, demanding to know which of the brothers had been responsible. Robert vigorously protested his innocence; and Charles, who returned to London on Monday, was soon being allowed to shoulder the entire blame for what had occurred.[90]

News of Charles's tactlessness was soon being circulated round the family; but it was rapidly overshadowed by a far more distressing item of family news: John, now on holiday in Devon, had 'only got a Third in Honours Mods – a great disappointment,' wrote APG in his diary, 'after the hopes Dr. James had raised in me by his "He has more than a sporting chance of a First." '[91] Alfred wrote wisely to his son;[92] but Amy sent John a stream of more or less anguished letters, and the more she endeavoured to sound sympathetic, the more clear it became that she regarded John's poor results as a terrible disgrace to the whole family.[93] Eventually Alfred calmed her down; and one good result of John's poor showing was that Robert's recent feelings of estrangement from his youngest brother suddenly dissolved. Nancy went back to Islip alone on 14 April, so that she could spend a few days getting everything in order before the others returned; and on the 15th Robert sent a message to John via their mother to say that you are very heartily invited to stay with them at Islip. ... I do not mind you accepting this [wrote Amy], as we have helped them considerably & if you feel a little hungry you can easily go out & get some eggs boiled hard for you or something else to eat out in the fields. If you quote this to Robert or N[ancy] I shall not forgive you. I know you need more substantial food than they can allow themselves.[94]

Robert had come to rely upon Nancy so much at this stage of their marriage that within hours of her departure for Islip he had begun to seem rather distracted. Alfred spent some time with him during the next two days; and on the 16th he noted grimly in his diary:

Robby ... is undoubtedly better but I have got to realize that he is hardly fit to be an Extension Lecturer yet. He hesitates greatly in speech and sometimes has to struggle hard to regain a dropped strand of thought. He protests too that railway travelling is a great trouble to him. I only trust he may grow out of these nervous conditions: I am not at all sure that his psychoanalysis is the best preparation for complete recovery from them.[95]

APG was also rather disappointed by Robert's *Whipperginny* collection, and began wondering whether Robert should not follow Diccon Hughes's example, and try his hand as a playwright. Why not revive the Hobby Horses idea, which had been gathering dust for the past sixteen months?[96] On the morning of Thursday 19 April, after an overnight visit to Barmouth to make sure that Dr Heath was still interested in collaborating with Robert, APG proposed that the three of them should work together on The Hobby Horses. Robert agreed, but without much pleasure.[97] He and Nancy had visited Heath at the end of March, and had found him so hostile to the idea of psychoanalysis that a coolness had sprung up between them.[98]

However, within a few hours Robert's initial reluctance had been transformed into enthusiasm. Isaacs, an Oxford friend of his who was now the Professor of English Literature at Bangor, arrived on Thursday afternoon at Erinfa intending to spend the night there. When he heard of the Hobby Horses idea, he warmly approved. The following morning Robert was due to return to Islip. The prospect of the train journey took away his appetite for breakfast; but he stepped into his railway carriage in a state of great excitement, with the plan for going to Nepal rapidly fading, and with Isaacs's encouraging words still ringing in his ears.

CHAPTER
9
'UNPROFITABLE WRITING'

As soon as Graves had returned to The World's End he began working hard on The Hobby Horses; and for a month or two some of his old self-confidence reasserted itself. Early in May he told his father that he believed that he could manage to write the play single-handed, though he would call upon APG if necessary;[99] and by the afternoon of 6 June Robert was up in London reading a completed draft to the singer and composer Frederick Austin, who had arranged the music for the successful revival of Gay's *Polly* which was then playing on the London stage. It was William Nicholson who had brought the two men together, as he liked Robert's new work, and thought it probable that an early London production might be arranged. Austin was non-committal; and Siegfried Sassoon, who was present at the reading, privately thought that the play was 'amusing but not dramatic'; but for the time being, Robert was in excellent spirits.

That evening, while Nancy and her father were out watching *Polly*, Robert and Siegfried had a long talk at Apple Tree Yard.

He is as stimulating as ever [Siegfried wrote of his old friend], and I take up my talk with him as though we hadn't been apart for months. He complains that he has too much domestic work to do, but his productivity seems to prove that the life agrees with him. Nancy and her father returned from Gay's *Polly* at 11.15. N. was grumpy (because I avoid going to Islip, I suppose). What a contrast R.G. is to O[sbert]. S[itwell]! He has all the humanity (and humility) which O. lacks. There is nothing mean or malicious about R.G. A happy evening. While R. discoursed, I sat puffing my pipe...[100]

But all too soon a familiar pattern in Robert's life began to repeat itself: enormous enthusiasm for a dubious project was followed by uncertainty, disillusionment, bitterness and exhaustion.

Towards the end of July *The Feather Bed* was published, and sold out rapidly. But there was no chance of capitalizing on this success with a cheaper edition because, as Robert explained bitterly in a letter to Edward Marsh, the Hogarth

Press were 'limited for type, which is a pity'. He added that he had been working all year

> on more or less unprofitable writing. My cursed treatise on poetry [the B.Litt. thesis] goes on plaguing me: time after time when I think I've finished, I have to rewrite three or four chapters. I wrote an opera for my father-in-law ['The Hobby Horses', now renamed *John Kemp's Wager*] to press on the Polly people; rather good fun but I don't see any hope in it; it was done on request and I spent weeks on it and then I have been editing a new *Owl* which is admirable in contents but if we sell all the 1000 copies at 10s. 6d. we will hardly be able to get the typing back.[101]

Apparently there was some talk of Heinemann's producing a collected edition of Graves's work; and he had completed a new 'book of philosophical poems [*Mockbeggar Hall*]'. But his latest set of hopes had come to nothing, money had run out, Nurse Engel had had to be dismissed, and Nancy was expecting another child. In the circumstances, Robert was once again reduced to asking for money, telling Marsh that:

> If the Brooke fund is still functioning as widow's cruse for us poetic Elijahs in this Samarian famine, a half-pint of oil and a cracknel or two will not come amiss. I can no longer meet the eye of the bank cashier any more than he can meet my cheques; Nancy is not in a condition to do as much of the work as usual and I have to be cook-housemaid-nurse-washerwoman all the time (no help from outside) and enjoy it very much and it's good for work but I find it hard to make ends meet. The children are extremely well, so am I, and so on the whole Nancy and I count ourselves the happiest of God's creatures when there is no deficit and no returned cheques. The house is spotless and all my poems scan and I have been re-elected local football captain.[102]

With help from Marsh, financial disaster was averted for another month or two; and when he was not busy with domestic tasks, Graves was able to stop worrying, and to concentrate both upon his B.Litt. thesis, 'The Illogical Element in English Poetry', which he renamed 'Poetic Unreason'; and upon his study of 'Conflict and Poetry', which was eventually published as *The Meaning of Dreams*.

Later Graves was to write that *The Meaning of Dreams* had been intended as 'a popular shillingsworth for the railway bookstall';[103] but at the time he took it very seriously, as a necessary link between *Mockbeggar Hall* and *Poetic Unreason*.[104] Classical Freudian ideas about the relationship between dreams and waking life and about the division of the personality into ego, super-ego and id are openly derided. Graves cannot accept that men and women have 'a sort of hidden bogey inside them, with the uncontrolled emotion of a child or savage, and as little sense of the decencies or refinements of civilized life'.[105]

Instead, he elaborates upon ideas from his own book *On English Poetry*, declaring that 'under the stress of difficult circumstances', the personality can split into 'two or more rival "selves"' and that 'when a person is in conflict between two selves, and one self is stronger than the other throughout the waking life, the weaker side becomes victorious in the dream'. Analysing dreams can therefore help to reveal the nature of a current internal conflict in the personality; and there is a clear link between 'dream-life' and 'the mood of poetic inspiration', since from the psychological point of view both of them derive from the same desire to reunify the divided mind.[106]

The Meaning of Dreams concludes with psychological studies of a number of poems including Keats's 'La Belle Dame Sans Merci', and Graves's own 'The Gnat'; but these investigations are perhaps less interesting than two new ideas which were to be an important part of Graves's thinking from this time on: the first was that literal truth was unimportant, and that an artist should be allowed to 'tell ... the truth by a condensation and dramatisation' of the facts; and the second, that 'associative thought is as modern and reputable a mode as intellectual thought'.[107]

This latter idea is taken up again in *Poetic Unreason* in which, after repeating and further elaborating his theories about how poetry comes to be written, Graves declares that poetry 'does not conform with those principles of logic which govern what I have been calling intellectual as opposed to emotional thought'.[108] In another interesting passage Robert discusses the relationship between the poet and the woman he loves. Such a relationship has become very difficult, in his view, because the poetic life involves an attitude towards women ('the deification of women, summed up in the idea of chivalry') which strongly conflicts with modern feminism.[109]

CHAPTER
10
UNCERTAINTIES

By mid-October 1923 debts were once again piling up at The World's End, and Robert wrote to his mother telling her that he owed some £40, and adding that Nancy was expecting a fourth child in the spring. Amy considered the matter for three days, and then sent him a cheque for £30; while Alfred, whose latest effort to find employment for Robert had recently come to nothing, wrote crossly in his diary: 'When will these boys stop pinching at her generosity?'[110]

Almost immediately more money was required, this time for house repairs. Robert wrote a long letter to his parents saying how much he and Nancy were devoted to The World's End, and making hopeful remarks about his work: poems of his had recently been taken by both the *Spectator* and the *New Statesman*, and it would not be long before his B.Litt. thesis was printed for presentation to the University authorities. Amy agreed that the necessary work should be carried out; though she mentioned that if and when she had any spare money, she should be using it to help her sisters, who had fallen on hard times in post-war Germany. In reply, she received 'a charming letter of gratitude' from Robert, who added that when their own situation had improved, he and Nancy both wished to play their part in helping the German aunts.

Mallik was now back in Nepal, but Robert no longer planned to follow him there. Perhaps Molly's words about the futility of such a move had struck home. In any case he hated travelling; and at last he had made his move depend upon T.E. Lawrence, who had also been invited. If Lawrence went, so would Graves. But Lawrence had declined. The strain of the war, and of the peace negotiations which followed, had finally caught up with him; the substantial success which he had recently achieved for the Arabs had come too late, and he was on the verge of a severe mental breakdown.[111]

In the circumstances Mallik's hold over Robert gradually decreased. He left behind him what has been described as 'a cloud of uncertain influence on all his associates'.[112] One of these, the young Balliol scholar Sam Harries, had often accompanied him to Islip, and now became Robert and Nancy's closest friend. The young poet Peter Quennell, a new arrival at Oxford, was also drawn into their circle. Quennell's poetry had been studied by both T.E. Lawrence and Marsh; while Robert Graves and Diccon Hughes had been impressed by his work since the spring of 1922, when Quennell was still a seventeen-year-old schoolboy; and Diccon's elderly mother, who was nobody's fool, had described Quennell admiringly as 'not cocky, but extremely well-read'.[113]

A more influential new friend was the author John Buchan, who lived not far away at Elsfield. Graves had been introduced to Buchan by T.E. Lawrence some time ago; but they only began to meet at all regularly when Robert moved to Islip, and used to captain the Islip football team against Elsfield. Buchan shared the Graves's dislike of Lady Ottoline Morrell, and once inveighed most memorably against her in his soft Scots burr as 'The worrst woman in the worrld!'[114]

Robert and Nancy had also made a number of new friends in Islip: in particular Edward Thompson and his wife, described by Robert as 'our closest neighbours here of the educated class'; he: 'a north country man & a Wesleyan Minister; a very good man', who played in the football team; and she: 'American & has lived a long while in Syria'.[115] When Clarissa spent Christmas 1923 at The World's End, she found her sister-in-law 'much more equable'; and part of Robert's thank-you letter to Amy, written shortly after Christmas, shows the extent to which he and Nancy had become a part of the community:

> We had a very happy Christmas indeed here with Clarissa. ... The children had everything that they could possibly wish. ... Then Mrs. Buchan sent us a turkey, & some friends, the Thompsons cooked it for us & helped us eat it & provided the plum pudding & Mrs. Buchan also sent us a Xmas tree & the Herdmans some more ornaments to put on it & Mrs. Webb some mince pies & two local people, apples: and Susy a cake & two other friends more cakes.
>
> We had our own Xmas tree (22 children & 20 grown-ups in our little room) & one at the Thompsons & one at the schoolmasters & three parties, two yet to come. A football match on Boxing Day, married against single. The married won for the first time in Islip history score 6–2. I shot 4 goals & was responsible for the other 2.

Amy had sent not only a parcel of presents, but a cheque for £10, described by her son as 'a magnificent present [which] puts me to the blush that I still owe you rent. "Only have patience & I will pay you all." I am not poor so much as uncertain until the New Year comes how things will turn out: it all looks very bright.'[116] Robert had some cause for optimism: no author can tell exactly how many copies one of his books will sell; but he had three works either ready or nearly ready for publication: *Mockbeggar Hall*, *The Meaning of Dreams*, and *Poetic Unreason*; and he must have hoped that at least one of them – perhaps *The Meaning of Dreams*, with its intriguing title – would meet with some popular success.

In the meantime, there was the excitement of waiting for Nancy's baby to be born; and indeed the new year of 1924 opened auspiciously with the birth on 4 January of 'a fine boy born early this morning',[117] and named Samuel after their friend Sam Harries. It was an easy birth, though Sam was a large 9lb baby; Nurse Engel had been reappointed to help out; Jenny, David and Catherine left The World's End for a few days to stay with the Thompsons; and within a fortnight Nancy was said to be 'making [a] splendid recovery & getting rid of goitre'.[118]

Nancy had now been subjected to the physical strain of bearing four children in under five years; she had also had to cope with the nervous strain of living on an uncertain income; while references to physical symptoms such as goitre, loss of hair and periods of exhaustion suggest that her health was frequently undermined by a thyroid problem which was aggravated by any unusual strain.[119] She was still only twenty-four, and she still had a healthy dislike of convention; but gone were the sudden youthful enthusiasms which Robert had found so refreshing after his years of soldiering. Often mildly depressed, she still loved and admired her husband; but she needed more financial security, and she had recently mentioned to her father-in-law that it would soon be necessary for Robert to take up some kind of paid employment.

Not long after Sam's birth, Robert had an unlucky footballing accident, hurting a leg so badly that he could not play again for five or six weeks. But he continued to arrange matches, and early in February he asked his brother John, who was now Captain of Soccer at St John's, to bring out a 'not too good' team to play against Islip. Afterwards there was tea for John at The World's End, where he could see that Robert was more than ever bound up with an almost constant round of domestic duties.

Robert, perhaps rightly, still regarded these duties as a bulwark against his mental troubles; though he realized that some people regarded him as a laughing-stock for being apparently tied to his wife's apron-strings, and he was ready to be seriously offended if anyone commented unfavourably on his situation. When in February 1924 Sassoon wrote asking whether a loan would be welcome, and commiserating with him about his 'drudging duties', Robert replied sharply:

As for my drudging domestic duties I have none; my domestic duties would kill you very quickly, but keep me happy and vigorous. As for money.

We are absolutely broke at the moment and I am awfully grateful for your offer and indeed perfectly ready to take money from you as a friend and to feel no obligation, but friendship at World's End implies friendship towards the whole damn lot of us, and until you realize that I am completely satisfied with this life, debts and all, and am not so far as I know Nancy's drudge or 'the Hen-Pecked Husband or Hammond's Depressed Villager or the Impoverished Genius with the Awful Wife and the Squalling Brats' (for these parts am I starred among literary gossipers), until then I say you and I are at too great cross-purposes to be really friends again for a while.[120]

Later on in the letter, however, Robert wrote warmly about Sassoon's recent poems, invited him to stay 'a night or two nights' at The World's End, and concluded: 'You will find Nancy perfectly reasonable if you treat her as a fellow human being not altogether lacking in wits or kindness. This letter is an awful muddle but I am really trying to put things right in my clumsy way.'[121] This drew both a friendly letter and a cheque for £25 from Sassoon;[122] and Robert, in acknowledging this generous gift, added a further word about Nancy, who was said to be 'much easier to get on with now, everybody seems to agree, especially if no particular effort is made to smooth her down'.[123] Sadly enough, this reconciliation was shortly followed by a further quarrel, once again over the Sitwells.

Edith Sitwell had now become a good friend of the Graveses. On one occasion she even came to stay at The World's End, where according to Robert 'she spent her time sitting on the sofa and hemming handkerchiefs'. For Robert it had come as 'a surprise, after reading her poems, to find her gentle, domesticated, and even devout'.[124] Edith not only liked Robert, but learned a good deal from him, though apparently she 'shied away from the [psychological] interpretations he insisted on making of her poetry'.[125] And unlike many of Robert's literary friends, she also liked Nancy: 'They are both most charming people', she wrote about them early in 1924.[126] But by the beginning of March that year Sassoon was once again feeling furious with the Sitwell clan. Osbert had played some silly practical jokes; Edith, when appealed to, refused to stop him; Robert defended Edith; and the result, as Arnold Bennett noted in his journal on 7 March, was that 'Siegfried won't speak to Robert Graves or vice versa.'[127]

Sassoon might have made more allowances for his old friend if he had fully appreciated Robert's frequently unhappy state of mind. In the circumstances, Robert depended more than ever upon Nancy; as might perhaps be deduced from his poem 'From our Ghostly Enemy', which begins:

> The fire was already white ash
> When the lamp went out,
> And the clock at that signal stopped:
> The man in the chair held his breath
> As if Death were about.
>
> The moon shone bright as a lily
> On his books outspread.
> He could read in that lily light:
> 'When you have endured your fill,
> Kill!' the book read.
>
> The print being small for his eyes
> To ease their strain
> A hasty candle he lit,
> Keeping the page with his thumb.
> 'Come, those words again!'
>
> But the book he held in his hand
> And the page he held
> Spelt prayers for the sick and needy,
> 'By God, they are wanted here,'
> With fear his heart swelled.

These chilling verses can be taken merely as a ghost story; but they are also a realistic depiction of a frightening delusion typical of a certain kind of severe depression or mental disturbance. Terrified by what has occurred, feeling that his own life is threatened, and 'filled with despairs', the writer goes upstairs to see his wife. He recounts to her sympathetic ear both this and earlier incidents, in one of which:

> 'In the garden yesterday
> As I walked by the beds,
> With the tail of my eye I caught
> "Death within twelve hours"
> Written in flowers' heads.'

His wife preserves him from danger by a remedy which seems simple, but is psychologically effective:

> She answered him, simple advice
> But new, he thought, and true.
> 'Husband, of this be sure,
> That whom you fear the most,
> This ghost, fears you.

'Speak to the ghost and tell him,
  "Whoever you bé,
Ghost, my anguish equals yours,
Let our cruelties therefore end.
  Your friend let me be."'

He spoke, and the ghost, who knew not
  How he plagued that man,
Ceased, and the lamp was lit again,
And the dumb clock ticked again,
  And the reign of peace began.[128]

When Alfred Perceval Graves came to spend a night at Islip towards the end of March, he found Nancy looking 'rather white'; but she and Robert appeared to be leading a very sociable life. APG had been met at the station by Sam Harries, who was staying at The World's End; more friends called during the afternoon, and then, as Alfred records, there was 'a jolly tea party', followed by 'Nuts and May with the children and bear fighting and recitations till supper'. Before APG left Islip the following morning there was time to read over Robert's newly published *Mockbeggar Hall*,[129] sadly but not surprisingly destined to be both a commercial and a critical failure; and he was also given a revised draft of Robert's *John Kemp's Wager* and asked for his comments.

By the time he arrived back at Erinfa that evening, Alfred had read through Robert's 'ballad play' three times, and on the whole he was impressed. Robert had told a love-story: how the brave John Kemp wins the hand of the beautiful maiden Virginia, despite a wicked postman who intercepts their letters, and despite the fact that he is honour-bound to perform a number of almost impossible tasks, which he has undertaken as a bet, or 'wager'. Packed with folk-songs, it is generally speaking both lively and entertaining; and with his own considerable experience of stagecraft APG reckoned that it was 'good $\frac{3}{4}$ way through and then tails off but this can be remedied'.[130] During the next ten days he did a great deal of work on all parts of the play, and sent Robert three successive letters packed with detailed suggestions, many of which were adopted. Unfortunately Robert refused to accept the most important change of all, which involved rewriting the last scene; and so the play still ends on something of an anti-climax.[131]

Robert's refusal to accept his father's advice in this respect was quite understandable. By the age of twenty-nine a man wants to stand on his own feet; and it must have been bad enough for Robert to have to keep asking his family for money, without having to be helped professionally by them as well. At least his father's help was reasonably straightforward. His mother's help, by contrast, must sometimes have been emotionally exhausting, because she was so adoring and so possessive. Earlier in the year APG had accused her with some justice of enjoying the role of martyr;[132] and in May, when it was Amy's turn to spend a night at The World's End she positively forbade John to come out to Islip with her, so that she could have Robert and his problems entirely to herself for a few hours.

Alfred himself was constantly trying to promote Robert's interests.[133] In the summer of 1924, for example, he reminded J.C. Squire, editor of the *London Mercury*, about Robert's poetry;[134] which prompted Squire to take 'a batch of longish poems'.[135] These included 'Ovid's Breeches' (later renamed 'Ovid in Defeat'), a plea for equality between men and women;[136] and the well-known 'Alice', based on 'Alice through the Looking-Glass', in which Robert writes most memorably about the separation between the world of normal reality, and the world of dream and myth:

> For Alice though a child could understand
> That neither did this chance-discovered land
> Make nohow or contrariwise the clean
> Dull round of mid-Victorian routine,
> Nor did Victoria's golden rule extend
> Beyond the glass: it came to the dead end
> Where formal logic also comes; thereafter
> Begins that lubberland of dream and laughter ...[137]

Early in June Robert took his family camping again;[138] but the holiday was a failure: Nancy and the children all went down with 'sharp marsh fever' and were ill for more than a week. When Amy heard of this, she invited them all to come to Harlech at once to recuperate; but Robert demurred, first writing about 'the danger on the roads to the children',[139] and then declaring more plainly that he would not be taking his family to Harlech that summer.

Probably Robert was wise: the atmosphere at Erinfa was heavy with anxiety about his brother Charles. Charles's career as a journalist was flourishing; but he had recently become engaged to a highly neurotic girl called Elvira Mullens, who had recently taken to her bed, explaining that she could not help being ill until she was married. 'I am disappointed', Amy commented in a family letter, '& Charles seem[s] uneasy. Love should not come in such a devastating way.'[140]

Despite having to see Nancy and the children through their convalescence, Robert continued to snatch occasional moments for his poetry. Sometimes he would get up very early in the morning, intending to cycle into Oxford and help one of his neighbours to collect the morning papers. But then, after they had cycled a mile or two, Robert would begin to look abstracted, fall behind, and then stop his bicycle altogether and start scribbling lines of poetry into the notebook which he habitually carried in his pocket. One long poem which Robert wrote very early in 1924 and which may have been begun in this manner was 'At The Games', a poem in honour of 'sportmanship in its pure form'. Although not very memorable, it had impeccable sentiments, and was awarded a silver medal at the Olympic Games that summer.[141]

Towards the end of June there came the devastating news that George Mallory, one of Robert's oldest friends, had died while making an attempt on Everest. He and his companion, Irvine, were last seen climbing strongly within five hundred yards of the summit when bad weather closed in. No one knows what happened thereafter; but, as Robert wrote some five years later, 'anyone who had climbed with George felt convinced that he did get to the summit, that he rejoiced in his accustomed way and had not sufficient reserve of strength left for the descent'.[142]

With so many uncertainties both in his private and in his professional life, the loss of friends was hard to cope with. Raleigh, Rivers, and now Mallory! It began to seem to Robert 'as though the death of my friends was following me in peace-time as relentlessly as in war'; and Islip, which had once appeared to be 'a country refuge' was now becoming clouded with 'many deaths and a feeling of bad luck'.[143]

William Nicholson helped them with an allowance that, in Robert's words, 'covered the extra expense of the new children';[144] and in July they went to visit him. Nancy's father was now living with his second wife 'in some state' at Sutton Veny manor house near Warminster;[145] and while Robert was staying there he was visited by T.E. Lawrence. Although Graves and Lawrence had corresponded occasionally, they had not seen each other since 1922, when Lawrence was in London working on *Seven Pillars of Wisdom*.

Later that year Lawrence had enlisted in the Royal Air Force under an assumed name as an ordinary aircraft hand, hoping to work his way through a mental breakdown; and the new life had just begun to calm him and cure him when his identity was revealed in the press, and he was thrown out of the R.A.F. as an embarrassment. Searching for another haven, he had been able to enlist in the Tank Corps in the spring of 1923 under the name of T.E. Shaw. This time the life did not suit him at all, and by the summer of 1924 his mental state had considerably deteriorated. He was already having himself birched, and before long he would be contemplating suicide. His only agreeable hours were spent away from the camp, which was at Bovington in Dorset; and he roared down the country lanes on his Brough motorbike, on his way to visit literary figures ranging from Thomas Hardy to the reclusive Theodore Powys.[46]

Despite his mental illness Lawrence remained a man with a sharp intelligence and great personal charm. Like many others who knew him, Graves was not fully aware of Lawrence's problems, and was therefore fascinated by his apparent renunciation of power and fame. This led Graves to write a fine poem, 'The Clipped Stater', which is ostensibly about Alexander the Great: in Robert's version of events, however, Alexander's death from fever is only a rumour. In reality, after being 'deified/By loud applause of the Macedonian phalanx', he has abandoned his temporal power for philosophical reasons, and has become a frontier guard in a foreign land. Then one day he is astonished to receive as his pay a clipped Alexandrian stater:

> ... he cannot fathom what the event may mean.
> Was his lost Empire, then, not all-embracing?
> And how does the stater, though defaced, owe service
> To a God that is as if he had never been?
>
> Is he still God? No, truly. Then all he knows
> Is, he must keep the course he has resolved on;
> He spends the coin on a feast of fish and almonds
> And back to the ramparts briskly enough he goes.[47]

However different writers and artists may be from the people whom they portray, they cannot help revealing almost as much about themselves as about their subjects; and Robert, with his present so insecure, and his future so uncertain, was to some extent describing his own state of mind. Like Alexander in the poem, 'all he knows/Is, he must keep the course he has resolved on'. Five years later, looking back at this period of his life, Robert wrote: 'I found myself resorting to my war-time technique of getting through things somehow, anyhow, in the hope that they would mend.'[48]

CHAPTER
11
'A FIRST FAVOURITE
WITH ME'

In the summer of 1924 Robert Graves still nursed hopes for the success of his serious work: *Poetic Unreason* now seemed unlikely to appear before 1925, but *The Meaning of Dreams* was to be published in the autumn; and Robert was busy arranging his poems for a collected edition: 'Secker wants to do them,' he told Sassoon, 'and it is only a matter of getting copyrights from Heinemann and Harold Monro.' However, money was still short; and while he was at Sutton Veny Robert wrote the first draft of what he described to Sassoon as 'a 30,000 word Biblical romance called "My Head, My Head[!]". ... In it I make my peace with Moses whom I used to loathe.'[149]

Graves wrote *My Head, My Head!* partly in order to find answers to a number of biblical questions which had perplexed him for some time: what, for example, were the relations between Elisha and the Shunamite woman? And why was it necessary for Moses to die within sight of the Promised Land? Although it is not a very satisfactory novel – as Graves himself acknowledged a few months later, when he told Diccon Hughes that Secker's decision to publish was 'his scheme and his funeral because it won't sell'[150] – it is important as the precursor of a number of books clearly based upon the 'associative thought' which Graves had praised in *The Meaning of Dreams*. Using 'associative thought' (he later called it 'analeptic thought'), Graves finds solutions to historical, religious, moral and poetic problems which cannot be solved by reason alone. *My Head, My Head!* was one of Graves's first steps upon a path which later led to such major works as *I, Claudius* and *The White Goddess*; and indeed it is in *My Head, My Head!* that he first outlines one of the central tenets of his later poetic creed, that society was once matriarchal, and that 'the beginning of our present misery' dated from the time when 'the mother lost her rule'.[151]

When Robert and his family returned to The World's End he began revising *My Head, My Head!*; and he was also working on a final revision of *Poetic Unreason*, and editing for English publication by the Hogarth Press a selection of poems by his American admirer and occasional editor of the *Fugitive*, John Crowe Ransom. Two of Robert's poems had now been published in the *Fugitive*, including this magical piece, which suggests that a poet's true origins are in a mythical realm far removed from the everyday world:

ON THE POET'S BIRTH

A page, a huntsman and a priest of God
  Her lovers, met in jealous contrariety
Equally claiming the sole parenthood
  Of him the perfect crown of their variety.
Then, whom to admit, herself she could not tell:
That always was her fate, she loved too well.

'But many-fathered little one,' she said,
  'Whether of high or low, of smooth or rough,
Here is your mother whom you brought to bed;
  Acknowledge only me; be this enough;
For such as worship after shall be told
A white dove sired you or a rain of gold.'[152]

Copies of the *Fugitive* were now to be found on the bookshelves at The World's End; and one day an English friend on vacation from a post in India was leafing through some back numbers when he was 'fired with excited interest' by the poems of a remarkable young American poet, Laura Riding Gottschalk.[153] Robert and Nancy took another look at a group of her poems which had appeared in February 1924, and which included 'The Quids',[154] a description of the sub-atomic structure of things, which managed at the same time to convey a series of wry philosophical comments upon human behaviour, as in this verse:

A quid here and there gyrated in place-position,
While many essential quids turned inside-out
For the fun of it
And a few refused to be anything but
Simple, unpredicated copulatives.
Little by little, this commotion of quids,
By threes, by tens, by casual millions,
Squirming within the state of things –
The metaphysical acrobats,
The naked, immaterial quids –
Turned inside on themselves
And came out all dressed,

Each similar quid of the inward same,
Each similar quid dressed in a different way –
The quid's idea of a holiday.

This was original work of rare quality. More of Mrs Gottschalk's poems
could be read in both earlier and later issues of the magazine; and when
Robert had also seen some of her unpublished work (forwarded to him by
Ransom at his request), he began hoping that he would find her an English
publisher. He still knew little about Laura Gottschalk apart from her work;
but in September, Ransom informed him not only that she was 'brilliant',
a fact which Robert must already have deduced from her writing, but that
she had been divorced from her husband, a Louisville college professor, earlier
in the year, that she was 'now in New York trying to make a living doing
hack literary work', and that, in Ransom's view, she was 'very fine personally,
but very intense for company'. Ransom also included some quite untrue but
highly intriguing details about Laura's childhood, suggesting that she had
come 'up from the slums, I think,' and had been 'much battered about as
a kid'.[155]

Robert was presumably very much interested in what was to be learned
of Laura Riding Gottschalk; but in the meantime another financial crisis had
to be dealt with. The first that Robert's parents heard of it was on Monday
18 August, when, as APG recorded in his diary, a 'bombshell wire from Robby'
arrived, announcing that he was raising money by letting The World's End
for a month, and asking 'to be taken in with his whole family on Thursday'.
Erinfa was already almost full of summer visitors, and more were expected
soon; but Amy could not bear to turn Robert away altogether, so she 'compromised after a family council by asking him to come in September instead'.[156]
However, The World's End was already let, and Robert had nowhere else
to go. On Wednesday morning Amy was walking through the village when
the postman handed her a letter in which Robert announced that he and his
family would be arriving the following afternoon.

Amy was furious. She had told Robert that there was no room at Erinfa,
and although it might just have been possible to squeeze them all into one
room, it would be very inconvenient, and she did not see why she should
back down. Within a few hours she had made alternative arrangements: they
were to camp at Cae Dhu, a farm above Harlech where they could have 'a
field to camp in, and the use of one good room'.[157]

On Thursday afternoon Robert and Nancy, both looking 'a bit fine drawn'
arrived at Harlech station in the same train as APG's brother Bob, now 'Sir
Robert' Graves, as he had recently been knighted for his services in the Middle

East. Alfred and Amy met the train, together with John and Rosaleen; Bob left for his hotel; and it took a lorry and a hired car to carry everyone else up to the site at Cae Dhu. A large tent was erected; the children were put to bed; and later Robert came down to Erinfa to borrow some mattresses for himself and Nancy.

He left his Olympic Games poem and medal for APG to admire; and also the poems by Ransom which were shortly to be published as *Grace after Meat*, with an introduction by Robert. Alfred was pleased by his son's poem; but described Ransom's work as 'clever, blasphemous and rather stilted productions. I'm sorry Robby is godfathering them.'[58]

Harlech was already full of Graveses, including Susan and Molly; and Friday saw the arrival of Robert's uncle Charles, his cousin Gerald, and his brother Perceval. Perceval had brought with him his fiancée, the professional singer Gwen Knight. That evening she took part in a family concert at Erinfa, and her beauty and talent both as a singer and as a pianist made her the star performer. Robert, leaving Nancy and the children in their tent, 'joined in ... & sang folk songs ... to Rosaleen's accompaniment'. For an hour or two, it might almost have been one of the prewar musical evenings of his youth.[59]

On Monday the weather changed for the worse, and, much to Alfred's relief, Amy began to relent towards her eldest son. A few days later, Robert and Nancy and their children were safely installed at Erinfa, where they stayed for the rest of their holiday.[160]

Before long they had contacted Diccon Hughes, who accepted an invitation to come over for an evening meal on Saturday 30 August. It was pouring with rain when he arrived at Erinfa; and he roared up the steep driveway on a motorbike with an open sidecar containing two very good-looking but very damp young women: Stella Watson and an artist friend of hers. After the visitors had dried out by a roaring fire, everyone sat down to supper, and then took turns in telling stories to one another until after ten o'clock.[161] When the weather improved again, Robert and Nancy took the children to the beach or the hills during the day; and played music or bridge in the evenings. Once Robert took Nancy to the Barmouth cinema, where they watched a film of Victor Hugo's *The Hunchback of Notre Dame*; and on 13 September they celebrated Nancy's twenty-fifth birthday with an outing in a hired car.

Happy episodes like these were interspersed with periods when Nancy showed signs of being in a highly nervous condition. It was always a great strain living at such close quarters with her formidable in-laws: Rosaleen and John were kind enough; but Clarissa, the only one who fully appreciated her artistic interests, was away; and Nancy could neither shine as a musician (like

Gwen Knight) nor make any very pointed or witty contribution to the endless family conversations, now so sharpened by years of sibling rivalry that it was extraordinarily difficult for any outsider to join in. There were days when Nancy took to her bed feeling 'rather low', or was 'on edge all day and hardly appeared';[162] and every time this happened, and either Robert was given yet more work to do, or Amy or Rosaleen kindly helped out, her feelings of inadequacy must have increased fivefold.

Luckily Robert accepted extra responsibilities without becoming embittered. Indeed, the harder he worked the happier he appeared to be, as there was less time for worrying overmuch either about Nancy's health or about his own continuing lack of success. He and his family returned to Islip on 20 September; and some weeks later Eddie Marsh came to visit him one afternoon, and found him 'radiantly happy at a teatable with five or six bread-and-buttery children and the village postmaster and wife'.[163] Soon afterwards, Robert wrote to Marsh saying that it was

> nice of you to walk over the other day and see the four reasons for my never coming to town; it is the life I have chosen and it suits me. In fact to have no leisure time on my hands at all has been the only possible cure for my neurasthenia from which I still suffer officially and actually, if I start at all a different life from this. Travelling is the one thing sure to upset me; a train journey to Oxford even leaves me utterly unstrung for the rest of the day. Can't quite explain it, but there it is.[164]

Money remained a problem. *The Meaning of Dreams* had received mixed reviews when it appeared in late September,[165] and was clearly going to earn very little. Squire had printed two of his poems, but had not even replied to a request for payment;[166] and Robert asked Marsh whether he was now owed any *Georgian Poetry* royalties, as 'a good time is coming perhaps but we want to live to see it'.

Robert was beginning to fear that he would eventually be driven to looking for some paid employment apart from his writing. If so, he would need qualifications; but he still had no degree. So at the beginning of December 1924, in the presence of his brother John, he finally submitted a typescript copy of *Poetic Unreason* to the University authorities as his thesis for a B.Litt. degree.

Alfred and Amy were delighted to hear this news when on 5 December they stayed at Islip for a night on their way home from a long and much-needed holiday in Austria. It was a great relief for them to feel that Robert's affairs were at last moving calmly ahead in the right direction, even if he was temporarily rather short of money.[167] His life contrasted favourably with that of his brother

Charles, who had recently been involved in some unpleasant scenes straight out of romantic fiction.

What had happened to Charles was that he had fallen out of love with the neurotic Elvira Mullens, and had very sensibly broken off their engagement. Elvira had then decided to commit suicide on the pavement outside Charles's window, having first alerted him by throwing stones at his window. Luckily Charles spotted the pistol gleaming in her hand, and arranged for a friend to distract her while he rushed from the front door and made 'a grab for the pistol. ... She tried to pull the trigger but the pistol fell out of her hand on to the pavement with a clang, and she fainted dead away.'[168] This might well have led to a considerable scandal, especially as in those days it was thought to be highly dishonourable for a man to break off an engagement, even if he did so having realized that marriage would lead to a lifetime of misery. Robert certainly felt that he was now justified in thinking of his brother as a 'cad', and some years later attempted to expose him as such.[169] However, Lord Beaverbrook, to whom Charles had made a clean breast of the whole affair, had allowed him to stay on at the *Express*;[170] and Alfred and Amy had also taken a more lenient view of Charles's actions.

Now they found everything at The World's End 'bright & pleasant', and they met several more of Robert and Nancy's friends, including Maisie Somerville, an undergraduate of the Oxford college which had been founded by her grandmother. Maisie had known Robert for about a year, very much admired him, and occasionally took friends such as the young Princeton graduate Tom Matthews out to Islip to meet him. APG, who had been told that Maisie was 'supposed to make every man fall in love with her', could not help feeling a little disappointed when she failed to stir his emotions in the slightest;[171] but she had her own particular appeal, and Matthews later described her as 'a large, blond, slow-spoken, cat like creature, with a cat's equivocal smile'.[172]

Although Robert had submitted his thesis as a necessary preliminary to finding employment, he still wanted to remain independent if at all possible, and he was working furiously at half a dozen new projects.[173] One of these he described to Marsh as 'a treatise on the various rival techniques of modern poetry; showing their historical necessity and meaning. Defending where defence is needed. About 8000 words, awful sweat.'[174] Dedicated to Edith Sitwell, it was to be published in 1925 by the Hogarth Press as *Contemporary Techniques of Poetry: A Political Analogy*. In this long essay Graves defends those poets, including himself, who made up a kind of moderate left-wing; and he quotes in full Laura Riding Gottschalk's poem 'The Quids', which he describes as 'a satire on traditional metaphysics; and a first favourite with me'.[175]

Robert was not alone in admiring Mrs Gottschalk's poetry. The December 1924 issue of the *Fugitive*, announcing the award of three prizes for distinguished work published in the magazine during the past year, stated that their most important prize,

> The Nashville prize of $100, offered by the Associated Retailers of Nashville, is awarded to Laura Riding Gottschalk, of Louisville, Kentucky. In the minds of the members of the group, who were the judges of the award, the poetry of Mrs Gottschalk stands out as the discovery of the year, and they deem it a privilege to be first in calling attention to the work of a young writer who is coming forward as a new figure in American poetry.[76]

Before long Robert Graves was to begin corresponding directly with Laura Riding Gottschalk; and this was to be the prelude of an important literary partnership which lasted for more than twelve years.

CHAPTER
12
'A QUESTION
OF IDENTITY'

At this stage of his life Robert was in desperate need of friends who believed in him, as he was full of self-doubt. On the surface everything was much as usual. Clarissa came to stay at The World's End for Christmas 1924, and enjoyed helping at a children's fancy-dress party at which Jenny was a fairy, David a pirate, Catherine a Coogan boy, and Sam a cupid with wings.[77] Soon afterwards, Rosaleen visited The World's End, and wrote to her parents praising 'the Charity girl of 13 taken in as Children's maid'.[78] This was Daisy, the daughter of 'an out-of-work ex-service man, a steam-roller driver by trade', whose wife had recently died, and who had called at The World's End to sell bootlaces, and ask for cast-off clothing. Nancy had offered to train Daisy in housework, so that she could later find a job as a maid; and her offer had been accepted with 'tears of gratitude'.[79]

Daisy's presence in the household made it easier for Robert to concentrate upon his writing; and it was a period when, as he wrote four years later, he was willing

> to undertake almost any writing job to bring in money. I wrote a series of rhymes for a big map-advertisement for Huntley & Palmer's biscuits (I was paid, but the rhymes never appeared); and silly lyrics for a light opera, *Lord Clancarty*, for which I was not paid, because the opera was never staged; and translations from Dutch and German carols; and rhymes for children's Christmas annuals.[180]

In January 1925 Robert enlisted his father's help with yet another project, a volume of ballads for schoolchildren. APG contributed some of his own verses, supplied him with ballad books and cleared a number of permissions; but although Robert was justifiably proud of his output ('Trump that, you idle fellow!' he wrote to Diccon Hughes in a lengthy letter detailing all his work in hand), it was clear that he had placed himself under enormous strain;[181] and this had its consequences. For example, a friendly letter of invitation from the father who had just been helping him was answered in the most wounding manner. Robert explained that he and Nancy had no intention of visiting Erinfa during 1925. He had learned from Nancy, he said, that the reason why she had kept on retreating to bed during their last visit was that she felt sick with worry to see her children being treated in so incorrect a fashion.[182]

Actions of this kind, apparently so hostile, sprang from an increasing sense of despair. Robert had made every attempt to make Nancy happy, but seemed unable to prevent her from drifting downhill into a state of nervous ill health. He had made every attempt to stand on his own feet as a writer; but he had been unsuccessful, and his latest tremendous efforts might well be similarly doomed. Constant failure was bringing about a kind of identity crisis. He seemed to have played many parts in his life; but what was the essential core of the real Robert Graves, and what was his purpose? Questions of this kind are formulated in a poem entitled 'A Letter from Wales' which Graves probably wrote late in 1924. The poem was subtitled 'Richard Rolls to his friend, Captain Abel Wright'; and despite Robert's disclaimer to the effect that 'The characters and incidents are unhistorical', Richard Rolls is clearly himself, and Captain Abel Wright is Siegfried Sassoon. The poem begins:

> This is a question of identity
> Which I can't answer. Abel, I'll presume
> On your good-nature, asking you to help me.
> I hope you will, since you too are involved
> As deeply in the problem as myself.
> *Who are we?* Take down your old diary, please,
> The one you kept in France, if you *are* you
> Who served in the Black Fusiliers with me.
> That is, again, of course, if I am I –
> This isn't Descartes' philosophic doubt,
> But, as I say, a question of identity,
> And practical enough. – Turn up the date,
> July the twenty-fourth, nineteen-sixteen,
> And read the entry there:
> > 'Today I met
> *Meredith, transport-sergeant of the Second.*
> *He told me that Dick Rolls had died of wounds.*
> . . .
> But then appeared a second Richard Rolls
> (Or that's the view that the facts force on me),
> Showing Dick's features to support his claim

> To rank and pay and friendship, Abel, with you.
> And you acknowledged him as the old Dick,
> Despite all evidence to the contrary,
> Because, I think, you missed the dead too much.
> You came up here to Wales to stay with him
> And I don't know for sure, but I suspect
> That you were dead too.

The two 'substitutes' go up to Wales, 'pretending a wild joy/That they had cheated Death'; but although on the surface they appear to be having a good time, sitting up to talk the nights away,

> They felt a sense of unreality
> In the proceedings – yes, that's good, *proceedings* –
> It suggests ghosts.

Later these two friends, 'the second of the series', go out to France again. The 'representative' of Abel Wright is once again killed; while the 'representative' of Richard Rolls 'died at Hove after the Armistice, / Pneumonia, with the doctor's full consent'. After this 'the I and you who then took over' felt 'a constraint in all our dealings'; and now, having been reminded of 'the second Richard' by finding 'A pack-valise marked with his name and rank', Richard Rolls begins to feel:

> ... badly confused,
> Being accustomed to this newer self;
> I wondered whether you could reassure me.
> Now I have asked you, do you see my point?
> What I'm asking really isn't 'Who am I?'
> Or 'Who are you?' (you see my difficulty?)
> But a stage before that, '*how am I to put*
> *The question that I'm asking you to answer?*'[183]

The publication in February 1925 of Graves's *Poetic Unreason* did nothing to place his literary career on firmer ground. At the beginning of April it received a destructive criticism in the *Manchester Guardian*; and a review in the *Times Literary Supplement* was regarded by Graves as 'a deliberate misrepresentation of my main points, because to concede them involves too much'. However, he learned that Sir Edmund Gosse was enthusiastic about his book; and Sassoon, the source of this information, responded to Robert's gift of *Poetic Unreason* (and perhaps to the 'Letter from Wales' poem) by sending a copy of his own latest book, with a double inscription to both Robert and Nancy. Robert was touchingly overjoyed by this gesture. 'Dearest Siegfried,' he wrote, 'You make us very happy by the double inscription: really to have you as a friend again is the best thing that has happened here for years. While there was a conflict on, it spoilt my relationship with Nancy as well as my relationship with you.'[184] On a lighter note, Robert mentioned that he and Nancy had been given a car valued at £7. 10s. 0d. As that value implies, it had seen better days. Robert's task was to go to the front of the car to 'wind up' the engine, and he later commented that 'the energy that I put into winding was almost equivalent to pushing it for a mile or two'.[185] Then Nancy did the driving; but although it gave them more freedom, it was also too expensive for them to run. 'The other night a wheel flew off on Boar's Hill', Robert told Sassoon; 'for which we owe mechanics a good deal.'[186]

Short of money again, they were bailed out in mid-April by Eddie Marsh with a cheque which, said Robert, 'came in the nick of time: (they always do)'.[187] On the strength of it, he took his family up to London on Monday 20 April, and they stayed for a week with Rosaleen and Clarissa, who were now in lodgings at Northwick Terrace, not far from Lord's Cricket Ground. Rosaleen had moved to London to continue with her medical studies; while Clarissa was working with the Christian Science movement as a spiritual healer.[188] On Tuesday evening Sassoon called in to see them after dinner, and

> found Robert, uncouth and charming, affectionate and impulsive, complaining that London upsets his nerves. And there was his younger brother Charles, who is 'assistant news-editor' of the *Sunday Express* and boasts that he has scribbled two thousand words a day for the last four years – a horrible achievement! And there was Nancy, queer and uncouth, concealing her shyness behind a mask of sharp-tongued reserve. The two sisters were friendly, but I bore the brunt, doing my best to 'make things go' by telling them anything that came into my head.[189]

It was arranged that on Friday Sassoon should meet them again, this time at the Zoo. When he arrived, Jenny, David and Catherine were waiting for a ride on a camel, while Sam, the baby, sat in 'an odd little folding perambulator' which was being pushed by Nancy. Sassoon noticed that

> R.G., as usual, was being gentle and patient with the children. It always touches my heart when I see him with them. They are countrified little creatures, chubby and frolicsome. William Nicholson and his son Ben (and wife) joined us, and after a long stare at the monkey house, we went into the Aquarium, which Robert enjoyed immensely, in spite of his parental

responsibilities. Then they all crowded into the tea-house and there I left them to it.[190]

Nancy was now more friendly towards Siegfried, though he still felt awkward with her; and she agreed that Robert should meet him for dinner that evening – 'quite a concession on her part', Sassoon commented in his diary.[191] But first Robert wanted to fit in a visit to Leonard and Virginia Woolf, whom he had never met despite the fact that they had now published several of his works.

Dashing from the Zoo, he arrived on their front doorstep in time to make a dramatic but not very favourable impression upon Virginia Woolf, whose account of the meeting was written three days later with a pen dipped in her accustomed mixture of insight and vitriol:

Figure a bolt eyed blue shirted shockheaded hatless man in a blue overcoat standing goggling at the door at 4.30, on Friday – 'Mrs Woolf?' I dreading & suspecting some Nation genius, some young man determined to unbosom himself, rushed him to the basement, where he said 'I'm Graves.' 'I'm Graves.' Everybody stared. He appeared to have been rushing through the air at 60 miles an hour & to have alighted temporarily. So he came up, &, wily as I am, I knew that to advance holding the kettle in a dishclout was precisely the right method, attitude, pose. The poor boy is all emphasis protestation & pose. He has a crude likeness to Shelley, save that his nose is a switchback & his lines blurred. But the consciousness of genius is bad for people.

Robert stayed with the Woolfs for more than two hours, telling them all about his way of life at Islip, and talking rather proudly about Nancy and her advanced ideas.

All this [wrote Virginia Woolf], sounded like the usual self-consciousness of young men, especially as he threw in, gratuitously, the information that he descends from dean, rector, Bishop, Von Ranke &c &c &c: only in order to say that he despises them. Still, still, he is a nice ingenuous rattle-headed young man; but why should our age put this burden of proof on us? Surely one could live simply without protestations. I tried, perhaps, to curry favour, as my weakness is. L[eonard] was adamant. Then we were offered a ticket for the Cup tie, to see wh[ich] Graves has come to London.[192]

Soon afterwards the Woolfs left to see a production of Shaw's *Caesar and Cleopatra*,[193] while Robert went on to the Reform Club, where he met Sassoon; and the old comrades-in-arms spent what Siegfried described as 'two enjoyable hours of dinner and discussion'.[194]

Two weeks later Sassoon saw Graves again: this time at Islip, where he called in at The World's End for tea, and found that George Mallory's wife was staying there. Nancy was resting in bed, and Daisy had left; so Robert was downstairs, busy looking after Sam, while the other children were outdoors playing with some of the village children. Daisy had opened Robert's eyes to the world of professional beggars, but in other respects she had not been a great success; and in any case when her father had called at the house again, a few weeks ago, he had said that he 'couldn't manage the little ones without her'.[195] Nancy came down for tea and was 'amiable' to Siegfried, who had brought some jam-roll and chocolates with him; and afterwards Robert and Siegfried rambled along the river bank and had, according to Siegfried, 'rather an unsatisfactory conversation' which ended in a downpour.[196]

Robert had now taken on yet another identity, as an Islip parish councillor.[197] A few years later this seemed to have no bearing upon what was important in his life, and he described with wry amusement 'another caricature scene: myself in corduroys and a rough frieze coat ... debating as [a] village elder whether or not Farmer So-and-so was justified in using a footpath across the allotments as a bridle-path.'[198] But at the time he was pleased to have been elected to office by his fellow villagers; and he did some important work for the community. In the autumn of 1925 Amy recounted proudly to John the story of how Robert had

> gone behind the authorities to get the shocking system of drainage at Islip and the consequent pollution of drinking water looked into. It is the more public-spirited of him, as his water supply is private and his drainage is by bucket and therefore quite harmless. Such things in you, my children give me a lovely feeling inside, you know how I feel![199]

Long before this, in the first week of June, Robert had heard that his thesis had been accepted; but before he could be awarded a B.Litt. he must undergo a viva voce examination.

The two examiners were to be Garrod, an expert on Catullus; and Gordon, the President of Magdalen. The prospect of a viva alarmed Robert, and he wrote defensively to John that he did not know the examiners, but that 'one has to be a pretty abandoned wretch to get either of their jobs'.[200] However, there was soon an opportunity to 'pull strings'. Robert left his family at Sutton Veny for a day or two, while he went down to give a lecture at Brighton. By good luck his father's friend the Bishop of Birmingham was in the chair; and afterwards Robert reported to APG that the Bishop had been 'sympathetic – thinks he can wangle [the] two examiners in the Viva Voce'.[201]

On 16 June 1925, the day of the viva, Robert had lunch with John, and borrowed from him the necessary 'white tie, gown and other academic disguise'.[202] The viva itself was as difficult as Robert had feared: but although Garrod and Gordon were clearly unconvinced by the arguments which he had put forward in *Poetic Unreason*, he came away with the impression that they were going to give him a degree. He was right. On 21 June Robert was able to wire the news to his father that he had been awarded an Honorary B.Litt., 'thanks', as he put it, 'to your persistence and assistance'. His parents were delighted by the friendliness of Robert's recent communications, so different from the hostile letters which he had written earlier in the year; and Amy, who had already sent Robert £25 to clear his outstanding debts, wrote a further letter offering to pay for his taking the degree, and for any arrears of fees.

Now that Robert had his degree, it was time to think again about his future. Despite the fact that most of his books had been published in America as well as in England,[203] his efforts to earn his living solely by writing had clearly failed for the time being. Secker and Knopf both published his biblical romance *My Head, My Head!*, but it made no significant impact on either side of the Atlantic; neither did a *Selected Poems* in Benn's sixpenny series later in the year; nor did *John Kemp's Wager*, though it came close: Robert lunched with Vaughan Williams, and for some weeks that great composer felt inclined to write the accompanying music. But that too came to nothing.[204] In the meantime, Nancy was worn out, and Robert himself was not merely exhausted but more than a little unbalanced by his recent ordeals. In the circumstances, as Robert later wrote, it was clear that 'cottage life with four of them under six years old, and Nancy ill, was not good enough. I would have, after all, to take a job.'[205]

CHAPTER
13
'THE MARMOSITE'S MISCELLANY'

Despite his lack of financial success, Robert Graves was still corresponding with a number of people who believed in his work, including Basanta Mallik, Laura Riding Gottschalk, and John Crowe Ransom.

Mallik in particular had been much in Graves's thoughts, partly because their mutual friend Sam Harries was planning to travel out to India to visit him in the summer of 1925;[206] and it was to Mallik that Graves dedicated a long poem, 'The Marmosite's Miscellany'.[207] The dedication took the form of another poem, in which Graves praised Mallik for having

> ...no ambition
> Except this only, to have no ambition.
> With no religion but our quiet faith
> That all religions are denial of God,
> Belittling what they most seek to applaud;
> With no support but friendship that makes light
> Of broad dividing seas, broad continents.

And he made it clear that it was this kind of friendship which enabled him to think lightly

> Of such calamities as whelm us both,
> The dragon darkness that piece-meal devours us,
> The sun that sucks our life.

The idea for the main poem had come to Graves during his visit to the London Zoo in the spring of 1925 with his family and Sassoon;[208] and in it he uses a marmoset, or monkey, as his mouthpiece in a lengthy dissertation first upon religion, and then upon his own personal philosophy, ending with a description of many contemporary authors written by the marmoset as though he were the great satirist Samuel Butler come back to life. Because of this last section, Graves thought it prudent to appear under the pseudonym of 'John Doyle' when the work was published later in the year by the Hogarth Press; but the satire was not very biting, and elaborate notes explain why remarks such as 'a stranded bream' in the following verse are not intended as insults:

> 'Blunden wore the sunset hues of a stranded bream,
> A shoal of Oxford minnows followed upstream,
> Edward Marsh was poised on the edge of a sofa,
> Hardy dribbled his umbrella,
> Belloc danced a tarantella,
> Aldous Huxley juggled up a skull and a loofah.'

More interesting is the section in which Graves (in the voice of the marmoset) writes about his principles, which include 'to reverence God, but not from any pew'; to treat other people on terms of equality, whether they are paupers or peers; and to listen carefully to ideas which on the surface appear to be no more than the 'maunderings' of a 'maniac': remembering that

> Thought comes often clad in the strangest clothing.
> So Kekulé, the chemist, watched the weird rout
> Of eager atom serpents winding in and out,
> And waltzing tail to mouth; in that absurd guise
> Appeared benzene and anilin, their drugs and their dyes.

This is another powerful plea for the exercise of 'associative' or 'analeptic' as against purely intellectual thought.

The idea that truth may reside in apparent madness leads on to these two verses which strongly foreshadow the future direction of Robert's thinking. They describe a world quite at odds with conventional life, a world in which the moon – seen for the first time as beneficent rather than always pointlessly cruel – presides over a timeless land of honeysuckle hedges and true lovers:

> 'The Moon is the Mistress of escape and pity,
> Her regions are portalled by an ivory gate.
> There are fruit-plats and fountains in her silver city,
> With honeysuckle hedges where true lovers mate,
> With undisputed thrones where beggars hold state,
> With smooth hills and fields where in freedom may run
> All men maimed and manacled by the cruel sun.

> 'Her madness is musical, kindly her mood,
> She is Dian no more when the sun quits the skies.
> She is the happy Venus of the hushed wood.
> So artless Actaeon may banquet his eyes

        At the crisp hair curling on her naked thighs,
        At her shapely shoulders, her breasts and her knees,
        She will kiss him pleasantly under tall trees.'

No doubt a copy of this poem reached Nashville, where since March 1925 'Mrs Laura Riding Gottschalk of Louisville' had been officially welcomed 'as a regular and participating member of the Fugitive group'.[209] Robert and Laura were now writing to each other; and Nancy, seeing the good effect upon Robert of mental contact with someone in whose work and outlook he found intellectual stimulation of a high order, had suggested that Laura be given an open invitation to come to England so that the two poets could work together more closely.[210]

    In the meantime Robert was looking for a job; and his own first thought was not that Laura should come to England, but that he and Nancy should travel to America, where Ransom and his friends might be able to find work for him as a lecturer.[211] Graves wrote to Ransom, who probably suggested that it would be best to have a definite offer of a job before crossing the Atlantic; and who put him in touch with Cornell University. Cornell showed interest; and towards the end of June 1925 Robert, who was then holidaying with his family at Sutton Veny, began collecting letters of recommendation.[212]

CHAPTER
14
'VERY MUCH
DISTRACTED'

Robert Bridges was one of the first to be approached: 'Money being scarcer than even usual', Graves wrote to him, 'I have more or less decided to take a University job in the States ... the Cornell people are ready to take me.'[213] Bridges wrote back on 4 July 1925 that it would give him 'great pleasure to be of any assistance to you';[214] and had soon supplied Graves with a valuable 'To Whom It May Concern' letter of recommendation. John Buchan, who had been joint dedicatee with his wife of Graves's *The Meaning of Dreams*, also supplied a testimonial; as did the Earl of Oxford, who had apparently 'taken a fatherly interest' in Robert, and often visited him at Islip; and a further letter was secured from the Vice-Chancellor of Oxford University.[215]

Armed with these recommendations, Robert Graves was now staying at Apple Tree Yard with Nancy, having left the children with their Nicholson grandfather at Sutton Veny. On Monday 13 July he was interviewed by a Professor Canby; but it appears that for some reason Graves was rejected.[216]

This great disappointment was followed not long afterwards by an unconfirmed report that Sam Harries, at that time their closest friend, had died while visiting Mallik in India. After a terrible three weeks during which both Robert and Nancy found it 'impossible to write letters or do anything ... we have been very much distracted', the bad news was confirmed. Harries had died of typhus. Nancy came very close to a complete breakdown, and in mid-August Robert once again left the children with their nurse and their grandfather, and took Nancy up to London for treatment.[217] Soon he was writing to Robert Bridges that Nancy was 'a good deal better under massage & we are hoping for a little peace after a succession of troubles'. He added that it had been 'too late to make satisfactory arrangements this year for America but next year should be favourable'.[218]

Shortly after arriving in London, Graves had called on Sassoon. Robert was looking 'worried'; and in his anxious state he upset Siegfried by tactlessly reporting a private conversation in which unkind remarks had been made about

Sassoon by Sassoon's landlord and supposed friend, the Australian poet Walter
Turner. For Siegfried that was a 'crisis'; and for the next ten days he spent
many hours in Robert's company, finding his presence 'a perfect godsend
for getting me through the days'.[219] On the 18th, for example, he drove Robert
and Nancy to Kew, where they spent the whole afternoon together; and on
the 19th Sassoon 'lunched at Apple Tree Yard (precious little to eat, as usual)
and then accompanied R.G. to the Broadcasting Headquarters, where he
underwent a voice-test'. Robert's friend Maisie Somerville, who was now working for the B.B.C., had arranged the test; and later in the day Robert and
Siegfried 'called at Heinemann's for some new books for R.G. to "talk about"
to the "listeners-in".'[220]

On the morning of 27 August, before he had had time to take part in
any radio broadcasts, Robert was compelled to leave London in a hurry. The
children's nurse had fallen downstairs and had been removed to hospital, and
it was necessary for him to take her place. Sassoon saw him off at Paddington
– apparently Robert was 'in a nervy state' – and then went on to lunch with
Nancy at Apple Tree Yard. There he met her Swedish masseuse, a Miss Halt-
man, whom he described as 'ugly, intelligent, kind, and humorous – not a
bad mixture'.[221] A few days later, when Nancy's course of treatment was over,
she too returned to Sutton Veny; and then went on with Robert and the children
to Islip.

Hardly had they reached The World's End when Alfred and Amy wrote
saying that they would like to see them, and asking if lodgings could be found
in the village. Robert and Nancy agreed; and so on Thursday 17 September
Alfred and Amy made the train journey to Islip, where they met Robert out
blackberrying with the children. Then they all walked back to the Beckleys'
house, where Alfred and Amy were to stay; and the grandparents had supper
there before going on to The World's End.

That evening there was much family news to discuss, chiefly about Robert's
brothers Charles and John. Charles had fallen in love at first sight with a
graceful, beautiful and utterly sane young woman from Georgia, called Margaret or more usually 'Peggy' Leigh. Tall, slim and elegant, she had aristocratic
connections, and was accustomed to wealth; but her rare combination of a
strong sense of duty and a very warm heart led her to spend her days as
a nurse in the children's hospital at Paddington Green. She and Charles were
now thinking of becoming engaged, though her parents had insisted that they
should not be married for at least four years, unless before then Charles could
earn enough money to keep her in the style to which she was accustomed.[222]
The news about John was that he had left Oxford with only a Third, having
spent too much of his time playing games for his college. Now he hoped to

go into publishing: but first he wanted to see more of the world. He had recently landed a job as private tutor to the son of an American millionaire, and was about to spend the next six months touring round Europe in great style.[223]

Robert himself sounded cheerful enough, and talked both about the six-penny edition of his poems being brought out by Benn; and about the possibility of Vaughan Williams composing music for *John Kemp's Wager*; while Nancy, though 'fine drawn', was 'more forthcoming than usual', and 'dressed charmingly in feminine costume'.[224] The children also seemed happy; and the next day, after a morning in Oxford, Alfred and Amy arrived back at Islip in time to see the village schoolchildren, six-year-old Jenny and five-year-old David among them, streaming out of the schoolyard for their midday meal. Three-year-old Catherine, dressed 'in little boy blue garb' was waiting for her brother and sister; and when her grandparents arrived the five of them walked back together to The World's End.[225]

It was an auspicious start to Alfred and Amy's visit; and at the weekend Maisie Somerville came to stay with Robert and Nancy, and pleased APG by asking him whether he would consider broadcasting some of his Irish poems at Christmas. But Robert's parents soon began to see the true state of affairs; and on Saturday evening APG noted in his diary: 'The children are less manageable and Nancy far from free from nerve trouble, and Robert evidently suffering sympathetically.'[226] They did their best to help, and on Sunday afternoon Amy kindly 'took care of the three elder, very lively & unruly children from 1.45 to 4 o.c. to give peace to their parents'. On their way back to The World's End, they were joined by the village schoolmaster and his wife; and then, to everyone's surprise, Molly arrived with three of her Preston in-laws, and talked a good deal about her life in Egypt.[227]

This busy afternoon left Nancy exhausted for several days. On Tuesday she actually took to her bed, and her children were 'rather difficult' that day, and 'very troublesome' the next.[228] On Thursday 24 September, when Alfred and Amy left Islip, they had much to think about. As usual, the most practical help which they could give was financial, and as soon as they had returned to Harlech (which was not until 8 October) APG wrote offering 'to pay Robert's remaining debts if he would give me particulars'.[229] The offer was gratefully accepted;[230] but it was not enough. Robert and Nancy could not continue much longer in their present condition without one or other or both of them suffering from a breakdown; and now their doctor told them plainly that if Nancy wished to regain her health it would be best for her to spend the winter in a 'dry, warm climate'.[231]

CHAPTER
15
THE CAIRO
PROFESSORSHIP

For some months Robert Graves had been letting it be known among his friends that he was looking for work; and within 'a week or two' of the doctor's ultimatum, Robert received an extraordinary morning post. One letter asked him to stand as a candidate for the Professorship of English at Liverpool University; while three further letters invited him to apply for the Professorship of English at Cairo.

Robert applied for both jobs, though it was the Cairo one which particularly interested him. Not only would it provide the 'dry, warm climate' which had been prescribed for Nancy, who was pleased at the idea,[232] and said that she would like to go to Egypt; but also the salary might be as much as £1,500 a year;[233] and the teaching duties were so light that Robert would have plenty of time to continue with his literary work. It was also flattering to have been put forward by such distinguished people. Robert told Sassoon that the letters about the Cairo professorship, a Foreign Office appointment, came from:

> Sir Sidney Lee, Sir Izzy Gollancz and my brother Philip who has secured George Lloyd's backing (isn't he High Commissioner of Egypt or something?). And apparently the 'little ray of sunshine' as I once heard T.E.L. queerly but accurately called, has been stirring in the matter.[234]

When Graves applied for the Cairo appointment (to the intense delight of his parents), he also forwarded the letters of recommendation which had been written for him earlier in the year by Bridges, Buchan, the Earl of Oxford and the Vice-Chancellor of Oxford. The only thing which alarmed Graves was that Arnold Bennett would be hostile, and he actually wrote him a letter 'begging [him] ... not at any rate to crab my chances'; but his alarm was needless: it turned out that Bennett had been one of those who had recommended him for the appointment.

For the first time for years, Robert's prospects looked excellent; but in the meantime he was once again short of money, and he asked Sassoon 'for

God's sake send me the ha'porth of tar to save the ship, and I'll pay it back in enamel of the purest white'.[235] Sassoon obliged with £10; and in his letter of thanks Robert remarked that he and Nancy were 'well enough but rather unhinged by this Cairo project'. Molly and Dick, two of Robert's closest relatives, both lived in Cairo, and might have been expected to help them through any difficulties in their early days in Egypt; but how welcoming would they be in such a traditional society to a socialist half-brother with a feminist wife? Robert and Nancy began to feel that they might be very isolated in Cairo; and, without detailing the reasons for his request, Graves asked Sassoon: 'I suppose it would be hopeless to suggest you coming to Cairo with us? It would make it so much more attractive for both of us. I suppose you wouldn't consent as my assistant, and pool the salaries?'[236]

As expected, Sassoon turned down the offer. This made no difference to his friendship with Robert; and when in mid-November Siegfried was staying in Oxford for a few days, he went out twice to Islip to see Robert and Nancy. They were able to tell him that Robert had now been formally presented with his B.Litt. degree; though he had had to rely upon Amy to pay the necessary fee of £20; and there was still no definite news about the Cairo appointment. Then came a period of chilly weather which gradually depressed the household at The World's End; and to add to her other ills poor Nancy suffered from an attack of ringworm, and had to have her remaining hair cut short.

Robert, his optimistic mood largely dispelled, busied himself more than ever with his work. 'The Marmosite's Miscellany' was published towards the end of November; another of his poems appeared in the *Spectator* at about the same time; and he was once again selecting poems for a possible collected edition – though this time it was Heinemann rather than Secker who were showing interest.[237] Another idea was for a further critical study of poetry; and since his prose works had failed to make much impact, Graves was now thinking in terms of collaborating with another writer. His chosen partner was T.S. Eliot, who had already made a reputation as the editor of *The Criterion* and as the author of *The Waste Land*; and his chosen subject was 'a book about modernist poetry to which we were each to contribute essays'.[238] Eliot had soon agreed in principle, though he warned Graves 'that he might find himself with very little time for doing his share of the work'.[239]

The chilly weather continued; and Amy, becoming anxious about Robert and his family, sent them a further £5 'to comfort them from the cold'.[240] She even mentioned her worries to Clarissa: not perhaps the wisest course of action, because Clarissa, while ostensibly looking on the bright side, succeeded only in underlining the difficulties of Robert's situation: 'I had no idea', she wrote to Amy, 'that it was so very doubtful whether Robert would get the Egyptian professorship. In any case it shows a willingness to come out into the world from his unnatural seclusion, and now that he holds a degree further opportunities will no doubt be offered him.'²⁴¹ But was Robert ready and willing 'to come out into the world'? At the very end of November he received a formal letter offering him the appointment. The terms of the contract, however, were not to be quite as rosy as he had hoped. The salary would be no more than £900 to begin with – a large enough sum, but not quite so exciting as the £1,500 which he had heard mentioned; he would receive no more than £75 towards his passage to Egypt; and he would have to agree to accept the appointment for a minimum period of three years. Faced with these less attractive terms, Robert balked at the prospect of tying himself down for so long a period, and wrote a letter in which he refused the appointment.

Sir Sidney Lee was immediately informed, and was not certain how to proceed. Should the refusal be taken as final? Or should Graves be given another chance to accept? He turned for advice to J.W. Mackail, a former Professor of Poetry at Oxford, and a shrewd Scot by whose judgment A.E. Housman set much store. Mackail told Sir Sidney to 'bide a wee'; and sure enough, by the next post Robert reversed his decision, and accepted. At the same time he wrote to his parents saying that he was disappointed by the reduction in salary, but that he was accepting the job because it would be so good for Nancy.

Once this final decision had been taken, Robert was overwhelmed with congratulations and good wishes. His parents and parents-in-law were particularly delighted by the thought that after so much uncertainty and dependence he would now be utterly secure and independent for at least the next three years. William Nicholson and his wife came down to Oxford to see Robert and Nancy and discuss their arrangements;²⁴² Amy, who had recently been left an inheritance of some £900 from one of her German relatives,²⁴³ immediately advanced Robert £300 'for a start & clearance of all liabilities';²⁴⁴ and Alfred, not to be outdone, passed on a family treasure: it was a letter from Wordsworth to Robert's great-uncle Robert Perceval Graves, and was sent with the hope, later fulfilled, that Robert would use it as the basis for an article. Further good news was that within a few days of Robert's accepting the professorship, the salary was 'raised from £900 to £1,120 per annum paid monthly', with a month's salary 'in advance towards his heavy travelling expenses'.²⁴⁵

On 16 December Alfred and Amy spent a night at The White Hart Hotel in Islip, on their way to London. Nancy was away, having 'gone up to town for Kit's birthday party at Apple Tree Yard';²⁴⁶ but Robert was busy with preparations for their journey to Egypt. He intended to set sail on 8 January

1926, and had booked passages for himself, Nancy, their four children and a nurse.[247] In the meantime there were many loose ends to be tied up. In particular, Graves wrote to Eliot, telling him about the professorship, and adding: 'I shall get on with my share of our projected volume and if I find that it's getting on too fast I shall possibily finish it myself. But not without giving you fair warning and a chance to collaborate.'[248]

With this letter to Eliot, Graves enclosed 'some criticism sent me by Laura Gottschalk', which he hoped that Eliot might use in *Criterion*.[249] It was now many months since Robert's plans for going to Cornell had fallen through; and soon afterwards, since they could no longer meet her in America, he and Nancy had invited Laura to come to stay with them at The World's End. There had been no immediate response to this invitation; but correspondence between them had continued, and Robert had become increasingly impressed by Laura both as a poet and as a critic.

In the meantime, Laura Gottschalk had begun to be intellectually isolated in America. Her association with the 'Fugitives' had not been altogether happy; and when in the autumn of 1925 she finally moved to New York she was disappointed by the literary milieu in which she found herself. As she later wrote, her American fellow poets appeared to her to be less than wholly serious both as poets and as individuals. While in their writing they did no more than employ individual variations of customary styles, she was searching for some altogether new mode of poetic expression which would enable her to describe the truth of things, in the most direct and powerful manner.[250] It was in these circumstances that Laura received an invitation to join Robert and Nancy on their journey to Egypt, in order to collaborate with Robert upon a book on modern poetry. Much to Robert's delight, she decided to accept.

Indeed, nothing could have pleased Robert more. He still had considerable misgivings about the way of life they would encounter in Egypt; and Laura's strength, for she was evidently a strong-minded woman, would enable both him and Nancy to face whatever lay ahead with greater confidence and greater equanimity. Robert explained to his family, who might otherwise have been surprised by this addition to his household, that Laura would be accompanying them as his 'lady-secretary' – a conception of Laura's status which was never communicated to her, and which she would have rejected if it had been. In reality she was going with them as their friend and as his collaborator.[251]

CHAPTER
16
THE ARRIVAL
OF LAURA

Towards the end of December 1925 Laura Riding Gottschalk made preparations for her voyage across the Atlantic. It was settled that she should accompany Robert Graves and Nancy Nicholson to Egypt; and Sassoon, visiting The World's End on 27 December, found 'both Robert and Nancy in good spirits – going to Egypt has enfranchised them'. Robert insisted on reading him some of Laura's poems. Suddenly it was a household full of happiness and hope.[252]

Until a few days previously one remaining shadow had lain across their plans: Sam had caught mumps earlier in the month; and although he had quickly recovered, there was the danger that one of the other children might be incubating the disease; in which case Robert would have had either to miss the sailing of the SS *Ranpura*, scheduled for 8 January 1926, or to travel out to Egypt ahead of his family. At various times both Jenny and David had exhibited symptoms of the disease, on one occasion much to the alarm of Diccon Hughes. Diccon had recently become engaged to Nancy Stallibrass, a lovely and charming girl whom he had brought to Islip not knowing that the children were still in quarantine. He and his Nancy were planning to get married in February, and the prospect of catching mumps shortly before their wedding was not a pleasant one.

However, by the time of Sassoon's visit the children were all in the clear, and a few days later Robert took his family up to Apple Tree Yard. He had intended to remain at Islip until 5 January, just three days before their boat sailed;[253] but he wanted to be in London to meet Laura Gottschalk, who had sent a telegram announcing that her ship would be docking at Portsmouth on Saturday 2 January, and that she would then come up to London by the boat train.[254]

Robert and his father-in-law were waiting to greet Laura when she stepped out of the train on to the platform at Paddington Station. They would have seen before them an attractive young woman a little below medium height, wearing a long dark coat buttoned down the front and a dark broad-brimmed felt hat.[255] Her face, serious in repose and always keenly intelligent, now wore the liveliest of expressions; her blue eyes were especially striking, and she had brown hair which was swept backwards from her forehead and fell on to her shoulders. Overall her outfit was smart but modest, and she later described it as being in 'unemphatic taste, suiting my 25 years'. Then, as she records, the two men busied themselves:

> with gathering in my luggage – a steamer trunk, and a suitcase, and a little carry-all I took in charge myself, holding toilette items. They wanted to disburden me of this, and I joked a little over the thing, saying 'It's just my beauty parlor.' And they took this in pleasant kind ... Mr. Nicholson ... had come just for the brief meeting-time. He departed, courteously, explaining that he had an appointment to keep.[256]

Robert then brought Laura back by taxi-cab to Apple Tree Yard, where she was introduced to Nancy, the children, and the nurse who had been engaged to accompany them to Egypt.

In the few days before embarkation Mrs Gottschalk made a pleasing impression upon several other members of the Graves and Nicholson families. They were struck both by her good looks ('Isn't she lovely?' Ben Nicholson said to his sister)[257] and by her evident practicality. Philip called round one day with his wife Millicent and their eight-year-old daughter Sally, who recalls seeing Robert sitting among piles of unpacked things. A few minutes later Nancy and Laura 'returned with last-minute shopping of first-aid kit, & children's things', and Sally 'immediately classif[ied] them as sisters', since apart from the fact that Nancy's broad-brimmed hat was light, and Laura's was dark, they were 'both dressed very much alike'. Soon Laura was sitting on a stool beside Millicent, who knew a great deal about Near Eastern housekeeping, and asking her advice about health, medicines, shopping, servants and so on, making careful notes all the while. Millicent was both flattered and impressed by her 'head for housekeeping'; and Laura herself later recalled that she sensed they would all have problems in 'dealing with unaccustomed modes – domestic and other, language problems etc.'[258]

Alfred Perceval Graves and his wife were also in London, where they were staying with Rosaleen, now the 'Senior Student' at the Charing Cross Hospital. APG had been doing everything within his power to give Robert a good start in Egypt, introducing him to those who knew something of the country and its people, and also securing letters of introduction which might be useful to him when he reached Cairo. Alfred had even been round to the Foreign Office, where much to his surprise he discovered that the F.O. representative for Egypt was 'a brother of Robert Nichols & a great friend of Robert's', and had already given him some sound advice about keeping clear of politics while he was abroad.[259]

APG met Laura for the first time on Tuesday 5 January, when he and Amy and Rosaleen had all been invited to Apple Tree Yard for supper. The children were in bed when he arrived, but he went up to see them, and found them 'very lively with nice nurse giving them syrup'.[260] They had all had so many inoculations for typhoid, para-typhoid and so on, that Catherine, now almost four years old, was promising to 'doculate' the Sphinx.[261] Downstairs, Alfred was introduced not only to 'Miss Gottschalk', but to 'Forster, a friend of Egyptian experience'. This was the novelist E.M. Forster, a friend both of Sassoon and of T.E. Lawrence, and a slight acquaintance of Robert's since about 1923. After spending several years in Egypt during the Great War, Forster had remained in touch with a number of influential Egyptians, and had apparently been one of those who had recommended Robert for the Cairo Professorship. His advice on Egyptian matters was welcome, but tiring; and after supper Robert relaxed by singing some folk-songs with Rosaleen.[262]

Wednesday was extremely busy. Not only was it Jenny's seventh birthday, but in the morning Robert was due to take Nancy and Laura round to see Virginia Woolf;[263] and in the afternoon Alfred, Amy and Rosaleen called once again at Apple Tree Yard. Robert was now becoming worn out by his parents' well-meaning but exhausting efforts to help; and he stayed at home both when his mother went out to buy as a farewell present the frock coat which he would need for ceremonial occasions, and when his father hurried off to discuss the Cairo professorship with Sir Sidney Lee.

Now in his eightieth year, Alfred remained indefatigable. On Thursday afternoon he arrived at Apple Tree Yard with yet another introduction, and yet more advice; later, although it was the very eve of Robert's departure, he would not leave until he had telephoned yet another Egyptian expert and persuaded him to come to see Robert at once. Then at last APG said 'farewell to R & N & babes', and left them in peace.

The following day was Friday 8 January 1926; and Siegfried Sassoon came to the docks to say goodbye to Robert, and to watch him and his household set sail for Egypt. But the SS *Ranpura* which would carry them to Cairo was also bound for Bombay; and Sassoon noticed that by a curious coincidence one of Robert's fellow passengers was an old acquaintance, a Royal Welch Fusilier nicknamed 'The Twisted Image', in a savagely ironic reference to the biblical proposition that all men are created in the image of their Maker. 'The Twisted Image' had not only been to Copthorne School with Robert, but had served with him at Wrexham and Liverpool, and had been wounded with the Second Battalion at High Wood, within a few hundred yards of the slope on which Robert had received his own near-fatal wound in the summer of 1916.

Now both men were on their way to the East: 'The Image' to join the First Battalion of the R.W.F. in India, and Robert to his Cairo professorship. The two men had never had anything to say to each other; but their meeting was a reminder for Robert of the distance which he himself had travelled since his Copthorne days. Then everything had seemed clear and straightforward. Since then certainty after certainty had been stripped away, until in recent years he had begun to feel as though a process of personal disintegration had begun.[264]

As he leaned over the ship's rail, waving goodbye to Sassoon, Robert was fortunate not to know where that process of disintegration would end. He was still more fortunate that he was sailing to Egypt with the woman who would one day help him to become whole again.

AFTERWORD

By 1926 Robert had won for himself the reputation of an interesting minor poet; and indeed he had already written some fifty of his best poems. Twenty-eight of them would later appear in his final volume of *Collected Poems* in 1975, including 'In the Wilderness', 'Love without Hope', 'Rocky Acres', 'The Pier-Glass', 'Children of Darkness', 'Alice', 'Full Moon', 'Sullen Moods', and 'The Lands of Whipperginny'. And at least another twenty poems of equal merit date from the first thirty years of Robert's life, poems ranging from 'The Clipped Stater' to 'The Poet's Birth', and from 'Goliath and David' to 'The Leveller'.

He had been brought up within a literary family in which it was taken for granted that artistic achievements were of great importance. He had also found from an early age that writing poetry helped him to cope with both external pressures and internal conflicts. Bullied assiduously during his first terms at Charterhouse, where the high standards of behaviour which he had assimilated at home made it difficult for him to be accepted by his peers, he had written how:

> Green terror ripples through our bones,
> Our inmost heart-strings thrill
> And yearn for careless day.

As he became less overwrought during the middle years of his Carthusian career, his writing lost the forcefulness of these lines; but he enjoyed words and the technical challenge of experimenting with new metres and rhyming patterns, and poetry became not only an escape, but a positive pleasure. From an early age Graves had been happy to take direction from someone whom he idealized; and his pleasure in writing poetry was heightened by the close friendship which developed between himself and 'Peter' Johnstone. This made writing poetry a celebration of the kind of idealistic friendship which A.E. Housman describes in the lines:

> When I would muse in boyhood
>   The wild green woods among,
> And nurse resolves and fancies
>   Because the world was young,
> It was not foes to conquer,

Nor sweethearts to be kind,
But it was friends to die for
That I would seek and find.

The stresses of Graves's wartime experiences at first strengthened his
reliance both upon Johnstone and upon other male friends such as Sassoon
and David Thomas; but these stresses also introduced into his work the horrify-
ing realism of lines such as those on the 'Dead Boche', who 'scowled and
stunk/ With clothes and face a sodden green'. At the same time his poetry
was improved by the thoroughgoing criticisms which he received from his
poetic mentor Edward Marsh. Towards the end of the war, recuperating from
shell-shock at a convalescent home in the Isle of Wight, Robert came to see
that in his poetry he had been conducting an 'Assault Heroic' in which he
had 'alchemized' unhappy experiences into poetic gold, writing:

I stood beneath the wall
And there defied them all.
The stones they cast I caught
And alchemized with thought
Into such lumps of gold
As dreaming misers hold.

The attraction for Marjorie, followed shortly afterwards by revulsion from
Johnstone and the belief that he himself had been treading down a dangerous
'pseudo-homosexual' road, was followed by marriage to Nancy. For a while
Robert and Nancy appeared to have much in common and attempted to live
in an enchanted world in which innocence and artistic ambition could flourish
side by side; but reality kept breaking in.

The stresses of married life, together with a recurrence of shell-shock,
sent Robert delving first into psychology, which immeasurably deepened both
his human understanding and the interest of his best poetry; and then (under
Mallik's influence) into philosophy, which threatened at one stage to make
his writing utterly obscure. The additional stresses produced by years of failure
to support himself by his writing, had begun to poison his relationship with
Nancy, to make her ill with worry, and to induce a kind of personality crisis
in Robert himself.

Whether Robert would remain an interesting minor poet, or whether he
would achieve something more, must have seemed an open question in January
1926. He needed above all some strong and self-reliant person upon whose
judgment he could rely, and in whose affection he could feel secure. Such

a person was to hand in Laura Riding. It was she who showed him the way out of his emotional and intellectual impasse; so that within three and a half years of their voyage to Egypt, Robert was nearing the end of *Goodbye To All That*, his heroic and partially successful attempt to rid himself of all the conflicts and unhappinesses of his 'historical' past.

Towards the end of the book, writing about his more obvious achievements and claims to distinction with that mixture of pride and contempt which he had learned from T.E. Lawrence, and which had been so cruelly observed by Virginia Woolf, Graves commented that:

> I seem to have done most of the usual storybook things. I had, by the age of twenty-three, been born, initiated into a formal religion, travelled, learned to lie, loved unhappily, been married, gone to the war, taken life, procreated my kind, rejected formal religion, won fame, and been killed. ... [While by 1926 he had also] ... won a prize at the Olympic Games, become a member of the senior common-room at one Oxford college before becoming a member of the junior common-room at another, [and] had a statue of myself erected in my lifetime in a London park.

All these things now seemed to him to be relatively unimportant. From the moment that he was joined by Laura Riding, Robert Graves had begun an important period of transition. The 'Assault Heroic', the struggle for survival, was gradually to be transformed into a struggle to achieve exact poetic truth, in a timeless world beyond normal reality.

NOTES

ABBREVIATIONS

1 UNPUBLISHED SOURCES

AMY An unpublished autobiography written by Robert Graves's mother Amalia Graves (née Ranke).

AUTHOR The vast collection of family papers built up by Robert Graves's brother John Graves (1903–1980), and now owned by John's son Richard, the present author. This collection has never been worked over before, except by John Graves (JTRG) who made use of some items for his incomplete and unpublished biography *My Brother Robert*.

BODLEIAN Letters owned by the Bodleian Library, Oxford.

BROTHER The incomplete typescript of *My Brother Robert* by his brother John Graves, now owned by John's widow Mary.

DIARY The 1911–1931 Diaries of Robert's father Alfred Perceval Graves (1846–1931), now owned by APG's grandson Richard, the present author. These diaries for the most part have been seen by no one apart from the present author and his father John Graves, who made some use of them for his unpublished work on Robert. However, APG himself published some extracts from the July to December 1914 entries, on pages 294–301 of his autobiography (see ALFRED below); and in letters to Martin Seymour-Smith John passed on a handful of extracts, some of which were used by MS-S in 'Robert Graves: His Life and Works' (Hutchinson 1982)

IMPERIAL Letters and maps owned by the Imperial War Museum, London.

LETTERS Letters from Robert Graves to his brother John, (JTRG), together with handwritten commentaries by John, now owned by John's widow Mary.

MAJORCA The collection of family papers held by Robert and Beryl Graves at their house in Deya. These have been studied previously by Martin Seymour-Smith.

PERCEVAL An unpublished autobiography by Robert's half-brother Perceval Graves entitled *Talk of Graves* owned by his widow Betty.

2 PRINCIPAL PUBLISHED SOURCES

ALFRED Alfred Perceval Graves, *To Return To All That* (Jonathan Cape 1930)

CHARLES Charles Graves, *The Bad Old Days* (Faber & Faber 1951)

GTAT29 Robert Graves, *Goodbye To All That* (Jonathan Cape 1929). I have quoted from this version wherever possible. The prose may not always be as polished as in the revised edition of 1957, but Robert's stylistic revisions were so extensive that, taken together with numerous excisions, they often make a considerable difference to the flavour and tone of what can only be described, in its original form, as a work of blazing genius. In any case the original account must usually be preferred as a document which is more contemporary with the events which it describes.

GTAT57 Robert Graves, *Goodbye To All That* (Folio Society 1981). This is an edition of the 1957 revised version. I have referred to it constantly to see what differences there are between the two versions, as these are sometimes illuminating in themselves. In addition, Robert sometimes mentions names in the revised version which he felt he could not publish in the original version.

MS-S Martin Seymour-Smith, *Robert Graves: His Life and Works* (Hutchinson 1982)

O'PREY(I) Ed. Paul O'Prey, *In Broken Images: Selected Letters of Robert Graves 1914–1946* (Hutchinson 1982)

SASSOON(I) Ed. Sir Rupert Hart-Davis, *Siegfried Sassoon Diaries, 1915–1918* (Faber & Faber 1983)

SASSOON(2) Ed. Sir Rupert Hart-Davis, *Siegfried Sassoon Diaries, 1920–1922* (Faber & Faber 1981)

SASSOON(3) Ed. Sir Rupert Hart-Davis, *Siegfried Sassoon Diaries, 1923–1925* (Faber & Faber 1985)

IMPORTANT NOTE ON THE POEMS

During his working life Robert Graves made many alterations to his poems. But when I am writing about his life in 1916, and decide to quote from a poem written in 1915 or 1916, then I believe that it is biographically more correct to quote from the version published in 1916 than from the slightly altered version published in 1918, or the substantially altered version published in the 1930s or later. So I have always tried to quote from the version of a poem which is most contemporary to the context in which it appears. The same principle has been used when quoting from the poems of Laura (Riding) Jackson.

INTRODUCTION

In the Introduction to this volume it is asserted that biography is an art rather than a science. Nevertheless, scientific elements are present. For one thing, it is clearly necessary to evaluate the claims of conflicting items of evidence. This is not always difficult. One soon learns, for example, that one contemporary document is usually worth fifty reminiscences. But even when examining a contemporary document such as a letter or a diary, one must ask oneself a number of questions about such things as the reliability of the witness, the aim that prompted him to write, the effect he hoped to produce, and so on.

Indeed, my chief problem in writing this book has been to find precise answers to questions beginning what, where, how, when and why. Robert, believing correctly that fact is not always quite the same as truth, was always more concerned to present the emotional truth of a situation than the precise facts of what occurred. *Goodbye To All That* is a great work of art, and tells the emotional truth about Robert's views and state of mind in 1929, but Robert himself says almost at the end of his autobiography (GTAT29 p. 441) that 'in many passages memory has been the only source', that there must therefore be 'many slight errors of one sort or another' and that some incidents 'are, no doubt, in their wrong order'.

Robert's terrible experiences during the 1914–1918 war, together with the considerable difficulties which he faced during subsequent years both in his private life and in his literary career combined, in my view, seriously to distort his memories of the past. This is no discredit to him, but a measure of the terrible ordeals through which he passed.

However, it would have been tiresome in the extreme to clutter up the text, in the manner of a number of biographers, with remarks such as: 'Up to now it has been widely assumed that', or 'In *Goodbye To All That* Robert states incorrectly that', or 'New evidence shows that'. Verbal tricks of this kind, whose only purpose appears to be that we should clap our hands at the cleverness of the biographer (often at the expense of the far greater man or woman who is the subject of the biography), have, I hope, found no place in the main body of the text, but where a biographer tells a story which is different from the one which has been generally accepted, he owes it both to his readers and to any biographer who comes after him to give a detailed account of his sources, and some idea of his reasoning. This I have tried to do in the notes which follow.

BOOK ONE
SOME PRELIMINARY SCENES
IN ENGLAND, IRELAND, WALES AND BAVARIA

Unless otherwise indicated, (see especially chapters one and three) the information in Book One is drawn largely from AMY.

CHAPTER 1
A CHILDHOOD MEMORY

The information in this chapter is chiefly drawn from my personal knowledge.

CHAPTER 2
AMALIA VON RANKE

1 There has been constant dispute within the family about the details of

both the Graves and the Ranke pedigrees. Martin Seymour-Smith alludes to this on p. 569 of MS-S. He declares that 'R.G. made many careless errors, but his brother John ... was not more accurate. I have relied mostly on anon., also a member of the family.' One of the problems is that when, in later life, Robert's memory began to fail, he became convinced of a number of 'facts' which are demonstrably untrue. For example, he believed at one time that his mother was born before the outbreak of the Crimean War, and was therefore several years older than anyone realized. This led to some altercation with John, who had access to the detailed family trees upon which the present account has been based. So far as the Ranke family is concerned, I have relied upon a bound volume entitled simply 'Ranke' with an introduction by Hermann Ranke dated 'Heidelberg, im September 1926'. This provides an entirely authoritative set of Ranke family trees.

Whichever member of the family provided Seymour-Smith with his alternative information was perhaps wise to remain anonymous. On pages 4 and 5 of MS-S, for example, there is mention of the 'genetic contribution' of Robert's ancestor Richard Graves, born in 1715 and author of *The Spiritual Quixote*. But that Richard Graves was one of the Mickleton Graveses, a branch of the family with whom it can be proved that the Irish Graveses had no connection whatever after the 1690s – and they may have had none before then, though family tradition decrees otherwise. If there was a French knight called Graves who landed with Henry VII at Milford Haven (MS-S page 4) there is certainly no way of connecting him with our family, as above the 1690s the Graves pedigree is lost in total obscurity. Incidentally, Sir John Perceval, described loosely on page 4 of MS-S as Helena Perceval's

'ancestor' was in fact her third cousin twice removed; while the Prime Minister Spencer Perceval, whom she very much admired, was her fifth cousin.

For this and other information about the Graves family trees I have relied principally upon (*i*) a printed family tree drawn up in the 1890s. (*ii*) a substantial leather-bound volume entitled *Graves Family* MSS. (This is a collection of deeds and MSS prepared in 1925, which has as its declared origin 'an attempt to solve the question of which of the English Graves families were the ancestors of the Irish branches'. It did not succeed in this, but it contains authoritative genealogical charts.) (*iii*) a manuscript family tree drawn up in association with (*ii*) above, which traces back the direct ancestors of Robert's father, Alfred Perceval Graves, (*iv*) a manuscript family tree drawn up by Robert's brother John Graves in the 1970s, which traces so far as was possible all the descendants of Robert's great-grandfather John Crosbie Graves.

2 ALFRED p. 274

3 Beryl Graves recently reminded me (July 1985) of Robert's story that Heinrich first went to Spain. While travelling in that country, his coach was attacked by bandits. Noticing that an English fellow passenger coolly ignored the attack, and carried on reading *The Times* in the midst of all the shooting, Heinrich decided to settle in England.

4 DIARY 28 November 1918

5 BROTHER

6 AMY

7 The account which Robert gives of this in 'Miss Briton's Lady-Companion' on pp. 192–202 of *The Crane Bag and Other Disputed Subjects* (Cassell 1969) was unfortunately written beyond the age at which Robert's memory was at all reliable. It will be enough to mention four of the numerous errors: the lady was known

as Mrs Tiarks; Amy was not sent to England in 1873 but in 1876, when she was still 18; nor was it to escape from the Bavarian Prime Minister, though it is true that in 1884 the then Bavarian P.M. proposed to her and was turned down; nor did Amy die of a nervous breakdown, but of cancer. My information on the first of these three points comes from Amy's own unpublished autobiography, and on the fourth from my aunt Dr Rosaleen Cooper (née Graves) who attended Amy in the last days of her final illness.

8 AMY
9 Ibid.
10 Ibid.
11 Ibid.
12 Ibid.
13 Ibid.
14 Ibid.

CHAPTER 3
ALFRED PERCEVAL GRAVES

Unless otherwise indicated, the information in this chapter is drawn not from AMY but from ALFRED.

15 AUTHOR
16 Alfred Perceval Graves, *Songs of Killarney* (London: Bradbury, Agnew & Co., Bouverie St., 1873) pp. 77–8. These lines are misquoted in GTAT29 p. 24
17 Alfred Perceval Graves, *Songs of Killarney* as 16 above, pp. 58–9
18 AUTHOR: Typewritten copy by the present author of a letter of 21 June 1874 in which Alfred writes to his Uncle Robert begging him to intervene on his behalf between his father and his prospective parents-in-law. The date of Alfred and Janie's wedding, as recorded in the Family Bible, was 29 December 1874, so RPG's intervention must have been a successful one.
19 The late Hugo R. Rice-Wiggin and Alfred Perceval Graves, *The Elementary School Manager* (London: Wm. Isbister Ltd, 56 Ludgate Hill, 1881)

20 Alfred Perceval Graves, *Irish Songs and Ballads* (Manchester: Alexander Ireland & Co., 1880); a third edition was published in London by David Bogue, 3 St Martin's Place, in 1882
21 APG therefore sold the song for £1. 12s. od. (see ALFRED p. 213) and not as MS-S p. 6 for one Guinea.
22 MS-S p. 6 says that APG 'never complained' but see ALFRED, pp. 213–14, which reads like a complaint to me.
23 AUTHOR: Janie Cooper to Alfred Perceval Graves 6 February 1882. Contrast the tone of this letter and the implications of the letter at 15 above with MS-S p. 8, that Jane Cooper 'practised no kind of piety'.

CHAPTER 4
A VICTORIAN COURTSHIP

24 PERCEVAL
25 Ibid.
26 AMY
27 Ibid.
28 Ibid.
29 PERCEVAL
30 AMY
31 Ibid.
32 Ibid.
33 Ibid.
34 Ibid.
35 AUTHOR: Amy to her son John (JTRG) 19 November 1920 gives the date of Amy's engagement to Alfred as 19 November.
36 AMY

CHAPTER 5
A SECOND FAMILY

37 Amy's daughter Dr Rosaleen Cooper in conversation with me in the summer of 1982.
38 AMY
39 Ibid.
40 AUTHOR: Typewritten copy by JTRG of a letter of 1 March 1884 to Janie.
41 AMY

42 AMY
43 ALFRED p. 17
44 AMY
45 An account of one episode in Charles and Selina's friendship with Mendelssohn is contained in AUTHOR: Selina's journal of a continental holiday in 1847, written in four slim exercise books.
46 AMY
47 AUTHOR: Amy Graves to the Bishop of Limerick from The Orchard, Taunton, 10 February 1892
48 PERCEVAL
49 AMY
50 AUTHOR: Amy to Charles Graves,

Bishop of Limerick, 23 April 1892
51 AUTHOR: Susan Macaulay (née Graves) to her half-brother John Graves September 26 (no year), from Hillside, Ewell
52 AMY
53 As 50 above, 7 November 1892
54 As 50 above, 22 December 1892
55 AMY
56 AMY
57 ALFRED p. 271
58 Sir Robert Windham Graves, *Storm Centres of the Near East* (Hutchinson 1933) gives a record of the personal experiences of its author during fifty years spent in the Near East.

BOOK TWO
ROBERT'S CHILDHOOD 1895—1909

CHAPTER I
UNDER THE SILVER MOON

1 AMY
2 GTAT29 p. 14
3 Externally Red Branch House looks today (1985) much as it did; but the garden is now smaller, and there have been internal alterations.
4 AMY
5 Ibid.
6 GTAT29 p. 28
7 Ibid. p. 32 (Emily's verse is not set out in lines in GTAT29)
8 GTAT29 p. 14
9 *Picture Lessons in Natural History*: the cover of this massive nineteenth-century volume, in the AUTHOR collection, is now so worn that it is impossible to distinguish the name of the publisher. The pages inside have been much repaired over the decades, and the backing sheet of paper which has been used to repair one half of the 'Rhinoceros' double-page spread is almost certainly the earliest surviving example of Robert's writing: a

'copybook' type of exercise, in which the names of MOTHER, FATHER and ROBERT have been written out in capital letters by an adult; and underneath Robert has copied the names in his own hand.
10 *30 Biblische Bilder zum Neuen Testament*, published by J.F.Schreiber in Stuttgart. No date is given; but on the title page of this volume, in the AUTHOR collection, Robert's sister Clarissa has written on 6 July 1953: 'This is a treasure – Mother used it to teach us the stories from the New Testament.'
11 Dr Rosaleen Cooper (née Graves) in a telephone conversation with me, 4 October 1982
12 AMY
13 Ibid.
14 This is in clear opposition to MS-S p. 8 where the author declares that Amy 'insisted that [Alfred] give up alcohol – he signed the pledge – for she was a ferocious missionary by nature, and saw alcohol as an obstacle to goodness'. In its context, the impli-

cation of this passage appears to be that Amy only agreed to marry APG on the condition that he sign the pledge; but that does not tally with my evidence. The truth appears to be that Alfred gave up alcohol on medical advice in the year 1898. Clarissa's annoyance about having had to renounce alcohol, and the occasional exceptions which she made to this rule, I recall myself from her visits to us at Holme Grange in the 1950s and 1960s.

15 AMY
16 Ibid.
17 Ibid.
18 From a supplementary list of dates appended by Amy Graves to AMY
19 Ibid.
20 ALFRED, p. 318
21 AUTHOR: A small notebook with a red cover, entitled 'The Red Branch Song Book'.
22 GTAT29 p. 27–8

CHAPTER 2
AN IRISH FUNERAL

23 Many of the objects mentioned in this chapter are still in the family. The marble portraits of Charles and Selina were sold to the Irish National Portrait Gallery in Dublin; but other portraits and furniture, the grant of arms in its tin case, and a share of the silverware, remain in my possession. The glass case haunted my own childhood and has been discarded.
24 ALFRED pp. 276–7
25 Ibid. p. 281
26 AMY

CHAPTER 3
CLOUDS AND SUNSHINE

27 AMY
28 ALFRED p. 318
29 GTAT29 p. 30
30 Ibid.
31 GTAT29 p. 53

32 AMY
33 AUTHOR: Article by Clarissa Graves
34 GTAT29 p. 44
35 Ibid. p. 53
36 AMY
37 Philip Graves to Alfred Perceval Graves [January 1900]; letter now owned by Mrs R.C. Chilver, Philip's daughter usually known as Sally.
38 PERCEVAL
39 GTAT29 p. 55
40 MAJORCA: Clarissa Graves to her brother Robert, 17 September 1953.
41 GTAT29 p. 53
42 Ibid. p. 28
43 Ibid. pp. 28, 27
44 AMY
45 Ibid. .
46 Robert Graves, *Over the Brazier* (London: The Poetry Bookshop, 1916). The copy at Canellun has, in Robert's hand: 'written at Wimbledon or perhaps Lancaster 1914. But it happened at Wimbledon in the Library. The second shelf from the bottom in the bookcase by the window.'
47 Rosaleen Cooper, *Games from an Edwardian Childhood* (David & Charles 1982) p. 11

CHAPTER 4
AN EDWARDIAN UPBRINGING

48 GTAT29 p. 38
49 Ibid. p. 30
50 Ibid. p. 31
51 Ibid. pp. 31–2
52 Ibid. p. 38
53 AUTHOR: Ash Wednesday 1903 Alfred Perceval Graves to Frau Professor von Ranke.
54 AUTHOR: John Graves quotes this in his poem 'To Robert' which he wrote for Robert's 80th birthday on 24 July 1975.
55 AUTHOR: Postcard Amy Graves to her mother Luise von Ranke, 8 March 1903
56 Ibid. 13 March 1903
57 GTAT29 p. 38

58 Ibid.
59 AUTHOR: Amy Graves (née Ranke) to her sister Agnes, 12 January 1904. The work, in three volumes, is *Life of Sir William Rowan Hamilton* by Robert Perceval Graves, M.A. (Dublin: Hodges, Figgis & Co., Grafton Street; London: Longmans, Green & Co., Paternoster Row, 1882)
60 GTAT29 p. 39
61 Ibid.
62 Ibid. pp. 39–40
63 AUTHOR: Amy Graves to her sister Agnes 23 December 1904
64 AUTHOR: Amy Graves to her sister Agnes 31 December 1904. Ill health continued into the spring; in March 1905 Rosaleen was at a convalescent home at Stanmore and Clarissa was left at a farm 'recommended by friends for children who want a change'. APG also was very depressed after being in lodgings for a while; and Amy herself felt that she had 'aged a good deal in the year, my teeth & hair show it also' (AUTHOR: Amy to Agnes 11 March 1905). Then APG had a long illness with carbuncles on the knee, and Robert 'violent & exhausting nosebleeding' (AUTHOR: Amy to Agnes 8 May 1905 from the Felix Hotel Felixstowe).
65 AUTHOR: Amy Graves to her father Heinrich von Ranke 2 June 1905
66 Ibid.
67 GTAT29 p. 28
68 MAJORCA: Alfred Perceval Graves to Robert 21 July 1930

69 GTAT29 p. 52
70 Ibid. p. 40
71 CHARLES p. 15
72 Ibid. p. 16, also AUTHOR: Postcard Amy Graves to her father Heinrich von Ranke 26 October 1905, and letter Amy to Heinrich 25 December 1905
73 GTAT29 p. 32
74 BROTHER
75 GTAT29 p. 41
76 CHARLES p. 17
77 AUTHOR: From John Graves's poem 'To Robert' written for Robert's 80th birthday on 24 July 1975
78 GTAT29 p. 47
79 CHARLES p. 20
80 Ibid.
81 GTAT29 pp. 49–50
82 ALFRED p. 275
83 Ibid. p. 319
84 GTAT29 p. 41. RG puts it more strongly: 'I found out later' rather than 'the story went round'; but it sounds somewhat implausible.
85 GTAT29 p. 42
86 ALFRED p. 319. For an appreciation of Rendall headed 'A Great Preparatory School Headmaster' see his obituary in *The Times* of 16 July 1937 which declares: 'His understanding of boys was exceptional, and their welfare was the main interest of his life.' [Obit. by J.T.R.G.]
87 AUTHOR: Robert Windham Graves to Alfred Perceval Graves 22 December 1909 from Constantinople.
88 ALFRED p. 319
89 GTAT29 p. 43

BOOK THREE
CHARTERHOUSE AND FAMILY
HOLIDAYS 1909—1914

CHAPTER I
OPPRESSION OF SPIRIT

1 Amy Graves to her sister Agnes von Aufsess 16 July 1909. MS-S p. 13 contains the odd remark that Robert was at Charterhouse for seven years; and the remainder of MS-S's account of RG's life at Charterhouse, as will be shown, is often unreliable so far as

the order of events is concerned. My evidence is that Robert was there from the autumn of 1909 to the summer of 1914, a period of five academic years.

2 CHARLES p. 27
3 GTAT29 p. 63. There were however periods when Robert was comparatively happy at Charterhouse, as succeeding chapters will show.
4 G.D. Martineau in ed. W.H. Holden, *The Charterhouse We Knew* (London: British Technical and General Press, 1950, pp. 53–4)
5 Ibid. p. 62
6 GTAT29 pp. 64–5. Other reasons given by RG are: being a scholar, not being outstandingly good at games, and not having enough money to treat his fellows at the school shop. In LETTERS 31 January 1920 Robert hopes that John is 'financially solvent which at Ch'ouse was always my nightmare'.
7 AUTHOR: Typed copy by JTRG of a letter from H.L. Gandell to John Graves 4 February 1974. In GTAT29 p. 64, Robert states that the 'von' in his middle name had hitherto been unknown to him, and was 'disconcerting'. Things became worse, in view of anti-Jewish prejudice, when 'the legend was put about that I was not only a German but a German-Jew'.
8 GTAT29 p. 63
9 Ibid. p. 65. MS-S pp. 15–16 adds that RG's Irish enemy described him as 'a fierce masturbator and secret seducer of boys'; and that his clothes 'were urinated on'. We are not told whether there is contemporary documentary evidence for these remarks.

CHAPTER 2
A PERSONAL HARMONY

10 AUTHOR: Clarissa and then Robert wrote out the story on a double sheet of lined paper which appears to have been pulled from the centre of a tall exercise book. In the original, all the names have been disguised. Thus Rosaleen has become Elizabeth, Robert has become John, Charterhouse has become Charchester, John has become Benjamin, and so on. John put in the correct names and a few additional words of explanation for BROTHER, and I have used his version.

11 CHARLES p. 23
12 On one notable occasion in September 1910 they sat round a table after luncheon and wasted the entire afternoon arguing about where to take their picnic tea.
13 This and the two previous quotations are from GTAT29 pp. 56–7
14 Ibid. p. 58

CHAPTER 3
PROOF OF INSANITY

15 LETTERS Sunday 29 January 1911
16 In GTAT29 p. 67 Robert dates his plea to leave Charterhouse to 'half-way through my second year', which clearly indicates the Long Quarter (spring term) of 1911. During that term, from the evidence of DIARY, Robert was only visited twice by members of his family: Amy and Rosaleen on 11 February, and Amy and APG on 28 March, the date of his Confirmation. My version of the story does not tally with GTAT29, in which it appears that Robert's Confirmation (GTAT29 p. 75), came some time after his plea to leave Charterhouse (GTAT29 p. 67), and also after the first appearance of one of his poems in *The Carthusian*, his invitation to join the Poetry Society, and the start of his friendship with Raymond Rodakowski (GTAT29 pp. 68–9). MS-S p. 19, following this, has, for example, 'In the term when he made friends with Raymond, Graves was being prepared for confirmation.' However, it seems that Robert's memory played him false. We know

that the date of his Confirmation was 28 March 1911 (DIARY of that date). We can also date the appearance of his poem in *The Carthusian* to June 1911 (see note 21 below). In the light of this evidence I believe that my order of events is the most likely one.

17 DIARY 28 March 1911
18 GTAT29 p. 67
19 In GTAT29 Robert does not mention that the idea of shamming insanity came from the Bible. This was added in GTAT57 p. 45, where he says, 'I got the idea from *The Book of Kings*, where David had scrabbled on the prison wall.' The incident occurs in verses 12–13 of Chapter 21 of 'The First Book of Samuel otherwise called The First Book of the Kings' from which this quotation is taken.
20 GTAT29 p. 68
21 *The Carthusian* June 1911, Vol. X, No. 349, p. 425
22 Robert Graves, *The White Goddess* (Faber and Faber Limited, 1948) p. 13

CHAPTER 4
FRIENDSHIP

23 DIARY 22 June 1911
24 DIARY 26 June 1911
25 BROTHER
26 GTAT29 p. 69
27 DIARY 1 August 1911
28 Ibid. 8 August 1911
29 Ibid. 11 August 1911
30 Ibid. 18–19 August 1911
31 APG had been given the Bardic name of 'Canwr Cilarne', or 'The Singer of Killarney'.
32 Ibid. 28 September 1911
33 Ibid. 10 October 1911
34 *The Carthusian*, December 1911, No. 354, pp. 534–5
35 ALFRED p. 319
36 DIARY 10 January 1912
37 'The Hushu Bird' is printed in ALFRED p. 320
38 DIARY 3 April 1912

CHAPTER 5
PILGRIMAGE TO CANTERBURY

39 GTAT29 p. 75
40 AUTHOR: Amy Graves to her son Charles 25 November 1911
41 DIARY 24 March 1912
42 Ibid. 22 July 1912
43 Ibid. 18 May 1912
44 AUTHOR: Amy Graves to Alfred Perceval Graves 18 March 1912
45 LETTERS 22 June 1912
46 AUTHOR: Amy Graves to her son Charles 8 June 1912. Perceval was 'better, but is looking for work again, which makes us anxious'.
47 LETTERS 18 September 1920

CHAPTER 6
SONGS AND POEMS

48 DIARY 10 August 1912
49 BROTHER
50 This song, described in DIARY 22 August 1912 as 'his [Robert's] song of "The Little Devils"', is taken from BROTHER
51 BROTHER; and see DIARY 7 September 1912 for Robert's next singing of 'The Whiskey Skin'.
52 Alfred Perceval Graves, M.A. ('Canwr Cilarne') President of the Irish Literary Society, London Representative of the Council of the Celtic Association, Member of the Executive Committees of the Folk Song Society and of the Welsh and Irish Folk Song Societies and Member of the Honourable Society of Cymmrodorion, *Welsh Poetry Old and New in English Verse* (Longmans, Green, and Co., 39 Paternoster Row, London, 1912)
53 Ibid. pp. xii–xiii
54 Ibid. p. 138. On 3 August 1912 Canon Edwards wrote to APG praising his new volume, but adding: 'I had noticed that your son's Englyn had several little flaws: and it is a pity it was not submitted to me before it was printed.' He suggested for example

that the first line would have been better begun with the words: 'See a gleam in this gloaming'.

55 *The Carthusian*, July 1912 Vol. x, No. 359, see pp. 605 and 607

56 GTAT29 pp. 83–4

57 Ibid. p. 84

58 *The Carthusian*, e.g., November 1912, No. 362, p. 28, when the Motion was 'That Civilisation is a failure'. Rodakowski spoke; and 'R. von R. Graves spoke on the helplessness of uncivilised man, and quoted Aesop's Fables to illustrate his point.'

59 *The Carthusian*, December 1912, No. 363, p. 48

60 GTAT29 p. 75

61 Ibid.

62 John Tiarks Ranke Graves was at Charterhouse from O.Q. 1916 to C.Q. 1921

63 LETTERS n.d. probably autumn 1919, from 'Wingle [sic] Cottage, Boar's Hill, Oxford'.

64 GTAT29 p. 80. Robert blames his father, 'my only link with books', for knowing nothing about these authors. This may be an exaggeration. Certainly [see DIARY] by 26 December 1912 APG had read Wells's *The History of Mr Polly* though he did not enjoy it, describing it as 'a very "drab" picture of the life of a half-baked shop assistant with some literary and artistic tastes. Probably a caricature tho' shows some knowledge but there is none of Dickens' geniality about it & no trust in "The Higher Powers". Funeral, Wedding, Family Life all caricatured. Leaves an unpleasant taste in the literary mouth. How far behind Galsworthy from the human point of view.'

CHAPTER 7
TWO LOVE STORIES

65 BROTHER

66 DIARY 19 December 1912

67 DIARY 22 December 1912. It was 'Why Jigsaws Went out of Fashion'.

68 DIARY 26 December 1912

69 DIARY 1 February 1913. [The 1913 diary has been lost, and all 1913 entries are taken from a transcription of some material by JTRG.]

70 BROTHER

71 CHARLES p. 25

72 GTAT29 p. 40

73 Ibid.

74 BROTHER

75 Ibid.

76 Ibid.

77 GTAT29 p. 76

78 See GTAT29 pp. 40–1

79 GTAT29 pp. 76–7

80 DIARY 1 February 1913 [but see note 69 above]

81 Ibid. 3 March 1913

82 Ibid. 6 March 1913

CHAPTER 8
'FALL NOT OUT BY THE WAY'

83 GTAT29 p. 59

84 DIARY 19, 20, and 21 April [but see note 69 above]. APG describes the party as including 'Mr. Mallory and Todhunter and young Percy'.

85 CHARLES p. 26. Charles writes, 'Term ended and there was no news'; but his memory, like Robert's, was far from perfect. APG had the news on 31 May in a letter from Fletcher. After the scholarship examinations, Charles probably spent a day or two at home, and it would have been then that the conversation with Amy occurred.

86 LETTERS Sunday 29 January 1911. Robert had felt acutely anxious about John at the very moment of John's accident, and had written at once to ask whether he was all right.

87 DIARY 22 June 1913 [but see note 69 above]

88 *Greyfriar*, March 1913, Vol. VI, No. 87, see pp. 87 and 88

89 *Green Chartreuse*, July 1913. RG also wrote 'One Hundred Years Ago', 'The King's Son', 'How to do Things', and 'The Miser of

Shenham Heath' [Higginson's bibliography p. 219]

90 RG reproduces this, with minor alterations, in GTAT29 pp. 81–3

91 *The Copthorne School Chronicle*, October 1913, Vol. III, No. 1, p. 50, 'The "Runabout" at Charterhouse', signed by R.R.G.

92 DIARY 22 June 1913 [but see note 69 above]

93 GTAT29 pp. 75–6

94 BROTHER

95 AUTHOR: Diary of Clarissa Janie Graves transcribed by her brother JTRG, n.d.; date from DIARY 10 August 1913

96 Ibid. n.d.

97 DIARY 20 August 1913 [but see note 69 above]

98 Ibid. 2 September 1913

99 Ibid. 1 September 1913

100 Ibid. 25 and 22 August 1913; and LETTERS 5 May 1914

101 Ibid. 23 July 1913

102 *The Carthusian*, October 1913, Vol. XI, No. 370, pp. 173–4. In his annotated *Over the Brazier* (London: The Poetry Bookshop new edition 1920) RG describes this poem as 'a reminiscence of Choir'.

103 *The Carthusian*, December 1913, Vol. XI, No. 372, p. 207

104 *The Carthusian*, November 1913, Vol. XI, No. 371, p. 187

105 DIARY 12–4 13/14 September 1913

CHAPTER 9
THE SHADOW OF FAILURE

106 GTAT29 p. 88

107 *The Carthusian*, December 1913, Vol. XI, No. 372, pp. 220–1. The official record contrasts with RG's memory of 'six voters against the motion'. [GTAT29 p. 88]

108 Christopher Hassall, *A Biography of Sir Edward Marsh* (Longmans, 1959). RG's published recollections of his first meeting with Marsh became increasingly unreliable. In GTAT29 p. 80 he correctly dates their first meeting to 1913, but includes a rebuke from Marsh about the quality of his poetic vocabulary which was not made until early 1915 (see Hassall p. 306 which appears to be supported by O'PREY(1) RG to Marsh 3 February 1915, pp. 30–1). In 1953 he repeated this error and added the further error that the first meeting came when he was sixteen and that it predated the publication of Vol. I of *Georgian Poetry*, which would have placed it in 1911–12 (see O'PREY(1) p. 28).

109 DIARY 10 December 1913

110 AUTHOR: Diary of Clarissa Janie Graves, 1914, extracts transcribed by her brother JTRG

111 DIARY 22 December 1913 [but see note 69 above]

112 DIARY 1 January 1914

113 DIARY 5 January 1914

114 GTAT29 pp. 94–5

115 RG did break one ski, which cost him ten shillings, but was not hurt himself.

116 DIARY 14 January 1914

117 AUTHOR: Clarissa Graves to her brother JTRG n.d.

CHAPTER 10
PERPETUAL DISCORD AND
'THE HERO OF THE HOUR'

118 *The Carthusian*, October 1913, Vol. XI, No. 370, pp. 173–4

119 *The Carthusian*, December 1913, Vol. XI, No. 372, p. 207

120 *The Carthusian*, November 1913, Vol. XI, No. 371, p. 187

121 Ibid. p. 188

122 As 118 above, p. 174. For the other poem see F. Higginson, *A Bibliography of the Works of Robert Graves* (London: Vane, 1966), p. 220.

123 AUTHOR: Amy Graves to her son JTRG 31 January 1914 describes the post as that of sub-editor; but Robert clearly had a greater influence on the magazine than the title of sub-editor suggests.

124 As 119 above, pp. 201–2

125 *The Carthusian*, February 1914, Vol. XI, No. 373, p. 225

126 *The Carthusian*, April 1914, Vol. XI, No. 375

127 Ibid. p. 267

128 Ibid. pp. 265–6

129 Ibid. p. 284

130 *The Carthusian*, June 1914, Vol. XI, No. 376, p. 285

131 GTAT29 p. 85

132 *The Carthusian*, April 1914, Vol. XI, No. 375, pp. 268–9

133 GTAT29 p. 77. Robert preserved 'cherry-whisky' for GTAT57 (see p. 53) but MS-S pp. 569–70 believes it was cherry brandy on the strength of a remark made by Robert in 1943, which he later retracted. Of such trivia are scholarly footnotes sometimes composed.

134 Ibid. pp. 77–8

135 AUTHOR: Charles Graves to his mother Amy n.d.

136 As 130 above p. 301

137 BROTHER

138 DIARY 6 April 1914

139 GTAT29 p. 93 Robert's account of these few days as 'a season' reveals how they stood out in his memory. But DIARY shows RG having supper with Rosaleen and Christopher Swayne at the Swaynes' house on the evening of 12 April; and he is back in Harlech playing golf with Charles against John and their father on the afternoon of 23 April.

140 Ibid. p. 95 quoted by RG from a contemporary essay of his on climbing.

141 Ibid. p. 97

142 Ibid. p. 98

143 DIARY 24 April 1914. APG persuaded Robert to enter for the Thackeray and Dickens prizes at Charterhouse.

144 DIARY 4 May 1914. APG begged RG not to publish this attack.

145 Christopher Hassall, *A Biography of Sir Edward Marsh*, p. 286

146 LETTERS 6 July 1914

147 DIARY 6 July 1914

148 GTAT29 p. 87 for this and the subsequent long quotation

149 Ibid.

150 DIARY 6 July 1914

151 GTAT29 pp. 61–2

152 DIARY 7 July 1914

153 GTAT29 p. 102. In the 1929 version, Robert pretended surprise that his uncle had been irritated; but in 1957 he simply wrote: 'This had infuriated him, as a good Victorian', p. 70.

154 DIARY 15 July 1914

155 GTAT29 p. 85

156 Ibid.

157 DIARY 20 July 1914

158 GTAT29 pp. 85–7

159 Ibid. p. 88

CHAPTER II
BELGIUM RAVISHED

160 AUTHOR: Amy to JTRG 18 July, no year. Internal evidence gives 1914.

161 ALFRED p. 296

162 ALFRED p. 295. APG adds that he applied to the OCC 'as Oxford cannot accept him till he has matriculated'.

163 *Punch* 7 June 1916, p. 376

164 DIARY 12 August 1914 omits the 'Royal' which appears before 'Welch' in ALFRED p. 296

BOOK FOUR
MILITARY SERVICE 1914–1919

CHAPTER I
'THE ONLY PLACE FOR A GENTLEMAN'

1 '1914 1.Peace' from *Poems of Rupert Brooke* (Thomas Nelson & Sons, 1952) p. 150

2 Alice Meynell, 'Summer in England, 1914' in *The Times*, 10 October 1914

3 Robert Graves, *Over the Brazier*. In MAJORCA RG annotates his 1920 edition with: 'Wrexham 1914 suggested curiously by the 3rd Bn. RWF regimental goat.'

4 GTAT29 pp. 118–19

5 Robert Graves, *Over the Brazier*, poem entitled 'Oh, and Oh!' MAJORCA RG annotates his copy: 'Lancaster 1914 in charge of a platoon guarding German POWS at the Wagon Works.'

6 AUTHOR: Amy Graves to her son JTRG 26 September 1914

7 LETTERS 14 October 1914

8 DIARY 20 October 1914. A version of this appears in ALFRED p. 300, edited and with the misprint of 'fatter' for the original 'taller'.

9 ALFRED p. 300 & DIARY 19 October 1914. See also DIARY 21 October, 6 November and 25 November for APG calling on *Punch* (twice) and *The Westminster Gazette* in attempts to find a home for this poem.

10 AUTHOR: Amy Graves to JTRG 24 October; see also DIARY 21 October 1914

11 AUTHOR: R.L. Arrowsmith, for many years a master at Charterhouse, had this from Humphrey Whinney, who went to Gownboys in 1913; and R.L.A. passed it on in a letter to the present author dated 9 September 1982.

12 IMPERIAL Special Miscellaneous M4: Robert Graves to Cyril Hartmann, 25 October 1914. Hartmann was now up at University College, Oxford.

13 When I visited RG for his 80th birthday party in 1975, he was proudly wearing a regimental tie, but talked sadly about the Germans he had killed. See also MS-S p. 567

14 LETTERS 14 October 1914

15 GTAT29 pp. 107–8

16 IMPERIAL as 12 above

17 AUTHOR: Amy Graves to JTRG 5 December 1914. From AUTHOR: Amy to JTRG 21 and 22 November 1914 we also learn that Amy was upset when Robert planned a weekend at Erinfa, as she wanted him to come home; but then all leave was stopped 'as they might be sent at a moment's notice to the East Coast'.

18 DIARY 7 December 1914

19 AUTHOR: Amy Graves to JTRG 12 December 1914

20 Ibid.

21 ALFRED p. 301

22 DIARY 28 December 1914. For the story of Jephthah's daughter see Judges 11:30 ff. Robert had recently (see O'PREY(I) p. 29) used the same simile in a letter to Eddie Marsh.

23 Ibid. 4 January 1915

24 DIARY 5 January 1915

25 O'PREY(I) pp. 29–30

26 In GTAT29 p. 80 Robert refers this rebuke from Marsh to his Carthusian days. However, the evidence of RG's poems in *The Carthusian* shows that he was using plenty of old-fashioned diction after his first meeting with Marsh; while O'PREY(I) RG to Eddie Marsh 3 February 1915 pp. 30–1 seems conclusive proof that the rebuke in fact came in late January or early February 1915. See also Book Three, Note 108 above.

27 O'PREY(I) p. 28 quotes this from RG's account in *Eddie Marsh, Sketches for a Composite Literary Portrait of Sir Edward Marsh*, compiled by Christopher Hassall and Denis Matthews, 1953. RG repeats his error of date, and elaborates upon his original story; but the emotional shock is still vividly recalled.

28 O'PREY(I) RG to Eddie Marsh 3 February 1915 pp. 30–1

29 DIARY 16 February 1915

30 GTAT29 pp. 122–3

31 DIARY 11 May 1915

32 DIARY 16 March 1915

33 Amy accompanied him to Charterhouse; they visited Charles first, and then Amy returned alone, leaving RG to stay till late in the evening.

34 GTAT29 pp. 108–9

35 DIARY 12 May 1915

36 Ibid.

37 DIARY 19 May 1915. This is a slightly edited extract, cutting out a repetition after the word war: 'it is a comfort to know, even in the most sanguinary war'.

CHAPTER 2
BAPTISM OF FIRE

38 DIARY 17 May 1915, has RG with 'six brother officers'; GTAT29 p. 127 has 'we six'; and the *Spectator* has 'the five of us Flash Mob'.

39 DIARY 15 May 1915

40 The *Spectator* 11 September 1915 contains contemporary letters of Robert's (their prose style occasionally polished by APG), some of which APG also published in ALFRED pp. 322–8. As a contemporary account, these letters must be taken to be more reliable than GTAT29 Chapter XII, which in any case Robert admits (GTAT29 p. 127) is a 'reconstituted chapter' of what was first written as an autobiographical novel. Thus in reality, on his first night he slept until stand-to, and did not take a watch at all; the incidents attributed to this mythical first watch in GTAT29 pp. 139–42 are no doubt a composite of various experiences during the next few days, though MS-S p. 35, despite knowing of the *Spectator* letters from ALFRED, appears to take GTAT29, Chapter XII at its face value.

41 GTAT29 p. 147

42 O'PREY(1) RG to Eddie Marsh 22 May 1915 pp. 31–3

43 GTAT29 p. 147. If both this letter (dated 22 May 1915) and 42 above are dated accurately, then RG wrote his letter to Marsh after the bombardment of 21/22 May which had made him sweat, but suppressed the information in favour of the news about a bombardment 'two nights ago' (i.e. 19/20 May) which had failed to wake him. However, the dating of the letters quoted in GTAT is unreliable, and their value as contemporary

documents is limited (see note 45 below). The likelihood is that the letter given in GTAT29 p. 150 should be dated 22 May, as it refers to returning to the trenches 'tomorrow'; while 42 above also mentions going into trenches 'tomorrow' and is reliably dated 22 May. The previous letters should therefore be dated earlier; and it is on that basis that I have written my narrative account.

44 Ibid. p. 152

45 ALFRED p. 324. There are some discrepancies in the evidence. APG describes this letter in DIARY 5 June 1915, so we can assume it was written before that date. Robert in GTAT29 p. 154 not only gives 6 June as the date, but then provides a version of the letter which differs enormously from the contemporary document as it appeared first in the *Spectator* for 11 September 1915 and then in ALFRED p. 324. If this letter is typical, which appears to be the case, then RG's dating of letters in GTAT29 is unreliable; and their value as contemporary evidence is also substantially reduced by heavy rewriting.

46 GTAT29 p. 155

47 ALFRED pp. 326–7 but first published in the *Spectator*, 11 September 1915; this letter appears in GTAT29 p. 155, with the correct date, but rewritten almost out of recognition.

48 DIARY 17 June 1915

49 AUTHOR: Amy Graves to her son JTRG 19 June 1915

50 See GTAT29 p. 156; also IMPERIAL who have some fine pictures of the ruined town; also AUTHOR: Amy Graves to her son JTRG 3 July 1915.

51 ALFRED p. 325 but first published in the *Spectator*, 11 September 1915.

52 DIARY 29 June 1915

53 A letter home from RG in the *Spectator*, 11 September 1915

54 DIARY 25 June 1915

55 DIARY 27 June: Clarissa had suddenly become 'scatter-brained & a little noisy' on her way back from a church service with Amy.

56 DIARY 29 June 1915

57 GTAT29 p. 163

58 Despite GTAT29 pp. 163–4 in which RG states clearly that the bad news came from his cousin (i.e. Gerald), MS-S p. 21 says that the news came from 'his brother John' who was at this time still at Copthorne.

59 Robert Graves, *Over The Brazier*; in the Canellun copy this poem is annotated by RG 'July 1915'.

60 GTAT29 p. 163. In AUTHOR: Gerald Graves to JTRG 17 March 1974 Gerald denies that he owed RG a grudge or wrote in spite. He recalls being persuaded to write to RG by Charles. By the winter RG's faith in Johnstone was entirely restored, and at Le Havre [see MAJORCA RG's annotated 'Over The Brazier'] he wrote the poem '1915' which includes the lines: 'And you've been everything,/Dear you've been everything that I most lack/In these soul deadening trenches.'

61 AUTHOR: Robert Graves to his 'Dearest Family', 2 July 1915. This letter exists only as a typewritten copy by JTRG. As a document it casts much doubt on the reliability of the letter of 24 June in GTAT29 pp. 156–9. MS-S p. 37 uses the GTAT letter, though realizing from the quotation from Skelton (then unknown to Robert) that 'this may be an error'.

62 AUTHOR: Quoted in a letter from APG to JTRG 6 July 1915

63 MAJORCA Robert Graves to his father, postcard 12 July 1915

64 *Spectator* 11 September 1915

65 GTAT29 p. 164

CHAPTER 3
DANGEROUS CLEAR LIGHT

66 GTAT pp. 164–74. When Robert was writing GTAT29, it suited him to play down the high moral earnestness of 1915, and to pretend that he went out on patrol largely to secure the type of minor wound which would have sent him safely back to England. See

also Frank Richards, who in *Old Soldiers Never Die* (Faber & Faber 1933) p. 109 writes: 'We had a young officer named Mr. Graves join the Battalion at this time and he was posted to the ['A'] Company. He was soon highly respected.'

67 MAJORCA: Robert Graves to 'Peter' Johnstone 5 August 1915. Much of this letter appears in MS-S pages 406–7.

68 The Gospel According to St Mark, 9:24

69 DIARY 20 August 1915

70 DIARY 31 August 1915

71 Robert Graves, 'Nursery Memories-III' in *Over the Brazier*; in the Canellun copy this poem is annotated by RG 'August 1915 (after a moonlight patrol near the Brickstacks).'

CHAPTER 4
ALONG THE SEA-SHORE

72 DIARY 9 September 1915; RG arrived in Harlech on the 3.15 train.

73 DIARY 9 September 1915

74 DIARY 21 July 1915. RG singled out APG's 'translations from the Irish which he thinks may become classical'.

75 DIARY 11 September 1915

76 DIARY 12 September 1915. The *Spectator* was dated 11 September 1915.

77 DIARY 14 September 1915

78 DIARY 15 September 1915

79 DIARY 16 September 1915

CHAPTER 5
THE BATTLE OF LOOS

80 GTAT29 p. 188

81 MAJORCA: Robert Graves to his family 20 September 1915

82 GTAT29 pp. 189–96

83 Frank Richards, *Old Soldiers Never Die*, p. 115

84 GTAT29 pp. 205, 208; GTAT29 p. 190 suggests that Robert and his fellow officers knew in advance that it was

just 'a subsidiary attack'; but o'PREY(1) RG to Eddie Marsh October 1915 p. 34 makes it clear that this was 'fortunately' not known until 'afterwards'.

85 As 83 above, p. 129

86 GTAT29 pp. 208–11

87 o'PREY(1) RG to Eddie Marsh October 1915, pp. 34–5

88 DIARY 8 October 1915. One of these poems may have been 'A Renascence' which was deleted from the 1920 edition of *Over The Brazier*. Soldiers are praised for learning 'to suffer and live clean'; and RG comments 'of their travailings and groans/Poetry is born again'.

89 MAJORCA: RG's marginal note in his 1920 edition of *Over The Brazier* reads 'October 1915 Annezin by a glass of Curaçao'.

CHAPTER 6
A STRAY BULLET

90 As 87 above, p. 35

91 Ibid.

92 ALFRED p. 302. APG was also chiefly responsible (see ALFRED pp. 303–5) for the setting up of the Fighting Forces Book Council, which sent thousands of books to the armed forces on every front.

93 AUTHOR: Amy Graves to JTRG 8 November 1915

94 DIARY 5 November 1915

95 AUTHOR: Amy Graves to JTRG 8 November 1915 and DIARY 8 November 1915. When writing GTAT29 (see p. 219) Robert surmised that he had been sent back 'for failing, one day when we were in billets, to observe a paragraph in battalion orders requiring my presence on ... parade'.

96 DIARY 13 November 1915. They lunched at Brooks's.

97 DIARY 18 November 1915

98 DIARY 15 November 1915

99 DIARY 22 November 1918. By the time he came to write GTAT29, Robert had

quite forgotten his hopes to return to England, and wrote instead (GTAT29 p. 218) what is in fact the opposite of the truth, that he was 'anxious to avoid' the 'disgrace' of being sent back to England.

100 SASSOON(1) 28 November p. 21

101 Siegfried Sassoon, *Memoirs of an Infantry Officer* (London: Folio Society, 1974), p. 82. As is well known, RG appears in this volume as David Cromlech.

102 DIARY 5 December 1915

103 o'PREY(1) RG to Eddie Marsh 10 December 1915, p. 37

104 SASSOON(1) For this paragraph I have drawn heavily upon the excellent introduction by Sir Rupert Hart-Davis (pp. 9–11)

105 Ibid. p. 21

106 Ibid. p. 21

107 Robert Graves, *Over The Brazier*, first published in *Westminster Gazette*, 13 March 1916, p. 2

108 As 106 above

109 GTAT29 p. 224; and see o'PREY(1) p. 37 for RG calling Sassoon 'a very nice chap but his verses, except occasionally, don't please me very much'.

110 o'PREY(1) RG to Eddie Marsh 10 December 1915 pp. 37–8

111 MS-S p. 43 quotes from the letter, probably held by the University of Texas at Austin. The name of the poem comes from DIARY.

112 GTAT29 pp. 227–31

113 DIARY 27 January 1916

114 Ibid. 27 January 1916

115 o'PREY(1) RG to Eddie Marsh 24 February 1916, p. 41

116 Ibid.

117 DIARY 21 February 1916. APG passed on the news that RG had given permission for them to appear in the *W.G.* to Marsh, who later told APG (DIARY 23 February 1916) that he had stayed up until two o'clock one morning, correcting them.

118 DIARY 8 March 1916

119 DIARY 10 March 1916. Just before this, RG had a bout of influenza (see DIARY 6 March 1916) which landed

him in hospital at Le Havre for a few days.

120 SASSOON(I) 19 March 1916, p. 45

121 GTAT29 p. 251

122 Robert Graves, *Goliath and David* London: Chiswick Press, Christmas 1916 – an edition limited to 150 copies published privately in booklet form. The poems it contains are 'The Bough of Nonsense', 'Goliath and David', 'A Pinch of Salt', 'Babylon', 'Careers', The Lady Visitor in the Pauper Ward', 'The Last Post', 'A Dead Boche', and 'Not Dead'. The copy which I consulted is in the Bodleian, Oxford.

123 GTAT29 pp. 251–2

CHAPTER 7
ON LEAVE

124 DIARY 27, 28 and 29 March; and 1 April 1916. Robert went into town with Clarissa and Rosaleen, travelled to Copthorne with Amy to visit John; and when he went to Charterhouse he took Rosaleen with him, and they had lunch with Charles. It was when he stayed on alone at Charterhouse for a second day that he spent time with Johnstone.

125 O'PREY(I) RG to Sassoon 2 May 1916, p. 46

126 DIARY 23 and 24 March 1916. Sir Alfred replied on 24 March disclaiming personal responsibility and suggesting that RG's case should 'go through the routine method'. But APG was no more in love with red tape and officialdom than his son, and took no notice.

127 DIARY 1 April 1916. At this point in the story, MS-S p. 47 mistakenly repeats RG's story from GTAT57 pp. 175–6 about an altercation with his parents over attending a Good Friday service. This did not appear in GTAT29, but was first published in Robert Graves, *But It Still Goes On* (Jonathan Cape, 1930), pp. 109–14. On Good Friday 1916 Robert was still in

hospital, where he was visited by Rosaleen who found him (DIARY Good Friday 1916) 'much better'. The circumstantial but utterly misleading details given by RG on p. 110 of *But It Still Goes On* show how easy it is for the memory to play tricks. In fact, the occasion when RG went to church in 1916 and had to push APG's bath chair was on 1 November (DIARY of that date).

128 DIARY 12 April 1916. Marsh also visited RG in hospital (DIARY 15 April 1916)

129 DIARY 26 April 1916. At the time it was believed that the operation had been a success, and in GTAT29 p. 253 RG states that it was performed by 'a first-class surgeon'; but in GTAT57 he changed his mind, said that the surgeon had 'bungled the job, and I still cannot breathe properly through one nostril'.

130 MAJORCA: A document shows that RG bought the cottage on 12 May 1916 for £29. 19s. od.

131 From 'The Cottage' in Robert Graves, *Fairies and Fusiliers* (Heinemann 1917). [The beechwood table is also described in O'PREY(I) RG to Sassoon 2 May 1916, p. 46.] First published in *The Carthusian*, November 1916.

132 GTAT29 p. 253

133 GTAT29 p. 331, and see BROTHER for the numerous additional details.

134 O'PREY(I) RG to Sassoon 2 May 1916, pp. 45–7

135 Ibid. n.d. [early May 1916], pp. 47–9. It was in June this year that CLG's affectionate poem about RG appeared in *Punch* (see Book Three, Note 163 above.) See also DIARY 15 May 1916

136 GTAT29 pp. 253–4; see also DIARY 18 May 1916

137 DIARY 22 May 1916. Later in the day RG saw Monro at the Poetry Book Shop, and was told that the trade had made advance orders for 150 copies of *Over the Brazier*. Then RG lunched with Marsh.

138 DIARY 25 May 1916. MS-S pp. 47–8

says oddly that RG was at Litherland
for two months starting in March. He
was actually at Litherland from 25
May to 25 June (see DIARY entries).

139 DIARY 27 May 1916

140 O'PREY(I) RG to Sassoon 27 May
1916, pp. 50–1

141 Ibid.

142 Ibid. 23 June 1916, pp. 51–3. See also
Ibid. 2 May 1916, p. 46, which shows
that RG had hoped for publication
of *Over the Brazier* on 1 May. But (see
DIARY 4, 6, 20 and 31 May) when
APG telephoned Monro on 4 May, he
talked of not going to the press until
about the 15th. However, by 6 May
APG had six advance copies; and
when RG went for his weekend to
Charterhouse, APG sat in the garden
at Red Branch House writing letters
about the book to various friends who
might promote it. It was at his request
that Strachey agreed to review the
poems.

143 DIARY 26 June 1916

144 DIARY 27 June 1916. Rosaleen
remained at home typing out RG's
latest poem; Clarissa, Perceval, Amy
and Alfred escorted him to the local
station; then the men went on with
him as far as Waterloo.

CHAPTER 8
THE BATTLE OF THE SOMME

Except where otherwise stated, material
from this chapter is drawn largely from
GTAT29 pp. 256–73. For background information I consulted John Harris *The
Somme: Death of a Generation* (Zenith
Books, 1966); & in August 1985 I visited
the sector of the line in which Robert was
severely wounded.

145 O'PREY(I) RG to Marsh n.d. [July
1916] pp. 53–4

146 GTAT29 p. 259

147 SASSOON(I) 12 July 1916, p. 91

148 O'PREY(I) RG to Sassoon 13 July 1916,
pp. 54–5

149 SASSOON(I) 14 July 1916, p. 93

150 Ibid. 21 July 1916, p. 98

151 Ibid. 16 July 1916, p. 94

152 From 'Letter to SS. from Mametz
Wood' in Robert Graves, *Poems
1914–1926* (Heinemann 1927), pp.
54–7. RG states that the eight lines
beginning '... today I found' were a
'Fragment included at the end of this
letter.' These lines were first published in RG's *Goliath and David*
(Chiswick Press, 1916), as the last
eight lines of 'A Dead Boche', which
begins:

To you who'd read my songs of
War
And only hear of blood and fame
I'll say (you've heard it said before)
'War's Hell!' and if you doubt the
same

Today I found [&c]

The 'Letter to SS from Mametz
Wood' (first published in RG's *Fairies and Fusiliers* (Heinemann, 1917)
was written in answer to a verse letter
of Sassoon's, sent to him a few weeks
earlier. RG's description of the
events from 9 to 15 July does not fit
in at all well with Sassoon's diary –
e.g. SSD makes it clear that the two
men conversed on the 14th, while RG
has it that it was not till the 15th that
he first tried and failed to get in touch
with Sassoon. The contemporary account is clearly preferable and I have
followed it. RG's confusion is quite
understandable; after his narrow
escape from death on 20 July many
wrong dates became embedded in his
memory; and by 26 July (see
O'PREY(I) p. 56) RG believed he had
enjoyed his long conversation with
Sassoon on the 16th. O'PREY(I) p. 55
follows the GTAT29 version of events,
and MS-S p. 48 believes that the poem
from Mametz Wood was written on
13 July, which was in fact the date of
RG's letter to Sassoon from Buire
(O'PREY(I) pp. 54–5).

153 GTAT29 p. 264

154 MS-S p. 48 says RG commanded 'B'
Company; but in both GTAT29 pp.
265–6 and GTAT57 pp. 185–6 RG

mentions that he was with 'D' company, and names 'Moodie' as the company commander. I can find no contrary evidence.
155 GTAT29 p. 265
156 Ibid. p. 271
157 Ibid. p. 272
158 Ibid. p. 273
159 MAJORCA: Colonel Crawshay to Amy Graves 30 July 1916

CHAPTER 9
'BUT I WAS DEAD,
AN HOUR OR MORE'

Unless otherwise stated, the material in this chapter is drawn from GTAT29 pp. 273–83
160 Ibid.
161 GTAT29 p. 274
162 Ibid. pp. 274–5
163 DIARY 24 July 1916; and see ALFRED p. 331
164 Ibid.
165 MAJORCA
166 DIARY 28 July 1916; and see ALFRED p. 332
167 DIARY 31 July 1916; and see ALFRED p. 332
168 O'PREY(1) p. 59 and GTAT29 p. 279
169 Ibid. p. 277
170 DIARY 1 August 1916 – on this day a letter arrived announcing the draining of the wound.
171 Ibid.
172 O'PREY(1) RG to Marsh 7 August 1916 pp. 58–60
173 Robert Graves, *Goliath and David*. The two damns in this poem later became curses; and 'Tickler's jam' was explained as 'ration jam'.
174 As 172 above p. 59–60. MS-S p. 51, despite the fact that thirteen-year-old John was not yet at Charterhouse, erroneously attributes the lines to him rather than to Charles. (John had just left Copthorne laden with prizes [see DIARY 1 August 1916], and went on to Charterhouse in the autumn.
175 Ibid. p. 58
176 DIARY 26 August 1916. In GTAT29 p.

283 RG seems to imply that Sassoon travelled up to Harlech with him; and this is assumed by MS-S p. 52. In fact Sassoon did not travel up to Harlech (see DIARY 29 August) until three days later, on Tuesday 29 August. RG's circumstantial account of meeting Sassoon at Paddington, and hearing the news about men killed on 3 September, cannot be at all accurate. Incidentally DIARY 24 August suggests that the plan was for Rosaleen to accompany Robert on the train journey. Whether she did or not is unknown.

This incident needs interpolating into SASSOON(1) p. 102 where at present Sir Rupert Hart-Davis has Sassoon 'at Weirleigh, riding and hunting'.

CHAPTER 10
ROBERT AND SIEGFRIED

177 DIARY 28 August 1916. It was at the holiday house of their Wimbledon friend Sir Maurice Hill; and one of the actresses was Clarissa's friend, the young Margaret Rutherford.
178 DIARY 29 August 1916
179 BROTHER
180 DIARY 30 August 1916
181 GTAT29 p. 288
182 BROTHER
183 DIARY 4, 5, 6 and 8 September 1916. JTRG pointed out to me that Charles was a better player than Robert, and suggested that Robert was annoyed by this.
184 GTAT29 p. 289. In describing his work at this time, RG refers to his *Fairies and Fusiliers* poems, which were dedicated to the regiment. But at this stage Robert was working on his more modest *Goliath and David* collection; and when he later began collecting poems for *Fairies and Fusiliers*, his first intention was that it should be dedicated to Sassoon.
185 Both 'Not Dead' and the subsequent lines from 'Babylon' come from

Robert Graves, *Goliath and David.*

186 GTAT29 pp. 289–90

187 MS-S pp. 196–7 describes a copy of GTAT29 annotated in 1929 by Blunden and Sassoon, though he does not say where it is to be found. But from MS-S's description of one of the annotations, and assuming that Sassoon's memory was reasonably reliable, it appears that RG's memory of leaving after one night is quite inaccurate. As we shall see in a future volume, Sassoon quarrelled violently with Robert's account of the visit in GTAT29, though he also admitted that he himself, in being irritated by his mother's behaviour, had 'behaved with very little courtesy or consideration' [see O'PREY(I), p. 207].

188 ed. Robert Gathorne-Hardy, *Ottoline at Garsington 1915–1918* (Faber & Faber, 1974) p. 152 shows that at some stage in 1916 Sassoon and Graves stayed at Garsington. This appears to be the only time when such a visit could have taken place. Further details in this paragraph are drawn from Sir Rupert Hart-Davis in SASSOON(I) pp. 102–3.

189 AUTHOR: Alfred Perceval Graves to his son John T.R. Graves 27 September 1916. DIARY 23 September 1916 shows that was the date upon which RG arrived at Llandindrod Wells. Other DIARY entries show that CLG left on 26 September, and APG on 5 October. Probably RG also left on that date and went on to Harlech.

190 GTAT29 p. 289 mentions RG working on this novel, but is not specific about the time, as he is concerned with laying a false trail to prevent people from connecting Sassoon with the 'First Battalion friend'.

191 DIARY 31 October 1916. DIARY 24 October 1916 shows that RG was then planning to go to Charterhouse first; but this visit probably never took place, as LETTERS RG to JTRG 15 December 1916 suggests that RG had not by then seen JTRG at Charterhouse.

192 Robert Graves, *But It Still Goes On*, pp. 109–14 contains Robert's bitter account of this affair. The details are not trustworthy (see note 127 above) but the incident certainly made a powerful impression upon him.

193 DIARY 1 November 1916

194 Ibid. 2 November 1916. RG also met 'young Asquith' on this occasion.

195 In GTAT29 p. 290 RG places this conversation or set of conversations with Sassoon in Litherland, in November. However SASSOON(I) p. 104 shows that Sassoon was not at Litherland until 4 December; while RG's letter to his parents received on 20 November (DIARY for that date) states his wish to return to France as soon as possible, and this is accepted by APG as a well-known piece of information. In the circumstances it seems reasonable to assume that the crucial conversation with Sassoon took place at an earlier meeting, most probably at lunch on 2 November 1916.

196 Clarissa Graves to RG n.d. but from internal evidence before 17 November 1916, the date of RG's Medical Board.

197 MAJORCA: Raymond Rodakowski to RG 12 November 1916. Incidentally RG had recently visited another O.C. friend, Nevill Barbour; but the visit was a disappointment & RG told APG that Barbour had 'rather hung fire intellectually and is very noncommittal' (DIARY 9 November 1916).

198 DIARY 13 and 14 November 1916. RG definitely failed to find Rodakowski in hospital early on the 13th before the round of engagements began. But on the 14th RG stayed on at Oxford for hours after APG left, and I have assumed, perhaps wrongly, that this was to meet his old friend.

CHAPTER II
BLACK VELVET DRESS

199 DIARY 5 December 1916

200 MAJORCA: Amy Graves to RG 21 November 1916
201 DIARY 12 December 1916
202 Ibid.
203 MAJORCA: Charles Graves to RG in 1916 folder, n.d. but see DIARY 28 November for APG receiving a similar letter on that date.
204 LETTERS 15 December 1916
205 See BROTHER and also JTRG's annotation to 204 above.
206 DIARY 26 December 1916. They 'made impromptu rhymes & told impromptu stories' as they walked over the Common. Amy and Rosaleen were not present for this.
207 SASSOON(I) 31 December 1916, p. 111
208 O'PREY(I) RG to Robert Nichols 7 January 1917 pp. 61–2
209 SASSOON(I) 18 January 1917, p. 121
210 DIARY 19 January 1917. It was a surprise visit.
211 O'PREY(I) RG to Sassoon 25 January 1917, p. 63
212 DIARY 21 January 1917. 'Robbie went into town to see a friend in hospital.'
213 GTAT29 p. 366 MS-S p. 83 says 'Nichols, although this is, decently, not stated in *Goodbye To All That*, had seen no active service.' But RG clearly states that RN was 'in no show'; and incidentally on page 39 of Robert Graves, *Poetic Unreason and Other Studies* (Cecil Palmer, 1925), RG states that RN 'levelled no revolver at Germans ... [was] ... never in the infantry at all ... [and] ... his service with the artillery in France was of the shortest.'
214 As 211 above
215 DIARY 24 October 1916. Ben was to be put in 'a large window'.
216 GTAT29 p. 331 gives no precise date; but 19, 20 or 21 January are the only possible dates if RG is broadly right, and the meeting occurred when he was going 'back to France in 1917'. It could not have been the day he left for France (22 January) despite his recollection that the meeting occurred on his way to the station. He was accompanied directly from

Red Branch House to the station by his parents; and the station was Waterloo and not Victoria [DIARY 22 January 1917]. 21 January seems to me the most likely date, as RG was making a special trip into town, not either dashing all the way down from North Wales (the 19th) or spending the day at Charterhouse (the 20th) [see DIARY for those dates].
217 DIARY 22 January 1917

CHAPTER 12
HOPE AND WET MATCHES

Unless otherwise stated, the material in this chapter is drawn from GTAT29 pp. 293–303.
218 MS-S pp. 52–3 says that RG was stationed in Harfleur; but on 25 January (O'PREY(I) p. 63) RG writes from Rouen; RG also talks of Rouen in GTAT29 p. 294. His mention of the [Havre near Harfleur] 'Bull Ring' in GTAT29 p. 295 appears to me to be a parenthetical comment based on his January 1916 experiences.
219 That this was only a temporary command becomes clear from AUTHOR: Amy Graves to JTRG 23 February 1917, with the report that Robert 'was no longer C.O. as they had a new Colonel'.
220 GTAT29 p. 297
221 O'PREY(I) RG to Nichols 2 February 1917, p. 65
222 GTAT29 gives Robert a larger role in preventing the attack. However, Sassoon's correspondence with RG in O'PREY(I) [see especially p. 200] makes it clear that although the attack may have been postponed at the conference in which RG participated, it was not finally called off until after a conference which RG did not attend, when it was realized that 'the German position could not be shelled owing to the formation of the ground'. In GTAT57 RG takes some note of Sassoon's complaints, and

alters 'hear the decision' to 'hear of my stand at the conference'.

223 AUTHOR: Amy Graves to JTRG 23 February 1917. This contemporary account differs in some details from GTAT29 p. 302

224 GTAT29 p. 303

CHAPTER 13
SHELL-SHOCK AND MARJORIE

225 GTAT29 pp. 106–7
226 Ibid. p. 330
227 DIARY 20 March 1917
228 Ibid. 21 March 1917. RG arrived home at 8 a.m.
229 O'PREY(I) p. 354 note 55 and RG to Sassoon 26 March 1917, pp. 66–7
230 Ibid. RG to Sassoon 21 April 1917, p. 68. DIARY 2 April 1917 shows RG in Oxford by that date; and DIARY 10 April 1917 reveals that news of RG's staff appointment reached Red Branch House on the 10th.
231 GTAT29 p. 306
232 Lester Pearson, *Memoirs 1897–1948: Through Diplomacy to Politics* (Victor Gollancz, 1973) p. 32
233 DIARY 28 April 1917
234 O'PREY(I) 22 April 1917, pp. 69–70
235 GTAT29 pp. 306–7. GTAT57 p. 216 adds Marjorie's name.
236 GTAT57 p. 216. Since details of Marjorie's name, peacetime occupation and father are only to be found in GTAT57 I have used it for this long quotation; but for other comments about her I have stuck to the original as being both closer to the events and less self-regarding. MS-S p. 55 adds that she 'tried to teach him about music', an elaboration of the GTAT material for which no specific sourse is given.
237 GTAT29 p. 310. Dating is approximate. O'PREY(I) pp. 69 and 71 shows RG still at large in Oxford on 22 April 1917. DIARY 7 June 1917 has 'Letter from Robby saying he is ordered for a month to Convalescent Camp at Osborne I of Wight.' Amy went to

Oxford at once to see him, but returned after an 'unsatisfactory visit ... Robby rude & depressed.' DIARY 18 June 1917 has 'No news of Robby but wired for it'; and DIARY 20 June has 'Card fr. Rob announcing safe arrival at Osborne.' Presumably the 7 June letter arrived after RG had been at Somerville with his cut head for a day or two; and probably he was not considered fit to travel until ten or eleven days later.

238 Ibid. p. 307
239 GTAT29 pp. 310–12
240 Robert Graves, *Fairies and Fusiliers*
241 GTAT29 p. 312
242 DIARY 30 June 1917
243 O'PREY(I) RG to Bob Nichols n.d. p. 73
244 CHARLES pp. 33–5; BROTHER agrees in most respects, but states C's punishment was for 'drawing in a corps lecture'.
245 BROTHER transcribes this from *The Carthusian* of June 1917
246 GTAT29 p. 319
247 GTAT29 p. 317; SASSOON(I) p. 173 has him in London from 4 June 1917
248 GTAT29 p. 321
249 SASSOON(I) p. 177
250 O'PREY(I) Sassoon to RG 7 February 1930, p. 199 states: 'I sent you on July 10 a *typewritten* copy of my statement.' In GTAT29 p. 319 RG very circumstantially misdates his first hearing of this news to late July, and to his receipt of a newspaper cutting dated 27 July 1917. Although Sassoon pointed out (still O'PREY(I) p. 199) that by then Sassoon was in Craiglockhart, RG did not revise his story in GTAT57.
251 O'PREY(I) RG to Sassoon 12 July 1917, p. 77
252 GTAT29 p. 220. This section is clearly written from memory, and the break with Johnstone is wrongly placed in October 1915. But RG was meeting Johnstone in e.g. January 1917 (see O'PREY(I) p. 63), and the break did not come until July 1917 (see O'PREY(I) p. 77). MS-S p. 75 notes that

RG has put the break with Johnstone back by 15 months, but 19 would be nearer the mark; and MS-S p. 21 gives 'early June 1917' for the news about Johnstone, but the first mention of this comes in O'PREY(I) p. 77, which shows that RG has received the bad news about Johnstone on 12 July 1917. Possibly MS-S was trying to reconcile the facts with RG's false recollection in GTAT that his meeting with Marjorie in early June 1917 (see BROTHER) came after the break with Johnstone. In GTAT57 p. 216 RG states explicitly that at the time of his meeting Marjorie, 'My heart had remained whole, if numbed, since Dick's disappearance from it.' This was artistically neat, but factually incorrect.

253 BROTHER

254 In GTAT29 pp. 40–1, RG writes about homosexuality at school in these terms: 'Many boys never recover from this perversion. I only recovered by a shock at the age of twenty-one. For every one born homo-sexual there are at least ten permanent pseudo-homo-sexuals made by the public school system. And nine of these ten are as honourably chaste and sentimental as I was.' MS-S p. 20 misquotes this, and then makes false comparisons on MS-S p. 20 between the GTAT29 and the GTAT57 versions. The revised passage reads as follows: 'Many boys never recover from this perversion. For every one born homosexual, at least ten permanent pseudo-homosexuals are made by the public school system: nine of these ten as honourably chaste and sentimental as I was.'

CHAPTER 14
SAVING SASSOON

MS-S p. 570 correctly states that 'Sassoon's version differs from R.G.'s' and then asserts, 'It is now impossible to sort out the true sequence of events. Probably Sassoon's is more accurate', but with the new

evidence which has become available we can at least make a try.

Here is a summary of the main events, in the order in which they appear in GTAT29, together with evidence about the dates on which they actually occurred.

(1) RG receives press cutting. This was not published until 27 July 1917 (GTAT29 p. 319).

(2) RG leaves Osborne. He left on 16 July (DIARY 16 July).

(3) RG writes to Evan Morgan. MS-S p. 58 quotes from this letter. From internal evidence (MS-S gives us neither date nor provenance for the letter) it was written after Sassoon arrived at Craiglockhart, which he did between 19 July (the day after RG arrived at Litherland [SASSOON(I) p. 182]) and 24 July (the day when Sassoon 'had great fun' on RG's birthday [SASSOON(I) p. 183]).

(4) RG writes to the C.O. He had received a reply before 17 July on the evidence of Robert Ross (SASSOON(I) pp. 181–2).

(5) RG receives letter from Sassoon. The dating is uncertain, but it was not written until the night of the 15th (SASSOON(I) p. 181) and so could hardly have reached RG before he left Osborne on the morning of 16 July (see 2 above).

(6) Morgan persuades the War Office to give Sassoon a Medical Board. In the light of the evidence at 3 above, this must be considered fictional.

(7) RG persuades Sassoon to go before a Medical Board. This must have been at some time between the date on which RG set out for Litherland (Wednesday 18 July, see SASSOON(I) p. 182) and the date on which RG writes in triumph to Eddie Marsh (Thursday 19 July, see O'PREY(I) p. 79).

So the real order of events now appears to be 4, 2, 7, 3, 1. The dating of 5 is uncertain (but probably just before or just after 7) and 6 never happened.

The waters are muddied a little by the

fact that in Sassoon's semi-fictional account, *Memoirs of an Infantry Officer*, his dating of the first few days appears to be accurate; but then he draws out the story so that it is not until Sunday (22nd) that Robert sees him – when all had been settled by the evening of the 19th. Perhaps this was simply a fictional device; or perhaps a few days seemed to him like many in his disturbed mental condition.

255 SASSOON(I) 19 July 1917 Ross to Gosse pp. 181–2 confirms the date that he passed through London as Thursday 12 July; and Siegfried Sassoon, *Memoirs of an Infantry Officer*, p. 230 describes the receipt of a telegram saying 'Report immediately' on a Thursday.

256 Ibid. Sassoon had spent Thursday night in Ross's rooms in London

257 GTAT29 p. 323; see also SASSOON(I) pp. 181–2

258 GTAT29 p. 324

259 SASSOON(I) p. 182. It seems reasonable to assume that RG knew of this, and it ties in with Sassoon's account in 260 below.

260 Siegfried Sassoon, *Memoirs of an Infantry Officer*, p. 242

261 GTAT29 pp. 324–5. RG's claim to have 'rigged' the Medical Board seems excessive. The authorities had been wanting to find Sassoon out of his mind for days.

262 O'PREY(I) RG to Eddie Marsh 19 July 1917, p. 79

263 SASSOON(I) p. 212. The other officer was S.W. Harper

264 Ibid. Sassoon to Ross 26 July 1917 p. 183

265 O'PREY(I) RG to Sassoon 31 July 1917 p. 80

CHAPTER 15
'THE FAIRY AND THE FUSILIER'

266 AUTHOR: Quoted by APG in a letter to his son Charles of 15 July 1917

267 DIARY 6 August 1917

268 DIARY 30 August 1917. RG arrived 'as usual without notice'.

269 BROTHER: Nancy had been born on 13 September 1899

270 GTAT29 p. 330

271 DIARY 27 September 1917

272 Robert Graves, *Fairies and Fusiliers* (Heinemann, 1917)

273 GTAT29 p. 332

274 Ibid.

275 DIARY 12 October 1917

276 GTAT29 p. 332

277 GTAT29 p. 52 has 'I was destined to be "if not a great man at least a good man."'

278 As 272 above, 'To Lucasta on going to the wars for the fourth time.'

279 SASSOON(I) pp. 191–2. Sassoon to RG 19 October 1917

280 ed. Harold Owen and John Bell, *Wilfred Owen: Collected Letters* (Oxford University Press, 1967) p. 499. The poem which RG was shown was 'Disabled'.

281 In his *Collected Letters* (as 280 above, p. 500), Owen writes: 'SS. said of [RG]: he is a man one likes better after he has been with one. So it turns out in my case.'

282 As 279 above

283 O'PREY(I) RG to Nichols n.d. pp. 88–9

284 Ibid. RG to Marsh 29 December 1917 p. 90. In GTAT29 p. 333 RG understates his responsibilities, recollecting thirty young officers and four or five hundred men.

285 SASSOON(I) Sassoon to Lady O. Morrell 21 November 1917 pp. 194–5

286 DIARY 22 November 1917, and see also RG to Rosaleen n.d. (photocopy lent by Rosaleen's son Paul Cooper) in which Robert apologizes for 'not actually coming to the station with the rest of the caravan'.

287 Ibid. In his letter to Rosaleen RG comments: 'Funny about that telegram: Mother was furious with me but I smoothed her down & now she's apologised.'

288 GTAT29 p. 332. RG mistakenly gives an October date for this meeting.

289 RG to Rosaleen n.d. as 286 above

290 GTAT29 p. 332

291 Ibid. and RG to Rosaleen n.d. (see 286 above)

292 O'PREY(I) RG to Sassoon n.d. pp. 87–8. Contrast this delightful contemporary description of Nancy by RG with his less enthusiastic view of GTAT29 p. 332. MS-S p. 74 suggests that RG was so 'haunted' by anxiety that he might be homosexual, that he was driven 'into an ill-considered marriage'; also that RG 'did not really love his wife any more than she loved him'. But Rosaleen in 1982 stated firmly that 'they were devoted to each other'.

293 GTAT29 p. 335

294 DIARY 18 December 1917

295 DIARY 19 December 1917

296 Ibid.

297 DIARY 22 December 1917

298 SASSOON(I) Christmas Day 1917 (Litherland) p. 198

299 GTAT29 p. 335

300 IMPERIAL: RG to Cyril Hartmann dated January 19[17]? but must be 1918. The MAJORCA copy of *Over the Brazier* shows that RG came to see his 'The Dying Knight and the Fauns' as a presage of Rodakowski's death.

301 O'PREY(I) RG to Sassoon 11 January 1918, p. 91 & GTAT29 p. 335

302 GTAT29 p. 337

303 O'PREY(I) RG to Sassoon 11 January 1918, p. 91

304 Ibid.

305 DIARY 22 January 1918

306 DIARY 23 January 1918

307 GTAT29 p. 335

308 O'PREY(I) RG to Sassoon 9 July 1918, p. 96

309 As 280 above, p. 528

310 For names of the guests see both IMPERIAL RG to Cyril Hartmann 27 January 1918 and DIARY 23 January 1918. Other celebrities present included E.V. Lucas, Festing Jones, Beerbohm Tree, and Belcher.

311 DIARY 23 January 1918

312 GTAT29 p. 336

313 DIARY 23 January 1918. AUTHOR: Amy Graves to JTRG 26 January 1918

has a farcical account of poor William Nicholson's afternoon, evening and night. His dog jumped into Nancy and Robert's car, so had to be brought back by them to Apple Tree Yard, where William had to say goodbye to his daughter again. The dog escaped again, William hunted for it till 2 a.m.; then the police called him at 3 a.m. to say that they had it at Marlborough Road police station, & he leaped from his bed and went to retrieve it. 'At 10 a.m.' writes Amy drily, 'he had to paint some generals, so he could not have been very fit, poor man!'

CHAPTER 16
ANOTHER WORLD

314 It should be stressed that although Nancy may not have been the easiest person in the world, she had many fine qualities, and all the contemporary evidence is that at the start of their marriage Robert was devoted to her, and she to him.

315 GTAT29 p. 336

316 IMPERIAL: RG to Cyril Hartmann 27 January 1918 is headed 'Llys Bach'

317 Robert Graves & Nancy Nicholson to Rosaleen Graves 28 January [1918]

318 DIARY 31 January 1918 has 'The Honeymooners part tomorrow. Sent "The Fairy and the Fusilier" to Nancy through Amy.' See also GTAT29 p. 336

319 AUTHOR: Amy Graves to JTRG 15 February 1918

320 Robert Graves to Rosaleen Graves 10 [?] February 1918

321 GTAT29 p. 337. For Robert's plans to secure this job see the letter to Rosaleen as in 320 above. The letter to Rosaleen as in 322 below shows that Robert started work with the 16th O.C. Bn. on 7 March 'best sort of job & very pleasant brother officers'.

322 Robert Graves to Rosaleen Graves 7 March 1918. The farmer's name was Jones. RG also passed on the news

that he had been put in for 'some foreign military decoration; rather fun if I got it: wouldn't Mother be pleased. But my God! (Yes, dear?) what rot it is, the 5th class of the order of the Purple eagle of Patagonia.'

323 Robert Graves to Rosaleen Graves 24 February 1918

324 DIARY 22 March 1918; see also Nancy Nicholson to Rosaleen Graves 25 March 1918

325 As 323 above

326 As 320 above. RG had shown Nancy most of these places, such as 'Coney's Slope' and 'Disappearing Man Place' during their honeymoon.

327 As 322 above

328 This, the earliest version of 'Vain and Careless' appears in the letter from RG to Rosaleen as in 320 above. A more polished version appears in RG's *Country Sentiment* (Martin Secker, 1920)

329 Robert Graves, *Country Sentiment*

330 DIARY 6 April 1918 has APG and Amy leaving for Harlech with family including Charles and Charles's Carthusian friend Diccon Hughes. [They had both just left Charterhouse.] 'Robby and Nancy who were to have "seen us off" only arrived to do that and no more; only a kiss hands as the train had started.' DIARY 6 May 1918 has Nancy in London while RG is on a course at Berkhampsted, which has lasted several weeks, but RG is due to join her in London on 7 May.

331 AUTHOR: Amy Graves to JTRG 20 June 1918, but referring back to RG's last London visit

332 As 329 above

333 Told to me by Sam and Anneliese Graves, Nancy's son and daughter-in-law in 1983

334 Nancy Nicholson to Rosaleen Graves 25 March 1918

335 O'PREY(I) RG to Sassoon 23 May 1918, pp. 93–4

336 SASSOON(I) 29 May 1918, pp. 258–9

337 LETTERS dated 'June 7th or so 1918'

338 As 330 above

339 AUTHOR: Amy Graves to JTRG 14 June 1918

340 GTAT29 pp. 340–1

341 AUTHOR: Amy Graves to JTRG 2 July 1918. Amy, very fed up, but trying to look on the bright side, commented that Rosaleen 'looks very pretty still, and her hair may grow stronger'.

342 O'PREY(I) RG to Sassoon 9 July 1918, pp. 95–7

343 As 334 above

344 RG to Rosaleen 24 June 1918. See also DIARY 19 February 1918

345 GTAT29 p. 336. DIARY 12 October 1917 shows that the Bishop of St Asaph first contacted Robert at APG's request. DIARY 22 March 1918 shows that Nancy made a good impression on the Bishop, and presumably kept her anti-clerical sentiments to herself.

346 As 342 above

CHAPTER 17
A TIME TO DIE

347 GTAT29 p. 341

348 O'PREY(I) RG to Sassoon 16 July 1918, pp. 97–8

349 Ibid. pp. 98–9. *The War Poems of Siegfried Sassoon* arr. & introduced by Sir Rupert Hart-Davis (Faber & Faber, 1983) publishes this poem dated 24 July 1918, pp. 130–2.

350 O'PREY(I) RG to Sassoon 27 July 1918, p. 99

351 GTAT29 p. 344

352 DIARY 4 October 1918

353 O'PREY(I) RG to Sassoon 26 August 1918, p. 101

354 Ibid. 11 September 1918, p. 102

355 AUTHOR: Amy Graves to her son JTRG 16 October 1918

356 DIARY for 12, 15 and 16 September shows that there had been an intervening visit to London by Nancy on her own

357 DIARY 21 October 1918

358 Ibid. In the light of this, Sassoon's comment in 1930 (see O'PREY(I) p. 207) that RG had been less than

generous to Ross in GTAT29 seems a fair one.

359 DIARY 9 October 1918

360 CHARLES p. 47 adds a vivid description of Amy tending Charles through his convalescence. On one occasion Charles asked Amy, who had never smoked a cigarette in her life, to light one and allow him to smell the smoke: 'She agreed at once, inhaled, and then blew a smoke ring as father used to do. I stared at her pop-eyed. "I just wanted to try out the paces of my charger," she explained amiably. But she never smoked another cigarette.' See also AUTHOR: Amy Graves to JTRG 22 October 1918.

361 GTAT29 p. 344

CHAPTER 18
DEMOBILIZATION

362 O'PREY(I) RG to Nichols n.d., pp. 104–5

363 Ibid.

364 O'PREY(I) RG to Marsh January 1919, pp. 107–8. The dates given in this letter reveal the inaccuracy of RG's memory in GTAT29 p. 347, where it is suggested that RG did not seek demobilization until 1919, after Jenny's birth, when he was in Limerick [see also MS-S pp. 70–1].

365 GTAT29 p. 345 RG says 'it took her years to recover', though Nancy went on to have several more children very rapidly

366 DIARY 13 January 1919

367 O'PREY(I) RG to Sassoon n.d., pp.

105–6. Since RG's subsequent letter to Sassoon was dated 13 January (a Monday), and RG had talked of going to Limerick 'on Wednesday' I have assumed that the next Wednesday was the 15th.

368 O'PREY(I) RG to Marsh January 1919, pp. 107–8

369 DIARY 27 January 1919. RG's later comment to MS-S (see p. 70) that whenever he was in Ireland 'he felt strangely oppressed by his ancestry' does not altogether tally with this contemporary account. See also a letter from RG to Rosaleen of 27 January 1919 (photocopy lent by R's son Paul Cooper) in which RG writes: 'Limerick is a lovely place isn't it? I feel absolutely part of it already & it provides the explanation of a great deal in me that I could only guess before.'

370 As 368 above

371 GTAT29 p. 349 and for additional details see DIARY 4 February 1919

372 GTAT29 pp. 349–50. In GTAT29 p. 350 RG wrongly dates these events to 13 February 1919 when DIARY shows that he arrived in Wimbledon on 4 February 1919.

373 Ibid.

374 DIARY 4 February 1919. RG in GTAT29 pp. 350–1 incorrectly recalls being demobilized before seeing his parents. When he met them, he brought them a pound of 'high' Irish butter. Amy seemed in a worse state than RG: she had fallen and broken her left wrist in slushy snow on 1 February.

BOOK FIVE
HARLECH AND BOAR'S HILL 1919–1921

CHAPTER I
'THE TROLL'S NOSEGAY'

1 For RG's first mention of the inac-

curate date see O'PREY(I) RG to Sassoon 1 March 1919, p. 108; and for his comment to William Nicholson see DIARY 11 February 1919

2 GTAT29, p. 352
3 AUTHOR: Amy Graves to her son JTRG 11 February 1919
4 DIARY 6 March 1919
5 GTAT29 p. 352
6 As 4 above
7 AUTHOR: Amy Graves to JTRG 20 February 1919
8 Robert Graves, *The Pier-Glass* (Secker 1921; Knopf, 1921)
9 GTAT29 p. 370. RG makes the wish a joint one in GTAT29; but as MS-S p. 83 points out, in GTAT57 RG attributes the wish to Nancy alone, and this seems more likely to be true
10 Robert Graves, *The Pier-Glass*
11 Robert Graves, *Whipperginny* (Heinemann, 1922)
12 O'PREY(1) RG to Sassoon 1 March 1919, p. 108
13 O'PREY(1) RG to Sassoon 13 January, p. 106
14 DIARY 6 March has APG visiting them at Apple Tree Yard on that day

CHAPTER 2
THE MUTUAL IMPROVEMENT SOCIETY

15 RG in GTAT29 p. 354 says incorrectly that they were there for a year, and MS-S p. 72 repeats this error. They were there from mid-March to mid-October 1919, a period of about seven months.
16 GTAT29 p. 354
17 Ibid. p. 355
18 Robert Graves to Rosaleen Graves 21 March 1919
19 AUTHOR: Amy Graves to JTRG, letters of 22 March and 28 March 1919. Charles was astonished by Robert's healthy appearance & wrote to Amy: 'Robby is looking very well & young, about 18.'
20 As 18 above and see AUTHOR: Charles Graves letter to JTRG n.d.
21 DIARY 3 April 1919
22 AUTHOR: Amy Graves to JTRG 5 April 1919
23 DIARY 11 April 1919. Robert wrote to say that he was delighted with them.

24 At this time there were a cook (Mrs Nelson) and a general servant (Mrs Jones) at Erinfa
25 DIARY 3 May 1919 Margaret was 'a Newcastle-on-Tyner who does not wish to live beyond 50'.
26 LETTERS RG to Amy Graves 3 May 1919 ('The cottage is now finished, we haven't finished planting the garden.')
27 DIARY 29 April 1919. On that date RG brought some poems for APG to look at, and accepted his criticisms.
28 DIARY 8 May 1919
29 As 27 above
30 DIARY 30 April 1919. I have no information about when Novello dropped out, but assume it was before RG showed his songs to Dr Heath on this date.
31 Charles was now bent upon a career in journalism [DIARY 29 April], switched from Classics to English & was awarded an English Exhibition [AUTHOR: Amy to JTRG 17 June 1919].
32 Amy went to London on 29 April, and APG followed on 9 May [DIARY entries for those dates]
33 AUTHOR: Amy Graves to JTRG 10 June 1919. Amy reassured John, who had worried that his sister was making a mistake. It was in fact an inspired move on Rosaleen's part: she was to become a superb doctor.

CHAPTER 3
FRESH IDEAS

34 DIARY 16 & 17 June 1919. APG also wondered whether he himself could find lecture work in the USA.
35 DIARY 12 June 1919
36 Amy to JTRG 2 July has RG and Nancy at Red Branch House on Sunday 29 June 'very nice though I regretted Nancy coming again in trousers'. Amy to JTRG postcard n.d. describes another visit to RBH by RG and Nancy, but on this occasion 'R. was not looking well & Nancy

was very quiet & hardly mentioned the rights of women'.

37 GTAT29 p. 357. The conversation may have taken place earlier at Harlech.

38 GTAT29 pp. 356–7

39 Told to me by Dr Rosaleen Cooper (née Graves), summer 1982

40 Robert Graves, *The Pier-Glass*

41 GTAT57 p. 234. This does not appear anywhere in GTAT29.

42 O'PREY(I) RG to Blunden 12 July 1919, p. 113

43 As 39 above. Rosaleen states that RG's actions created no scandal of the kind suggested in GTAT29 p. 358.

44 AUTHOR: Amy Graves to JTRG 10 March 1920 shows Amy still trying 'to persuade Robert about Jenny'.

45 DIARY 21 August 1919

46 DIARY 28 August 1919

CHAPTER 4
MOVING TO OXFORD

47 DIARY 15 September 1919

48 DIARY see entries for 27 August, 6 and 10 September 1919. By his amiable conversation Sassoon had made it clear to Amy and APG that he had not become the dangerous revolutionary of their fears.

49 DIARY 5 September 1919. Marsh was accompanied by Lady Juliet Duff and her new husband.

50 DIARY 7 September 1919. RG and Nancy also talked to Queen Mary's Private Secretary on this visit.

51 DIARY 18 September 1919. The job was taken by Perceval instead, and he stayed at St Ninian's for several terms.

52 DIARY 25 September 1919; and see RG to Sassoon 21 April 1917, p. 68, for RG's letter of introduction to Masefield from Gosse; see also RG to Sassoon 3 July 1917, pp. 74–5 for an indirect message from Masefield; and RG to Sassoon n.d., pp. 87–8, for a 'ripping' letter from Masefield.

53 SASSOON(I) pp. 281–2 contains a good description of Masefield in

November 1918 which I have used here.

54 O'PREY(I) RG to Blunden 14 August 1919, pp. 113–14

55 For descriptions of Constance see GTAT29 pp. 365–6 and MS-S p. 82. This paragraph is partly speculative as there is no firm evidence that this was the occasion upon which RG and Nancy met Constance Masefield. MS-S p. 82 quotes interestingly from Mrs Masefield's diaries, but does not say where they are to be found.

56 AUTHOR: APG to Amy, postcard, 26 September 1919

57 AUTHOR: Susan Macaulay (née Graves) to Amy Erinfa Sunday n.d. (from internal evidence 12 October 1919)

58 AUTHOR: APG to AMY 27 September 1919. The first plan was for RG and Nancy to renew the lease, and then sublet it for income; but AUTHOR: 30 September 1919 shows Amy sensibly scotching this plan, as she learned that serious trouble was brewing about payment for dilapidations on the property since William Nicholson had first leased it.

59 AUTHOR: Rosaleen to Amy and APG 12 October 1919 has most of the preceding details; but the place of honeymoon comes from AUTHOR: Amy to John 11 October 1919.

60 As 57 above

61 AUTHOR: Susan Macaulay (née Graves) to APG and Amy, Erinfa Friday n.d. but from internal evidence 10 October 1919

62 As 59 above. Rosaleen was at the 'Home Student' College.

63 AUTHOR: Amy to JTRG 11 October 1919

64 DIARY 11 October 1919. Red Branch House had sold for £3,000.

65 DIARY 17 October 1919

CHAPTER 5
'AWFULLY HAPPY IN SPITE OF IT ALL'

66 GTAT29 pp. 359–60

67 GTAT29 pp. 360–6
68 DIARY 15 November 1919. They arrived in Oxford on this afternoon. On returning to the Roebuck they dined there with Rosaleen.
69 Earlier in the day APG and Amy called on Charles and saw Leonard Morgan and other friends
70 DIARY 16 November 1919
71 GTAT29 p. 371
72 DIARY 16 November 1919
73 LETTERS n.d. but from internal evidence autumn 1919
74 Ibid. 30 November, or so, 1919 pp. 116–17. In his n.12 p. 358 O'PREY wrongly describes this 'tiny book' as *The Feather Bed*.
75 Robert Graves, *The Treasure Box*. I have consulted the copy in the Bodleian Library, Oxford. It is described on the title page as 'Privately Printed 200 copies Christmas 1919.' The poems it contains are: 'Morning Phoenix', 'Catherine Drury', 'The Treasure Box', 'The Kiss', 'Lost Love', 'Fox's Dingle', and 'Four Rhymes from "The Penny Fiddle"', comprising: 'The Dream', 'The Fiddler', 'The Gifts' and 'Mirror Mirror'.
76 Ibid.
77 From the tone and content of GTAT29 p. 370 it would appear that RG now felt quite indifferent to Johnstone; my modifications to this account are based upon O'PREY(I) RG to Marsh n.d., p. 150, where as late as the summer of 1923 RG writes: 'Of Peter Johnstone I can't think sanely. ... it will be a long while before I can meet him again without being extremely upset because I was once very fond of him and am not so any longer.'
78 LETTERS 8 December 1919
79 LETTERS n.d.
80 LETTERS 31 January 1920
81 Ibid. In the same letter RG accurately forecast that *The Treasure Box* would become 'a literary curiosity of colossal value'; and he also advised JTRG to buy as investments Blunden's *The Waggoner* (which he had been helping

Blunden to see through the press) and Nichols's *Aurelia*.
82 LETTERS 24 February 1920. AUTHOR: Amy to JTRG 17 February 1920 shows that Amy had refused John permission on the grounds that moving house had been too expensive.
83 LETTERS 24 February 1920. Also see AUTHOR: Amy to JTRG 7 February 1920 about Holbrooke's backing out.
84 DIARY 8 March 1920. AUTHOR Amy to JTRG 10 March shows that Amy and APG had only recently heard that Nancy was pregnant, and were not expecting the birth until the autumn.
85 AUTHOR: Amy to JTRG 10 March 1920. DIARY 16 March 1920 shows that shortly after John David's birth, Margaret had a holiday and Nancy's Aunt Fanny looked after the family. Fanny then went down with influenza, which very much alarmed Amy, who suggested ways in which she could help, and sent them a cheque for £25. But it was a storm in a teacup, as no one else became ill.
86 O'PREY(I) RG to Blundens 5 April 1920, pp. 117–18
87 Ibid.
88 DIARY 6 April 1920

CHAPTER 6
'LET US BE AS WE USED TO BE'

89 AUTHOR: Amy to JTRG 30 May 1920
90 In GTAT29 p. 403 RG suggests that it was not until after he had completed *The Pier-Glass* collection of poems that he ceased attempting to write for the ordinary reading public, but this process seems to have begun after the publication of *Country Sentiment*. While writing many of his *Pier-Glass* poems, as he pointed out in March 1921 (see O'PREY(I) RG to Blunden 10 March 1921, pp. 123–4), he was trying to come to terms with his shellshock, a very different matter from looking for commercial success. The

concluding ideas in this paragraph come from RG's *On English Poetry*, which he was writing during the period of the *Pier-Glass* poems.

91 O'PREY(I) RG to Eddie Marsh 15 June 1920, p. 119

92 DIARY 1920. They arrived by motor 'from Aberystwyth where they had been carried through misdirection'. It had been an expensive journey but DIARY 24 July 1920 shows that Amy and APG deliberately made up for this the following month by giving RG a generous £10 birthday present. AUTHOR: Amy to JTRG 16 June 1920 shows that Nancy had kindly found Amy a college cook from Oxford to work at Erinfa for the summer. Harlech was to be full of Graveses, with APG's brothers Arnold and Charlie arriving 'next week', and his sister Lily and his son Dick later on. Rose Gribble also visited Harlech; and [AUTHOR: Amy to JTRG 12 July 1920] Diccon Hughes returned to his cottage.

93 AUTHOR: Amy to JTRG 7 February 1920. APG organized several pageants at Harlech over the years; they were set in the castle, involved many family, villagers and visitors, and were enormously hard work.

94 AUTHOR: Amy to JTRG 12 July 1920

95 Ibid.

96 DIARY 1 July 1920. They went to the concert with Rosaleen.

97 GTAT29 pp. 366–9. From RG's account one might deduce that this incident [omitted from GTAT57] took place in January 1920; but DIARY shows that he & Nancy did not stay at Erinfa until June that year; John arrived on 27 July, and Robert left Harlech on 31 July, so the incident must come between those dates.

98 GTAT29 p. 369 has 'I was sick and shaking for weeks after this'; but in view of DIARY 30 July 1920 'days' seems more likely; a period of time which may have indirect confirmation from O'PREY(I) RG to Marsh 7 October 1920, pp. 119–20, where RG

says: 'I never seem to see anybody these days and when I do they excite my shell-shock so that I am useless for days.'

99 Robert Graves, *The Meaning of Dreams* (Cecil Palmer, 1924) pp. 159–65. 'The Gnat' appeared in *The Pier-Glass*.

100 Title poem of *The Pier-Glass*. MS-S pp. 91–3 argues that Graves, in speaking as a woman, invents 'a destructive female figure' who foreshadows the White Goddess. In view of RG's description in 1917 (O'PREY(I) p. 65) of the poet as 'a woman suffering all the hardships of a man' this may be over-elaborate.

101 GTAT29 p. 374

102 Ibid. pp. 374–9

103 Ibid. p. 379

CHAPTER 7
THE SHOP ON PARNASSUS

104 Ibid. pp. 379–80. But for the cost of the shop see AUTHOR: Amy to JTRG 16 October 1920

105 LETTERS 18 September [1920]

106 O'PREY(I) RG to Marsh 7 October 1920, pp. 119–20

107 Ibid.

108 AUTHOR: Amy to JTRG 16 October 1920. In GTAT29 p. 381 RG reports that the gross weekly takings rose to £60 per week, giving an even higher weekly income of twelve pounds and ten shillings. The unknown factor is how much interest Nancy and Mrs Howard were paying the bank on borrowed money, as after its initial success the shop was enlarged and two or three hundred pounds' worth of stock purchased. However, interest charges should not have made a serious dent in such considerable profits.

109 *Isis*, 20 October 1920, No. 566, p. 11

110 Passing on local stories to the national press has always been a useful source of income for editors of *Isis*, and I have assumed (perhaps wrongly) that

this is how the story reached London. AUTHOR: Amy to JTRG 23 October 1920 mentions the *Mirror* and *Mail* articles.

111 I have assumed this. RG would also have been irritated by the fact that (AUTHOR: Charles Graves to JTRG 29 September 1920) Charles had recently turned down some work by RG, describing it to JTRG as 'a simply dud article for *The Isis*'. Later on RG and Charles were to become equally jealous of each other: Charles for Robert's reputation in the literary world, and Robert for Charles's financial success. At this stage (see AUTHOR: Amy to JTRG 19 November 1920) Charles was so well-known in Oxford that Rosaleen, at dances, found that she was no longer asked whether she was Robert's sister, but whether she was related to the journalist. [And at the end of term Charles hurried to London to spend a fortnight on the staff of the *Daily Express*.]

112 O'PREY(I) RG to Marsh 7 October 1920, p. 120

113 As 109 above

114 *Isis*, 27 October 1920, No. 567, p. 5. Higginson's bibliography p. 226 says RG later 'acknowledged' authorship; but the style and content and other evidence are at odds with RG's memory.

115 LETTERS 30 October [1920]

116 Ibid.

117 GTAT29 p. 371

118 Ibid. pp. 371–3. In the GTAT57 revision Nancy is written out of the Vachel Lindsay lunch.

119 Robert Graves, *The Pier-Glass*

120 Robert Graves, *Whipperginny*. In the early 1920s Lawrence wrote to Lionel Curtis [see Richard Perceval Graves, *Lawrence of Arabia and his World* (Thames and Hudson, 1976)]: '... isn't it true that the fault of birth rests somewhat on the child?' An example of an influence in the other direction: TEL's view in 1923 that 'Marriage-contracts should have a clause termi-

nating the engagement upon nine months notice by either party' [see John E. Mack, *A Prince of our Disorder: The Life of T.E. Lawrence* (Weidenfeld & Nicolson, 1976) p. 422] sounds very much like RG talking under Nancy's influence.

121 *The Carthusian*, Vol. XIII, No. 416. JTRG edited Nos. 416–422 inclusive. His first *Carthusian* contained a number of contributions from family and friends, including 'The Naked Head', a short story by Diccon Hughes.

122 LETTERS 30 October [1920]. 'Delilah's Parrot' appears on p. 32 of 121 above, and can be found as Part IV of 'The Coronation Murder' in *The Pier-Glass*.

123 O'PREY(I) RG to Marsh 15 June 1920, p. 119

124 Ibid. 7 October 1920, p. 120

125 DIARY 12 November 1920

126 DIARY 5 June 1921

127 AUTHOR: Amy to JTRG 19 November; 30 November; 16 December. It appears that John was in Oxford from about 5 to 20 December. He was put up by Leonard Morgan for some days [certainly while taking his first set of exams] and then went out to Boar's Hill.

128 DIARY 10 January 1921. APG saw much of Diccon Hughes during his holiday, and on 16 January Hughes and a friend called Thorpe joined Robert and Nancy and APG for supper in APG's room. APG commented: 'There was too much irreligious talk – & I said there is such a thing as irreligious as well as religious cant' (DIARY 16 January 1921).

129 DIARY shows e.g. 11 January APG visits Professor Jacks; 15 January Gilbert Murray; 17 January Blackwell

130 DIARY 12 January 1921; APG and RG worked in the shed, where Nancy brought them lunch

131 Ibid. APG took time off for tea with Keating, the landlord of the ground on which the shop stood.

132 DIARY 17 January 1921

133 Ibid. The cost of the holiday is mentioned in another AUTHOR document whose reference I have mislaid.

134 DIARY 6 February 1921 refers to this offer as having been turned down at some time in the past, and I have felt it appropriate to mention it here

135 DIARY 17 January 1921. *The Hobby Horse* later became *John Kemp's Wager* and was published as No. 11 of 'The British Drama League Library of Modern British Drama' (Oxford: Basil Blackwell, 1925). In his introduction RG states that the origin of the play was a request from 'a prominent citizen' of the Berkshire village of Sunningwell for a play to be written in time for Boxing Day, to be performed at Sunningwell. This request came a few days after a successful performance of morris-dancing and folk-songs at Sunningwell had coincided with a visit by the inhabitants of 'the hated-rival village of W ...' to 'a play of Euripides in English, given by the well-intentioned highbrows who colonize a neighbouring hill'. The point of the play would be to 'maintain the success of the folk-song performance ... and most particularly put the hated rivals' noses out of joint'. This cover-story is easily penetrated: Sunningwell is near Boar's Hill; the rival village was probably Wootton; the neighbouring hill is clearly Boar's Hill, and the play was not by Euripides but by Aristophanes. But to go one stage deeper: APG records that on 17 January 1921 there was no question of a performance at Sunningwell: the initial intention, as he commented in his DIARY was: to 'try to get it produced at Harlech'. So *John Kemp's Wager* did not start in the way Robert records. A possible explanation is that Sunningwell later asked for a play similar to the one on which RG was already working; and he decided in his own mind that this was the 'real' origin of the play.

136 DIARY 18 January 1921. Thorpe played Hippolytus and Mrs Keating the nurse.

137 DIARY 20 January 1921. Amy and the others had been at Wengen.

138 DIARY 21 January 1921

CHAPTER 8
FINANCIAL WRECKAGE AND
'THE LOWEST OF SPIRITS'

139 DIARY 17 January 1921

140 AUTHOR: Amy to JTRG 18 February 1921 shows that Amy understood Margaret to have had a nervous breakdown; AUTHOR: APG to JTRG 23 February 1921 talks of 'a breakdown after heart trouble'.

141 AUTHOR: Amy to JTRG 4 February 1921

142 Ibid. for the date of M's arrival; remainder from 143 below.

143 DIARY 6 February 1921

144 SASSOON(2) 5 February 1921, p. 38. On 6 February Sassoon visited the Graveses.

145 O'PREY(1) RG to Blunden 10 March 1921, p. 123

146 AUTHOR: Amy to JTRG 12 February 1921. Amy received the letter on Saturday 12 February, but 'asked leave to wait till Monday, as [Margaret] has had a bad night & will be more able to bear it then'.

147 AUTHOR: Amy to JTRG 18 February 1921

148 AUTHOR: APG to JTRG 23 February 1921

149 DIARY 2 March 1921. See also 146 above for RG's agreeing to pay wages.

150 DIARY 5 March 1921. And DIARY 15 March 1921 mentions a further letter from Robert, 'but he says nothing about repaying us'.

151 GTAT29 p. 383

152 O'PREY(1) RG to Blunden 10 March 1921, pp. 122–3 and note 20, p. 358. The articles were draft chapters of *Seven Pillars of Wisdom*; T.E.L. recalled one of them, and RG sold the others to America.

153 O'PREY(I) RG to Marsh 13 April 1921, p. 124

154 This is not apparent from GTAT29 p. 383 where RG claims that he decided to cure himself after reading the modern psychological books and applying them to his own case. This entire section about the poor state of RG's mental health was expunged from GTAT57.

155 GTAT29 p. 384

156 O'PREY(I) RG to Marsh 13 April 1921, pp. 124–5

157 ed. Anne Olivier Bell ass. by Andrew McNeillie, *The Diary of Virginia Woolf, Vol. 3, 1923–1930* (The Hogarth Press, 1980); from the entry for Monday 27 April 1925, pp. 13–14. This is more contemporary than RG's description in GTAT29 pp. 385–6, by which time it appears, like any good story-teller, to have made a few improvements upon the original tale. Both versions, though artistically pleasing, are considerable over-simplifications of the truth.

158 DIARY 14 April 1921

159 DIARY 23 April 1921

160 DIARY 25 April 1921. John is not mentioned as the fourth at bridge; but he was at Erinfa and played in another four on the 26th; while Nancy is not described as learning the game until the 27th.

161 DIARY 27 April 1921

162 DIARY 28 April 1921

163 DIARY 10 May 1921

164 AUTHOR: Amy to JTRG 20 May 1921

165 DIARY 24 May 1921; a wire arrived on the 24th from the vendors' solicitors; it was confirmed by post on the 25th, and Amy wrote to Preston, the family solicitor, asking him to examine the title and act for them.

166 To be strictly accurate I should have peppered the last part of the last sentence in this paragraph (from the word 'timber' onwards) with the word 'perhaps'. Contemporary evidence has by now shown up some of the inaccuracies in GTAT29 pp. 384–7 (the pages on the shop failure, and

the move to Islip). In particular, the order of events has been significantly altered, but many aspects of Robert's financial affairs at this time remain mysterious. What was the full extent of his debts, and when were they finally paid off? DIARY 31 May 1921, for example, shows that RG had just repaid £25 of the £50 he had borrowed from Leonard Morgan. This small debt was hitherto unknown, and there may have been others. One very significant piece of new information comes from a postcard which RG wrote to Diccon Hughes on 25 October 1921 [a photocopy was very kindly sent to me by Hughes's literary executor Mrs Lucy McEntee]. This shows that by 25 October 1921 the Boar's Hill shop had not yet been sold; and there were still outstanding debts to the wholesalers. In conjunction with the evidence already adduced (especially that of O'PREY(I) RG to Marsh, pp. 124–5) this demolishes much of the relevant passage in GTAT29 p. 385, and leaves the way open for a good deal of speculation.

167 O'PREY(I) RG to Sassoon 29 May 1921, pp. 126–7

168 GTAT29 p. 387. This section about RG's 'affinity' with Skelton was removed from GTAT57.

169 Robert Graves, *Poetic Unreason and Other Studies* (Cecil Palmer, 1925) p. 240

CHAPTER 9
On English Poetry

Except where otherwise stated, all the material in this chapter is taken from Robert Graves, *On English Poetry: Being an Irregular Approach to the Psychology of This Art from Evidence Mainly Subjective* (Heinemann, 1922). My principal references are to pages vii, 19, 22, 33, 84–5, 95, 96–7, 119, 123–4 and 134–7. [Also published by Knopf in 1922.]

170 Robert Graves, *On English Poetry*, p. vii

171 See Richard Perceval Graves, *A.E. Housman: The Scholar-Poet* (Routledge & Kegan Paul, 1979) pp. 253–5
172 As 170 above p. 19
173 See page 72 of this volume
174 Robert Graves, *Country Sentiment*
175 Robert Graves, *Whipperginny*. RG states in an 'Author's Note' that 'Unicorn and the White Doe' was 'bankrupt stock of 1918, the year in which I was writing *Country Sentiment*'.

CHAPTER 10
A LETTER FROM CHARLES

176 DIARY 31 May 1921
177 AUTHOR: Amy to JTRG 16 June 1921
178 DIARY 4 June 1921

179 Ibid. DIARY 5 June shows that Simpson, Charles's Eng. Lit. tutor, blamed Powell, his college tutor for not informing him. And apparently (see AUTHOR: Amy to JTRG 16 June) Charles 'could have got absolved on a/c of war service if his tutor had told him to apply for this in time'. In the event (AUTHOR: notes by JTRG in a typescript of extracts from APG's diaries) Charles wrote to John in the autumn, asking him: 'What day am I to be sick on?'; but JTRG found that he had passed an exempting examination at Charterhouse in 1917.
180 As 177 above
181 Ibid.
182 It had been decided early in June to let Dorothy go. AUTHOR: Amy to JTRG 3 June 1921 has 'Nancy's nurse may come back to me as a cook'.

BOOK SIX
THE WORLD'S END 1921–1926

CHAPTER 1
AN ISLIP SUMMER

1 O'PREY(1) RG to Blunden 12 July? 1921, pp. 127–9
2 Ibid. The main problem with the house, incidentally, was the poor water supply. See DIARY 10 September 1921 which has an account of Leonard Morgan visiting R and N at Islip and finding them 'still without water'; see also DIARY 21 November 1921 for Amy's comments.
3 AUTHOR: An unpublished Diary by John T.R. Graves which runs from 12 October to 8 December 1921. See entry dated Friday 14 October. See also DIARY 16 September 1921 which has Robert declaring that 'Sir Walter Raleigh assures him of a B.Litt. on the strength of his new book on Poetry to be published next winter here and in the "States"'. In fact the thesis, with the new title of *Poetic Unreason and Other Studies* did not appear until 1925.
4 Robert was co-editor with Diccon Hughes and Alan Porter. It was published in November and [RG to Hughes, as in Book Five, note 166 above] Blackwell gave the editors a dinner to celebrate the occasion.
5 O'PREY(1) RG to Blunden 12 July ? 1921, p. 127
6 For the correspondence between Graves and Bridges between 1921 and 1926 see BODLEIAN MS Don d. 113 184–202 (for SPE tracts see earlier items in this collection); and also BODLEIAN Dep Bridges 109 fols. 162–6. RG's letter appeared in Tract No. VI, published in 1921.
7 BODLEIAN Dep Bridges 109 fol. 162
8 AUTHOR: Amy to JTRG 23 July 1921.

DIARY 20 and 22 July 1921 shows that Robert and Nancy had met him through another friend, Roger Fox, who was shortly to become a friar in Father Giles's order, and who had recently been a welcome guest at Erinfa.

CHAPTER 2
THE ARRIVAL OF JOHN

9 AUTHOR: Amy to JTRG 12 July 1921. Charles was almost fatally gassed in an accident in his rooms soon after Finals; but he survived to give an entertaining account (see CHARLES p. 58) of a viva voce examination in which the two senior examiners were Sir Arthur Quiller-Couch and Sir Walter Raleigh. Sir Arthur's sole question was: 'Did you know that your father was an old friend of mine?'; while Sir Walter asked whether Charles knew that his grandfather Bishop Graves had been a famous Gaelic scholar.

10 AUTHOR: As 4 above, JTRG's entry for Friday 14 October 1921

11 Ibid. JTRG's entry for 12 October 1921. At their first meeting, Pearson, a future Prime Minister of Canada, had told JTRG that he 'hopes to be a journalist and has introductions to Beverley Baxter and Lord Beaverbrook'.

12 Ibid. JTRG's entry for 6 November 1921

13 See Book Five, note 166 above for the uncertainties about RG's precise financial state at this time. In GTAT29 p. 395 he points out that his army pension was his only certain source of income, his exhibition and government grant having ended when he moved to Islip and gave up his BA degree. He calculates in GTAT29 p. 397 that his total income, including birthday and Christmas presents from relatives, was about £130 per annum. But much of his income was too uncertain for an annual average

to be very informative; nor do we know what his outgoings were, or what, if anything, he still owed.

14 AUTHOR: Amy to JTRG 11 November 1921

15 AUTHOR: Amy to JTRG n.d.

16 AUTHOR: As 4 above, JTRG's entry for 18 November 1921

17 Ibid. JTRG's entry for 19 November 1921

CHAPTER 3
CLARISSA HELPS OUT

18 DIARY 21 November 1921; see also AUTHOR: As 3 above, JTRG's entry for 21 November 1921, showing that John and Rosaleen had twenty minutes with Amy (at her request) while she changed trains at Oxford. Amy was 'quite nicely dressed & look[ing] well'. [Her children were often embarrassed by her dowdy appearance.]

19 DIARY 25 November 1921

20 AUTHOR: Amy to JTRG 1 December 1921

21 DIARY 30 November 1921

22 DIARY 5 December 1921

23 DIARY 6 December 1921

24 DIARY 9 December 1921

25 *Isis*, 7 December 1921 p. 2 [reviewer TWH]

26 Robert Graves, *Whipperginny*

27 BODLEIAN MSS Gilbert Murray 541 fol. 75 RG to Lady Mary, Monday December 1921

28 O'PREY(I) RG to Sassoon 31 May 1922, p. 134

29 William Shakespeare, 'The Phoenix and the Turtle', verse 7

30 AUTHOR: A Diary of Clarissa Graves, p. 7

CHAPTER 4
'THE LANDS OF WHIPPERGINNY'

31 GTAT29 p. 404

32 See this volume p. 250

33 Robert Graves, *Whipperginny* (Heinemann, 1922; Knopf, 1923)

34 Ibid.

35 Robert Graves, *The Feather Bed* (The Hogarth Press, 1923)

36 O'PREY(1) RG to Marsh 17 December 1921, pp. 130–2

37 In *Whipperginny*

CHAPTER 5
THE BIRTH OF CATHERINE

38 Catherine was born on 3 February 1922; see DIARY 4 February 1922; and AUTHOR: Amy to JTRG 8 February 1922

39 MAJORCA: Nancy to Clarissa n.d.

40 AUTHOR: Amy to JTRG 18 February 1922. Amy writes: 'Robert is coming instead of Clarissa.'

41 DIARY 19 February 1922. RG made a friend of H.G. Wood of the publishers Nisbet's.

42 AUTHOR: Amy to JTRG 23 February 1922

43 Ibid. They were uncomfortable, as Amy economized by moving them from their hotel to a bed and breakfast establishment. But APG gave three lectures which 'went excellently', and interested John Murray in his autobiography. This interest was not followed up, and DIARY 1 May 1922 shows Nisbet declining APG's autobiography as 'such a very slight sample of the whole'.

44 DIARY 28 February 1922. APG and Amy had supper at The World's End.

45 AUTHOR: A testimonial to Clarissa from one John Abercound(?) of Milfors, Co. Carlow

46 MAJORCA: RG to Clarissa n.d.

CHAPTER 6
LOSING FRIENDS

47 DIARY 5 April 1922. Earlier DIARY entries show that APG had consulted a Mr Hutchinson about the possibilities, and had sent on H's reply to RG on 7 March.

48 DIARY 7 April 1922

49 O'PREY(1) RG to Marsh n.d., pp. 141–2

50 See O'PREY(1) pp. 132–3 and related note; and also SASSOON(2) p. 103, and pp. 150–1

51 Ibid.

52 O'PREY(1) RG to Sassoon 29 May 1922, p. 133

53 Ibid. pp. 133–4

54 Ibid. RG to Sassoon 31 May 1922 pp. 134–5

55 Ibid. RG to Blunden n.d., p. 139

56 Ibid. p. 139

57 Ibid. RG to Blunden n.d. [after 20 June 1922]

58 GTAT29 p. 406

59 O'PREY(1) RG to Sassoon n.d. [July 1922], p. 143

60 GTAT29 pp. 398–401 and local memories. Beckley is described in 1985 by Arthur Bateman of 2, Collice Street, Islip, in conversation with the present author as 'a painter and decorator' – perhaps a later career.

61 See GTAT29 pp. 391–2. But O'PREY(1) RG to Blunden n.d. [August 1922], p. 144 has a contemporary account, which I have preferred where the evidence is conflicting.

62 DIARY 29 July 1922 has some details of RG's itinerary

63 O'PREY(1) RG to Marsh n.d. [June 1922], p. 137

64 Robert Graves, *On English Poetry*, p. 38

65 Robert Graves to Diccon Hughes n.d. 1922; from a photocopy kindly lent me by Hughes's literary executor Mrs Lucy McEntee

CHAPTER 7
MALLIK AND *Mockbeggar Hall*

66 O'PREY(1) RG to Blunden n.d., pp. 145–6: RG says it has taken him '12 months since the 1st draft' to finish it

67 ed. Nigel Nicolson, *The Question of Things Happening: The Letters of Virginia Woolf*, Vol. 2, 1912–1922 (Hogarth Press, 1976), p. 552. Virginia

Woolf, writing to Carrington on 24 August 1922 has: 'Captain Graves, the poet Graves, wants us to print a poem, with a portrait by Eric Kennington – who is he?'

68 The portrait of Mallik is drawn from O'PREY(I) pp. 148–9; and from GTAT29 pp. 404–5. All mention of Mallik and *Mockbeggar Hall* has been removed from GTAT57.

69 GTAT29 pp. 405–6 (deleted from GTAT57, see 68 above). RG's comment here that psychology became 'of secondary interest' to him, though literally true, may nevertheless give a false impression. Psychology was still extremely important to him: for one thing he was about to embark upon a period of psychoanalysis, a period to some extent glossed over in GTAT29 p. 383, and omitted altogether from GTAT57.

70 AUTHOR: Amy to JTRG 22 November 1922

71 Robert Graves, *Poetic Unreason and Other Studies*, p. 13. RG states that he sat for Kennington while preparing an address given (p. 1) at Leeds University in December 1922.

72 Quoted in O'PREY(I) pp. 142–3

73 AUTHOR: Amy to JTRG 22 November 1922 is interesting in this respect, as Amy talks first of the new *Georgian Poetry*, and later of reviews of A.E. Housman's *Last Poems*.

74 DIARY 14 December 1922

75 DIARY 2 January 1923

76 AUTHOR: Amy to Clarissa 15 January 1923

77 GTAT29 p. 355 talks of RG's 'technique of endurance'; see also p. 390

78 This is a subject upon which (see note 69 above) RG was understandably reticent. It is only from contemporary comments by his father in DIARY that we hear the word 'psychoanalysis' applied to RG. GTAT29 p. 383 suggests that Robert decided to stop all work and cure himself by reading modern psychological books in the spring of 1921. On p. 243 (and see Book Five, note 154 above) a more

accurate account of that period of his life appears. From DIARY 27 January and 23 March 1923 we can learn of RG's psychoanalysis during 1922–3; though no hint of this appears in GTAT. Whether he was now sensibly consulting someone as he had done briefly in 1921, or whether he was trying to treat himself, remains a mystery.

79 Robert Graves, *Mockbeggar Hall* (The Hogarth Press, 1924), p. 59

80 Ibid. pp. 8–9 (First appeared in *Winter Owl* November 1923)

81 Ibid. p. 58 (First appeared in *Winter Owl* November 1923)

82 Ibid. pp. 14–15

83 Ibid. pp. 23–4

84 DIARY 26 and 27 January 1923; and AUTHOR: APG to Amy Saturday n.d. RG mentions his work on 'Conflict and Poetry' in a letter to Sassoon in (n.d.) February 1923 (see O'PREY(I) p. 147).

85 DIARY 29 January 1923

86 See *The Times* for 16, 17 and 18 August 1921

CHAPTER 8
HARLECH INTERLUDE

87 DIARY 24 February 1923

88 O'PREY(I) RG to Sassoon n.d., pp. 147–8. They were staying with 'Toronto', the nickname given to the Canadian farmer poet Frank Prewett.

89 DIARY 28 March 1923. The following morning they arrived back at Erinfa just in time to enjoy a second breakfast.

90 AUTHOR: Amy to JTRG 14 April 1923 [misdated 13 April]. DIARY 10 and 11 April 1923 shows that the storm about the review blew over so quickly that on Tuesday 10th, the day after Charles's departure, Mrs Hughes came to stay at Erinfa; and the following day there was a happy picnic on the seashore, after which, in APG's words: 'The children slept while Rob & I played golf on sand & Robert sunbathed with Nancy & then bathed.'

91 DIARY 7 April 1923
92 AUTHOR: APG to JTRG 8 April 1923
93 AUTHOR: e.g. Amy to JTRG 7 and 14 [misdated 13] and 17 April 1923
94 AUTHOR: Amy to JTRG 15 April 1923 [misdated 13 April]
95 DIARY 16 April 1923
96 DIARY 15 November 1921 has APG writing 'to Robert returning the Hobby Horse'; and DIARY 29 December 1921 has APG writing a New Year's letter in which he suggests 'that Claree and Robert should do The Hobby Horses together'.
97 DIARY 18 and 19 April 1923. On the 19th, APG explained RG's reluctance in the words: 'I think his mind was in the throes of a poem at the time and hence his want of manner.'
98 This is partly speculative; but we know from DIARY that APG visited Heath at Barmouth on 23 March 1923, '& confabbed with him about Robert'. Heath was of the opinion that 'this Psychoanalysis is doing him harm and even disimproving his verse'; but he said that he would ask Robert to lunch one day. We also know from DIARY that Robert and Nancy visited Heath on 31 March 1923.

CHAPTER 9
'UNPROFITABLE WRITING'

99 DIARY 5 May 1923. See also DIARY 8 May 1923, when APG learns that RG 'is doing the Hobby Horses with his father-in-law'.
100 SASSOON(3) p. 34 entry for 6 June 1923
101 O'PREY(1) RG to Marsh n.d., pp. 149–51
102 Ibid.
103 GTAT29 p. 403. This description omitted from GTAT57. MS–S p. 119 appears to take *The Meaning of Dreams* at RG's 1929 valuation, and describes it as 'a hurried hash-up of Freudian dream-theory'; though at the time of writing TMOD RG had already rejected both Freud and Jung. [See RG, *The Meaning of Dreams* (Cecil

Palmer, 1924) p. 164.] [Also published in New York by Greenberg, 1925.]
104 Robert Graves, *Poetic Unreason and Other Studies*: see 'Author's Note'.
105 Robert Graves, *The Meaning of Dreams*, p. 16
106 Ibid., quotations from pp. 20, 24, and 164
107 Ibid., quotations from pp. 109 and 56–7
108 As 104 above, p. 117
109 Ibid. pp. 246–7

CHAPTER 10
UNCERTAINTIES

110 DIARY 23 October 1923. See also DIARY 28 August 1923 which gives news of a 'Letter from Robby offering bond for future payment of £80 paid by Amy for storage of his furniture. Amy gave him a quittance of the amount, however.' Earlier in the year RG had had some trouble himself in getting rent from one Palmer Stone who was in his Harlech cottage (see e.g. DIARY 18 May 1923).
111 O'PREY(1) RG to Sassoon n.d., p. 152. See also my *Lawrence of Arabia and his World* (Thames & Hudson and Charles Scribner's Sons, 1976) pp. 92–5
112 AUTHOR: Laura (Riding) Jackson to me 8 June 1985. Mrs Jackson adds that one of Mallik's theories was that 'when difficulty arose between people, no one in particular was to blame. All should withdraw, stand apart as from something of common responsibility.'
113 DIARY 24 April 1923, from which it appears that Diccon Hughes may have had Quennell to stay at his mother's cottage in North Wales.
114 Janet Adam Smith, *John Buchan* (Rupert Hart-Davis, 1965), p. 224. Lady Ottoline Morrell is not mentioned by name, but from the context it seems reasonable to assume that she is the woman in question.

115 LETTERS RG to Amy n.d. [December 1923]
116 Ibid.
117 DIARY 4 January 1924
118 DIARY 16 January 1924
119 This view is reinforced by and partly derived from AUTHOR: Laura (Riding) Jackson to me 8 June 1985, in which Mrs Jackson says that Nancy had 'a constitutional (physical) deficiency – a glandular, thyroid problem'.
120 O'PREY(I) RG to Sassoon n.d., pp. 151–2
121 Ibid.
122 O'PREY(I) p. 153; but for the amount of the cheque see SASSOON(3) entry for 21 February 1924, p. 92
123 O'PREY(I) RG to Sassoon 19 February 1924, pp. 153–4
124 GTAT29 p. 406
125 Victoria Glendinning, *Edith Sitwell: A Unicorn among Lions* (Weidenfeld, 1981), p. 57. I have replaced VG's 'Freudian' with the word 'psychological' because 'Freudian' suggests a faith in Freud which by this time RG had lost.
126 Ibid. p. 100
127 Quoted in Ibid. p. 86
128 Robert Graves, *Welchman's Hose* (London: The Fleuron, 1925) pp. 5–7; first published in the London *Mercury* by Squire in December 1924.
129 DIARY 30 March 1924. AUTHOR has a copy of *Mockbeggar Hall* which is inscribed: 'Father & Mother with love from Robert and Nancy. 1924'.
130 DIARY 31 March 1924
131 Robert Graves, *John Kemp's Wager*. In his 'Author's Note' RG does not acknowledge APG's help, though he sent him a copy inscribed 'Father & mother with love from' and an arrow pointing to his name; and on p. XIII he declares that 'The wicked postman theme is a reminiscence of an Irish comedy, *The Post Bag*, written by my father, Mr. A.P. Graves. The wager itself is about my only original contribution, except for the last scene, which, I am informed, is an anti-cli-

max: and the fantastic geography.'
132 AUTHOR: Amy to JTRG 24 February 1924. John gradually became Amy's confidant during the last seven or eight years of APG's life [APG died in 1931 at the age of 85] and on this occasion she told him of APG's accusation, and defended herself by saying that: 'I just think of the situation as a whole & then do what I think best.'
133 DIARY 5 February and 28 March 1924 shows APG discussing RG's poetry and possible work with Harold Monro; and DIARY 29 February 1924 finds him corresponding with John Buchan, who 'strongly favours [Robert's] going in for lecturing'.
134 DIARY 27 May 1924 has RG 'much bucked by an interview with Squire, most friendly to Philip and Robert (whose work impresses with every book he writes & whom he'd like to see in town)'.
135 DIARY 17 June 1924 has RG writing to APG to tell him that '[APG has] done him a good turn with Squire'.
136 Robert Graves, *Welchman's Hose*, pp. 11–13. This contains the poem under its later title; but its earlier title is retained in a line of the poem 'To an Editor' [from which we learn that the other poems sent to Squire included 'Alice', 'Burrs and Brambles', and (from RG's description) 'From our Ghostly Enemy'].
137 Ibid. pp. 1–2
138 SASSOON(3) entry for 2 June 1924, p. 132 has: 'R. Graves sends me his *Mock Beggar Hall*. He is camping in a tent on Prewett's farm at Abingdon this week, and wants me to go there.' The note on p. 132 explains that Frank Prewett had encountered SS at a convalescent home in 1918.
139 DIARY 18 June 1924
140 AUTHOR: Amy to JTRG 7 June 1924
141 In *Welchman's Hose* as 128 above, pp. 50–61. A note by RG states that it was written in January 1924. See also O'PREY(I) RG to Sassoon 19 February 1924, p. 153. The poem 'has

been taken by "English Life", and I have entered it also for the Olympic Games Prize'.

142 GTAT29 p. 92

143 GTAT29 pp. 406–7

144 Ibid. p. 407. Their income was now about two hundred pounds a year.

145 Hilary Spurling, *Secrets of a Woman's Heart: The Later Life of Ivy Compton-Burnett 1920–1969* (1984), pp. 138–9. Nicholson's grandchildren 'ran wild all over the Noyeses' house and garden, next door to their own except for an orchard'.

146 See my *Lawrence of Arabia and his World* (Thames and Hudson and Charles Scribner's Sons, 1976); and my *The Brothers Powys* (Routledge & Kegan Paul, 1979 and Charles Scribner's Sons, 1980)

147 In *Welchman's Hose* as 128 above, pp. 40–4. The poem appeared in RG's *Poems (1914–1926)* (Heinemann 1928), subtitled 'To Thomas Edward Shaw'; was subsequently dropped from RG's collected works; but reappeared in a revised form in *The More Deserving Cases* (Marlborough College Press, 1962) in which it is subtitled: '(To Aircraftman 338171, T.E. Shaw)'.

148 GTAT29 p. 407

CHAPTER 11
'A FIRST FAVOURITE WITH ME'

149 O'PREY(1) RG to Sassoon n.d., pp. 154–5

150 Robert Graves to Richard Hughes n.d.; from a photocopy kindly lent me by RH's literary executor Mrs Lucy McEntee

151 Robert Graves, *My Head! My Head!* (Secker, 1925) p. 52 [& Knopf 1925]

152 Robert Graves, 'On The Poet's Birth' in the *Fugitive*, Vol. 1, No. 4, December 1922, p. 103; p. 112 of the same issue contained 'A Valentine'; both these poems had previously appeared in *Whipperginny*. The *Fugi-tive*, Vol. 1, No. 3, October 1922, had contained an excellent review of RG's *On English Poetry*.

153 AUTHOR: Laura (Riding) Jackson to me 8 June 1985. Mrs Jackson recalls that the friend's name was 'Tommie', and that 'Nancy was given to saying that she wished I could have known Tommie; she was very respectfully fond of him.'

154 Laura Riding, 'The Quids' in the *Fugitive*, Vol. 3, No. 1, February 1924, pp. 10–11. The poem was later considerably revised in part. The same issue contained 3 other poems by Laura Riding.

155 O'PREY(1) p. 162 quotes Ransom's letter. Mrs Laura (Riding) Jackson tells me in letters of March and April 1986 that she was not divorced until early in 1925; and that 'As to "hack literary work", [she] was working for publishers and editors, but [she] was also writing poems.' Indeed, she asserts that the letter is 'a fabrication. Not Ransom's, I feel sure.'

156 DIARY 18 August 1924. AUTHOR: Amy to JTRG 7 May 1924 shows that RG was reviving a scheme he had thought of earlier in the year, when he was 'trying to let his house & go for a holiday'.

157 DIARY 20 August 1924

158 DIARY 21 August 1924

159 DIARY 22 August 1924

160 DIARY 23–25 August 1924. Just for the record: On Saturday Robert, Nancy and Amy took the children to the beach, where they bathed and then had a lunch cooked by Robert over a spirit-lamp on the sea-shore. On Sunday they were invited to lunch at Erinfa. On Monday night, after a 'grand family gathering', RG and his family were allowed to spend a cramped but dry night at Erinfa. On Tuesday night they were back at Cae Dhu; but on Wednesday Perceval and Gwen went back to London leaving rooms free, and they moved into Erinfa.

161 DIARY 30 August 1924 Nancy and

Robert had driven over to Llan-frothen and spent the day there with Diccon before escorting him back to Erinfa. At 10.15 John and Rosaleen went off to a dance at the St David's hotel; and Diccon and his friends departed 'after long delays owing to the state of the side-car in which D. brought the two girls'. RG and Nancy saw Diccon twice more on 13 and 18 September 1924. [See DIARY entries for those days; on the second of which they also met a celebrated local poet, Mrs Jones.]

162 DIARY 11 September 1924
163 Quoted in O'PREY(1) pp. 156–7
164 Ibid. RG to Marsh n.d., pp. 155–6
165 DIARY 25 September 1924 records: 'Good notice in Star ... a bad one in the Spectator.'
166 The two poems were 'Alice' and 'Burrs and Brambles', according to the poem 'To an Editor', subtitled 'A Satiric Complaint in the Old Style', which appears on pp. 15–19 of Robert Graves, *Welchman's Hose*, and which is the published version of a verse letter which RG sent Squire after months of unsatisfactory dealings with him. In this version, Squire appears lightly disguised as 'John Cole, Esquire', and the letter concludes:

> Then John Cole, Esquire,
> If it be your pleasure,
> It is now my desire
> To be paid in full measure
> According to my hire.

RG records that 'John Cole' took the letter 'in good part, and after a time replied with a cheque and acceptable explanations of the delays of which the poem complains'.

167 DIARY 6 December 1924 Amy gave Robert '£10 as a Xmas present, as Squire has not paid up and he is short.'
168 CHARLES pp. 82–3
169 Robert Graves, *But It Still Goes On*, pp. 130–2. The full story of this episode belongs to a future volume.
170 As 168 above. CHARLES p. 84 relates

that a few years later Elvira was charged with the murder of an acquaintance of hers in the early hours, possibly in similar circum-stances. She was however acquitted.

171 DIARY 5 December 1924
172 T.S. Matthews, *Under the Influence* (Cassell, 1979) pp. 118–19
173 MS-S devotes much of pp. 117–18 to '"The Shout", a story [RG] wrote in 1924.' Just to set the record straight, and in case any critic wonders why there is no mention of it at this stage, I would point out that according to the best contemporary evidence, 'The Shout' could not have been written before January 1926, when RG first set foot in Egypt. The story appears in Robert Graves, *But It Still Goes On*, pp. 79–104. On p. 79 there is an introductory passage in which RG states, 'This story occurred to me one day while I was walking in the desert near Heliopolis in Egypt ... [&c &c]'. Probably MS-S was misled by the date given in an introduction RG was asked to write in 1965 to a volume of his short stories collected by Cassell. 'The Shout' appears, but without the introductory passage which would have enabled RG to recall the date of writing more accurately.
174 O'PREY(1) RG to Marsh n.d., pp. 155–6
175 Robert Graves, *Contemporary Techniques of Poetry: A Political Analogy* (The Hogarth Press, 1925), p. 19
176 The *Fugitive*, Vol. 3, No. 5/6, December 1924, p. 130

CHAPTER 12
'A QUESTION OF IDENTITY'

177 DIARY 27 and 30 December 1924 and 3 January 1925. Being dressed as a 'Coogan boy' meant adopting the dress of a charming urchin, typically wearing a peaked cap with the peak pushed to one side, as popularized by the child film star Jackie Coogan.

178 DIARY 9 and 13 January 1925
179 GTAT29 pp. 393–4
180 Ibid. p. 409. RG was also [p. 419] doing 'some verse-reviewing for the *Nation* and *Athenaeum* but by 1925 I found it more and more difficult to be patient with dud books of poetry'.
181 Robert Graves to Richard Hughes n.d.; from a photocopy kindly lent me by RH's literary executor Mrs Lucy McEntee
182 AUTHOR: Amy to JTRG 23 February 1925. DIARY 24 January 1925 and AUTHOR: APG to JTRG 23 January 1925 & 28 January 1925 show further mild clashes between RG and APG, this time on the subject of family history. APG was arranging for genealogical charts to be drawn up by a professional; and was hoping that RG would put him up for a night or two, and then accompany him to Mickleton in Gloucestershire, home of an important branch of the Graves family. RG declined on all counts; though AUTHOR: Amy to JTRG 9 February, etc. show that Charles and John both went along, knowing how much the journey meant to their seventy-eight-year-old father.
183 'A Letter from Wales' appears in Robert Graves, *Welchman's Hose*, pp. 31–8. The date of composition is uncertain; but from (possibly misleading) internal evidence it was probably written at Harlech in August/September 1924.
184 O'PREY(I) RG to Marsh 2 April 1925, pp. 157–8
185 GTAT29 p. 389. No evidence is given by MS-S for his assertion [p. 121] that Nancy drove the car 'with a recklessness which became the talk of Islip.' It sounds totally out of character. Nor is evidence given for his assertion that RG had to 'hotly defend her mistakes to indignant neighbours.'
186 As 184 above
187 O'PREY(I) RG to Marsh n.d., p. 157
188 DIARY 15 April 1925. See also AUTHOR: Clarissa to Miss Edith Weir 24 September 1925, which shows

Clarissa hoping to join a close woman friend of hers who was living and working in Florence.
189 SASSOON(3) 21 April 1925, pp. 234–5
190 Ibid. 24 April 1925, p. 237
191 Ibid.
192 ed. Anne Olivier Bell, *The Diary of Virginia Woolf*, Vol. 3, 1923–1930, entry dated Monday 27 April 1925, but referring back to 'Friday' e.g. Friday 24 April 1925.
193 Ibid. Virginia Woolf unkindly suggests that RG stayed till 7.15, and had to be encouraged to leave so that she and Leonard did not miss their play. But RG had an appointment with Sassoon; and SASSOON(3) [see 194 below] makes it clear that RG was with Sassoon from 7 p.m. to 9 p.m. that evening. ['De literatis ubi est veritas?']
194 SASSOON(3) 24 April 1925, p. 237
195 GTAT29 p. 395
196 SASSOON(3) 5 May 1925, p. 246, refers back to 4 May 1925
197 Unfortunately the minutes of the Islip Parish Council for these years have been lost
198 GTAT29 pp. 398–9
199 AUTHOR: Amy to JTRG 23 November 1925
200 LETTERS n.d. from Islip
201 DIARY 11 June 1925
202 As 200 above
203 Knopf published *Fairies and Fusiliers* (1918); *Country Sentiment* (1920); *The Pier-Glass* (1921); *On English Poetry* (1922); *Whipperginny* (1923) and *My Head, My Head!* (1925). Greenberg published *The Meaning of Dreams* (1925).
204 DIARY 23 June has news of RG lunching with Vaughan Williams; DIARY 26 June 1925 has APG meeting VW, who tells him that he is 'much taken with [Robert] and his folk-singing and Hobby Horses for which he is inclined to write music'. This conversation took place in Aberystwyth where Amy and APG were having a short holiday. [Holst was also there.]
205 GTAT29 p. 407

206 In GTAT29 p. 407 RG incorrectly recalls that Sam Harries's fatal visit to Mallik in India took place in 1924. RG's letter to Robert Bridges which refers to recent news of Harries's death (see BODLEIAN Letters to Robert Bridges Dep. Bridges 109 fol. 165) is undated; but it contains details about RG's plans and about Nancy's health and treatment by massage which in the light of DIARY 9 June 1925 and of entries in SASSOON(3) [pp. 270–5 passim] place the episode firmly in 1925.

207 [Robert Graves using the pseudonym] John Doyle, *The Marmosite's Miscellany* (The Hogarth Press, 1925)

208 SASSOON(3) p. 237 has this footnote by Sassoon to his entry for 24 April 1925: 'This monkey house visit, combined with some volumes of 'Curious Characters' which I gave him [Graves] last Xmas, caused him to write 'The Marmosite's Miscellany'. SASSOON(3) p. 270 entry for 17 August 1925 has Sassoon reading 'with pleasure' 'the proofs of his [RG's] new poem, "The Marmosite's Miscellany"'.

209 The *Fugitive*, Vol. 4, No. 1, March 1925, p. 31

210 This sentence is to some extent speculative, as details of correspondence between RG and Mrs Gottschalk [as Laura (Riding) Jackson then was] do not appear to have survived. But AUTHOR: Mrs Laura (Riding) Jackson to me 8 June 1985 states of Nancy: 'The conception of my coming to join them, and join in their life, was hers.'

211 DIARY 9 June 1925

212 BODLEIAN Letters to Robert Bridges Dep. Bridges 109 fol. 163 RG to Bridges n.d. shows the interest from Cornell; but the penultimate sentence in this paragraph is partly speculative as I have no proof that it was Ransom

who introduced RG to Cornell. But if not he, then who?

213 Ibid.

214 BODLEIAN R. Bridges to Graves 1921–1926 MS Don d.113 184–202 4 July [?1925]

215 GTAT29 p. 408. We know from O'PREY(1) RG to Sassoon n.d. [October 1925], p. 159, that Robert Bridges's letter of recommendation, obtained in July, was re-used later in the year when RG applied for the Cairo professorship; and it seems likely that the other letters of recommendation mentioned in that October letter were also first obtained in July.

216 Had RG been accepted, one would most probably have heard, but the interview is followed by complete silence on his part, and is never referred to again. Possibly his views were too original to meet with approval. Possibly it was only an exploratory meeting, which he felt unable to follow up after the shock of hearing about Harries's death.

217 SASSOON(3) entry for 17 August 1925, p. 270, shows RG and Nancy arriving; and for 27 August 1925, p. 275, mentions Nancy's masseuse

218 BODLEIAN Letters to Robert Bridges Dep. Bridges 109 fol. 165 RG to Bridges n.d.

219 SASSOON(3) 17 and 19 August 1925, pp. 270–1

220 Ibid.

221 Ibid. 27 August 1925, pp. 274–5. RG had also seen Sassoon on the 20th and the 23rd [when they called on Edmund Gosse].

222 See CHARLES pp. 94–6 and also DIARY 12 and 18 May 1925. Charles first saw Peggy in about November 1924; he had proposed to her within a fortnight of their first meeting, and fairly frequently thereafter. To begin with it was a very loose engagement.

AUTHOR: Amy to JTRG 22 December 1925 has Amy writing: 'She [Peggy] struck me as more beautiful than ever & good, but it seems she cannot quite make up her mind to marry him [Charles]. ... How I hope Charles will win such a treasure. It makes me cry as I write it.'

223 DIARY 8 June 1925 & 23 and 30 July 1925. See also AUTHOR: Two notebooks of JTRG's Diary describing his extensive travels during the course of which he flew in an aeroplane in Germany, went deer-hunting in Austria, fell in love with a girl whom he had glimpsed in a church at Arcachon, and played tennis with Ezra Pound at Rapallo.

224 DIARY 17 September 1925

225 DIARY 18 September 1925. That afternoon Nancy drove them out in the car for a picnic tea and some blackberrying.

226 DIARY 19 and 20 September 1925

227 AUTHOR: Amy to JTRG 20 September 1925

228 DIARY 23 September 1925

229 DIARY 8 October 1925

230 DIARY 10 October 1925. Robert accepted £15.

231 In GTAT29 p. 408 RG specifies Egypt, which makes the better story; but AUTHOR: Amy to JTRG 11 December 1925 makes it clear that the recommendations were limited to 'a dry, warm climate'.

CHAPTER 15
THE CAIRO PROFESSORSHIP

232 AUTHOR: Amy to JTRG envelope 30 October 1925. What became of his application to Liverpool University is unknown to the present author.

233 Various sums were mentioned to RG. AUTHOR: Amy to JTRG 30 October 1925 mentions £1,250 a year; but SASSOON(3) entry for 21 October 1925, p. 291, mentions £1,500 a year.

234 O'PREY(1) RG to Sassoon n.d. [October 1925], p. 159

235 Ibid.

236 O'PREY(1) RG to Sassoon n.d., pp. 159–60

237 O'PREY(1) RG to Sassoon pp. 160–1 [misdated by O'PREY December 1925; from internal evidence 'We did enjoy you last week' about 22 November 1925]. The poem published in the *Spectator* was 'Four Children' on 28 November 1925. A second poem, 'Bargain' was published in the *Spectator* on 19 December. [See F. Higginson, *A Bibliography of the Works of Robert Graves*, p. 234.]

238 GTAT29 p. 410

239 O'PREY(1) pp. 161

240 DIARY 19 November 1925; and see AUTHOR: Amy to JTRG 24 November 1925

241 AUTHOR: Clarissa to Amy 22 November 1925

242 SASSOON(3) entry for 9 December 1925, p. 298, shows that on 4 December RG lunched with Sassoon in London; and then they travelled back to Oxford. Sassoon stayed at the Randolph, where he found William Nicholson and his wife also staying.

243 DIARY 3 November 1925. The precise sum was £950; and now that Robert had a degree Clarissa wanted one too, and was hoping that Amy would give her part of the money for that purpose.

244 AUTHOR: APG to JTRG 11 December 1925

245 Ibid.

246 DIARY 16 December 1925

247 AUTHOR: Amy to JTRG letters of 3 and 14 December 1925

248 O'PREY(1) RG to Eliot n.d., pp. 161–2

249 Ibid.

250 Laura (Riding) Jackson in *Contemporary Poets* (1975) see MS-S p. 128

251 AUTHOR: See e.g. Amy to JTRG 8 January 1926, in which Laura is described as a 'Lady Secretary'. But in a letter to me of March 1986, Mrs Laura (Riding) Jackson states definitely: 'No such conception of my status was, ever communicated to me. I would have rejected it if it had been.'

CHAPTER 16
THE ARRIVAL OF LAURA

252 SASSOON(3) entry for 27 December 1925, p. 306

253 AUTHOR: Amy to JTRG 28 December 1925

254 I take the date from MS-S p. 129; but AUTHOR: Mrs Laura (Riding) Jackson to me (5 April 1985) makes it clear that Laura docked at Portsmouth, and came to London on that boat train – not, as MS-S p. 122 has it, 'from the boat train from France'.

255 AUTHOR: Sally Chilver (Philip Graves's daughter) to the present author 1985 has some details of LRG's dress, including the long black coat. The following impressionistic description of her appearance is taken partly from near-contemporary photographs modified by some information passed on to me by Mrs Jackson's friend and authorized bibliographer, Mr Alan Clark, to whom I am much indebted for his careful consideration of everything which I have written about Mrs Jackson.

256 Mrs Laura (Riding) Jackson to me 5 April 1985. This story is very different from that in MS-S p. 122, and some of the detailed description such as the word 'courteously' has been included as a direct response by Mrs Jackson

(as she explains in her letter to me of March 1986) to what has been written about this meeting in the past. MS-S appears to rely heavily here upon T.S. Matthews, *Under the Influence* pp. 121–2, though Matthews himself makes it clear that this was only one version of the story, and therefore not reliable.

257 Ibid.

258 AUTHOR: As 255 above. See also AUTHOR 14 March 1986 Mrs Laura (Riding) Jackson to me.

259 DIARY 30 December 1925

260 DIARY 5 January 1926

261 AUTHOR: Amy to JTRG 8 January 1926

262 As 260 and 261 above. See also ed. Mary Lago and P.N. Furbank p. 38. Forster had done much to champion the work of the great Egyptian poet C.P. Cavafy.

263 ed. Nigel Nicolson, *The Letters of Virginia Woolf*, Vol. 3, 1923–1928, VW to Vita Sackville-West [Tuesday 5 January 1926]: 'Do come tomorrow as early as possible – I'm threatened with Robert Graves, Mrs R; and Nancy [*sic*] Gottschalk ... so come early.'

264 See the interesting comments in GTAT29 p. 439 (omitted from GTAT57) in which RG states that 'By the summer of 1926 the disintegration was already well-advanced.'

SELECT BIBLIOGRAPHY

For a full bibliography the reader should turn to F.H. Higginson's *A Bibliography of the Works of Robert Graves* (Nicholas Vane, London 1966). What follows is a guide to the more important sources.

I RELATING TO ROBERT'S FAMILY HISTORY, AND HIS LIFE UP TO 1926

ed. Bell, Anne Olivier *The Diary of Virginia Woolf*, Vol 3 1923–1930 (The Hogarth Press 1980); contains a memorable account of Robert's first meeting with Virginia Woolf.

Cooper, Rosaleen (née Graves, Robert's sister), *Games from an Edwardian Childhood* (David and Charles 1982); contains a useful introduction full of memories about her childhood and that of her brothers and sisters.

ed. Gathorne-Hardy, Robert *Ottoline at Garsington 1915–1918* (Faber & Faber 1974); shows how Robert Graves and Siegfried Sassoon appeared to Lady Ottoline Morrell.

Graves, Alfred Perceval (Robert's father) *To Return To All That* (Jonathan Cape 1930). The bulk of this work is a straightforward and constantly entertaining autobiography, which had been written though not fully revised long before Robert began writing his *Goodbye To All That*. However, after the success of Robert's book a new chapter was added in which APG replied to some of his son's criticisms and corrected some of his inaccuracies, and the present title was decided upon. This has given to many people the misleading impression that the whole book is simply an attempt to fight back at Robert.

Graves, Charles (Robert's brother) *The Bad Old Days* (Faber & Faber 1951). This book is chiefly interesting as a somewhat impressionistic account of life in Fleet Street in the 1920s, 1930s and 1940s; but it also contains details about Robert's childhood, and about Charles's attitude towards his brother, which do not appear elsewhere.

Graves, Robert *Goodbye To All That* (Jonathan Cape 1929; revised edition 1957). My narrowly academic reservations about this superb autobiography appear on pp. 330–1.

Graves, Robert *But It Still Goes On* (Jonathan Cape 1930); contains interesting comments by RG on material in *Goodbye To All That*, and some other not very reliable autobiographical material on the pre-1926 years.

Graves, Sir Robert Windham *Storm Centres of the Near East* (Hutchinson 1933); has some information about members of the family, especially Philip and Dick, during these years.

ed. Hart-Davis, Sir Rupert *Siegfried Sassoon Diaries 1915–1918* (Faber & Faber 1983); *Siegfried Sassoon Diaries 1920–1922* (Faber & Faber 1981); and *Siegfried Sassoon Diaries 1923–1925* (Faber & Faber 1985). Sassoon is a highly reliable witness, and these superbly edited volumes contain much valuable information not only about Robert Graves and Siegfried Sassoon but about many of their mutual friends and acquaintances such as Robert Ross, John Masefield, T.E.Lawrence and others. For the biographer they provide an indispensable corrective to *Goodbye To All That*.

ed. Holden, W.H. *The Charterhouse We*

Knew (London, British Technical and General Press 1950). G.D. Martineau gives many telling details of Carthusian appearance, manners, habits of work and so on at the time when both Martineau and Robert were schoolboys.

Matthews, T.S. *Under the Influence* (Cassell, London 1977); contains some recollections of Robert Graves and his family at Oxford prior to their departure for Egypt. Maisie Somerville is also introduced.

Perceval family information may be found in Part V of *Histories of Noble British Families With Biographical Notices Of The Most Distinguished Individuals In Each* (London, William Pickering 1844). See also Vols I and II of *A Genealogical History of the House of Yvery*; in its different branches of Yvery, Luvel, Perceval, and Gournay (London, printed for H.Woodfall, jun. 1742).

Ida, Lady Poore (Alfred Perceval Graves's sister and Robert's aunt), *An Admiral's Wife in the Making* (London: Smith, Elder & Co., 15 Waterloo Place, 1917); a source of much additional information about A.P. Graves's childhood.

ed. Owen, Harold and Bell, John *Wilfred Owen: Collected Letters*. This volume is important for the light it throws upon the relationship between Wilfred Owen and Robert Graves.

ed. O'Prey, Paul *In Broken Images: Selected Letters of Robert Graves 1914–1946* (Hutchinson 1982). This volume has been of the utmost help to me during the last four years. As with all collections of letters, it has the great value of allowing the writer to speak directly and clearly to us across the lengthening period of intervening time. It will remain an essential companion both to *Goodbye To All That* and to all subsequent biographies.

Richards, Frank *Old Soldiers Never Die* (Faber & Faber 1933); describes life in the Royal Welch Fusiliers, and contains one or two memorable

sketches of Robert.

Sassoon, Siegfried *Memoirs of an Infantry Officer* (Folio Society, London 1974). An account of Sassoon's service with the Royal Welch Fusiliers, which contains a memorable portrait of Robert, who appears as 'David Cromlech'.

Seymour-Smith, Martin *Robert Graves: His Life and Works* (Hutchinson 1982). My numerous disagreements with the author of this pioneering work are fully set out in the reference notes of the present volume and do not need further elaboration. As a literary critic, however, Seymour-Smith is always interesting; and as a biographer he has set much material before the public for the first time.

2 PRINCIPAL PUBLICATIONS BY ROBERT GRAVES UP TO JANUARY 1926

1916 *Over the Brazier* (London: The Poetry Bookshop) [Poems]
Goliath and David (London: The Chiswick Press) [Poems: 150 copies]

1917 *Fairies and Fusiliers* (London: William Heinemann) [Poems]

1918 *Fairies and Fusiliers* (New York: Alfred A. Knopf) [Poems]

1919 *Treasure Box* (London: The Chiswick Press [Poems]

1920 *Country Sentiment* (London: Martin Secker; and New York: Alfred A. Knopf) [Poems]

1921 *The Pier-Glass* (London: Martin Secker; and New York: Alfred A.Knopf) [Poems]
Oxford Poetry 1921 (Oxford: Basil Blackwell) [Editor with Alan Porter & Diccon Hughes]

1922 *On English Poetry: Being an Irregular Approach to the Psychology of this Art, from Evidence Mainly Subjective* (New York: Alfred A.Knopf; and London: William Heinemann) [Critical]
Whipperginny (London: William Heinemann) [Poems]

1923 *Whipperginny* (New York: Alfred A.Knopf) [Poems]

The Feather Bed (The Hogarth Press) [Poem]

1924 *Mock Beggar Hall* (The Hogarth Press) [Poems & Philosophical Play]

The Meaning of Dreams (London: Cecil Palmer) [Critical]

1925 *The Meaning of Dreams* (New York: Greenberg) [Critical]

John Kemp's Wager (Oxford: Basil Blackwell) [Play with Folk-songs]

Poetic Unreason and Other Studies (London: Cecil Palmer) [Critical]

Welchman's Hose (London: The Fleuron) [Poems, 525 copies]

My Head! My Head! (London: Martin Secker; and New York: Alfred A. Knopf) [Historical Novel]

Contemporary Techniques of Poetry: A Political Analogy (The Hogarth Press) [Critical]

Robert Graves [A 6d. selection of his poems] (London: Ernest Benn) [Poems]

The Marmosite's Miscellany (The Hogarth Press) [under pseudonym John Doyle, poem]

INDEX

RG stands for Robert Graves, APG for Alfred Perceval Graves.